July 10, 1990

For Betty E. Schwesinger –

With very best wishes –

Jean Maddern Pitrone

TANGLED WEB

Legacy of Auto Pioneer John F. Dodge

By Jean Maddern Pitrone

Avenue Publishing Co.
Hamtramck, Michigan 48212

Dedication

This book is dedicated to the memory of two people who shared this writer's intense interest in the Dodges. To the late Amelia Rausch Cline who continued to offer her personal reminiscences of the Dodge family until a few months before her death in February, 1982, at age 95. And to the late George McCall who collected Amelia's papers and memor- abilia.

The writer also wishes to thank Mike and Vivian Boutell and Nancy McCall for their generosity in permitting access to the George McCall Collection.

A sincere thank you must go, also, to the Dodge Brothers Club for its enthusiastic interest in the book project and to the staff at Meadow Brook Hall for their cooperation.

The 1989 publication of this book salutes the seventy-fifth anniversary of the date—November 10, 1914—when the first sturdy Dodge Motor Car chugged its way out of the gates of Dodge Brothers' factory (Dodge Main) in Hamtramck, Michigan. The popular Dodge automobile, which still rolls off the assembly lines of Dodge Division of Chrysler Corporation, was the product of the inventive and mechanical genius of those strong-willed, inseparable brothers...John Francis Dodge and Horace Elgin Dodge.

Table of Contents

Chapter 1: The View from the 13th Floor   1
Chapter 2: A Car and a Courtship   15
Chapter 3: A Mansion and a Marriage   26
Chapter 4: A Money Tree—The Model T   38
Chapter 5: The Dodge-Ford Affiliation Fractures   49
Chapter 6: Parallel Births   58
Chapter 7: Separate Lives in Different Molds   70
Chapter 8: Prosperity in Modest and
             Immodest Proportions   81
Chapter 9: The Inseparable Dodge Brothers—
             Together for Eternity   94
Chapter 10: Tragedy Strikes the Widowed Matilda   109
Chapter 11: The Wilson Era Begins   121
Chapter 12: Mistress of Meadow Brook   137
Chapter 13: Romances of the Unwelcomed Kind   153
Chapter 14: Tragic Honeymoon   167
Chapter 15: The Known and the Unknown   179
Chapter 16: Evidence of Origin   190
Chapter 17: Struggles for Independence   207
Chapter 18: Epitaphs and Testaments   222
Chapter 19: A Link is Discovered   236
Chapter 20: The Second Frances   249
Chapter 21: Probate Limbo   263
Chapter 22: Up Against the "System"   276

Chapter 1

The View from the 13th Floor

A bitter December wind whips along the gray Detroit River. Gusts sweep across the riverfront plaza and through the maw of a towering, doughnut-shaped structure—the Dodge fountain, its inefficient valves turned off for the winter. Opposite the plaza, the wind whirls furiously at the corner of Jefferson and Woodward where jurors, defendants, clerks, and a swarm of attorneys push their way into the glass and marble interior of the City County Building in downtown Detroit.

With one hand firmly holding a small brimmed, black hat to her pale blond hair, Lucille Mealbach enters the building. Frances Lucille Mealbach, she calls herself now, trying to become accustomed to the first name. The 70-year-old Frances Lucille is a solidly built woman, voluptous but not fat, whose shapely legs flash beneath a well fitted, black suit made on her own sewing machine. No one guesses she makes her own clothes—Dodge women wear designer costumes, not homemade creations. And she is certain she is a Dodge as she walks, with her daughter Sharon, into an elevator filled with men carrying attache cases.

The elevator swooshes up to the 13th floor where passengers step into a hallway leading to offices of Wayne County Probate Court. Here it will be determined whether Frances Lucille will inherit a fortune or will continue depending only on social security payments plus her earnings as a saleslady.

Frances Lucille hesitates near the elevator as her blue eyes catch sight of newspaper reporters rising from benches that line the walls. She hurries past the reporters and into the courtroom of Probate Judge J. Robert Gragg. Journalists—local reporters and writers from New York, Palm Beach, and other cities—have already written so much about her in recents weeks. The lurid headlines infiltrate her dreams at night. Every time she thinks of them, her pulse beats faster.

"Is 'Siamese Twin' a Dodge Heiress?"
                              —*The Detroit News*

"A woman's amazing claim that she is the long-lost Siamese twin of an heiress to the $40 million estate of auto pioneer John Dodge has set off a weird dispute over the tycoon's fortune..."
                              —*The National Examiner*

"Frances Mealbach, a 69-year-old Detroit housewife, has gone to court to prove her claim—and set the stage for a bitter and bizarre legal battle that could rival anything on Dynasty and Dallas..."
                              —*The Star*

Since the articles first appeared in late 1984, Frances Lucille has observed her 70th birthday and endured several court hearings in preparation for a March, 1985, jury trial. At this morning's December 14, 1984, hearing, Frances Lucille and her daughter slide onto a front bench in the small courtroom. Her attorney, James P. Cunningham, is already there, his guileless hazel eyes looking at them from behind glasses that seem too large for his face. The glasses slip down his slender nose as he riffles through a sheaf of documents. He stabs the lenses back into place with an index finger.

At Cunningham's left, ten sleek attorneys, faces bronzed from the Florida sun or in the tanning booths of plush health spas, chat as they wait to represent the interests of nine previously designated Dodge heirs, plus the Matilda R. Wilson Fund. Named earlier this year by the Michigan Supreme Court after persistent in-fighting among the Dodges, the chosen heirs expected a quick division of the $40 million trust fund set aside by John Dodge at the automotive pioneer's death in 1920. They did not expect the intrusion of the unknown Frances Lucille with her claim that John and Matilda Dodge discarded her at birth as an unwanted child.

Frances Lucille's face sets in a stern mold, now, as she averts her eyes from the Dodge lawyers, clone-like in their expensive, tailored suits. Bruised by their references to her, in previous hearings, as a fortune hunter and parasite, and expecting more sarcasm and insults at today's hearing, she is tense, her cheek muscles twitching.

A clerk polls the collection of Dodge attorneys, noting that the first lawyer requests to address the court for ten minutes. A second lawyer specifies five minutes. Their self assurance frightens Frances Lucille despite her frequent assertions that they—the attorneys—are the ones who have been feeding off the John Dodge trust fund for 60 years.

Everyone stands as Judge Gragg enters the courtroom and sits at his desk. A recently appointed black judge in his mid-fifties, he presses his fingertips together in a contemplative pose. He announces that Attorney Cunningham has filed a petition for "production and inspection" of Mrs. Mealbach's adoption records and for her original birth certificate.

Frances Lucille, previously denied access to either of these records, listens closely to Jim Cunningham citing reasons why the adoption records should be unsealed. He claims that Frances Lucille is a John Dodge daughter and the Siamese twin of deceased heiress, Frances Dodge Van Lennep. Reinforcing this assertion, he reminds the court of the two "surgical" scars at the back of Mrs. Mealbach's head and base of her neck. He points out that the two birth certificates, city and state, issued in 1914 for his client's "twin"—Frances Dodge (Van Lennep)— contain discrepancies indicating a cover-up of important facts. This conflicting information was filed on forms intended for the registration of multiple births, he adds.

Frances Lucille's head nods affirmatively as her lawyer tells the court that almost every major newspaper in the country has picked up the Mealbach-Dodge story, attracting public attention to the hearings. His client, he argues, has a "psychological need to know" the truth of her heritage now that the matter has been "elevated to enormous public interest."

Cunningham's voice rises as he tries to make a final impact on the court. "Since Mrs. Mealbach's biological parents are presumed dead, and since her adoptive parents are also deceased, the right of privacy no longer applies," he insists. In recent years, Michigan has amended earlier restrictive adoption laws, he reminds the court, so that adoptees may obtain their records from the state—unless biological parents object—if they were adopted after September, 1980. Armed with numbers and statistics for other cases concerning adoptees throughout the country, he supports his arguments for permission to review and inspect Frances Lucille's adoption records and original birth certificate.

Sharon and her mother nod in agreement. Their lawyer's presentation reinforces their own belief that Dodge attorneys cannot reasonably argue against delaying distribution of the trust fund until the records are opened.

Perspiration dots Frances Lucille's brow, though, as Dodge attorneys also cite numbers and statistics to support the opposite view. None of them observes his self-imposed time limitation as each rejects Cunningham's interpretation of the "twin" markings on Frances Dodge Van Lennep's birth certificate from the state. "The vast notoriety given the case has been orchestrated by the petitioner," one lawyer charges. "Mrs. Mealbach's attorney is aware," he adds, "that her claims are frivolous. Mr. Cunningham's persistence shows callous disregard for laws of the state."

The judge's impassive face seems carved from mahogany as the crossfire of arguments persists until noon. When Frances Lucille and her daughter leave for lunch, they express their worries about the judge's detachment during the heated exchange between lawyers. They wonder why the judge is aroused from apathy only when annoyed by Cunningham.

The women have already been warned by Cunningham that if the judge rules to unseal the adoption records, he will break precedent and establish a new law in Michigan, where adoption records never have been opened by court order during a trial. The Mealbachs question whether Judge Gragg, on the bench for only eight months, might feel pressured by the need to rule on such an important matter and if he blames Cunningham for the pressure.

Judge Gragg resumes the hearing at 2:15 p.m., but Cunningham is not in the courtroom. Frances Lucille shifts uneasily on the hard bench when Gragg drums his fingers on his desk. She glances at her daughter, as if reminded by her daughter's profile of the resemblance between childhood photographs of Sharon and a photograph they have seen of Frances Dodge Van Lennep's daughter. They are cousins... Frances Lucille is convinced of that. She believes that this eerie resemblance reflects the likeness in her own blue eyes and blond complexion, her wide face and strong jawline, to John Dodge.

When Cunningham hurries into the courtroom, ten minutes late, Frances Lucille breathes a sigh of relief. Ignoring his own 30-minute tardiness this morning, Gragg reprimands the attorney for lack of respect. "It is a concern to me and an affront to the court," the judge scolds.

The hearing goes on with Cunningham, still breathless, explaining that the law severing the rights of adoptees to share in estates of natural parents was not passed until 1953. Mrs. Mealbach, he points out, was born in 1914, and John Dodge died in 1920—long before the 1953 law took effect.

Before an opposition attorney has a chance to speak, Frances Lucille freezes in alarm as Judge Gragg leans across his desk and looks in her direction. "Are you interested?" he demands.

A voice behind her asks, "Who me?" Frances Lucille recognizes the voice as that of the female newspaper reporter sitting behind her.

"Yes, you," the judge snaps. "Were you sleeping?"

The reporter holds up her notebook. "I was taking notes," she explains.

Even a reporter, working quietly with her head bent down toward her notebook, is a target for the judge's wrath. Frances Lucille shifts position on the bench. She looks at her watch.

Three p.m. Dodge attorneys are still pleading for "accelerated judgment" based on "unreasonable delay" by Frances Lucille in filing her claim after first suspecting her links to John Dodge.

"Mrs. Mealbach sat idly by and now comes out of the woodwork," one attorney sneers.

Frances Lucille flinches at the comparison to a roach.

Four p.m. The hearing ends with no immediate ruling. As with previous hearings, the judge says he will write his opinion later.

"I think I must have aged ten years since this all began," Frances Lucille answers a reporter as she leaves the courtroom. She knows that within three days she must submit to hours of interrogation by Dodge lawyers taking her deposition.

At the Mealbachs' modest home in Dearborn, the daughters try to cheer the sagging spirits of their usually good-humored mother. Frances Lucille shakes her head. "I'm ready to forget the whole thing," she tells her daughters. She has felt content with her life, especially in late years, she says—not for the first time. And she doesn't need the aggravation of court trials and squabbling. She has no desire to possess great wealth. "Money can't buy happiness," she insists, reminding her children of the tragedies marring the lives of the affluent Dodges.

Her three daughters and two sons resist her protests. They deserve to know their roots, they say. They have a rightful claim to the Dodge fortune if they can prove their mother is a Dodge. They are not willing to settle for anything less. Nor will Cunningham's law firm, working on a contingency basis, willingly abandon the case after a heavy investment of time and effort.

They are right. Frances Lucille recognizes that. She sees no way out. Whatever the cost, she must continue to battle for what she believes is her birthright.

Surrendering to a sense of fatalism, she re-reads the description that one reporter wrote of the proceedings. "The story that is unfolding is like a dark fairy tale." The words express her own mystical feelings about her origin. But her children insist that the story is not a myth, but a true saga that reaches back, for its beginnings, to the turn of the century. To the birth of the automobile industry. To the accelerated rags-to-riches transformation in the lives of hard working mechanics,

John and Horace Dodge. And, especially, to the hiring of a young secretary, Matilda Rausch, at Dodge Brothers machine shop.

By 11 p.m. on December 31, 1900, crowds of Detroiters spilled out of streetcars at City Hall, waiting to celebrate the turn of the century at midnight. When the 1 1/2-ton bell clanged in the clock-tower of City Hall, downtown Detroit burst into light. Thousands of red and white bulbs outlined windows of the city's two skyscrapers—the Hammond Building and Majestic Building, looming ten and fourteen stories against the sky line.

Rockets arced toward the river. Bands blared. Church organs thundered. Detroit, along with the rest of the nation and world, was moving from the Gay Nineties into the Twentieth Century.

In the earliest years of the 1900s, the dawning automotive age staggered the imaginations of Detroiters who had depended on bicycles and horse drawn streetcars for transportation. When the last horse drawn car was replaced by an electric streetcar in 1896, the city became a model of efficient transit. In 1900, Detroit was listed as the thirteenth largest city in the country with a population of 285,000—mostly Germans. The city also had the greatest percentage of inhabitants who could not speak English—nearly twelve percent.

Although the Anti-Saloon League was gaining national membership and Carry Nation had begun her crusade against "Demon Rum," the large immigrant population of Detroit supported or tolerated the glut of taverns flourishing in the city. Saloons lined tawdry Monroe Avenue. More sedate "drinking emporiums" were found on Woodward Avenue.

Most of the city's breweries and many taverns were owned by Germans, as was George Rausch's saloon on St. Aubin Street in the lower east-side. Teamsters from Voight Brewery drove their teams of draft horses down St. Aubin to the Rausch saloon where neighborhood workmen came, after 10-to-12 hour workdays—six days a week, to guzzle beer in the company of friends. And the sounds of rough voices and laughter drifted from the saloon up the stairs to the second-floor flat where the Rausch family lived.

In the late summer of 1902, the saloon proprietor's 200-pound wife, Margaret Rausch, worked behind the bar until six p.m., at which time her husband came downstairs to take over the bartending. Regular patrons were accustomed to the ill-matched appearances of the husband and wife who operated the saloon, but visitors to the tavern occasionally remarked on the scrawniness of the bar owner, but kept silent about the ponderous bulk of his wife. Rausch took no offense at the remarks, obliging with his standard explanation that he had "some meat on his bones" when he came to this country. But he had been plagued with a recurrent fever and took so much sulphur for it that the marrow in his bones "froze."

When Rausch began tending bar after eating his evening meal in the upstairs flat, his wife slowly climbed the stairs to the family's living quarters. As she came into the kitchen, her older daughter, Matilda, hurried to the wood-burning cook-stove to spoon the contents of a steaming pot into three plates for the mother and the two daughters. She put a lesser amount on her own plate. The dainty Matilda, nearly 19 years old, abhorred the idea of gaining weight, even though a full, fleshy figure epitomized the ideal woman.

Matilda's aversions included more than a disdain for weight-gain. With her mother spending so much time downstairs, working in the "business," things weren't really organized. Matilda hated eating meals in shifts—father first, mother and daughters afterward. In the opinionated Matilda's view, if Margaret Rausch did not have to tend bar, she would have more time to teach 15-year-old Amelia how to cook and clean and keep a supply of linen napkins ironed and ready for use. Sadly, it seemed to Matilda that neither her mother nor her sister had much concern for observing the amenities that were so important to the elder Rausch daughter.

Her mood brightened when, as the three women sat down to eat, Margaret Rausch inquired about Matilda's secretarial job interview at Dodge Brothers machine shop that afternoon. The interview had gone well, Matilda told them, after the red-haired Mr. Dodge learned that she had attended Gorsline Business College for a year and that she already had a year of experience working as a stenographer at E.J. Kruce Cracker Company. She could report for work at Dodge Brothers the next morning, she said triumphantly.

She did not confide her suspicions to either her younger sister or her mother that she detected something personal in John Dodge's appraisal at the interview...in the way his eyes studied her face and her coiled, glossy, dark brown—almost black—hair. "Black, like Mother's hair," Amelia often teased, taking perverse pleasure in adding that her own pigtails were "brown, like Father's side of the family."

Both girls were short, like their parents; Amelia scarcely one inch over five feet, the older sister an inch taller. Matilda, who hated being short, held herself proudly erect to give an illusion of height, and was pleased that her petite, small-waisted figure had no need for tightly laced corsets. Although women of the era pined to acquire an "hourglass"-Lillian Russell figure—full hips and well rounded bosom—the word "bosom" was never mentioned by either sister in the St. Aubin Street flat. Still, the sensitive Matilda was aware of Amelia's critical gaze at the older sister's small, high breasts when Matilda stood in front of the bedroom mirror and waited for Amelia to hook the back of her dress, padded with ruffles and flounces.

The stoic nature of the grossly overweight and plain Margaret Rausch, who wore dark and shapeless clothing, concealed a core of romanticism that revealed itself when she named her daughters. Matilda. Amelia. Elegant names, she thought, befitting charming little girls whose embroidered and beribboned dresses and matching bonnets and pantaloons were carefully tailored by their mother, who sewed as well as she cooked and tended bar.

When the sisters, in their early teens, seemed consumed by an insatiable interest in newspaper society notes, Margaret worried that her daughters might be living in a fantasy world that could never be a part of the lives of daughters in a working class German family. But it would be a part of her life someday, Matilda vowed as she coaxed Amelia to walk with her through more fashionable neighborhoods where the sisters pretended to be ladies of wealth, admiring the handsome homes and spinning dreams of the future.

On her daughters' return from these excursions, the mother was not disinclined to complain that the sisters had too many fancy ideas for girls who lived upstairs of their family's saloon; that perhaps she and George Rausch had spoiled their young daughters by giving them too many luxuries. For the Rausches, there were no chamber-pots, nor kitchen washtubs for bathing, like those of most ordinary families. The Rausch flat contained a sink with running water. And a modern water closet.

Still, Matilda freely expressed her disdain for her parents' occupation and for the living quarters above the saloon, even though the Rausches had never required—not would have permitted—their daughters to work downstairs at, or near, the bar. Both parents agreed that the saloon quarters were verboten for the girls.

Despite Matilda's penchant for aristocratic airs, Margaret had to admit that her older daughter was very capable at cooking and cleaning—a housekeeping perfectionist, in fact, whose demands for not only a clean and sweet-smelling icebox, but also for perfectly arranged contents, galled the mother. Amelia was different. She avoided household chores unless Matilda supervised her closely, not daring, then, to defy the older sister and expose herself to Matilda's peppery temper.

In those early months of employment in the office of Dodge Brothers, however, Matilda's calm and efficient manner gave no hint of her stormy temperament. Her compulsion to bring order and neatness out of chaos pleased the Dodges, who carelessly tossed order blanks, receipts, business letters, and records into piles, drawers, and cubbyholes during the two years since they first set up their own machine shop in Detroit. They had begun by leasing the Boydell Building in September, 1900, and by staking their meager resources in a push for success with their own business.

Even before that, they had gambled once for business success, although not in Detroit—and lost. But Detroit, at the beginning of the century, was attracting men skilled with tools—blacksmiths, machinists, wagon-makers—to join the earlier influx of immigrants who crowded into the city, working in Detroit's tobacco and cigar factories, its furniture and shoe factories, boiler shops, iron foundries, brickyards and breweries. The more highly skilled men came to work in Dimmer Machine Works or Leland and Faulconer Manufacturing Company, and in the Olds plant which employed 300 men, or, for a short time, in the smaller Detroit Automobile Company where young Henry Ford worked as chief engineer.

Only grit and endurance kept Dodge Brothers machine shop in business in Detroit through the first terrible year of personal misfortune. John Dodge's wife, 37-year-old Ivy Hawkins Dodge, died in October, 1901, of tuberculosis, leaving three children—the youngest only three years old.

John, also 37 years old when his wife died, worried about his children until his sister-in-law, Anna Dodge, offered a suggestion. Anna's friend of childhood days, Isabelle Smith, was willing to move into John's Trumbull Street home as a housekeeper. She agreed to care for the three children and for John's mother, Maria Dodge, an invalid.

Anna and Horace Elgin Dodge, almost four years younger than his brother, John, also had two young children by this time. Dodge Brothers' finances were so meager in 1901 that the brothers had borrowed money to buy a joint plot of eight grave sites in which Ivy Dodge was the first to be buried at Woodlawn Cemetery.

Despite John's personal problems, the Dodge brothers struggled determinedly to survive in a tough, blue-collar city where machine shops were multiplying and competing for business. Working at his lathes and flywheels, mechanical wizard Horace could pattern, mold, and shape any object—including iron stove parts, much in demand—for which John snared an order.

The brothers often worked long past midnight to fill orders, then slept on benches in their shop until six a.m. when they started up their machines. Even after they employed twelve men and young appren- tices, John and Horace worked late, making designs and castings. Each of the Dodges drew a salary of forty cents an hour; the employees were paid from five cents to thirty-five cents an hour.

The wage scale increased when the need suddenly ended for searching the city to acquire orders. This occurred in 1901, soon after a fire gutted the Olds Motor Works—the first automobile company organized in Michigan.

Although the fire consumed Ransom Olds' plant and its contents, the blaze consumed none of Olds' eagerness to get his one-cylinder, curved-dash Oldsmobile on the market. He decided to resort to a different plan, searching out machinists with reputations for accuracy to make parts for his car, after which Olds would assemble the parts into the finished product.

Although the accepted ratio of precision for the machining of auto- mobile parts was one sixty-fourth of an inch (0.016 in.), Olds knew that engineering genius Henry M. Leland had shared his expertise in precision-machining with Horace Dodge when both Horace and Leland's son, Wilfred, had worked at Leland, Faulconer & Norton in 1898. Henry Leland, who soon would design the Cadillac automobile, relied on micrometers for accuracy instead of on the usual rule-of- thumb measurements, and was gradually gaining the ability to refine this precision ratio to one ten-thousandth of an inch (0.0001 in.)— assuring perfect fit of parts and smooth meshing of gears.

When Ransom Olds offered Dodge Brothers a contract to build 3000 transmissions, they signed quickly even though gearing up to turn out transmissions involved a preliminary expenditure that strained their finances.

The Leland and Faulconer shop also contracted to produce motors for Olds. When Detroit's first automobile show attracted a crowd to the Armory Building in 1901, spectators grouped around the platform holding the Olds exhibit where two Olds motors, made from the same pattern, ran at equal speeds—the speed of each indicated on a large meter.

Henry and Wilfred Leland passed along the story of the two motors to their family, and the tale was later told in a biography of Henry Leland written by Mrs. Wilfred Leland. She wrote of a young Henry Ford—attending the auto show and goaded by curiosity—quietly moving behind the platform to inspect the two motors. Unnoticed there, he discovered that one motor was slowed to the speed of the second one by a brake load applied to the fly wheel. The faster motor, he learned, was the Leland machine which could deliver 3.7 horse-power. The second motor, made by Dodge, delivered 3 horsepower.

By the end of 1901, Olds assembled 425 of his light-weight cars, each selling for $650, and the Dodges tasted the first flavor of financial success as Olds' payments began to arrive. The brothers continued fulfilling their contract in 1902, a year in which Olds would sell 2500 of the spunky little cars which trundled along the road on bicycle-type wheels fitted with pneumatic tires.

Shortly after the Dodges began producing transmissions for Ransom Olds, their Boydell shop on Beaubien Street became choked with piles of steel and supplies, newly installed lathes, and grinding machines. Using the profits from Olds, the brothers had a building of three stories—50 by 138 feet—constructed on Monroe Avenue at Hastings, just east of Woodward Avenue, to house their flourishing business. They moved into the new building in 1902, then had hired their secretary, Matilda Rausch, to join the male bookkeeper already employed in their business office.

While the new Dodge shop hummed with activity, Matilda Rausch relished her increasing responsibilities. She basked in the approval of her florid-faced, bull-chested employer when he came into the business office and complimented her for a letter she had typed. But there were other times when she bit her tongue and fought to control her quick temper when he roared his way into the office, demanding to know why a certain business letter or blueprint was not on his desk. Matilda invariably located the missing papers without too much difficulty, under a notebook or a set of tracings that her boss had carelessly tossed on his desk. And John's tempestuous outbursts faded as quickly as they had erupted.

Conflicts with Horace were rare, because the younger brother was occupied with the mechanical operation of the shop, not with business affairs. But when this younger, better looking brother did get angry, his rage was as explosive as John's. Unlike John, however, Horace then sank into a moody silence lasting for days.

Matilda's sharp brown eyes closely observed the red-headed brothers in the early days of her employment. She was impressed by their strength as they lugged heavy pieces of machinery into the shop, and by their determination to succeed. When a machine broke down, Horace, in coveralls, and John, grabbing a leather apron, made the repairs—then traded jokes with their shopmen-buddies.

Matilda often heard John talking on the telephone. "My brother and I think..." he would say. "My brother and I have decided..." Horace spoke, always, in the same manner. There seemed to be none of the rivalry that, despite her own closeness to Amelia, existed between the Rausch sisters.

Not long after she began working at the Dodge shop, Matilda became acquainted with Mrs. Horace Dodge who came into the office to leave two-year-old Horace Junior in the secretary's care while Mrs. Dodge went shopping. Holding her three-year-old daughter, Delphine, by the hand, Anna Dodge headed for the downtown department stores of Mabley and Co. and J.L. Hudson.

Young children held no particular appeal for Matilda. Still, the baby sitting did not annoy her when she found that Anna Dodge was pleasant and unpretentious. Since John Dodge was a widower, there was no sister-in-law to join Anna in buying luxuries that had previously been beyond the Dodge budget.

After Anna's return from one of her shopping sprees, John confided to Matilda that his wife had been dead for a year. He said no more, but his eyes, the color of the faded blue overalls that Horace wore when he repaired machines, slowly moved over her—from the gleaming dark hair piled high on her head to her small feet in the leather boots that fit so closely around her dainty ankles.

It was not possible to work in the Dodge shop and not hear reports of the brothers' Saturday night drinking binges. The Dodge brothers impartially patronized Monroe Avenue taverns, Woodward Avenue "drinking emporiums," and then went on from bar to bar, in all parts of the city, acquiring reputations as hard drinking brawlers.

In Matilda's life above the Rausch saloon, she had seen and heard the crude behavior and rough talk of drinkers, so she was not shocked at the brothers' bar-hopping habits. But she felt an intense distaste for drinking men.

On Monday mornings, when her employers showed no signs of hangovers, Matilda recognized that the brothers did not permit their weekend drinking sprees to interfere with work. For John Francis Dodge, the shop represented growing power and accomplishment—a triumph over a poverty-burdened early life. For Horace Elgin Dodge, the machine shop represented art and beauty—a ballet of cogs and levers and shuttles coming together in a symmetry of movement.

Because Matilda spent hours each day in John Dodge's office, she often saw him take a medicine bottle from a shelf and drink from it. When she saw him rush to get the medication each time he was gripped by a coughing spell, she recognized his dependence on the compound prescribed by his friend and physician, Dr. William R. Chittick.

Matilda soon learned, from rumors in the shop, that tuberculosis had caused the death of John's wife. The secretary could easily sympathize with her employer's anxiety. The disease was such a terrible scourge that people chose not to admit its existence in their families and referred to it only as the "white plague" or "consumption."

When the wiry, energetic Henry Ford first came to the Dodge office, the brothers were intrigued by Ford's plans for a car. Closing John's office door against the noise of the shop, they studied the plans, drawn up for Ford by C. Harold Wills. The younger Dodge brother immediately felt an affinity for Wills whose first name, Childe, was even more of an embarrassment, Horace felt, than his own name. More important, Horace was fascinated with Ford's idea for building a two-cylinder, eight-horsepower motor that could be made to operate by explosion from drops of gasoline—a combustion engine.

For the past several years, mechanics had attempted to build cars, powered by internal combustion engines, that were simple enough in design to be machine-produced rather than custom built. Henry Ford already had achieved some success in building custom-designed racing cars, but he could not make a success of the Quadricycle that he had worked on for two years. By 1902, he had failed twice in the automobile manufacturing business. Such failures were not uncommon. Of 502 American automobile companies formed by 1908, only 200 would survive past that year.

When Ford came to the Dodges in 1902, his designs were his only asset. Because of his earlier business failures, he could not get financing when he searched for money to manufacture a car from his latest plans. Coal dealer Alexander Malcomson, a shrewd promoter, became attracted to Ford and his car-manufacturing plans after Malcomson was captivated by Ford's hand-constructed, 80-horsepower race car—the 999, which would be raced by daredevil cyclist Barney Oldfield to a record breaking win at Grosse Pointe in 1902. The five mile contest was Oldfield's first as a car driver.

Since Henry Ford worked with ordinary tools in a small garage-workshop, he envied the Dodges who owned a new and well equipped machine shop. He respected the Dodges' success in producing transmissions for Ransom Olds and desperately wanted the use of Dodge Brothers shop as the essential womb for the birth of his automobile.

The Ford-Wills engine, with its two cylinders placed vertically instead of in the usual horizontal position, roused Horace to enthusiasm with his appreciation of the additional power, and less vibration, created by the vertical cylinders. He convinced John that they should work with the plans, even though their own profitable commitment to Oldsmobile production demanded most of their time and resources.

Before the end of 1902, the Dodges turned out the prototype for the new car. Ford and Wills were as pleased with the results as were John and Horace, who had redesigned the rear axle and made some adjustments to the motor.

To Ford, it seemed logical to expect the Dodges to re-equip their entire shop, at their own expense, for the production of Ford chassis—engines, transmissions, and axles. This meant that the Dodges would have to give up their money-making Olds contract and risk a heavy investment in new machinery. It meant gambling with the financial well being of their families and of possibly sliding back into the same poverty they had so recently escaped.

It also meant a chance for a better business deal, however, if the Ford car were successful. By this time, the Dodges were so captivated by the idea of the new car that their gambling instincts could not be muzzled. The brothers decided to stake their future on a hazardous business venture with a man referred to by many Detroiters as "Crazy Ford."

Chapter 2

A Car and a Courtship

Within weeks after John Dodge hired Matilda, the 19-year-old secretary began to lose her awkward feelings in her employer's presence. When she turned quickly, catching a feverish look in his blue eyes, she held herself a little taller and enjoyed the awareness of her own dainty femininity. She quickly accepted when he invited her to a concert at the Detroit Opera House, and went with him on following weekends to vaudeville performances at the Avenue Theater and to dinner at the Russell House.

At the Rausch flat above the saloon, Amelia and her mother chattered endlessly, speculating on the relationship between Matilda and her employer. Intrigued with John F. Dodge's courtship of Matilda, who never before had a "beau," Amelia and Margaret Rausch wondered if the youthful Matilda's interest in her much older employer stemmed only from her enjoyment of Detroit's flourishing entertainment circuit and appearances of such popular stars as the Cherry Sisters and comedienne Marie Dressler.

In the presence of her older daughter, Margaret Rausch carefully avoided chattering about John Dodge. Occasionally she asked a prudently phrased question which Matilda either airily answered or completely ignored, depending on her mood. And Dodge continued inviting Matilda to the theater on Friday or Saturday nights, even in the early months of 1903 when the Ford-Dodge venture wobbled off to a perilous start.

If John and Horace Dodge worried about the contract they had signed with Ford and Malcomson at the end of February, 1903, they were too busy installing additional machinery and hiring new employees to brood about expenditures rising to more than $60,000.

Too busy for sharing their apprehensions...that only the promises of Ford and Malcomson stood between the Dodge Brothers and financial ruin.

By signing the agreement, the Dodges committed themselves to immediately begin producing chassis for purchase by Ford and Malcomson at $250 each. The Dodges promised to deliver 650 chassis, including transmissions, engines, frames and axles—complete auto- motive skeletons ready to be sheathed in shiny enameled body-shells and mobilized with sets of wheels. The responsibility for acquiring bodies, wheels and accessories belonged to Ford and Malcomson, who would assemble the cars. The two men took on an even more pressing responsibility of making monthly progress payments of $5000 each to the Dodges beginning in mid-March. If Ford and Malcomson failed to make the payments, the Dodges could appropriate the "holdings" of Ford & Malcomson Ltd.—plans, patents and a few tools and machines. Years later, renowned Ford biographer, Nevins, wrote that these "holdings" were given "a highly artificial estimate."

At that time, the Dodges must have trusted Malcomson's ability to raise money quickly, because the first $5000 payment became due only two weeks after they signed the contract. But the glib trader and huckster, Malcomson, met nothing but frustration in two weeks of frantic search for financing. To financeers, horseless carriages were little more than flimsy, balky, noisy, faddish contrivances.

Malcomson beseeched the Dodges to continue working on the chassis while he appealed for help from his uncle, John S. Gray, president of the German American Bank. The Dodge brothers agreed to proceed with their work and to wait for payment until Malcomson could convince Gray to put up the money for his nephew's project.

Another month passed, with another $5000 owed to the Dodges, before Malcomson could draw Gray's attention to the car manufacturing enterprise. Before agreeing to advance funds, Gray came to look over Dodge Brothers machine shop. Impressed by the array of machines and skilled workers, the banker consented to furnish $10,500 for payment to the Dodges so the work could continue, but Gray attached certain demands to the funding. He wanted to form an automobile company in which he would own 10.5% of 1000 shares of stock to be issued. Gray also insisted on becoming president of the company.

With the incorporation of Ford Motor Company in June, 1903, President John Gray owned 105 shares of stock valued at $100 per share. Malcomson and Ford, who invested no money, each took ownership of 255 shares. John and Horace Dodge each acquired 50 shares, paid for with $7,000 of materials supplied to the company, plus a note for $3,000 payable in six months. Remaining shares went to seven other investors, including Malcomson's coal-business associate, James Couzens, and Albert Strelow, whose shares paid for the lease of his one-story wagon factory on Mack Avenue for assembly of the cars.

C. Harold Wills, co-designer of the original Ford engine, had no money for stock. Because Ford wanted Wills as chief engineer for the company, he made a verbal promise to pay Wills a salary plus ten percent of any proceeds that Ford received from manufacture of the cars. And within two weeks of the incorporation of the new company, the Dodges began delivering completed chassis on horse-drawn hay ricks to Strelow's former wagon factory, now boasting the name, Ford Motor Company, in large white letters painted on the front and sides of the flat-roofed building.

The pressures of dealing with new mechanical procedures and an expanded work force heightened tensions within Dodge Brothers' Hastings and Monroe plant in those early months of 1903. The little secretary in Dodge Brothers office perceived these tensions stretched to the breaking point by the diversity of temperaments among the men launching the new company.

The powerfully built, blunt-spoken Dodge brothers, whose appetite for liquor was as keen as was teetotaler Henry Ford's distaste for alcohol, clashed repeatedly with the no less opinionated and willful Ford who resented the brothers' persistent tinkering with the innards of a machine about which Ford was obsessively proprietary. The brothers clashed even earlier and more often with Malcomson, whose extrava- gant claims to the media enraged the Dodges. Hot tempered James Couzens, his bull-doggish appearance matching his determination, was equally contentious. But since Couzens was a whiz with figures, the other men tolerated his belligerence while they made concessions to Gray because of his financial stranglehold on the company.

At this point, Couzens projected total costs for all components for the car at $389, of which the Dodges would collect $250. The remaining $139 would pay for wheels, tires, a body, and seat cushions. Couzens' projections included a $20 assembling cost for each car, with selling expenses pegged at $150. The finished automobile would sell for $750, payable in advance. An optional back-seat attachment, known as a tonneau and shaped like a curved love seat, would boost the price an extra $100.

The prim and fastidious Matilda shuddered at the ferocity of John Dodge's frequent arguments on the office telephone with Ford or Malcomson or Couzens. Upset by her employer's surliness after such arguments, Matilda sometimes conceded that her 16-year-old sister,

Amelia, might have made the better choice of careers after all. Following graduation from eighth grade at Duffield School the previous February, Amelia began taking dressmaking classes.

Since the Rausches had sent both their daughters to kindergarten and first grade at a German seminary where only the German language was spoken, each sister had been required to repeat the first grade on entering public school. Both girls, nearly 16 years old when com- pleting the eighth grade, had been relieved to graduate.

Matilda's concerns about the background of hostility at work vanished with the sale of the first Ford car in the middle of July, 1903, when the mood at Dodge Brothers changed to one of buoyant optimism. By this time, Dodge Brothers had 150 employees, while only 12 men worked at assembling the cars for Ford Motor Company.

The two-cyclinder, eight-horsepower Model A emerged as a sturdy, little open car. Although it had no door nor running board, with only a carriage step to hoist driver or passenger up to the leather upholstered seat, nothing of the "cycle" look marred the appearance of this first Ford automobile. On the right, a tall column and steering wheel accommodated the driver, perched high above the motor. Slender fenders, like plucked eyebrows, arched above substantial 28-inch, wood-spoked wheels. Two headlamps, plus a rear lantern, were both a convenience and shiny adornments to the machine.

Following the sale of that first Model A to a Chicago dentist, a spurt of orders arrived from physicians looking for convenient transportation in making house calls. By October of 1903, 195 cars—159 of them complete with tonneaus—were sold. The wrangling among the Dodges, Ford, Malcomson and Couzens moderated because no one could argue with success confirmed by payment of the company's first dividend as early as November, 1903—$10,000, of which the Dodges collected $1000.

Stimulated by the smell of success, Ford began enlarging the assembly building. The Dodges signed another contract to deliver 1,890 chassis by July of 1904 at $175 each, and prepared to expand their Monroe shop with two more buildings. Ford Motor Company advanced $25,000 to the Dodges for the expansion, to be paid back without interest the following summer.

Again in January, 1904, the company's spiraling success yielded a payment of $20,000 in dividends to investors. Within the Dodge shop, however, John and Horace fumed over Couzens' complaints of loose flywheels and faulty brakes in the Model A. Since Dodge employees now were paid on a piecework basis, John and Horace hired more supervisors to prevent workers from hurriedly turning out botched brakes and engines. The defects were eliminated in the 1904 models, and the experience led, later, to a revised pay system in the Dodge shop, combining an hourly wage with piecework credits. At the time of the complaint, Couzens also reminded the Dodges of an agreement they had previously signed in which the brothers promised not to make any changes in the chassis without permission from Ford, still determined to retain total control.

By the end of March, 1904, the company's sales totalled 658 automobiles. Assembling costs per car climbed to $37 instead of Couzens' projected $20. And profits per machine averaged $150.38. But total profits ballooned to $98,951.96, elevating the company—whose assets had amounted to only a couple of hundred dollars the previous July—into the ranks of million-dollar firms.

When the board of directors met in Couzens' office on June 15, 1904, John Dodge, supported by vice-president Henry Ford, moved that $68,000 of profits should be distributed to stockholders. Including this third distribution, each stockholder now received 98% of the original investment made only 14 months earlier.

Since the Dodges also profited from their production of chassis, the incoming flow of money began changing their lives. John Dodge abandoned the use of streetcars in late 1903 and drove a Ford car to pick up Matilda at the Rausch flat. Dressed for an evening at the opera house, the fleshy-figured Dodge wore a high silk hat and well tailored suit that, Matilda knew, was one of two identical suits ordered by Horace Dodge from his tailor.

Because the older brother, John, had little interest in his own wardrobe, Matilda considered it fortunate that the younger and more dapper brother, who had a wife to brush and press and hang up his clothes, never ordered a new pair of trousers or a suit for himself without ordering a similar item for John. The two brothers usually arrived together at the shop in the mornings, worked together, consulted each other on every important decision, locked up the shop together in the evenings, and, at regular intervals, drank themselves into rowdy drunkenness at one of their favorite saloons.

John Dodge exhibited no signs of rowdy behavior on the weekend evenings he spent with Matilda. Nor was it his style to permit conversation to lag, largely because he never seemed to tire of reminiscing about his early life with his family in Niles, Michigan. Matilda listened closely when he compared his impoverished youth to his current financial status and expectations of even greater wealth—as if the exuberance he felt in his self-made success were too great to be contained. The earthiness of the man, whose passions lay so close to the surface, held a peculiar magnetism for the inhibited Matilda, who rarely spoke of her background and who choked on the word saloon as if she bit into a gooseberry.

Each time John spoke of his early life, Matilda sensed, more fully, the strength of the Dodge family bonds. John and Horace—the inseparable, hard working brothers. Their older sister, Della—a paragon of intelligence and elegance, according to John, and a writer of poetry of utmost grace and beauty. The father, Daniel Rugg Dodge—working for years at a blazing forge in the Niles foundry in which his brothers, Caleb and Edwin, shared ownership and profits which were miserably inadequate to nourish three families. John deeply regretted, he often confided to friends, that his father died in July, 1897, without knowing of the business success his sons would achieve.

Above all, John spoke tenderly of his mother, Maria Casto Dodge—as proud of her Pennsylvania-Dutch and French heritage as her husband, Daniel, was of his English ancestry that could be traced back to 1627 and the arrival of the Dodge family's immigrant ancestor on New England soil. The mother's philosophy became a stimulus to her three children as she stressed their moral duty to observe the precepts of the Methodist Church...to value honesty and to refrain from the vices of drinking, smoking, dancing and card-playing.

The young Dodge brothers, who wore oddly assorted and patched clothing and were often reduced to barefoot discomfort in cold weather, dutifully followed the tenets instilled by their mother. They regularly attended Methodist Sunday School classes and worked at odd jobs to earn a few coins.

John Dodge's stories of his boyhood invariably included poignant memories of driving a cow three miles, twice daily, for the magnificent sum of 50 cents a week, and, in his later teen years, working full time at the Krick factory in Niles where he earned $6.25 a week. The latter sum substantially improved family finances.

The Canadian-born Matilda knew little of poverty, although she certainly had observed the struggles of her parents. She chose to tell John nothing about the Princess Saloon—the business that her father, George Rausch, had opened in 1884 when Matilda was not yet a year old. The Rausches and their baby daughter lived in second-floor quarters above the saloon, located near Detroit's riverfront and catering to sailors and shipworkers. For Matilda, it was no less tainted to confess to a lifetime—20 years—of living above a "thirst emporium" than to admit that her mother, Margaret Rausch, had opened the neigh- boring Dry Dock Hotel and served 25 cent home-cooked meals to the same customers who visited the saloon. But when Margaret became pregnant with a second child in the summer of 1886, the Rausches sold the Dry Dock Hotel and Margaret began helping her husband in the Princess Saloon until the birth of the second daughter, Amelia.

John Dodge's enthusiam for tracing his life from poverty to prosperity remained undampened by Matilda's reluctance to discuss her own background. Certainly she had no inclination to talk about her schooling. Not after her employer boasted of his sister Della's graduation, with honors, from high school in 1879 at age 16. Three years later, John pleased his mother by graduating from the same Niles school.

The father, Daniel Dodge, was more concerned with the proficiencies of both his sons at the forge and lathe in his shop where he trained the young brothers to repair marine engines. But as Niles became a railroad center in 1879, the demand for marine-engine repair faded.

Through an earlier marriage between Silas W. Dodge and Sally Upton in Allegan, Michigan, the Daniel Dodges claimed a family relationship to the more prosperous Upton family which, like the Dodges, had relatives spread across southwest Michigan—in Niles, St. Joseph, Benton Harbor, Battle Creek, and neighboring towns. When the Daniel Dodge family learned that James S. Upton planned to move his Upton Manufacturing Company from Battle Creek to Port Huron, on the east coast of Michigan, both John and Horace Dodge supported their father's decision to move across the state and to take jobs with the company at its new plant. John's married half-sister Laura—daughter of Daniel Dodge and his first, deceased wife—was the only family member to remain in Niles.

Located just south of the city of Port Huron, population approaching 12,000 inhabitants, the Upton Manufacturing Company became a self-sufficient settlement known as Uptonville, with stores, houses, and its own post office adjacent to the "Upton Works" built with a quarter-million-dollar capitalization along the Grand Trunk Railroad. There, the Dodges—parents, 19-year-old John and 15-year-old Horace, their sister, Della, and their older half-brother, Charlie—settled into an Uptonville house, showered with soot and grime from snorting switch engines, that trembled with each bellow and rumble of passing freight trains. The company, manufacturer of huskers, shredders and threshers, had various Uptons on its payroll, including Edward Frank Upton as vice-president, when the Dodges came to work in Port Huron. As they trained under the guidance of company superintendent Uriah Eschbach and attended the same church as the staunchly Methodist Uptons, the link between the two families was strengthened.

Four years before the sale of Upton Manufacturing Company in 1890, the Daniel Dodge family reluctantly parted from their many friends in Port Huron to move 70 miles south to Detroit. Their friend and boss, Uriah Eschbach, left Port Huron at the same time to go into the cleaning and dyeing business in Ann Arbor.

Although the gutsy city of Detroit was recovering from a financial depression that had crippled the economy of 1884-85, the husky Dodge brothers quickly found work in 1886—building boilers and repairing boats at Tom Murphy's boiler shop. They started at a weekly wage of $18 each, and 23-year-old John Dodge soon won a promotion to shop supervisor.

Seventeen years later as the 40-year-old Dodge indulged in reminiscences over dinner at the Russell House, Matilda listened attentively to her employer's vivid memories of those early years in Detroit. The brothers' lucky break occurred in 1892 when they found jobs, at $150 monthly salaries, across the Detroit River with the Dominion Typography Company in Windsor, Canada. There, both Horace and John gained valuable experience in working with precision tools—micrometers and calipers—to produce patterns and dies.

One year later, another financial depression stifled the economy in Detroit where 25,000 men roamed the streets in search of work. When business slowed, also, at the Dominion Typography Company across the river, the company's decision to begin manufacturing bicycles excited the Dodge brothers.

The Dodges' fascination with wheels reached back to their schooldays when the first high-wheeled cycle appeared in Niles. The $200 contrivance, fitted with a lofty seat, was an unaffordable luxury for most townspeople, and certainly for the indigent Dodges. But the young Dodge brothers devised their own conveyance by steaming a strip of wood and bending it to shape a rim for the high front wheel, and then inserting spokes. Using the small wheel from a baby carriage at the rear, they put together the second high-wheeled cycle ever seen in their hometown.

But in 1893, the popularity of high-wheeled cycles faded as low bicycles with two wheels of equal size came into vogue. Young men ("scorchers") raced up and down the streets of Detroit on the machines, and young women (considered quite immodest by more inhibited females) also rode the new "safety" bicycles. Laborers pedalled them to work, and doctors and postmen rode them on their rounds.

Still entranced by cycles, Horace invented a four-point, adjustable, ball-bearing mechanism. He then leased the dirt-proof bearing-device to his Canadian employer who began to manufacture the Maple Leaf Bicycle (also known as the Evans & Dodge Machine). The employer promised royalty payments to the Dodges for the use of the ball-bearing device.

In 1896, when the failing Canadian typography company was listed for sale, the Dodges took every dollar they could drain from their family budgets to try to lease the company's building and fixtures. Horace even managed to borrow $200 from his wife, Anna—savings she had accumulated by giving piano lessons. Obtaining the lease, the brothers started operating their own business, but it survived only a short time.

Matilda sensed an evasiness in John Dodge's quick-skimming account of the three years following 1897...of selling the business to another Ontario, Canada, firm while the brothers continued working for the new owners, although John had to move, with Ivy and the children, to Hamilton, Ontario. There, John worked at the company's Hamilton plant while Horace remained in Windsor until the company failed—owing royalties for the ball-bearing device to the Dodges. In lieu of royalties, the brothers were given their choice of machinery from the plant.

With this machinery, the brothers set up their first machine shop in Detroit's Boydell Building in 1900. To attract customers, they asked their sister, Della, to help them write an advertisement:

DODGE BROTHERS

Builders of Simple, Compound, Triple and Quadruple Expansion Marine and Stationary Engines.
We also build and repair any kind of machinery, do all kinds of difficult punch, die and tool work; do internal, external and surface
grinding, millings, gear cutting and punch work.
Linotype machines repaired skillfully and promptly.

Few people knew that the muscular John Dodge had been ill with tuberculosis in the late 1890s. But Matilda finally deduced, from tidbits of gossip at the shop, that tuberculosis had not only taken the life of Ivy Dodge but had, even earlier, threatened John's life and prompted his use of alcohol—as medication. In December, 1904, a <u>New</u> <u>York</u> <u>Times</u>
headline—"Whiskey, Beer & Wine Useful for Consumption"—would

quote the opinion of Dr. Wiley, chief chemist of the U.S. Department of Agriculture, who endorsed this method of treatment. Knowledge of John's earlier illness provided Matilda with new insight into the erratic pattern of Dodge business affairs in the late 1890s, when Horace—who, until that time, had always worked with his brother—went to work for Leland. She could understand, too, why John Dodge never smoked, although Horace occasionally smoked cigars.

At the time Matilda came to work in the Dodge office, few of the restrictive tenets of the Methodist Church were observed by the brothers. But John Dodge did not play cards nor did he know how to dance. Matilda was not unwilling to set aside her romantic dreams of gliding across a dance floor in the arms of a dashing male partner—since no such partner had sought her company—for acceptance of the widower Dodge as her escort and means of ingress to the kinds of entertainment in which she took pleasure.

Before the end of 1903, Matilda began to accept the reality of her employer's intrusion into her very proper and prudish life as more than a convenience for entertainment-excursions. John Dodge could no longer completely restrain his passion for his young secretary whose dark hair and slim figure reminded him of his first wife, Ivy. Although the sexually naive Matilda may have been unaware that her cool restraint served only to inflame the hot blooded Dodge, she soon thrilled to a feeling of power over the vigorous man who trembled with the fevor of his desire for the virginal secretary...a desire enkindled by the strange mixture of eager girlishness and sedate maturity exhibited by Matilda.

The tiny secretary realized, by this time, that she could not hold off John's advances indefinitely and that she had a decision to make. In her usual deliberative manner, she considered both the advantages and disadvantages of continuing the relationship and, even, of becoming Mrs. John Dodge. She was unconcerned that Dodge was old enough to be her father, but much more concerned with the three Dodge children for whose care she would be responsible if she married her employer. Despite Matilda's lack of warmth for children, she was reasonably confident of her ability to manage the youngsters, and to do a conscientious job if she decided to assume such a responsibility.

She also faced the unpleasant fact that John Dodge was a drinking man, even though he had not touched liquor until he was 30 years old. Matilda was horrified by a story, circulating within the shop, of an intoxicated John pointing his revolver at a saloon proprietor and forcing the hapless owner to dance on a table to the shattering applause of glasses tossed at the bar by Dodge. Still, her horror was not devastating enough to eclipse her perception that great success appeared to lie within the grasp of the Dodge brothers. The rapid expansion of the Monroe Avenue plant signified such success. So, too, did the new contract for more chassis...the mushrooming payments from Ford Motor Company...the soaring popularity of the Ford Model A.

Matilda decided to bide her time and to be certain of the range of John Dodge's affluence before committing herself to the idea of becoming the future Mrs. John F. Dodge.

Chapter 3

A Mansion and a Marriage

In 1904, the number of automobiles in Detroit became a growing menace. The city soon established a speed limit of eight miles an hour in the downtown area, but snorting motorcars continued to threaten the safety of pedestrians and cyclists, of citizens traveling in horse-drawn carriages, and of teamsters making deliveries from horse-drawn drays.

Nonetheless, the rising popularity of the motorcar boosted Detroit's economy. The automobile industry spawned several related businesses as manufacturers and retailers supplied auto accessories—lamps, horns almost as large as tubas, and baggage carriers. Although few women attempted to drive the bucking motorcars because of the need to crank the machines to a start and then leap into shuddering vehicles already jerking forward, the auto industry began influencing fashions. Stores stocked loose dusters made of linen or pongee for feminine automobile passengers who also bought chiffon veils to tie around their large hats when they "went motoring." For men, there were dusters, visors, and thick goggles.

Ford Motor Company brought out three models in 1904—an $800 Model C runabout, a $1000 Model F touring car, and a larger, four-cylinder Model B selling for $2000. In August, the company pressured the Dodges to contract to manufacture 2500 chassis for the small Ford model within the first six months of 1905. Because the Dodge plant was already working at capacity, the brothers agreed to furnish only 2000 rigs.

Other disagreements occurred at weekly Monday-morning board of directors' meetings. Malcomson insisted that payments to the Dodges for chassis should be reduced, since Ford Motor Company was now averaging a profit of only $80 per car. John Dodge fiercely protested Malcomson's suggestion, pointing out that the Ford company's overall profits were growing as increasing numbers of cars were sold. The payment reduction to the Dodges was voted down, but John Dodge nourished a lasting dislike for Malcomson.

Malcomson and Ford argued tempestuously, Malcomson demand- ing that the company should build more expensive models in response to a demand for large and comfortable cars, while Ford persisted with his idea of quantity production of one simply designed car to sell at the lowest possible price. Despite personal animosities among the direc- tors, the company thrived and distributed a hefty $200,000 dividend in mid-year, 1905. By this time, the company had outgrown its Mack Avenue quarters and had erected a three-story brick factory on Piquette and Beaubien.

With his share of profits from Dodge Brothers plant, Horace indulged his ardor for boats—a passion that had gripped him ever since, as a youngster, he watched cargo ships moving along the St. Joseph River to Chicago. Because his brother, John, had so little interest in either the river or its ships, it is likely that Horace was the only person who suspected the scope of the older brother's fear of deep water. The earth—forest, orchard and farmlands—was John's love. As a boy hiking through the lush valleys of Niles, John dreamed of owning a country estate—the dream as vivid as was Horace's vision of cutting through the waves with a powerful craft of his own.

In 1904, Horace took his designs for a 40-foot steam launch—the Lotus—to a boat works where a racing launch was also being built for Ransom Olds. When Horace's Lotus was completed, he raced it along the Detroit River, spent countless hours fine-tuning the mechanisms of the craft, then built another engine for a second 40-footer, the Hornet.

Unlike Horace Dodge and Ransom Olds, Henry Ford cared nothing for boats, but still retained his fascination for race cars. By January of 1904, Ford was back into racing—using his race car, the Arrow, as advertising for the four-cylinder Model B, since the engine for the Arrow and the Model B were almost identical. With Ford at the wheel, the race car hurtled along a 15-foot-wide clearing, covered with cinders, on frozen Lake St. Clair to break the previous world's record with a speed of 91.37 miles an hour.

John Dodge had neither time nor inclination for boats or race cars. He was still absorbed with his passion for the trim and immaculately attired Matilda Rausch, whose smooth fragrant skin and brilliant dark eyes excited his hunger to possess his young secretary.

At the Rausch flat on St. Aubin Street, Amelia Rausch's big, round eyes widened each time her older sister chose to share some of her experiences at the busy Dodge office. Matilda talked freely about Horace Dodge's love affair with his boats and his purchase of a large new home on Forest Street. And she entertained her parents and sister with descriptions of some of the automotive men who came to confer with the Dodges.

Matilda talked much less of John Dodge, which hardly surprised Amelia who was familiar with her sister's reticence in personal and sensitive matters. But Matilda's reticence did not restrain Amelia's avid curiosity about the relationship between her sister and her middle-aged "beau."

Each time that Matilda returned home with an extra program from a concert or play or vaudeville performance that she attended with Dodge, Amelia carefully saved the program in a bureau-drawer collection of mementos. Her vicarious enjoyment of what she perceived as her sister's eventful life influenced Amelia to abandon the boredom of dressmaker classes and to enroll in shorthand and typing classes at Miles Business College. Although Amelia considered herself as quicker and more clever than her older sister ("Matilda had to study very hard to make things stick in her mind," the younger sister insisted), she was not ambitious enough to follow Matilda's example by taking bookkeeping classes.

Amelia completed her business-school training and then gratefully accepted the chance to work in the Dodge office when Matilda offered her the job. The younger sister, still wearing her hair in pigtails, began working at the Dodge plant in June, 1905, assisting Matilda and the bookkeeper, whom 18-year-old Amelia addressed as "Mr. Stone." John Dodge, of course, had been "Mr. Dodge" to Amelia ever since he first came to the Rausch flat to pick up Matilda.

Although senior workmen at the Dodge shop called John Dodge by his nickname, "Frank," even the newer employees called Horace "Ed." For years, the younger Dodge brother had resorted to using a series of nicknames to avoid the name he disliked—Horace. For a time, he used his second name, Elgin. Later, he called himself Delbert. Dellie. Ed. And eventually, "H.E."

Advised by Matilda to address Horace, like John, as "Mr. Dodge," Amelia tried to please the sister who reigned over the office. But she noticed that Anna Dodge called her husband's secretary "Tilly," ignoring Matilda's distaste for the nickname. Matilda took her revenge by reminding Amelia, each time that Anna left the office, that Mrs. Horace Dodge was nothing more than a Scotch immigrant who worked in a cookie factory before her marriage.

Still, Amelia could see that her proud older sister tried to be pleasant to Anna Dodge when the two women met. For Amelia, dominated by her willful sister, there was some satisfaction in observing Matilda's conciliatory overtures to the coolly aloof Anna Dodge. Amelia concluded that the alliance and loyalty between the two Dodge brothers were strong enough to force her proud sister to bend in deference to family unity.

Before the end of 1905, Matilda discovered the reason for the chill that altered Anna Dodge's once friendly manner. Margaret Rausch's brother, Harry Glinz, stomped upstairs to the Rausch flat one evening with a warning for the family. Closing the kitchen door, Margaret talked with her brother and then called Matilda into the kitchen. In Matilda's presence, the uncle repeated his message. He had been told by several customers who came into his Third Street barbershop, Uncle Harry said accusingly, that John Dodge was married to the woman known as the "housekeeper" at Dodge's Trumbull Street home. "Her name is Belle Smith," Harry Glinz asserted. "But she calls herself Mrs. Dodge."

Certain that his message would immediately impel George Rausch to sever the relationship between Matilda and the much older Dodge, the barber returned to his shop. A short time later, Glinz was incensed to learn that his nieces still worked at Dodge Brothers office and that the relationship continued between Matilda and John Dodge.

Once again, Harry Glinz stormed over to the Rausch flat. Because Glinz had previously boarded with the Rausches and had pampered and indulged his young nieces in those earlier years, his ties with his sister and her family were strong. Now, however, George Rausch begged his brother-in-law to lower his voice so the young, innocent Amelia would not hear.

Matilda's insistence that the neighbors' talk was idle gossip did not pacify her Uncle Harry. From the other side of the kitchen door, Amelia clearly overheard her uncle's angry voice. If his sister and brother-in-law allowed Tilly to bring scandal to the family by associ- ating with a married man, he threatened, he would never again speak to any of the Rausches.

Shut out from the family discussions that followed, Amelia knew that Matilda, though under pressure from her parents, was still determined to remain in charge of her own life. In December, 1905, the younger sister was dismayed when, a few weeks after Uncle Harry's visit, Matilda informed Amelia that she was leaving the Dodge office. "I think it would be best for you to do the same," she advised Amelia in the firm tone that always commanded quick compliance from the sister.

Matilda immediately found a new job at the Detroit Lumber Company. Standard Electric Company hired Amelia who complained, at home, that "they wanted a cheap office girl."

Matilda ignored the complaint as thoroughly as she ignored Amelia's curiosity about the reason for their abrupt departure from Dodge Brothers. Amelia assumed there had been a quarrel between Matilda and John, and that Dodge would no longer be a part of the Rausches' lives.

Matilda had no intention of confiding in Amelia or her parents—no intention of letting them know that John Dodge had, indeed, married his housekeeper in a secret ceremony performed in Walkerville, Canada. He had reluctantly confessed to the marriage when Matilda demanded the truth, telling him of the rumors her uncle had heard. Stunned by Dodge's admission, Matilda recalled seeing Belle Smith—an attractive, well-built woman—just once when she came, unannounced, into the Dodge shop. Introduced brusquely by John as "my housekeeper," the woman was whisked out of the office before anything more could be said.

Unable to control her dismay at John's admission, Matilda insisted on knowing when the marriage took place. Dodge's answer — December of 1903—shocked her into silence. 1903—while he regular- ly escorted her—Matilda Rausch—about town! Two years of deceit...while he led her to believe that marriage was in their future...while she considered becoming the wife of a man of wealth and power. And all the time he knew that he could not marry her.

The enormity of the deceit enraged her as John Dodge pleaded that he was making every effort to force Belle Smith out of his home. He explained, desperately, that he originally hired the woman at Anna Dodge's suggestion...that Anna and Belle had been neighbors and friends since their grade-school days. So close were the two women, he added, that Belle had even accompanied Anna to the neighborhood homes of piano students who took lessons from Anna Thomson in the years before she married Horace.

John admitted that he found housekeeper Belle Smith's presence in his home most convenient. Belle ran the house efficiently, did a fine job of supervising the motherless children, and gave John's invalid mother the kind of tender care that endeared the housekeeper to the wheelchair-bound Maria Dodge. The subtle pressures from the mother whom John cherished, from Anna Dodge, and even from Horace, gradually became less subtle as Belle Smith made herself indispensable in the Trumbull Street household.

Despite John's explanations, Matilda found it difficult to believe that the forceful and robust Dodge allowed himself to be pushed into a marriage of convenience. She found it impossible to be persuaded that, even if John had been drinking at the time, he could be maneuvered into making a quick trip to Canada where he and Belle were married by a Methodist minister with Horace and Anna as witnesses.

Distraught at the possibility of losing Matilda, John Dodge vowed that he would get Belle Smith out of his home immediately...that he would divorce her as quickly as possible...that he would build a fine mansion for Matilda if only she would give him the chance to straighten out his life.

His pleas were useless. Matilda reminded him, sternly, that she could never marry a divorced man. Divorce was an ugly, scandalous affair and she could never again hold her head high if she became a party to it. Their relationship was ended. She would never again set her dainty foot inside John Dodge's office.

For Amelia, clacking away at a heavy typewriter at Standard Electric, workdays became humdrum affairs. After-work hours at the St. Aubin flat were dulled by the presence of a moody and listless Matilda who perked up only when annoyed, like a streak of heat lightning flashing unexpectedly on a clear night.

Although Amelia worked for Dodge Brothers less than six months before coming to Standard Electric, she missed the sense of excitement and adventure that pervaded the Dodge office. She suspected that Matilda felt the same, although the older sister never mentioned her former employer. Pining for the excitement of her former job, Amelia clipped and saved every article published in Detroit newspapers that carried accounts of Ford Motor Company and of transactions conducted by its board of directors, including John Dodge. While still working for Dodge Brothers, Amelia often had listened to John Dodge's expressions of personal dislike for Malcomson. Now, she had no way of knowing that Dodge was supportive of Henry Ford in Ford's devious plan to force Malcomson out of the flourishing company.

The conflict between Ford and Malcomson had escalated in direct proportion to increased Ford Motor Company automobile production, amounting in 1905 to 25 cars each day. Finding it unbearable that the quarrelsome Malcomson's shares in the company equalled his own, Ford formed a new company incorporated in November of 1905 as the Ford Manufacturing Company, with Henry Ford as president and John F. Dodge as vice president. Malcomson was offered no stock in the new company.

The Dodges—now manufacturing parts for a new Ford machine, the luxurious, six-cylinder Model K touring car—went along with Ford's plan to have the newly formed Ford Manufacturing Company on Bellevue Avenue make the chassis for the latest and most popular Ford car...the Model N. The Model N would have four cylinders and a torque-drive, but would be priced at a reasonable $600.

At a January, 1906, meeting of Ford Motor Company's board of directors, it was determined that the company would buy 10,000 Model N chassis from Ford Manufacturing Company "at no more than $206" per chassis. But Malcomson realized that the new manufacturing company would be able to boost its prices for Model N chassis at the will of Ford, John Dodge and other directors. In this way, Ford Motor Company profits could be drained into the coffers of the new Ford Manufacturing Company in which Malcomson held no shares.

By this time, Malcomson, who had promoted the more expensive Model K, recognized that Ford's maneuvers had placed him in an untenable position. In July of 1906, when a faltering national economy contributed to Henry Ford's deliberate erosion of Ford Motor Company earnings, Malcomson reluctantly sold his stock to Ford for $175,000 ($45,000 of that amount borrowed from the Dodges.) Strelow sold his 50 shares for $25,000 with his announced intention of going out West to invest in a gold mine. Three other minor stockholders sold their shares, also, increasing Couzens' holdings to 110 shares but swelling Henry Ford's holdings to 585 shares—giving him control of the company. At that point, the new company had accomplished its purpose and it was absorbed into the Ford Motor Company in 1907.

Even before Malcomson sold his stock, John Dodge and Matilda resumed the relationship that was ruptured in December of 1905. To Amelia's astonishment, Dodge appeared at the Rausch flat on a Saturday evening, as if nothing unusual had happened. He collected Matilda—her hair puffed and pinned into a high, glistening pompadour, her shirtwaist starched and scented with lavender—and the two calmly went down to his waiting car. The puzzled Amelia could learn nothing of what transpired when she questioned her mother, who confessed to being equally perplexed.

Matilda said little, assuring her mother only that "there will be no scandal about which you need concern yourselves." She did not intend to explain further...to tell them that the Dodge "housekeeper" had already left the Trumbull Street house...that the marriage had been kept a secret as far as the newspapers and Dodge associates were concerned and that the neighbors' suspicions had never been verified...that John Dodge was determined to get an equally secret divorce, and was friendly enough with several judges to ensure that it remained a secret...that he was already planning to build a quarter-million-dollar home on East Boston Boulevard for her—Matilda. Until these things were accomplished, Matilda was willing to wait.

In the several weeks between her departure from the Dodge office and her reconciliation with John, she took time to consider her position. She was 22 years old and not a great beauty, and never had a "beau" apart from Dodge. She was not remotely interested in marrying a son of any of her parents' German friends when that type of marriage would commit her to the same kind of hard working life that her mother had endured.

Because John Dodge could endow her with the trappings of wealth, Matilda decided she could compromise her principles if his second marriage remained a secret. She recognized the risk that information about the divorce might leak out at some future time. That, to Matilda, would be a disgrace as bad as having to wear the badge of an adulteress. Deciding that the prize overbalanced the risk, she consented to give John Dodge time to rectify his mistake.

When the John Dodge family moved into its new three-story, multi-gabled home in 1906, the first floor bedroom remained unoccupied. John had planned the spacious room, fitted with an extra wide door to accommodate wheelchair entrance into a large, private bathroom, for the use of his mother, Maria, even though the mother protested that she would never live in the new house. Unmoved by the installation of central heating, thick rugs, and gold-plated bathroom fixtures, Maria stubbornly clung to the threat she made when her son forced Belle Smith out of his Trumbull Street house. Opposed to divorce and suspicious that her son wanted to marry his secretary, the mother issued her edict. She would never enter the new house that John was building. No matter how well appointed it might be. No matter how fashionable the neighborhood.

Because of the desirability of the East Boston Boulevard environs where Malcomson built a fine home next door to the Dodges, John easily persuaded his sister, Della, to come to Detroit with her husband and to move into the great house where she would supervise the servants. Like her brothers, Della aspired to a better and more affluent way of life. She had been 20 years old at the time the Dodge family had moved to Port Huron where 38-year-old Uriah Eschbach trained John and Horace as workmen at Upton Manufacturing Company. Nine years later, the widower Eschbach had come to Detroit to ask Della Dodge to become his wife. At the age of 29 and still unmarried, Della was not averse to the 45-year-old Eschbach's proposal.

Married in 1892, Della moved to Ann Arbor where her husband continued operating his laundry business. Within a short time, Della changed her husband's name from Uriah Eschbach to one that Della considered more aristocratic—Rie Ashbaugh. Like Horace, Della never liked her own name, so she re-christened herself Delphine Ashbaugh.

Uriah, who suffered a bullet wound in his jaw as a young soldier in the Civil War, was 51 years old and in failing health when John Dodge asked his sister and brother-in-law to move to Detroit in 1906. Enchanted with the idea of living in grandeur, Della assured her brother that she could talk their mother into moving to Boston Boulevard.

The Eschbachs (Ashbaughs) settled into 33 East Boston Boulevard where Della smoothly adjusted to her upscaled lifestyle. She en- countered problems, however, with her mother who insisted on going to Decatur, Michigan, to live with her two sisters. Although Della and her brothers liked to think of their mother's stay in Decatur as a visit with their aunts, the Decatur address turned into a permanent home for Maria Dodge who died there the following year, August, 1907.

After more than 20 years in the saloon business, George Rausch sold his saloon in 1906 and bought a grocery store on Kercheval Street.

Like the Rausches' previous businesses, the store had an upstairs apartment into which the family moved. The change of businesses and living quarters occurred so quickly that 19-year-old Amelia, who began to feel that her family would never change their thinking of her as "Baby Rausch," tried to understand the reasons for the sudden transition.

When Matilda left her job at Detroit Lumber Company at the same time, Amelia wondered if Matilda's resignation was linked with the sale of the saloon. The younger sister was even more perplexed at Matilda's increased interest in self-improvement as she enrolled in culinary classes at the YWCA. A private tutor, Miss McDonald, began coming to the Rausch grocery store-flat to instruct Matilda in elocution, English literature and piano studies. Because the Rausch girls no longer remembered their early-life German language studies, Matilda also enrolled in German classes. And when Amelia returned from work in late afternoons, she often saw her sister studiously reading a book entitled <u>Simple</u> <u>Notion</u> <u>of</u> <u>French</u>.

Such persistent studying and memorizing remained outside the scope of the more vivacious Amelia's inclinations. But for Matilda, the long hours of studies were a kind of expiation for the guilt that gnawed at her conscience. She had tried to purify her life by persuading her parents to rid themselves of the saloon, and to work at an untainted business. And still the nagging guilt persisted. She attempted to bridge the guilt with a boardwalk of goals, determining to equip herself to become a cultured lady who would work for charitable causes. She resolved to be a supportive wife and model housekeeper and, above all, a helpful and caring stepmother to the young Dodges, setting an uplifting example to both the father and his children.

Sometimes Matilda envied Amelia, her frivolous ways and light- hearted personality. The younger sister made no secret of her delight when, in 1906, John Dodge asked Amelia to return to work in the Dodge office. She switched jobs again, happy to be a part of the busy world of automotive entrepreneurs. Following the death of banker John S. Gray in July of 1906, John F. Dodge became vice-president of Ford Motor Company as Henry Ford became its president.

Ever since the formation of the Ford Manufacturing Company for the purpose of forcing Malcomson to sell his Ford stock, Ford continued to make the essential parts for its own small and popular Model N. The Dodges still manufactured parts exclusively for the heavier Model K Ford selling for $2800. In the lagging economy of 1906 when many automobile companies collapsed as financially pressed customers cancelled their orders for cars, the demand for expensive Model K's also declined. John and Horace began to worry about the danger of making parts exclusively for a single customer.

Aware that Ford Motor Company would be making even more of its own parts in the future, the Dodges began to consider alternative plans for their factory. They had no intention of selling their Ford stock, however. They regarded Strelow as foolhardly in selling his shares, even though the brothers never suspected that an insolvent Strelow would return, later, to stand in the Ford Motor Company employment line to ask for work.

By 1906, Horace Dodge became convinced that his older brother was totally committed to marrying Matilda Rausch...which meant an equal and prior commitment to divorce Belle Smith. Although John had maneuvered Belle into a separation, she refused to become a divorcee because of the attached stigma at a time when only a major charge such as adultery provided a legal basis for divorce.

Horace finally joined with John in importuning Belle Smith Dodge to cooperate in divorce proceedings. She would be financially secure for the rest of her life, they promised. And if her concerns for secrecy equalled those of John, not a word of the marriage or divorce would be reported to Detroiters...she would not be publicly known as a divorcee.

Influenced greatly by Horace, the husband of her dear friend, Anna, Belle yielded to the pressure and filed divorce papers in a small Michigan town, attempting to disguise names with the use of "Minnie" and "Frank" instead of Isabelle and John. The charge, "desertion", was accurate, but the payment to Belle, according to the October 29, 1907, settlement papers, was $2000—far less than accurate. Although John Dodge was now a wealthy man of influence, no newspaper printed notice of the divorce.   Nor did Dodge acquaintances learn of it.

It galled Matilda, though, to realize that Anna Dodge knew of the divorce and could disclose the secret to others if she chose. Matilda trusted Horace—no one could question his unqualified loyalty to John. But she knew that Anna's sympathies lay with her close friend, Belle. It was clear to Matilda that John expected her to do everything possible to win Anna's tolerance and good will, because of the value that John and Horace Dodge placed on family ties and bloodlines. An even more compelling reason was to win the assurance of secrecy from Anna.

One of the more bothersome parts of Amelia's job was recording the unfamiliar names of illiterate immigrants, hired as employees by the Dodges, on payroll sheets. Andrea Bozzio, a young Italian who came to work at the Dodge shop in 1907, had managed to get past immigration authorities at Ellis Island without a change of name. In Detroit, he went to work for the Michigan Stove Company until he learned to operate a drill press with enough proficiency to look for a better paying job—at Dodge Brothers.

On his first payday at the Dodge shop, Bozzio lined up to collect his money at the office window.   Other employees walked away with their wages while Bozzio waited as the clerk called out "Henry Batz."   When Bozzio protested that his name was not "Batz," he was told that "if you want your job, your name is Henry Batz."

Bozzio-Batz wanted the job. He also liked the Dodges, especially John Dodge who frequently came into the tool room and worked along with the rest of the men, joking and talking as if they were his closest friends. Batz soon learned that several of the tool-room men were hunting and fishing companions of Dodge. Drinking companions, as well. But Batz had no time for hunting and fishing, nor drinking in saloons. As the oldest son of a family still living in Italy, it was his responsibility to work hard and send as much of his wages as possible back to his parents, who would then send Andrea's younger brothers to America. Batz, who took this responsibility very seriously, would work for the Dodge company for 49 1/2 years without taking a single day off.

On December 10, 1907, as Amelia typed invoices at her desk, John Dodge burst into the office to tell her that she could have the afternoon off. She looked up in surprise to see a wide smile creasing his face. "Your sister and I are going to be married today," he told her.

Fluttering with excitement, Amelia hurried home. In the flat above the grocery store, Matilda whirled about in a frenzy of activity— packing a suitcase and curling the tendrils of hair framing her face. A strange, shrinking sensation crept over Amelia as she saw the hurt and confused look on her mother's face and realized that neither she nor her parents were included in Matilda's sudden wedding plans.

She and John were simply going before a minister, Matilda told them firmly. Horace and Anna would be the only witnesses. There would be no reception. The newlyweds would return to the Dodge home to have dinner with the children.

Never before had the parents and sister felt so totally shut out of Matilda's life as on that December afternoon when the 24-year-old Rausch daughter walked out of the Kercheval Street flat.

As Matilda had briefly told them, she and John spoke their wedding vows at four p.m. at the home of the Reverend C.S. Allen. Then they drove to the elegant East Boston Boulevard manor to meet John's sister, Della, and the three Dodge children—all complete strangers to Matilda. The date was exactly six weeks after the Dodge-Smith divorce became final. Uncle Harry Glinz had not spoken a word to the Rausches since his last warning to them—and would not speak to them for many years to come.

Chapter 4

A Money Tree—The Model T

To the new Mrs. Dodge, John's sister, Della, seemed to have all the admirable qualities of which both John and Horace boasted. A tall, auburn-haired woman of regal bearing, Della spoke with a precise diction that prompted Matilda to be grateful for her recent "elocution" lessons. Matilda was impressed, too, by Della's writing skills and by the collection of poems she planned to have published, courtesy of her brother John.

Della also had acquired significant connections with various organizations. The Detroit Federation of Women's Clubs—already on her way to becoming its president. The American Red Cross. Women's Auxiliary of the Salvation Army. The Republican Party.

Still, Matilda had prepared herself to become mistress of the Boston Boulevard mansion and now, as John's wife, she steeled herself to firmly take control of the household that Della Eschbach had been managing. When Della willingly deferred to Matilda in matters of household management, the youthful Mrs. John Dodge turned her attention, with some relief, to shaping a good relationship with her three stepchildren.

To 13-year-old Winifred and 11-year-old Isabel Dodge, their father's bride looked much too young to be seriously considered their "Mother"—the name their father insisted they must use to sanction his choice of 24-year-old Matilda as his wife. The attractive, dark-haired Dodge daughters, who resembled the deceased Ivy Dodge, were quiet and polite in Matilda's presence but preferred to seclude themselves in the twin bedrooms and bath they shared in the large home that afforded such privacy.

The close companionship of the two sisters left their nine-year-old brother, John Duval, excluded from their girlish diversions and exchanges of confidences. "Don't bother your sisters. They're studying," the boy's Aunt Della warned, concerned that her nieces should be good students at Liggett School—Detroit's most prestigious private day school.

Matilda focused much of her attention on John Duval. The lonely little boy listened willingly while she read stories to him, but resisted her attempts to monitor his schoolwork.

Matilda's own quest for self-improvement continued with marriage to John Dodge. She carefully read collections from the works of Longfellow, Tennyson, Byron and Keats in her eagerness to learn more about poetry and to speak knowledgeably with Della concerning such subjects.

From the beginning, the management of the house and its six servants brought as much satisfaction to Matilda as had her experiences in creating order from disarray in Dodge Brothers office in 1902. Under her sharp-eyed supervision, the servants learned what was expected of them—furniture polished to shining perfection, curtains always crisp and clean, windows and mirrors sparkling. The servants listened politely to the instructions until their mistress began to speak fervently of "inventories." Linens, towels, cutlery, silver, china, hardware items, cleaning supplies—everything had to be categorized, labelled and recorded. Lists had to be kept of all purchases, including food supplies, and even of menus served.

The cook, treasured by the Dodges, threatened to find another job when Matilda instituted the new, stiff rules. She was persuaded to remain when she saw that her employer worked harder than anyone else at labelling storage closets and kitchen compartments. Plus, there was the matter of convenience for the Irish-Catholic cook, who was able to slip out the back door of the Boston Boulevard house for early mass at Blessed Sacrament Church, just back of the Dodge home. She could return in time to serve breakfast at eight a.m.

The evening meal also was served on schedule, even if John Dodge had not yet arrived. Although John was not a solitary drinker, he still relished visiting saloons with his drinking buddies, some of whom were shop employees. On such occasions, he had no concern for time nor for the silent disapproval he could expect from his wife. When he arrived home, he always went to bed at once.

Matilda learned to harness her own quick temper after her marriage to John, whose irascibility worsened when he had been drinking. As long as her husband did not create a public disturbance in a saloon,

Matilda could endure his periodic carousing with Horace and their friends, although she tried to think of ways to distract John from his weekend sprees.

In early childhood, Matilda and Amelia lived for several months at their maternal grandparents' sheep farm near Walkerton, Ontario, while George and Margaret Rausch had taken a trip to George's native Germany. Matilda, who had been born in Walkerton and brought to Michigan at one year of age, retained pleasant memories of her grandparents' farmlands and of the sheep and horses. Since John also loved the countryside, the interest that Matilda expressed in farms quickened his own eagerness to buy a country place.

In early spring, 1908, John began his search for a country home north of Detroit. When he found a 14-room farmhouse for sale, situated on the highest point of rolling acreage that resembled the farmlands of Niles, John was captivated by the property and the spring-fed brook that ran through the land. Barns and outbuildings dotted the 320-acre farm located four miles west of the small town of Rochester. John offered the owner, Higgins, $50,000 for the property.

With this purchase, the Dodges wanted to get capable people as caretakers. John and Matilda could think of no one who would be more dependable nor industrious than George and Margaret Rausch who, the new owners assured themselves, surely would thrive in the exposure to fresh air and to the simple lives of farmers.

The obliging Rausches sold their grocery business and moved out to the Higgins farm, which John renamed Meadow Brook Farm. The former housekeeper did not keep her promise to stay on at the farmhouse to assist the new caretakers for a few weeks, and George and Margaret Rausch, overwhelmed by the demands of the job, had to plunge into management of the hired help and the operation of the sizeable farm.

When the Rausches sold their home and business in Detroit, Matilda invited Amelia to live in the Boston Boulevard mansion, assigning her to the "pink room" previously occupied by Della and Uriah Eschbach. The Eschbachs moved up to a bedroom, sitting room and bath that John built for them on the third floor of the house.

Since the "pink room" had a connecting bath to John Duval's bedroom, Amelia suspected that John and Matilda viewed her arrival with some relief—an excuse to move the Eschbachs further away from the family after Uriah Eschbach's fits of coughing aroused the suspicions of the Dodges. Now that the older man was ensconced in comfortable third-floor quarters, it was no longer feasible for him to make his way down two flights of stairs to join the family for meals.

When Della came down to the dining room, a maid took Uriah's dinner up to the third-floor sitting room...later, as his tubercular condition worsened, he ate from a bedside tray. Despite John Dodge's dread of tuberculosis contamination, he permitted the ailing Uriah to remain in the house and commissioned his long-time friend and personal physician to care for Eschbach. Riding in a carriage pulled by a snow-white horse, Dr. William Chittick made regular house calls to the Dodge mansion.

The short walk from the Boston Boulevard home to the corner of Woodward and Boston made it convenient for Amelia to catch the Woodward Avenue streetcar for a ride downtown each day to the office. Now that she was a working girl no longer living with her parents, there were times—when she was away from Matilda's presence—that Amelia felt she had shed her "Baby" Rausch role.

She enjoyed dressing fashionably to go to work. And she changed her hairstyle. A hairdresser charged 50¢ to brush out her pigtails and to wave Amelia's brown hair at the sides, gathering it into a loose bun at the back of her head. When, one day, she wore a net to hold stray tendrils of hair in place, John Dodge remarked that he liked the tidy arrangement. From that date, Amelia wore a hairnet every day—throughout her life. "Because Mr. Dodge liked it that way," she would say in later years, carefully patting at her coiffure encased in its fine netting.

In Amelia's presence at the office, Horace and John frequently discussed Ford Motor Company's purchase of a former racetrack along Woodward Avenue in Highland Park—60 acres of land on which the company planned to erect a four-story building with a glass, saw-toothed roof to admit light. A machine shop, foundry, office building, and gas-engine plant would also be built to help speed the production of Henry Ford's newest creation—the four-cylinder Model T. The Model T was announced to the public in March of 1908, although the car did not actually go into production until the end of the year, selling for $825.

The solid, angular machine, with its planetary transmission and flywheel magneto, included no frills nor cosmetics except for a choice of colors offered the customer—red, blue, gray, green, or black. One of the T's innovations—left-side positioning of the steering wheel to facilitate a better range of vision for the driver—soon was adopted by all U.S. car manufacturers.

The Model T was, at last, the automobile that captured the spirit of Henry Ford...that represented the essence of what Ford believed made up the backbone and greatest treasure of the country—the common man. Owners of the Model T soon tagged it with inelegant nicknames. Tin Lizzie. Flivver. Family Horse. Later, Ford biographer David Lewis fittingly dubbed it "the indomitable little rattletrap." The plebian terms delighted Henry Ford who scorned the more graceful names with which other manufacturers endowed their automobiles. Jewell. Pungs-Finch. Peerless.

Perceived by the public as a taciturn man in contrast with the ebullient, talkative John Dodge, Henry Ford yearned for the facility of glib speech to put his ideas into expressive phrases. Unfortunately, he muddled his words when he spoke publicly. He had a similar frustrating problem when trying to sketch his ideas for mechanical plans, and had to rely on Wills and other employees to draw his designs from his verbal descriptions.

With the manufacture of the first Model T's, Ford identified totally with the utilitarian automobile as the embodiment of his own philosophy, planning and goals. "I want to make a car for the multitude," he said. The "multitude," in his mind, encompassed the factory worker, the storekeeper, and, above all, the farmer who could rely on the homely Model T to ford streams and straddle rocks on rough rural roads...who could trust the loose-jointed, three-point suspension system of the car to hold together through jolting ruts...who could repair the car from the average man's tools—screwdriver, wrench, hammer, pliers and a roll of wire.

The Dodges, each of whom drew monthly salaries of $2000 from their own shop by this time—plus $60,000 in 1908 as their combined share of Ford dividends, had their fortunes considerably improved in November of that year by a $190,000 payment when Ford Motor Company stock split, 20 to one. By this time, the Dodges had enough faith in Ford's new Model T to expect that their dividends would increase with the sale of T's in 1909.

During the process of renovating the farmhouse at Meadow Brook that summer of 1908, John and Matilda took their first trip away from home. Accompanied by the three children, they left for California by train. Soon after their return to Detroit, they drove a team of horses and a carriage out to Meadow Brook Farm to observe the progress of the renovations.

In the farmhouse, carpenters worked at enlarging the kitchen and adding a milk room, laundry room, storage room for boots and lanterns and stacks of firewood, and a back basement with a furnace and water-storage tank. Until bathrooms were installed and the water tank completed so the water could be pumped up for the toilets, the family had to use an outhouse.

During the installation of automatic pumps and a filtering plant for drinking-water, the family continued to pump water from the well-house. The Dodges liked the drinking water so much that John took bottled spring-water back to Boston Boulevard each time the family returned home.

By the winter of 1908-09, John replaced the oil lamps at Meadow Brook by installing a Union Carbide tank under the ice house and piping acetylene gas into the house. But soon afterwards, the Detroit Edison Company brought electricity to the area, and the farmhouse was wired and an electric refrigerator installed in the kitchen.

Although the inconveniences at the farm contrasted with the smoothly functioning elegance at Boston Boulevard, the John Dodges went regularly and eagerly to Meadow Brook, transported by horses and sleigh in the wintertime. They relished Margaret Rausch's savory German cooking and often brought guests to share their meals. They returned to Detroit with eggs, milk, cream, freshly churned butter, and even ham and sausage after the fall slaughter of pigs at the farm.

At Christmas time, 1908, John gave Matilda an electric automobile. The Model T Ford, with its irritable crank and its tendency to precipitate itself into forward movement at unexpected times, was not the type of machine that she wanted to drive. Horace bought a similar electric automobile for the use of his wife, Anna.

The Horace Dodges, in the flush of financial success, purchased a piece of property on Lake St. Clair in Grosse Pointe. They lived in a modest cottage on the property while they planned to erect a magnificent home that would impress Grosse Pointers who had refused country-club membership to the newly rich Horace Dodges.

Horace often visited at Meadow Brook Farm, bringing Horace Junior, two years younger than John Duval, to play with his cousin. But Horace rarely brought his daughter, Delphine, to the farm and, among themselves, the John Dodges complained that Anna was raising Delphine "to be a princess."

The home the Horace Dodges ordered built in Grosse Pointe was certainly suitable for a princess. The red sandstone edifice, named Rose Terrace, faced Jefferson Avenue; the back of the elegant home overlooked tiered rose gardens descending to Lake St. Clair where Horace could dock his boats.

In his predeliction for "common folks" and "plain-style living," Henry Ford scorned the Dodges' increasingly lavish expenditures for luxuries. After 17 years of constant shifting from one nondescript rented house to another, and even moving in with Henry's father,

William Ford, for a time, Henry finally built a substantial home at Edison and Second and moved into the red brick house with his wife and son, Edsel.

As much as Ford disdained the Dodge Brothers' drinking excesses, Henry was able to work with the high-living Dodges for a greater good—the benefit of Ford Motor Company. It was questionable how much longer Ford would work in harmony with C. Harold Wills, upon whose expertise Ford relied for so many years. Childe Harold also was adopting a lavish lifestyle, including the purchase of rare gems and a yacht, which Ford found offensive.

When Wills began coming into work at his own convenience in the mornings, the two men were alienated. Eventually, Ford stopped putting work on Wills' desk, completely ignoring his presence. By 1919,Wills would feel compelled to resign with a settlement of $1 1/2 million—a move which, like that of Strelow, later led to financial problems for Childe Harold.

The Dodges collected $180,000 in Ford dividends in 1909... $200,000 in 1910 with rising production and sales of the Model T. The brothers now manufactured parts in quantity for the Model T, but they still considered the possibility of manufacturing a car of their own, bearing their own name.

In 1909, tiring of the constant price-cutting competition with other shops vying for Ford contracts, and aware that Ford's expanding facilities were making it possible for the company to produce more of its own parts, the Dodges bought a piece of property in Hamtramck—a town entirely surrounded by Detroit and Highland Park and largely inhabited by Slavic immigrants. The brothers planned to build a 5.1 million-square-foot factory on the acreage...a factory in which they would build Ford parts for now. Later, the factory could be used for the manufacture of their own car.

In June, 1910, workmen dug the foundation for the Dodges' forge plant at Hamtramck. Before the end of the year, the brothers moved into the new Hamtramck administration building. John's executive office—richly paneled in gleaming oak with leaded glass cabinet doors and with a huge fireplace—was located at one end of the second floor; Horace's drafting office was at the opposite end. Amelia's secretarial office was centrally located, accessible to either of her employers.

Since Amelia now had to take two streetcars to reach the Dodges' Hamtramck plant, she frequently rode to work with John in his Packard motorcar—another source of disgruntlement to Henry Ford who proudly rode in his Model T. When John had spent the previous evening in saloons with his drinking companions, however, he slept later in the mornings. Then Amelia relied on streetcar transportation.

Success brought more leisure time, as well as money, to the Dodges. John and Horace spent much of this time with their friends—not only with workmen pals from earlier years, but also with men of prominence in Detroit and Wayne County politics. Among them were the Stein brothers, Wayne County Judge Christopher Stein and Edward Stein, who soon would become Wayne County Sheriff. Detroit's Mayor Codd also frequently visited at Meadow Brook. In 1905, Codd had appointed John to the Detroit Water Board which, during John's five-year tenure as water commissioner, completed a new and modern pumping station for the growing city.

The brothers and their political friends frequently boarded Horace's new diesel steam yacht, the 100-foot Hornet II, for a 30-knot spin on Lake St. Clair. At such times, John's liking for convivial male companionship and the pleasures of hearty drinking and eating aboard the craft offset his fear of water.

Oscar Marx, an upcoming politician with aspirations of becoming mayor of Detroit, was another Dodge crony and family friend from Port Huron days. John and Horace backed Marx's political forays with generous financial contributions.

Caught up in the fervor of politics and power, and influenced by his wife's eager pursuit of self-improvement and education, John Dodge began collecting information on a political historical figure whose federalist views he admired—Alexander Hamilton. Although Henry Ford was widely quoted as saying "History is more or less bunk," John Dodge persisted in his quest for Hamilton memorabilia, eventually contributing his materials to writer Arthur H. Vandenberg for a Hamilton biography.

Matilda followed Della's lead, joining the same organizations and working at the same kind of philanthropic activities in her pursuit of culture and of acceptance by the elite of Detroit. Her ingratiating efforts to win the good will of Anna Dodge prevailed as Horace's wife succumbed to the warmth that her sister-in-law could project when she chose to do so.

With justification, Matilda complimented Anna on the attractive wardrobe for which the older woman had been fitted at the "Fashion Row" salon of Ruth Joyce, where elegant models pirouetted in a swishing of silks and taffeta petticoats. To Anna, who remembered when a family neighbor, Mrs. Flanagan, had hurriedly sewed an all-purpose dress for the bride at the time of Anna's quick and quiet marriage to Horace, a Ruth Joyce wardrobe helped provide the self-assurance she needed when she attended meetings of society-women benefactors for the new Detroit Symphony Orchestra.

Matilda also became an early patron of the orchestra, and, as she encouraged her husband in his Hamilton research, she hoped to channel John's considerable energies away from the saloon excursions with Horace that were so unacceptable to both their wives. Since both sisters-in-law were proud, introverted women, they rarely discussed their concerns for their husbands' reputations and safety as a result of the drinking sprees. Nonetheless, these same unexpressed concerns drew the women closer together.

Nor did Matilda Dodge ever complain to Amelia about her husband's cronies and their drinking habits. But Amelia saw the cold glitter in her sister's dark eyes at every mention of these men by John Dodge. The younger sister continued to marvel at Matilda's unprecedented control of a temper that had intimidated the Rausches all through Amelia's earlier life.

Amelia knew, from her mother's own admission, that Margaret Rausch had pampered her elder daughter in childhood, following the year-old Matilda's nearly fatal bout with diphtheria, resulting in an emergency tracheotomy. But, in Amelia's opinion, her sister's explosive temper was as much a part of her lineage as were her dark eyes and black hair—a "bad seed" kind of inheritance from some unknown ancestor...surely not from her quiet and industrious parents.

The most formidable test of Matilda's control of temper occurred abruptly in early January of 1911. Observing the tight set of Matilda's lips and the smoldering fire in her eyes, Amelia suspected that another of John's drinking capers had brought embarrassment to the family. This anticipation of embarrassment did not prepare Amelia for the degree of humilation the family suffered when a Detroit newspaper published a damaging news item on its front page.

Crippled Attorney Kicked and Beaten by John Dodge and Bob Oakman in Schneider's Saloon.

The story beneath the headline was as sordid as the caption. A horrified Amelia read the unsavory details; that Dodge and Oakman, while drinking at the saloon, had been introduced by Schneider to two lawyers—Thomas J. Mahon and Edmund Joncas, the latter a Frenchman. Within minutes, it became apparent that Dodge was not pleased, either with Joncas's accent or with what Dodge and Oakman perceived as affectations in the lawyers' conversation. Suddenly accusing Joncas of being "a damned foreigner," Dodge flew into a drunken rage when both lawyers responded in a patronizing way.

With Oakman's accusation to the lawyers of spouting "college talk," the confrontation escalated as Mahon warned that he already knew of the rowdy reputations acquired by Dodge and his friend. Although Mahon walked with the aid of a cane, on two wooden lower legs, Oakman sprang at the handicapped attorney, hitting him in the face and knocking him to the floor. Dodge vaulted at Joncas at the same time, but Joncas fled from the saloon while Mahon, in an effort to swing his cane for protection as he lay on the floor, was kicked by Dodge.

With some trepidation that she might be walking into a combat zone, Amelia returned to Boston Boulevard after work the next day. An unnatural quiet lay over the house while its occupants moved about cautiously, as if fearing that contact with each other would dissolve the uneasy stillness and explode into turbulence. Dinner was served on time, and then the children and adults escaped to their rooms. But the following day, and the next, brought more notoriety about the fracas...more details of John Dodge's bullying and brutish behavior.

Matilda remained tight-lipped on the matter even when, two weeks later, a newspaper reported that Mahon was still incapacitated as a result of "the beating and kicking" he had received...even when Mahon filed a $25,000 damage suit as Dodge and Oakman were arrested, then released on bail. The damage suit was dropped later, and Amelia was sure that John Dodge made a generous out-of-court settlement with the injured man.

More humiliation followed when John Dodge responded to an imperative summons from Ella Liggett—who, along with her sister and minister-father, had founded the ultra-conservative Liggett School. Headmistress Liggett firmly expressed her repugnance for such uncivil behavior on the part of a parent of any of her neatly uniformed Liggett girls, who were being imbued with every possible advantage of gentility, decorum and savoir-faire. Mr. Dodge would have to remove his daughters from the school in the event of any more unfavorable publicity, the headmistress warned.

For a time, the John Dodges were dispirited, not only because of the bad publicity but also because George and Margaret Rausch left Meadow Brook Farm, saying the work was too demanding. With regret, John replaced the Rausches with his widowed sister, Laura Stineback, and her daughter and son-in-law—all of whom had lived near Niles. The new arrangement did not work out well in 1911 because Laura and her family objected to doing the milking and other extra chores when hired hands did not show up for work.

When the Dodges came out to the farm, they missed the bountiful meals the Rausches had provided. John and Matilda decided to appeal to the Rausches to return, promising to hire more help so that George and Margaret would not have to work so hard.

Even though their wealthy son-in-law was already buying adjacent farms to add to Meadow Brook's acreage, the Rausches complied with the Dodges' wishes. Once again, John and Matilda could bring extra weekend guests to the farm to enjoy Margaret's hearty cooking.

Daughters Winifred and Isabel were still at Liggett School, from which Winifred expected to graduate soon. And John Duval, growing into his restless teenage years, left for boarding school in Gainesville, Georgia. Matilda fervently hoped that John's recent unhappy experience at Schneider's saloon had influenced him to be more prudent in the future so that their home life, on Boston Boulevard, could settle into the pattern to which Matilda always had aspired. A pattern of respectability and dignity.

Chapter 5

The Dodge-Ford Affiliation Fractures

In late April, 1913, John and Matilda boarded the <u>Mauretania</u> for passage to England where they planned to tour historical sites of London and the green countrysides of both England and Ireland. Unlike Horace, who already had taken Anna on a European tour, John was not a zealous traveler; he preferred vacationing at Meadow Brook to crossing the Atlantic Ocean on the lavishly appointed <u>Mauretania</u>. But Matilda's studies of English literature and history honed her desire to explore the ancient habitats of Tudor royalty and of England's famous writers and poets. She was determined to see the tourist attractions that lured wealthy Americans to board steamships bound for the English port, Southampton.

John Dodge, recently appointed to the Detroit Street Railway Commission, had a different mission; the study of public transportation systems in London and Manchester. However, neither the boat trip, the change of water and climate, nor the constant moving-about agreed with the hefty John. He returned with few evaluations of English transportation systems, leaving the train at Detroit with both hands clasping his expansive paunch in relief to be home where he could recover from the queasiness that plagued him throughout the journey.

Although, in later years, Amelia Rausch frequently complained that her life was "separated from the social circles in which my sister moved," the younger sister had accompanied John and Matilda—along with the 14-year-old John Duval and a maid—to the British Isles. For Matilda, Amelia became the perfect, eager and tireless companion as the two trudged about London and Dublin on similar pairs of short and slender, bowed legs—shaped that way, both believed, because the sisters were given coffee, rather than milk, to drink in their youth.

On the family's return from England, Amelia excitedly unpacked her souvenirs, dresses and Irish lace—gifts from Matilda during their travels. Then the younger sister happily went back to the secretarial job she loved and which, by the end of 1913, would pay her $105 monthly—a most generous salary at a time when the average female office employee in Detroit was paid $1.80 per day.

In the cold and early-morning dark of wintertime, Amelia usually rode to work with John to avoid dealing with street-car transfers. She sat stiffly beside him, sensing that he shared her fear of a gunshot blast as the car approached the plant where a watchman stood at each side of the gate. At the dinner table at home, John talked angrily of "foreign radicals" trying to infiltrate both the Dodge and Ford factories. Threatening letters arrived at the Dodges' Boston Boulevard home, and union organizers infuriated John by approaching the gates of the Dodge plant where they handed out circulars urging workers to come to Industrial Workers of the World meetings.

In efforts to fight unionism, John and Horace hired their own secret agents to attend union meetings and spy on the proceedings, providing their employers with names of workers who joined the union movement. Even while he traveled in England, John had received mail from the Dodge plant superintendent with information about union-organizing activities. One of their agents reported that 20 people joined the IWW at a single night's meeting where an organizer, Matilda Rabinowitz, urged workers to use sabotage in case of a strike. "Killing time," Rabinowitz told the workers, was another form of sabotage that was effective during working hours.

Matilda Dodge recognized that John's stomach problems had worsened at his separation from the factory while in England where he worried about the union-inspired turmoil that John felt was jeopardizing the contentment of Dodge workers. He and Horace perceived themselves as benevolent employers who enjoyed an unusual camaraderie with their shopmen. Some of these shopmen—Silas Burgett and Rudolph Grandt among them—were confidants of John and Horace Dodge as they drank together in the saloons of Hamtramck and Detroit.

During morning and afternoon breaks in the Dodge factory, the brothers supplied sandwiches and free beer, brought in barrels from a saloon across the street. Workmen poured the beer into four-quart pails for distribution to perspiring men who labored, stripped to the waists, in the blistering heat of the forge and foundry. And the Dodges set up a medical clinic for employees, along with a private fund—which soon amounted to $5 million—for aid to sick or injured workers or for widows of former employees.

When John's stomach problems subsided soon after he came back to the plant, he decided to avoid any further inconveniences to either Amelia or himself in the mornings by giving his sister-in-law the electric motorcar that he had bought as an earlier Christmas present for his wife. After Matilda protested that the "electric" ran out of power and stalled at inconvenient times, John provided his wife with a new gasoline-powered automobile and a chauffeur to drive it, while the "electric" sat, unused, in the garage.

Accustomed to making use of her sister's rejects, Amelia drove the "electric" to work and, one evening, to the home of a friend on Detroit's east side. As she returned home at midnight, the car stalled near the Belle Isle bridge. Abandoning the paralyzed machine on Jefferson Avenue, Amelia simply waited for a Jefferson streetcar, then transferred to a Woodward streetcar and arrived at the Boston Boulevard address with the pleased feeling that she had outgrown her "Baby Rausch" image.

John and Horace were pleased, too, with their own images as tycoons as they collected more than one million dollars in 1913 from Ford Motor Company dividends as sales of the Model T proliferated. Even though a federal income tax took effect in 1913, the flow of profits—from dividends and from the Dodges' production of rear axles, transmissions, drop forgings and steering devices for the Model T—burst the barrier of whatever inclinations toward frugality that the brothers retained from their deprived childhoods.

When Horace admired a Rinaldi oil painting displayed at the Woodward Avenue saloon of Charlie Churchill, John decided to acquire the painting as a surprise gift for his brother. He offered Churchill $5000 for the artwork, depicting four monks playing cards in a monastery at the moment of their discovery by an abbott. When Churchill refused the offer, John sent his employee and drinking buddy, Rudolph Grandt, to the saloonkeeper with a letter and a check for $10,000.

"...If you would sooner have this check than your dear old monks, give Rudy Grandt the picture, " John wrote. "If you would sooner have the picture, give him back the check. If I were in your place, I would give him back the check, but you are to suit yourself in the matter."

Churchill accepted John's check and the Detroit Journal reported that $10,000 was the largest amount ever paid by a Detroiter for a painting. John then had the painting delivered by drayman's wagon to his brother's Grosse Pointe home. A bauble—a small and whimsical token of affection for Horace, his devoted companion.

Together, the brothers indulged their passion for outdoor life with the Stein brothers at the Detroit Hunt and Fish Club near West Branch, Michigan. At other times, they made 350-mile trips up to their own isolated hunting lodge south of Sault Ste. Marie.

When the brothers went off on their hunting or fishing trips, Matilda's anxieties subsided. With her husband away, she was unworried about complications arising from John's drinking at local saloons or at Detroit's Harmonie Club, where the brothers consumed quantities of German food and steins of lager beer, singing lusty beer-hall songs with their comrades.

At Meadow Brook, John planned to construct a clubhouse, a $49,000 golf links, and a swimming pool. When completed in 1915, these would be more of an attraction to his family and friends than to himself. His own favorite pastime at Meadow Brook, with Horace, required no expensive props as the brothers boisterously played their version of "autopolo"—a fad introduced in Wichita in 1912 by a Model T dealer. The Dodges adapted the game to Meadow Brook's hills, racing about in automobiles as they tried to butt a four-foot ball between two goalposts.

Horace's favorite diversion remained unchanged. Still obsessed with boats, the younger Dodge brother ordered construction of a $150,000 yacht, the Nokomis, with a gross weight of 303 tons and measuring 180 feet long. Henry Ford made no secret of his contempt for what he felt was Horace's ostentation in building such a palatial yacht. But Horace was not entirely preoccupied with the ornateness of the boat—the rich mahogany interior of the cabins, the soft glow of Tiffany lighting fixtures. He was, rather, enraptured with the yacht's structure and texture, the turbines and energy that propelled the craft through powerful currents at a top speed of 19 knots, and the precision of balanced designing that endowed the weighty vessel with its buoyancy.

In a burst of sentiment, John and Horace paid a visit to their hometown of Niles and to the graves of their parents in 1913. John Dodge found it impossible to be humble as the brothers offered a $100,000 gift to Niles for a park. "...(the amount) is nothing to us now," he blustered. "H.E. and myself are worth fifty million dollars."

Although city officials rejected their offer of a park, the sentimental Dodge brothers returned to Niles annually and gave private financial help to needy townspeople. An old, paralyzed, black man, who once worked for Daniel Dodge in his forge shop, was one beneficiary of a monthly check from the Dodges.

Unlike Henry Ford, who showed no concern for his two impoverished brothers, John Dodge distributed money to peripheral family members and friends and provided generously for his sister, Della Eschbach. Because of Della's activities in the Detroit Federation of Women's Clubs, John purchased the former Butler home at Second and Hancock Streets for $35,000, then rented it to the federation as a headquarters for one dollar monthly.

Henry Ford scorned the Dodges' extravagant expenditures and their zeal to match, and even surpass, the fashionable lives of wealthy, old-family Detroiters. While the Dodges ardently supported the Detroit Symphony Orchestra (and Horace even considered personal ownership of it at one point), Henry and Clara Ford danced stiffly at square-dancing parties, hiring early-American fiddlers to entertain at their social affairs.

And while the high-living Dodge brothers gratified their hearty appetites for heavy meals and hard drinking, the wiry Ford ate sparingly of raw vegetables and nuts. In his loathing for alcohol, he drank quantities of carrot juice and acquired a fetish for milk derived from soybeans. Most of all, Ford detested the Dodges' continuing, personal use of Packard motorcars when their profits poured in from sales of the plain and sturdy Model T, in whose utilitarian ugliness Ford took great pride as a symbol of the laboring man's disdain for snobbery and opulence.

Ford became haunted with the idea of stripping the Model T to nakedness—spare tire, headlights and even the windshield were sold separately to shrink the price on the basic auto so that every worker could afford the car. He believed that the resulting rise in car sales would make it possible to further decrease the price of the Model T, creating a spiral of mounting sales and declining prices.

When Ford replaced brass radiators and lamps with black-painted steel radiators and lamps, he wanted to reduce the price to something less than $500. He reached his goal in 1914 when buyers could no longer purchase a Model T in any color except black; price, $490.

At his Boston Boulevard home, John Dodge fumed at Ford's enduring refusal to consult with his board of directors in determining policy. In the years following the introduction of the first Model T, John complained to Matilda and Amelia about the narrowing margin of profits in turning out Ford parts as the price of the auto continued to drop, squeezing the suppliers. In July of 1913, the Dodge brothers notified Ford, in accordance with their contract, that they would discontinue their manufacture of Ford parts within a year's time.

In August of 1913, John Dodge resigned from the vice-presidency of Ford Motor Company to avoid a conflict of interest as he and Horace began enlarging their Hamtramck factory for the production of their own car. "I am tired of being carried around in Henry Ford's vest pocket," John told reporters.

Newspapers across the country carried the announcement of John Dodge's resignation from Ford Motor Company's board of directors, and of the brothers' intention to manufacture a Dodge car in 1914. Since the automotive world recognized the Dodges' contributions to the success of Ford automobiles, the brothers' revelation that they would build a moderately priced, four-cylinder Dodge car received respectful attention in the nation's journals. Matilda escaped humiliation when newspapers did not report embarrassing details of an announcement party tossed by the Dodges at the Book-Cadillac Hotel—details of an inebriated John Dodge celebrating by wielding a cane to smash light bulbs in the hotel's expensive chandeliers, one after the other.

Amelia cut the car-announcement articles from journals and saved them. By this time, young John Duval was away at another boarding school and the Dodge sisters had graduated from Liggett School— Winifred in 1912, Isabel in 1913. The girls were spending the summer in Nantucket when their father brought more notoriety to the family.

This time, John drove his Packard along Jefferson Avenue with his usual disregard for speed limits. As he accelerated the Packard through a construction site and sideswiped a Hupmobile traveling in the opposite direction, he simply roared on down Jefferson Avenue as if the Hupmobile were a bug that splattered against the side of the larger car. Even when he observed a motorcycle officer chasing the Packard, John merely grinned at his friend, Detroit Mayor Oscar Marx, sitting in the passenger seat of Dodge's automobile.

Since the Hupmobile's occupants were injured only slightly , the incident might not have attracted the attention of newspapers except for the insolent responses to the policeman from both Dodge and Marx. "That'll teach them to keep to the right!" Dodge snapped...a retort disclosed in the next day's papers.

Mayor Marx's blustering made matters worse when reporters pursued him to his City Hall office. Marx's response to their questions, printed in local papers with substitutions for cuss words, revealed his "good-old-boy" loyalty to Dodge. "John Dodge could buy your blankety-blank old paper and turn your plant into a machine shop," Marx was quoted.

The notoriety resulted in a warrant charging Dodge with reckless driving. A suburban justice-of-the-peace then conducted a private, at-home examination of the defendant. This cozy arrangement did not appease journalists who promptly printed a rash of editorials censuring the partiality afforded the wealthy and politically powerful by the courts.

It seemed that John's satisfaction in the outspoken loyalty of his friend, Marx, outweighed any displeasure he felt because of the notoriety. But Matilda was affronted. Already planning an early December debut for her stunning, svelte-figured stepdaughter Winifred, she resented having the affair shadowed by reports of John's unruly behavior.

Anna Dodge, whose husband had not been involved in either the humiliating Schneider's saloon fracas or the automobile accident, exuded kindness to her sister-in-law in the wake of these embarrassing occurrences. Quivering from wounded pride, Matilda silently accepted what she felt was condescension from Anna—the woman who already held the power to reveal the John Dodge-Belle Smith secret marriage and divorce, and who could destroy Matilda by such a revelation.

The accident notoriety rapidly faded from the news, if not from Matilda's keen and enduring memory. Still, she was pragmatic enough to realize that favorable publicity about John Dodge outweighed the bad ever since the terrible Mahon-confrontation two years previously. And Anna Dodge certainly semed sincere in her friendly overtures.

One of Winifred Dodge's closest friends—Josephine Clay, niece of the late department-store magnate, J.L. Hudson—also made her debut that season. For Winifred's dinner-dance, Matilda ordered the transformation of the Pontchartrain Hotel ballroom into a formal English garden several days before Christmas so that Isabel Dodge, now a student at Briarcliff, would be at home for the event.

Beneath a vine-entwined ceiling, the twittering of songbirds emanated from borders of boxwood and yew trees as Winifred, a dark haired beauty in white net over white chiffon and satin, stood with her stepmother, Matilda, in primrose velvet, to receive 150 guests. Nearby stood the ruddy-faced John Dodge, a high collar—stiff as celluloid— biting into his fleshy neck, faded blue eyes criss-crossed with tiny red lines.

For John, the debut was a party to be endured rather than enjoyed. The only party he might have enjoyed less would have been one of Henry and Clara Ford's tidy little square dances, with soda pop as a thirst quencher. At Winifred's dinner-dance, cocktails were served, but John knew the petite Matilda closely monitored his behavior. To John, who liked his whiskey "straight-up," cocktails were only a cut above Ford's soda pop, in any case.

Young Edsel Ford, Henry's son and only child, remained a close friend of Isabel Dodge and her neighbor and chum, Eleanor Clay. For a time, Isabel's sharp-eyed stepmother, Matilda, entertained the opinion that young Edsel was seriously attracted to Isabel. Matilda and Amelia, in their fascination with the idea of such a close Ford-Dodge family relationship, talked privately about the possibility of an Edsel-Isabel liaison. Matilda's dark eyes glowed with excitement as she pointed out to Amelia how vast a range of power and influence could be commanded by such an inter-family merger of automotive titans.

Amelia had more concern for personalities. She admired young Edsel as a pleasant fellow—soft-spoken and gentlemanly, and cast in a different mold from his perverse and acerbic father. It seemed to Matilda and Amelia that Isabel, who soon would make her own debut, and the 20-year-old Edsel Ford might make a most suitable match in the near future. Their speculations dissolved a short time later, however, when Edsel gave an engagement ring to Isabel's friend, Eleanor Clay, who also had come from a lower-class background into wealth inherited from her bachelor uncle, J.L. Hudson.

Ever since he began producing the Model T at the expanding Ford facility at Highland Park, Henry Ford continued experimenting with different devices and improvisations to get greater production by means of a conveyor-assembly line for parts. In August of 1913, when John Dodge separated himself from the Ford Motor Company, the Ford chain of moving assembly lines was making it possible to achieve faster production than ever before. But even while customer demand for the Model T still exceeded production quotas, some of the assembly procedures remained in a crude stage as each Model T body plunged from the second-floor body shop into a huge sling which dumped the body over a chassis newly emerged from the assembly line.

Immediately following the Dodges' announcement that they would build a Dodge car of their own design, 13,741 (22,000 before the end of 1914) applications for dealer franchises poured into the Dodge office from businessmen with faith in the Dodges as expert mechanics who had built "the working parts" for the Ford car for many years. In a magazine article published several months before the Dodge car appeared on the market, the <u>Michigan Manufacturer and Financial Record</u> reported that the Dodge brothers "are reputed to have refined the engine for the Ford machine...they built it for many years...then they (Dodge Brothers) kept on at the (Ford) axles and other parts..."

The publicity aroused even more interest in the new Dodge. As incoming dealer-applications deluged Amelia with extra paperwork, she felt most deserving of her $105 monthly salary. She also had to put up with the testiness of both John and Horace who busily re-equipped their foundries, drop-forging and heat-treatment departments, and machine shops with new patterns, tools, jigs and fixtures. They constructed several huge buildings to double the size of their facilities to 20 acres of floor space—a new 876-foot-long and four-story assembly building, a 600-foot-long sheet metal shop, an addition to their brass foundry, and a carpenter shop. As Horace devised an assembly system, with monorail, the brothers prepared to augment their work force (2000 in January of 1913) until, in early 1915, there would be a payroll of more than 7000.

To Amelia's relief, John and Horace also hired additional office employees as a Dodge sales organization was set up to work with dealerships. One of these new employees was 22-year-old Frank Upton, who had recently moved to Detroit with his parents, the Adelbert Uptons. Although Frank and his brother Floyd might have sought work with their Niles-St. Joseph relatives (Frederick and Louis Upton) who recently had invented an automatic washer and founded the Upton Machine Company (forerunner of Whirlpool), the young Uptons chose to remain in Detroit and apply for work at the Dodge factory.

John and Horace delighted in hiring old family friends and relatives to work in their plant. They signed up Floyd Upton as a stenographer; Frank as an accountant who soon became a trusted employee, handling the brothers' personal and business affairs.

Horace and John worked together at plans for their new car model, but the younger brother was largely responsible for designing and constructing the four separate test models that evolved. The brothers ran the models hard, frequently over the hills at Meadow Brook as they experimented with the machine that was to bear their name. They built a wooden track, with high trestles supporting a steep ramp and descent, roller-coaster fashion, for further testing at the Hamtramck factory.

When the Dodges incorporated their firm on July 17, 1914, with a capitalization of $5 million in common stock, there was no need for them to become testy about obtaining financing. The money invested was their own, and the capitalization would increase to $10 million within three years...to $15 million within another three years.

John and Horace Dodge took great pride in exercising total control to run their business as they pleased and to make all their own decisions. And in this, they were, after all, like Henry Ford.

Chapter 6

Parallel Births

In early spring, 1914, Matilda suspected that, at age 30 and after six years of marriage, she might be pregnant. When spasms of nausea gripped her each morning, it was easier for the inhibited Matilda to confide her suspicions to her personal maid, Mary Matthews—a black woman with children of her own—than to her husband. John's noisy exuberance and his habit of talking openly of family affairs to his drinking companions offended Matilda's sense of privacy.

When she finally told John that she was expecting their first child, he was pleased with the idea of becoming a father, again, in November, when he would be 50 years old. He liked the idea of a Dodge heir and a Dodge automobile destined for birth at the same time.

But while Amelia's collection of news clippings swelled as newspapers and magazines reported every stage of gestation for the Dodge automobile, Matilda hugged the knowledge of her pregnancy to herself and pledged John to secrecy.

Matilda was certain that, if her child were a boy, the new heir to the Dodge automotive empire would be blessed with a fortunate combination of his father's ambition and mechanical skills plus her own relish for education and excellence. She was sure the child would be very different from young John Duval, who strained the limits of his father's patience as he shifted from one boarding school to another, expelled from each for truancy.

John Duval's irresponsible behavior was not the only source of his father's indignation in 1914. The year began, in the bitter cold of a Midwest winter, with an unexpected announcement on January 5 by Henry Ford. The daily wage for workers at the Ford complex would be raised to $5 for an eight-hour day, a tremendous increase from the $2.50 to $2.70 earned by most Ford workers at that time for a nine-hour day.

Thousands of jobless men collected near the entrance to the Ford Highland Park plant on the same day of the announcement. They jostled for places in lines that turned into a frantic mob battling for the chance to register for work. Early the next morning, city police came to protect Ford deputies who shouted through megaphones that there were no jobs. They hoisted a huge No Hiring sign in front of the employment office. And still the crowd of 12,000 waited, muttering and shifting about as a cold wind raced up Woodward Avenue.

For the past decade, so many immigrants poured into the Midwest to work in foundries and factories that the Detroit labor market could no longer absorb them. Now, as Poles, Italians and Hungarians roamed Detroit's streets in search of work, Ford's $5-a-day policy also enticed men from Michigan's farms and small towns to rush to Detroit by train or bicycle. One week after Ford's announcement of the $5 workday, a mass of job-seekers pushed against the doors of the employment office until guards dispersed them with streams of icy water from fire hoses in the nine degree weather.

Ford's new policy infuriated other automotive industrialists who already faced pressure to raise wages as unions gathered strength. John Dodge wrote a letter to Henry Ford, protesting the increased wage scale and the influx of excess workers and unrest created by Ford's actions.

The Dodges disagreed with Ford on more than just the wage scale. Since Ford dropped the selling price of the Model T to $490, the brothers complained of dissatisfaction with their 1914 dividends— $1,220,000. They resented Ford's habit of referring to stockholders as "parasites."

Nor did the Dodge brothers relish Henry Ford's emerging image as champion of the laboring man. A number of years would elapse before historians pointed out that 30% of Ford workers were not receiving the $5-a-day payment two years after its adoption. The high wage was not paid to women workers, nor to divorced men, single men under 22 years of age, nor to probationers who worked for Ford less than six months. Probationers received $2.70; 7500 of them were hired in 1916, then fired within six months and replaced with new employees.

Irving Berlin's "I Want to Go Back to Michigan—Down on the Farm" became popular in 1914, partly because Berlin's lilting melodies caught public attention and partly because many workers did exactly that...returned to the farm. Still, Detroit's population zoomed to 725,000 in 1914, the year that Billy Sunday began his campaign to convert Americans to his religious beliefs, decrying the vulgarity of dance fads such as the Bunny Hug and the latest craze—The Tango—made popular by Vernon and Irene Castle.

The rhythmic music appealed to Amelia Rausch, even though she lacked opportunity to go with her friends on slightly wicked weekend excursions to music halls. On Friday nights, Amelia dutifully traveled to Meadow Brook to stay with her parents for two days.

In June, Amelia visited as usual at Meadow Brook on the Sunday when George Rausch suddenly "took a spell." Doctors were called to the back bedroom of the 66-year-old Rausch, but their ministrations were useless. Amelia and Margaret Rausch sat at the bedside, keeping vigil for 36 hours until he died.

The burial site was the eight-grave Dodge plot in which John Dodge had buried his first wife, Ivy, 13 years earlier. When the Dodges became wealthy, John ordered Ivy's body exhumed and placed in a magnificent mausoleum the brothers built for the repose of their own bodies and those of their immediate families. At that time, the Rausches bought the original Dodge plot where George Rausch's body was now interred.

Following the funeral, Amelia remained at Meadow Brook, intending to stay for a few weeks to help her mother adjust to her changed life. When it seemed that Margaret Rausch's interest in Meadow Brook lagged in the period following her husband's death, John and Matilda worried that the widowed Margaret might leave the farm. Matilda decided to speak to her younger sister, suggesting that their mother needed companionship now that her husband had died...that it would be better for all the family if Amelia stayed at the farm—permanently.

When Amelia protested, tearfully, that she did not want to give up the job she loved at the Dodge office, John reinforced Matilda's arguments. There was an important job for Amelia right at Meadow Brook, he pointed out. Doing the bookkeeping and taking inventories. Taking care of the farm business.

Amelia wavered, and Matilda seized the opportunity to settle the matter. "It's the best thing...the right thing to do," she insisted.

Amelia knew that, if she decided to stay at the farm, her mother would be pleased. So, although the pulse of the city had beat persistently in her veins since her birth at the flat above the Princess Saloon, Amelia packed her suitcases and moved out to Meadow Brook. As much as she resented her separation from the glitter of Woodward Avenue shop windows and theater lights, she realized that for her—the docile "Baby" Rausch who had matured into "Melie" Rausch—the guilt from satisfying her own desires would have been too great to bear.

Matilda came only rarely to the farm that summer. She was not at Meadow Brook on the weekend that John Dodge came into the kitchen to tell Margaret Rausch that she would soon be a grandmother. Both Margaret and Amelia stared at him in silence for a moment. The only sound was the bubbling from a pot of beans, John's favorite food, simmering on the cookstove. Then, Margaret reached out her hand to offer good wishes to John.

Neither woman felt hurt or surprised by Matilda's failure to share her secret with them. They were accustomed, by this time, to being shut out of intimacies with her.

For Matilda, the summer passed quietly as she remained secluded in her fashionable home in the months preceding the birth of her first child. Since the propriety of a woman appearing in public while in such "delicate" condition depended on whether she "showed," Matilda, whose petite body rapidly swelled, avoided leaving her home. For a time, her life slowed to a dullness matching Amelia's life at the farm.

At the Hamtramck factory, workdays for the Dodge brothers became noisier and busier as they geared up for production of their new automobile. Within the expanded plant, the brothers adapted their systems of routing and arrangement—the complete chain of traveling cranes, monorail cranes, locomotive cranes, lifting magnets, elevators and trucks—to turning out the Dodge motor car. Their modern brick office building now fronted 30 acres extending from Joseph Campau Avenue to Clay Avenue, along which concrete factory buildings—four stories high with rows of fenestral windows—were prepped for the processes of mechanized labor and delivery.

In paternalistic concern for their employees' welfare, the Dodges decided to pay their workers, who received $3 a day, in cash instead of by checks in 1914. This method, they expected, would end the temptation for workers to stop at neighboring saloons to cash their checks, spending part of their earnings in the saloons before going home to their families. The plan backfired when handling so much cash proved to be a cumbersome task. Moreover, workers griped about the hard-drinking Dodges trying to control their workers' spending habits. The cash payment experiment soon expired.

While John Dodge spent long hours at the plant that summer, fans whirred monotonously within the great tree-shaded Dodge home as Matilda waited out the long, hot days of July and August. There was more time for her to read, now, than ever before. When she tired of reading the classics, she read magazines and local newspapers, mildly diverted by advertisements for "ready-made" clothes at department stores, even though her own wardrobe was custom-made by a dressmaker. The ads showed "Mary Pickford Caps"—full at the side and flattened on top, banded around the forehead—with a signature of the star in each cap selling for $1.95. Buttoned-up, mid-calf boots advertised as "Gaitor Tops," at $5 a pair. Ostrich plumes at $1.98.

Lurid details of alienation-of-affection suits were routinely splashed across the front pages...Widow is Love Thief. Inside pages contained the speculations and opinions of columnists on the possibility of war in Europe, following the assassination of Archduke Francis Ferdinand of Austria-Hungary on June 28, 1914. Still, Americans were shocked when, on July 28, Austria declared war on Serbia, after which major European countries plunged into the conflict. When Great Britain responded to the invasion of Belgium by declaring war on Germany on August 4, it seemed that disaster threatened the world.

Wealthy families of America's growing leisure class, who sailed to England on Cunard steamships for lengthy vacations and who strolled along London's Park Lane as often as along New York's Fifth Avenue, read daily reports of a war which, to them, seemed unreal. In the United States, prices of commodities escalated and the labor market tightened. Still, despite concern about American "preparedness," life continued as usual for most Americans.

On November 10, 1914, the first Dodge automobile—a shiny, black touring car with self-lubricating springs and a body of welded steel, instead of the wooden bodies used by other car makers—was unveiled to newsmen at a luncheon at the Dodge plant. Then, the blue-eyed brothers—hefty, twin-like figures in their hard bowlers, high stiff collars, diamond stickpins and identical topcoats—sat proudly on the leather back seat with the car-top rolled back. A chauffeur drove the four-cylinder automobile out of the factory gates to Boston Boulevard where photographers waited at John's home.

From her cloistered second-floor sitting room, Matilda parted the window drapes to look down on the men and the solid, 110-inch wheelbase, $785 Dodge Brothers automobile. Measuring 13 feet long and six feet, nine inches high, the car had an "L" type engine, a cone clutch and a pressurized fuel system. Matilda's personal interest in the new motor car lay in the innovations that made the Dodge a practical machine for women drivers—a self-starter system of 12-volt capacity employing a combined starter and generator driven by a silent chain. The car rarely needed cranking. The driver pressed a starter on the floor after which starter-cranking resumed automatically to prevent the engine from coughing and stalling when the armature voltage fell below the battery voltage.

Another dashboard improvement featured an air-pump handle used to propel air into the rear-mounted gas tank to bring gasoline foward to the carburetor. This made it possible for the Dodge car to climb a steep hill without forcing the driver to put his car into reverse gear and to ascend the hill backwards, as drivers of some Model T Fords had to do.

But since automobile repair shops were almost non-existent at this early date, owners had to service their own Dodge cars by following detailed how-to manuals supplied by Dodge Brothers—instructing owners in the art of sliding underneath their autos to apply grease and oil to some 50 fittings. Although John told his wife that manufacturers would introduce 120 different makes of new automobiles in 1914, Matilda never doubted the abilities of John and Horace Dodge to succeed despite a competitive market that would bring failure to a large percentage of the others.

Two and one-half weeks after the birth of the Dodge car, Matilda Dodge went into labor. At six p.m. on November 27, a baby girl and heiress to the Dodge fortune, was born. On the original birth certificate—a multiple-birth form—filed in Lansing for Frances Dodge, a line was marked through the word "twin" and another line through the word "triplet" in a box containing the phrase "twin, triplet, or other." In a second box indicating "number in order of birth," the word "1st" was inserted.

Wayne County was the only indication of where, in Michigan, the child was born. The line indicating the city or township where the birth occurred was left blank. The street address also was blank.

A birth certificate for the blue-eyed, fair-complexioned Frances Dodge filed at the Department of Health in Detroit, which should have been identical to the record filed with the state, was unlike the Lansing document. The signature of the "delivering physician," William Chittick, on the Detroit certificate did not appear to be identical to the Chittick signature on the Lansing certificate. And the Detroit document, which also was a form intended for multiple births, had only the numeral "1" placed inside the first box. The box indicating order of birth was left blank.

The Detroit certificate also contained a definite place of birth—the East Boston Boulevard home of the John Dodges in Detroit. But the childless Amelia Rausch, the little sister whose life centered around her collection of myriad details of, and significant events in, the lives of the John Dodge family, recorded a different place of birth for her first niece—Frances Dodge. Amelia noted the birthplace as Harper Hospital—the institution to which John Dodge had contributed a generous donation for a new building in 1912 and the hospital to whose board of trustees John Dodge would be named the following September. "Doc" Chittick, whose teenaged daughter was also named Frances, served, of course, on Harper Hospital's staff.

At the other end of the state, on the shores of Lake Michigan and only 16 miles from the Niles birthplace of the Dodge brothers, a blue-eyed infant of fair complexion was brought to the Michigan Children's Home in the Berrien County seat of St. Joseph in late November, 1914. The Michigan Children's Home Society (later changed to Child and Family Services of Michigan) had been founded in St. Joseph in 1892 "to become the friend and protector of helpless little children, uncared for and unwanted," with the goal of placing these children with foster parents.

The cornerstone for the first, two-story, frame house for the children's home was laid in 1892 with a program featuring "little Katie Smith in songs and recitations." In 1906, the society built a larger home of two stories mounted with curved dormers. The nursery, to which the infant was brought from Detroit in 1914, held several cribs and a cradle beneath the sloping roof of the dormers. A rug, covering the center of the floor, cushioned the tread of the nurses' high shoes. A round coal stove warmed the nursery, flames reddening its iron belly and roaring up the tall stovepipe when a nurse opened the damper.

In March, 1915, the baby girl was taken from the Children's Home to a foster home, and a few weeks later, to a modest home in a working-class neighborhood—Hogarth Avenue—on Detroit's west side. A childless couple, Robert and Minnie Manzer, lived at the Hogarth address. The couple had cared for foster children previously as a way of earning extra income, while living in Belleville, Michigan. When the Manzers lost their Belleville home to foreclosure, they moved to Wayne, Michigan, where the husband worked for a carriage company. A short time later, after moving to the house Manzer built on Hogarth Avenue in 1914, Robert Manzer came up with enough money to hold a clear deed to the house.

Through the foster care program of the Methodist Children's Home in Detroit, the Manzers, active Methodists, had become friends of Frank Upton, John Dodge's trusted employee. Although all the children previously taken into the Manzer home came from the Methodist home, on whose board Upton served, the baby girl came from the Michigan Children's Home Society in St. Joseph. And her placement was not temporary. Robert and Minnie Manzer were already in the process of adopting the child, even though the baby was weak and ailing.

Minnie Manzer provided her adopted daughter with meticulous care in the first year of the child's life as the little girl rapidly gained weight. But it was Robert Manzer who leaned over the crib, patiently coaxing the first smiles and coos from the baby and exulting when the child, whom they named Lucille, started to crawl and then to take her first steps.

The John Dodges employed a nurse to care for the infant Frances at East Boston Boulevard. As Matilda recovered slowly from giving birth, she edged into a whirl of social life beginning with the John Dodges' announcement of the engagement of John's eldest daughter, Winifred, to William J. Gray, Jr., son of a prominent Detroit family. Together, Matilda and Winifred planned an October, 1915, wedding.

John Dodge's friend, "Doc" Chittick, still made regular house calls to the Dodge home in the early months of 1915, ministering to Della's husband, Uriah Eschbach. Eschbach died of tuberculosis at age 73 in early June.

Soon after Uriah's funeral, Matilda tried to hide her anger when she learned that, without asking anyone's permission, Della invited a woman-friend—43-year-old Helen Bovee—to live with her in the third-floor suite of the Dodge home. The Bovee family's friendship with the Dodges dated back to John and Horace's employment with the Upton Manufacturing Company in Port Huron.

Knowing how loyal John was to his sister and how strong his old-boy relationship was to friends in Niles and Port Huron, Matilda dared not protest the presence of Helen Bovee in her home. A while later, when Matilda learned that her sister-in-law and her very close friend were absorbed in psychic experimentation, she decided to express her concerns to John. Because John scoffed at Henry Ford's belief in reincarnation and at Ford's public statements that he had been Leonardo da Vinci in a previous life, Matilda expected her husband to react with similar intolerance to his sister's clairvoyant interests and her study of reincarnation.

"Damn it. Don't interfere in Della's concerns," John warned.

Galled by his rebuff, Matilda transferred her indignation at John's unfairness into additional animosity toward Della and, especially, to the companion. In John's presence, she dared not risk showing any resentment toward Della. But Matilda was cold and aloof to her sister-in-law during John's frequent absences from the home while he worked at the factory, stayed at Meadow Brook, or socialized with his brother and their rowdy friends.

Silas Burgett, still employed at the Dodge factory, greatly admired the free-spirited John Dodge with whom he sometimes fished on the Huron River. On one such expedition, as their boat moved through a narrow part of the river lined with small cottages, the men saw two steaming pies cooling on a window sill. Maneuvering the boat to the water's edge, John Dodge jumped out, grabbed the pies from the ledge, and ran back to share the apple pastries with his hungry pals.

Silas' admiration for the impetuous Dodge seemed unaffected even by a secret which he claimed was confided to him by his employer over drinks in a Hamtramck saloon. Later, an awed Silas revealed to his wife the secret which he said John Dodge had disclosed...that Mrs. Dodge had given birth to Siamese twins—both girls; that the babies were separated and that the Dodges kept one of the infants.

Similar stories circulated among other tool-room workers and reached the ears of Henry Batz, who puzzled over the reasons why a wealthy man and wife might give away a child. He repeated the story to his brothers, who had recently come to Detroit from Italy, omitting only the word "Siamese"—an unfamiliar term to him. How could anyone give away his child, Batz continued to ask his brothers in Italian. Years later, he would still ask his family the same question, in broken English, as he pondered the past and recalled the early years of his employment at the Dodge factory.

When the Dodges left their Monroe-Hastings shop for their new factory in Hamtramck, Batz had taken his drill press from the Monroe shop and kept it as a memorial to his early years with Dodge...a testimonial to his loyalty to Dodge Brothers. Each look at the drill press sparked his memories of John Dodge working in the tool room and telling "his boys" that he would remember them in his will for their help in producing the first Dodge motorcar.

By the end of 1914, John and Horace were planning for major production of Dodge cars in 1915, introducing a two-passenger roadster with rear luggage compartment, and a first closed car—a center-door sedan. In October, 1915, the fuel system for Dodge cars was changed to a vacuum type as total production, largely touring cars and roadsters, rose to 45,000 automobiles that year.

As early as January, 1915, the Dodges sent their first agent to Europe to arrange for overseas dealerships, although the six-month-old war in Europe continued. Despite their liking for German food and camaraderie, the Dodge brothers supported the British-French alliance against the Kaiser, and strongly promoted American preparedness. They organized a Dodge Brothers Industrial Band, made up of factory workers who played rousing marches, rehearsing after each man completed a full day's work.

In the spring of 1915, the torpedoing of the Lusitania killed 114 Americans and heightened emotions in the United States against Germany. While Dodge Brothers Industrial Band played the popular

"Keep the Home Fires Burning," Henry Ford expressed disapproval of band performances designed to stir patriotic emotions.

Refusing to take part in preparedness drives, Ford came under the influence of Madame Rosika Schwimmer, a Budapest journalist and believer in achieving peace through mediation at Geneva, Switzerland. Inspired by Schwimmer, Ford seized upon the idealistic notion of chartering an ocean liner and financing a delegation of influential people who would sail for Europe and sway public sentiments to his own pacifist beliefs.

When Ford took up a cause, he spent money lavishly. Naming his chartered ocean liner Peace Ship, he tried to entice men and women whom he admired to sail with the peace seekers whose goal was, Ford announced to news reporters, "to get the boys out of the trenches by Christmas."

The press ridiculed Ford's expedition. President Wilson refused to authorize the pilgrimage. James Couzens, embarrassed by Ford's bitter pacifism and the notoriety given the Peace Ship project, resigned in October, 1915, as treasurer and vice-president of Ford Motor Company. But Ford suffered his sharpest disappointment when Jane Addams, William Jennings Bryan and Thomas Edison failed to join the diverse collection of pilgrims when the Peace Ship sailed for Norway on December 4, even though Ford offered Thomas Edison a million dollars to take part in the expedition.

Buffeted by the Atlantic under leaden December skies, the Peace Ship became a microcosm in which Ford's attention was finally focused entirely on his fellow passengers, including journalists who observed the bickering among the pompous and opinionated travelers. Ford began to wrestle with the notion that the mission might be doomed to failure. Suffering from a severe cold by the time the ship docked in Norway, he quickly arranged for return passage on the next available liner while the rest of the group went on to Copenhagen, continuing the exercise in futility at Ford's expense.

Henry Ford, his kingpin image considerably diminished, slunk back to the Ford Motor Company where production, now amounting to 200 cars a day, was establishing records never imagined except by the shrewd inventor of the Model T. At the close of his workdays, he returned to the secluded Dearborn-area home into which the Ford family moved in late 1915—a newly built, gray limestone manor named Fair Lane.

As much as Henry professed to despise the showplace homes of wealthy residents of Grosse Pointe or Detroit's Indian Village, his own Fair Lane was a sprawling and costly structure. He justified the lavishness of the 56-room Fair Lane by its location in surroundings to which he and Clara Ford were sentimentally attached—where both had been born and where they were married. In this wooded Dearborn haven, with guards for protection, Henry and Clara and their son, Edsel, could have the privacy the parents desired.

Here, the Fords enjoyed their quiet hobby of bird watching and practicing bird calls—whistling, chirping and warbling to greet each other within the great, echoing expanses of Fair Lane. But even in this Dearborn sanctuary, removed from the bustle of Detroit and the intrusion of people looking for jobs or handouts, Henry Ford always carried a gun.

While the <u>Peace Ship</u> was still in its planning stages, Winifred Dodge became the bride of William J. Gray, Jr., in a Saturday afternoon wedding, October 30, 1915, at First Presbyterian Church. John Duval and Isabel took part in the wedding as Winifred, in white silk tulle piped with silver, swept down the center aisle on the arm of her father.

Matilda, wearing a mushroom chiffon and velvet dress and a magnificent black velvet hat with a bird-of-paradise plume, returned to East Boston Boulevard immediately after the ceremony to receive wedding guests at a reception held at the Dodge home. Since Isabel would make her debut before the year's end, the wedding reception provided an opportunity for Matilda to present this second stepdaughter to family friends at the same time.

Dressed in her wedding finery, flowing champagne satin and brown chiffon with garlands of green and autumn foliage hanging from one shoulder to the back hem of her gown, Isabel might have been mistaken for a wood nymph in a pagan festival scene. But her manners were the product of Liggett School and eastern finishing schools as she curtsied to one after another of her parents' guests to the bobbing accompaniment of red berry-clusters wreathing her brown crepe hat.

The bride and groom departed for an East-Coast wedding trip, secure in the knowledge that a spacious new home in Detroit's Indian Village awaited them on their return. The home was a $250,000 gift from John Dodge.

In late November, Matilda planned a small dinner party to celebrate the christening of her one-year-old daughter, Frances Matilda. The Reverend Dr. Joseph Vance, who came to East Boston Boulevard early on Saturday evening to baptize the child, marvelled at the highly emotional reactions of the little girl's father, John, and godfather, Horace, during the brief ceremony. The two, tough Dodge brothers gripped hands, tears streaking their faces, as the minister spoke the ritualistic words: "I baptize thee, Frances Matilda..."

The society paper, *Detroit Saturday Night* of November 27, 1915, described the affair as "A lovely party, full of home sentiment." It listed the dinner guests as Dr. Vance, pastor at First Presbyterian Church on Woodward Avenue (and an appointee, along with Anna Dodge, in November 1914, to an Advisory Committee for the Social Service Department of Harper Hospital); Dr. William Chittick (Vance's neighbor at Edmund Place) and his lovely wife, Adeline Kent Chittick; Mr. and Mrs. Horace Dodge; and the former mayor of Detroit, the Honorable George P. Codd, and Mrs. Codd.

The remaining social function for Matilda to manage in 1915 was Isabel's official debut party. When this party—a dinner dance at the Pontchartrain Hotel during Christmas week—turned out well, Matilda felt that her ability to handle such affairs with poise and assurance had been successfully tested. To the proud and serious-minded Matilda, propriety and decorum were of utmost importance.

Chapter 7

Separate Lives in Different Molds

Propriety and decorum loomed importantly, also, in the life of Amelia Rausch, who persisted in wearing mourning clothes for more than a year after the death of her father. "Why don't you stop wearing those damned dark clothes?" John Dodge complained when he visited at the farm. "You're too young to go around looking so dreary."

Wounded by John's insensitivity, she was equally wounded by her widening separation from her sister. "My sister forgot how it was for me," Amelia still would insist, years later, as she compared her own secluded life at the farm with Matilda's eventful life.

Amelia's "dreary" disposition quickened John's awareness of his sister-in-law's negative reaction to the sequestered farm environment. To brighten her life, he sent a factory employee on the 1 1/2-hour drive out to Meadow Brook with a Dodge car for Amelia's use. The employee, instructed to teach Mrs. Dodge's sister how to operate the automobile, drove Miss Amelia the few miles to Rochester and back to the farm. The man then parked the touring car near the farmhouse and returned to Detroit.

Amelia decided that the car could become her means of access to a livelier world and that she had better conquer the formidable one-ton vehicle immediately, before the instructions became muddled in her mind. Sitting on a plump pillow that boosted her high enough to see over the steering wheel, and stretching her short legs to reach the clutch and brake, Amelia cautiously maneuvered the car, which could reach speeds of 50 miles an hour, on a solo trip along the rutted road to Rochester—returning triumphantly to the farm.

Soon afterwards, when John came alone to the farm for a weekend, he brought something else for Amelia's use and protection. A pistol. Amelia's dislike for guns was as intense as her fondness for the Dodge car. Still it never occurred to her to resist learning how to load and fire the pistol.

She knew that whenever John left the farmhouse at night, he carried a rifle. Despite his camaraderie with most Dodge factory workers, there were some dissatisfied workers, former employees who had been laid off, and union activists who were a threat to the Dodges, John pointed out in justification of following Henry Ford's practice of carrying a firearm.

Amelia recognized the truth of what he said, realizing that the isolated location of Meadow Brook was little protection from anyone who wanted to seek out John Dodge. She also saw some of the written threats that had arrived at the Dodge office. Even so, Amelia sensed another puncture in the John Dodge power image...he feared darkness she was sure, as much as he feared water and as much as he dreaded becoming ill, again, with tuberculosis.

Still, John seemed determined not to permit these fears to control his life; he often boarded Horace's <u>Nokomis</u> or the Oakmans' <u>Mamie-O</u> for excursions with friends to roadhouses along the Canadian shoreline. And he continued coming out to Meadow Brook regularly on weekends—alone, or with Matilda, the baby Frances, and her nanny.

On these weekends, Matilda's strong attraction to the farm frequently clashed with what she perceived as her obligations to the smooth operation of the Boston Boulevard household or with attendance at certain social functions. Usually, she settled for summer weekends at the farm—not only because of the appeal of abundant orchards and lush meadows where cattle grazed peacefully, but also because the ghost of John's second, secret marriage constantly shadowed her life.

Well acquainted with her husband's impetuous nature and robust sexual appetite, she frequently observed the soft gleam of admiration in Amelia's eyes when John, with a few thrusts of his powerful shoulders and body, raised a heavy timber into place or tossed feed sacks off a wagon as if they were fluffy pillows. Moreover, she knew that the second-floor master bedroom, at the top of the wide three-turn staircase rising from the front entrance hall, adjoined Amelia's bedroom with a connecting door. Despite Amelia's conviction that "my sister forgot how it was for me," Matilda recognized that the younger sister was lonely at Meadow Brook—and susceptible. Matilda determined to be vigilant; to accompany John on his Meadow Brook excursions as often as possible.

Matilda's life of increasing wealth and prestige as Mrs. John Dodge never erased the memory of her early years as the introverted daughter of saloonkeepers. The recollection of those years left her with a hidden sense of tarnish that made her resentful, even now, of Amelia's modest self-esteem and unembarrassed acknowledgment of the same working-class background.

Each time the younger sister dropped little insinuations regarding the twist of fate resulting in Matilda getting married first, to the only man she ever dated, while Amelia, who enjoyed so many friends of both sexes, remained unmarried, the insinuations irked Matilda. "Remember whens" galled her if either her mother or sister spoke of the temper tantrums and breath-holding episodes of the older sister's childhood...of the several times Margaret Rausch was summoned to school by teachers concerned about Matilda's isolation from her classmates. The adult Amelia's attachment to their childhood neighborhood annoyed Matilda who resolutely tried to separate herself from the painful past at St. Aubin Street and to live only in the present and the future.

Whenever the John Dodges came out to the farm, often with extra guests, life at Meadow Brook took on an increased tempo. To Margaret Rausch, it seemed she prepared as much food—for family, guests, hired help, extra waitresses, and even for caddies and chauffeurs—as she had prepared in her younger days at the Dry Dock Hotel.

For farm manager John Cline, who first came to work at Meadow Brook in 1910, weekends could be inquisition sessions when he was accountable to his employers for all farm projects and, what was much worse, had to pretend enthusiasm for whatever new project that Mrs. John Dodge wanted to incorporate into Meadow Brook operations. Bees, for example. The responsibility for hiring a beekeeper and for collecting Meadow Brook's own honey. Building racks in the basement for storage of vinegar, made at Meadow Brook, in huge jars. Putting up more basement shelving for two-quart jars of tomatoes and other farm produce canned by Margaret Rausch. Fitting rows of cupboards with locks for storage of liquor and gingerales and tins of caviar on the north wall of the basement, adjacent to the newly built clubhouse.

It became Cline's responsibility, also, to hire extra men for butchering hogs and lambs; to see to it that bacon and hams were hung in the smokehouse for curing. The keys to the smokehouse, the liquor vault, to the extra china and glassware storage, the cider racks, the canned goods cupboards, the clubhouse...all remained in Amelia's possession, jangling from huge rings which she guarded as if she were a mother-superior protecting the doors to her convent and novices.

The acreage that Cline managed at Meadow Brook continued expanding as John Dodge bought properties from neighboring farmers. And in Hamtramck, the Dodge brothers expanded their 20 acres of factory floor-space in 1914 to 72 acres in 1916—constructing an eight-story building 310 feet long and 125 feet wide, and making both vertical and horizontal additions to existing structures.

A universal stand, invented by Horace for holding engines on the assembly line, speeded the factory's automatic conveyors to substantially increase production. The younger Dodge brother also discovered that insulators, formerly used only for refrigeration purposes, were superior to insulating materials currently used in enameling-ovens. By converting the refrigeration materials into insulating components for enameling ovens, Horace reduced oven heat loss to one-tenth of its former leakage. At that point, the Dodge enameling plant reached a capacity of 400 cars a day, providing four coats of enamel baked on the metal body of each car as it traveled 800 feet through loops of conveyors and electric ovens.

Each fully equipped car could now be driven away from the end of Dodge Brothers assembly line only two hours and 35 minutes from the moment the frame-skeleton began its assembly-conveyor journey. The brothers boasted of the swiftness of their assembly line...of the testing of axles, drive shafts and similar parts by a torsion machine (one of only two in use in the world) that could exert a torsion strain of 230,000 inch-pounds...of the fitting of their cars with mohair tops, side-curtains and upholstery made in their own plant from a daily consignment of 8000 pounds of interlaced hair and more than 625 full-sized hides...of the introduction, in 1916, of a removable winter top, complete with glass windows, that could be purchased for an additional $165 with the Dodge touring car or roadster.

The Dodges took even more pride in their automobile in March of 1916 when they received commendations for the splendid performance of Dodge cars in the Mexican Badlands as U.S. troops pursued Pancho Villa and a raiding party across the border into Mexico. Under the command of General John J. Pershing, young Lieutenant George S. Patton led the first U.S. motorized attack against an enemy as three Dodge cars, packed with a couple of dozen men, lurched across a patch of rough desert toward one of Pancho Villa's strongholds. Although Villa escaped and continued to elude his pursuers, Pershing was sufficiently impressed with Dodge cars to notify the U.S. War Department that he wanted only Dodge Brothers automobiles for use in the Mexican campaign. A total of 250 Dodges soon churned their way in low gear through desert sand and along narrow rutted mountain paths.

The rugged and dependable Dodge had become, even earlier, the first car ever driven to the bottom of the Grand Canyon and back up the steep ascent under its own power. It climbed higher up San Francisco's twin peaks than any other car of that era.

By the fall of 1916, the Dodge factory had turned out 100,000 cars which, since April of that year, had multiple disc type clutches replacing the former cone type. Like Ford, the Dodges were incited by success to aspire to even greater expansion of their business. They planned to use their Ford dividends to help finance this expansion.

When Ford stated his intentions, in the summer of 1916, to turn much of the accumulated profits of the Ford Motor Company back into the business, the Dodges strenuously objected. They viewed Ford's plans for enlargement of his company as grandiose enough to command the greater part of company dividends for many years. Ford's designs included the purchase of 1000 acres of land at the Rouge River where a blast furnace and foundry would be built for production of glass and steel for Ford cars. He also planned to double the size of the Ford Highland Park plant.

This was not to be done at stockholders' expense, the Dodges determined. In September, 1916, the Dodges drafted a letter to Ford demanding a distribution of 50 percent of Ford Motor Company's $58 million cash surplus to stockholders. At Ford's refusal, the brothers made a second demand—that Ford should buy their stock for $35 million. Since Ford already owned controlling shares in the company, he refused to rush into the purchase of more stock. This left the Dodges with only one option; to sue Ford for distribution of larger dividends.

By November 1, when Henry Ford's son, Edsel, married Eleanor Clay, the Dodge brothers' suit against Ford had not yet been announced. A small group of curious onlookers gathered on East Boston Boulevard outside the former Malcomson home—purchased by the late J.L. Hudson and still occupied by Hudson's sister Eliza Clay and her two daughters—to gape at the wedding guests as they arrived that evening to attend the home-ceremony.

The parents of the groom arrived first—lean-figured Henry Ford and his short, plump wife, Clara. Thomas Alva Edison, the white-haired inventor, followed, always managing to look slightly dishevelled, no matter what the occasion. A ripple of excitement stirred the onlookers as they watched the famous inventor, who had traveled to Detroit to accommodate the wishes of his friend, Henry, slowly approach the front door of the stone house and disappear inside. Still, it was the arrival of the florid-faced Dodge brothers and their stylishly dressed wives, who walked from the John Dodge manor to the neighboring Hudson home, that stimulated the spectators to press forward to catch a closer look at the wealthy brothers and their wives.

By contrast, the 22-year-old groom, Edsel, was a colorless figure—slim like his father, but shorter at five feet, six inches. As he arrived at the Hudson home in early evening, Edsel smiled broadly. He looked happy to be marrying 19-year-old Eleanor Clay. Even happier, said those who knew the Fords, to be separating himself from the suppressive supervision of his parents.

Henry and Clara Ford, who expected their son and his bride to live at commodious Fair Lane or to build an adjacent home, were pained at the decision of Edsel and Eleanor to live on Detroit's Iroquois Avenue, near the new Indian Village home of Winifred Dodge Gray. But no hint of problems appeared on the evening of the wedding as the Fords, Edison, Dodges, and various guests mingled and chatted—and drank grape juice.

Among the many homespun philosophies spouted by Henry Ford was his belief that "you don't have to agree with a man to get along with him." On the day following the wedding, Ford's philosophy was tested when newspaper headlines announced: Dodge Brothers Sue Ford. The Dodges, the article explained, had filed a minority stockholders' suit to force Henry Ford to distribute 3/4 of Ford Motor Company's cash surplus as dividends.

While Dodge attorneys handled the brothers' problems with Ford, John asked Matilda to accompany him to his four-bedroom northwoods hunting lodge near Munuscong Lake for a week in the company of Mayor Oscar Marx and his wife. The men hunted in the thick woods surrounding the lodge and the women walked near the camp and enjoyed the unbroken quiet of the forest. When John and Marx returned for their evening meal, conversation inevitably turned to criticism of the man whose arbitrary rule of the Ford Motor Company burdened John's mind. Ford. His scorn of stockholders who had made possible the very existence of the company...his insistence on reducing the price of the Model T runabout, in 1916, to a new low of $345 at a time when 500,000 Model T's produced still did not meet demands of buyers waiting to purchase the cars.

John's indignation always became more explosive with mention of Ford's opposition to the Dodge brothers; his temper cooled only when conversation turned to reminiscences of Ford's eccentricities. The Peace Ship, of course. And another absurdity ridiculed by newspapers the past spring, April, 1916—Henry Ford's obsessive interest in the invention of a 70-year-old Long Island resident...a secret formula which, the inventor claimed, could change water into gasoline. With gasoline prices inflated to 30¢ a gallon because of the war in Europe, Ford was intrigued by the water-into-gasoline inventor's claim that his formula could produce gasoline at a cost of one-cent per gallon.

After a secret meeting between Ford and the inventor—Louis Enricht, a New York newspaper printed an article unveiling Ford's gullibility. The article revealed that Enricht previously had swindled other businessmen who invested in the self-styled inventor's earlier recipes for turning wood shavings into finished railroad ties and changing dirt into concrete bridges.

Ford appeared to be unaffected by the newspaper story. He held still another meeting with Enricht, during which, Ford disclosed afterwards to reporters, he decided to overlook the inventor's former indiscretions. Moreover, he announced, he intended to provide a Ford car and expense money for the inventor to proceed with his water-gasoline experimentation.

As much as the Dodges and Marx scoffed at Ford's stubborn refusal to admit errors in judgment, even they could not have foreseen that six years later, Enricht would be arrested and tried for grand larceny; then sentenced to Sing Sing.

Soon after the John Dodges returned from their hunting lodge to Boston Boulevard, it was time to celebrate the second birthday of their daughter, Frances, in late November. The child had been left in the care of her nurse while the parents were at the lodge. And by this time, Matilda was quite sure that she was pregnant again.

At the Manzer home in Detroit, two-year-old Lucille, who was never left in the care of a nanny or sitter, also celebrated her second birthday in the fourth week of November. Although her father liked the outdoors and, occasionally, went off on hunting or fishing excursions with friends, her mother, Minnie Manzer, was always at home to carefully brush her daughter's blond hair into curls and to take the child by the hand when she walked to the neighborhood grocery store or to a Ladies' Aid meeting at church. It was a comfortable and secure kind of life for the little girl who pressed her nose to the window pane and eagerly watched for her father's return from a day of fishing. He would take her out in the fishing boat when she was older, Robert Manzer often promised his daughter.

For John Dodge, it was a rarity to take his wife to his hunting lodge. He still preferred to make the trip up to Munuscong Lake with his brother, Horace, and their male friends. On their return from one of these excursions, the brothers discovered that a newly promoted young superintendent decided to act as an efficiency expert in his employers' absence and had closed the "playpen"— a special workshop the Dodges set aside for the use of retirees in their leisure hours. In the well equipped workshop, retirees were free to come and go as they wished and to build whatever they chose from a generous supply of scrap materials—until the day the superintendent locked the door.

Matilda would have covered her ears if she had been within the considerable hearing-range of her husband's loud voice as he tongue-lashed the bungling superintendent. Then John drove off to personally visit the home of each retiree accustomed to using the "playpen," inviting each man to again make use of the facilities—the kind of generous gesture that made Matilda proud of her husband.

At the time of Edsel Ford's wedding, half of the 48 states already were dry as the Anti-Saloon League and Prohibition Party exercised growing political clout. Outspoken teetotaler Henry Ford was the hero of Prohibition activists who prompted a write-in, Ford-for-president, primary campaign in 1916, previous to the November election in which Woodrow Wilson won a second presidential term.

Although the United States had not entered the war, shortages of materials and equipment—including a shortage of freight cars that could be used for shipment of civilian goods—plagued the country. A Dodge dealer in Superior, Nebraska—Mrs. Zona Berg—wrote to the Dodge plant, asking: "Can you ship cars or, if not, can you give me some if I come after them?"

In February, 1917, Zona, her 58-year-old mother, her 12-year-old son, and three male employees arrived by train in Detroit. On February 11, with thermometers in Detroit registering 15 degrees below zero, Zona and her entourage started out with four new Dodge automobiles on the 1200-mile trip back to Nebraska. Zona drove one car. Her very young son drove another. Two of her mechanics drove the remaining two cars while Zona's mother and a third man went along as relief drivers.

They stopped periodically in Michigan to shovel snow from the roads. In Iowa, they learned that Dodge cars "skated along very well over ice," Zona reported after the caravan arrived safely in Superior— an early pioneer in "drive-away" operations.

By this time, young John Duval Dodge was already at work in his father's factory, his employment resulting from unhappy circum- stances—another truancy episode. Both John Duval and his cousin Horace Junior had sneaked away from their schools to meet in New York for a good time on Broadway. When their money ran out, the cousins returned to their schools, but an angry headmaster promptly delivered John Duval to the train depot and sent him home to Detroit.

Furious at the unexpected appearance of his son, John Dodge threatened to send the boy to work in his factory. Matilda demurred. She wanted her stepson to finish prep school...to be a credit to the kind of training she had tried to give him at home. Young Horace was back at Manlius Institute, Matilda pointed out, after Horace and Anna appealed to school administrators to readmit their son. The Horace Dodges already were planning to present the institution with a sizeable endowment.

John Dodge silenced his wife with a reminder that John Duval was two years older than Horace...that an 18-year-old was old enough to start learning the automobile business if he would not study for an education. He did not remind Matilda that the country might soon be at war, and that if his son were working in the factory, he might avoid induction into the armed forces. Patriotism, it seemed, was superseded by concern for his son's safety.

For John Duval, factory work held no more appeal than schoolwork. He partied at night, dawdled at the factory during his enforced work hours, and tried to shield his ineptitude with a veneer of insolence that aggravated other employees.

The father, John Dodge, made no secret of his envy of Henry Ford in having produced an industrious and loyal son—the soft-spoken Edsel, who took a keen interest in all the workings of the Ford Motor Company and prepared himself to assume the responsibilities of directing the Ford empire. Since Matilda Dodge could find no graceful way to express her own opinion that her husband never really spent much time with his son—either in his very early or teen years—while Henry Ford always gave Edsel a great deal of time and attention, she remained quiet when John compared his own willful son with Henry's model offspring.

With the United States' declaration of war in April, 1917, Dodge automobiles increased $50 in price as the production of munitions commanded greater allotments of steel and other materials. Despite the war, Dodge Brothers added a convertible coupe and a convertible sedan to their models, each with removable side-window and center-post pillars, available in deep blue with wire wheels in cream enamel. The 1917 Dodge featured headlamps that could be reversed to furnish light for making repairs or changing tires at night. The dependable four-cylinder engine remained unchanged, however, and company policy remained unaltered: "Constant improvement but no yearly model change."

In May, 1917, the government required all men between 21 and 31 years of age to register for military service. Edsel Ford, included in this prime-age group, came under pressure from his father to request a deferment on the basis of his indispensability to the efficient operation of the Ford Motor Company, as Ford prepared to produce Liberty engines for the war effort. John Duval Dodge would not be required to register for the draft until the following year, when Congress amended the Selective Service Act to include men as young as 18 years.

Henry Ford always seemed impervious to the public furor aroused by his actions or public utterances, many of them regarding his earlier pacifist sentiments which included a threat to burn down his Highland Park factory before he would agree to turn out war materials. But Edsel preferred facing induction into the armed services rather than asking for the deferment demanded by his overbearing father who now took up the cause of producing military supplies as enthusiastically as he had previously promoted pacifistic causes.

When Edsel obediently followed his father's directive, newspaper editorials labelled young Ford a "slacker"—the popular word for those who tried to avoid serving their country. The criticism stung...and lingered in Edsel's memory for years after the war ended.

In the same month that conscription began, Horace Dodge donated his Nokomis I to the U.S. government as a submarine chaser. His sister, Della, carefully fashioned a poem for the sentimental farewell ceremony planned by Horace, who ordered booklets printed with a cover photo of the Dodge brothers standing on the pier at Rose Terrace, gazing solemnly at the trim and elegant yacht. On the day of departure for the Nokomis, Horace and John and their closest friends clustered at the end of a Detroit River pier to wave farewell as Navy personnel boarded the yacht. The Dodges then handed out copies of the commemorative booklet featuring Della's poem.

> "The wind is lashing the somber lee,
>   And the foam-flecked waves roll high,
> And my heart is stirred like the stormy sea,
>   As you sail from the shores of 'Used-To-Be'
>   Goodbye, Nokomis, Goodbye."

Some of the sacrificial sheen of the sentimental affair was corroded by the fact that, only four months earlier, Horace went to Wilmington, Delaware, for the launching of a new 243-foot-long steam yacht, built to his specifications by Gielow and Orr, top-flight naval architects. Electrically lighted and equipped with a thermo-fan heating system, the yacht, christened Nokomis II (later Delphine I), provided comfortable living for its owners and guests in large staterooms and luxuriously furnished dining room and living room. If Horace could have known that one year after his <u>Nokomis</u> I went into governmental service, his <u>Nokomis</u> II would also be requisitioned by the government, his eagerness to purchase the new yacht would have been dampened.

Within the Dodge plant, Liberty Loan posters, framed with flags and bunting, reminded employees of their patriotic duty to buy war bonds. Inspired by a desire to sell war bonds, Della Dodge Eschbach trekked across the state and country, accompanied by her friend Helen Bovee, rallying women to sign up for the American Red Cross and rousing support for the Liberty Bond campaign.

Matilda, remaining in seclusion as she awaited the birth of her child in the early months following America's declaration of war, felt grudging admiration for the sister-in-law with whom her relations were so strained. Della's leadership role in the home-front war effort was the kind of strategy Matilda would have emulated if she had not been in her present "delicate" condition.

On July 23, 1917, Matilda went into Harper Hospital for the birth of a healthy baby boy, named Daniel George Dodge for both grandfathers. Three-year-old Frances, blond and blue-eyed like her father, now had a baby brother who, as his eyes changed to dark brown within weeks of his birth, resembled his mother. "And this one looks like a Rausch," the baby's Aunt Amelia and Grandmother Rausch frequently congratulated each other, as if the child's dark hair and bright eyes were a personal tribute to themselves.

Dodge employee, Frank Upton, and his wife, Viola, visited frequently at the Manzer home on Detroit's west side in these years. Three-year-old Lucille Manzer enjoyed the attention she received from the Uptons, but Minnie Manzer began to wonder if her adopted daughter might be spoiled by all the pampering given to an only child.

Since Robert Manzer was equally indulgent of his young daughter, Minnie was relieved when, after a period of unemployment, her husband took a job with Ray Harroun, who leased part of the Dodge Power Building on Jefferson Avenue to build the first models for his new Harroun Motor Car. Soon after the war ended, the Harroun Motor Car Company lanquished for lack of capital, then went into bankruptcy. Manzer again became a self-employed carpenter with free time to spend with five-year-old Lucille when she returned home from kindergarten classes.

Chapter 8

Prosperity in Modest and Immodest Proportions

In May, 1917, spectators crowded the courtroom when the Dodge-Ford trial began in Michigan Circuit Court where the Dodges sought distribution of surplus profits to stockholders by the Ford Motor Company. Extra police came to restrain the throng of people trying to view the spectacle of the independent auto-magnate, Henry Ford, forced to spar with Dodge attorney, Elliot Stevenson.

Throughout the questioning by Stevenson, Ford clung to his claim that his company was not organized for the purpose of making profits, but "...to do as much good as we can, everywhere, for everybody concerned." With a flourish, Ford insisted that "business is a service, not a bonanza."

Normally unhandy with words, the determined Ford surprised Stevenson by answering in ways that impressed spectators with his altruism. The Dodge lawyer hastily abandoned that line of questioning and turned to Ford's introduction of the five-dollar day. Was it not true, he demanded, that Ford had stated that the greater pay and reduced workday made his workers "hustle" to the extent that they had "no more hustle left" at the day's end?

Ford responded with difficulty to Stevenson on that point. More difficulties followed when the lawyer pointed out that Ford acted as a one-man board of directors. "Can you mention one example of a veto by the Ford Motor Company board of directors in regard to something you requested them to approve?" Stevenson wanted to know.

The courtroom was quiet as Ford squirmed in the witness chair. "I don't recall any examples," he finally admitted.

The defendant's uneasiness intensified as Stevenson intruded into a still more sensitive area—the origin of the Ford Motor Company.

Ford, the attorney claimed, started out with only the model of a car which the lawyer branded as "a pretty poor model." Under the attorney's barrage of questions, Ford admitted that Dodge Brothers made "part" of the first cars.

That "part," Stevenson maintained, consisted of motors and frames—total cars except for tires and bodies which were put on "completed cars" at Ford's "carpenter shop."

At the close of the arguments, the judge ruled that Ford must pay a special dividend of $19 million within 90 days, of which the victorious Dodges would collect $1.9 million.

The court ruled that future earnings must be distributed in a similar manner. Despite the rigors of the trial, Ford refused to capitulate, demanding an appeal to the Michigan State Superior Court.

At the time of the circuit court decision, America's involvement in World War I steadily encroached into all areas of the home front with rationing of sugar and a scarcity of coal. While 65,000 Detroit and Wayne County men went into the armed forces in 1917-1918, the list of employees, serving their country, grew longer on placards displayed at Dodge Brothers factory. The brothers hired replacement employees and began producing cars for government use. The cars, fitted with heavy canvas tops and with army serial numbers stencilled in white on the hoods, were sent to U.S. military installations and overseas to French battlefields.

The first Dodge screen-side trucks, weighing 2600 pounds and placed on passenger-car chassis equipped with heavier springs, left the factory in November, 1917. The U.S. government ordered these, as well as Dodge closed panel-side trucks, for use as ambulances.

Still, the strategic core of Dodge Brothers' wartime contributions turned out to be not its cars and ambulances, but, rather, its response to an unusual appeal from the French government. France needed assistance in producing a recoil mechanism for the French 155-millimeter Howitzer gun essential to Allied battle troops. The mechanism made the gun safer for the handler and more lethal to the enemy because of a faster refiring action. In French factories, the sensitive recoil mechanism was being painstakingly made by hand in quantities too small to satify the demand.

When Secretary of War Newton D. Baker called upon Dodge Brothers in late October, 1917, to work with the mechanism, John Dodge left for Washington. He arrived, confident in his conviction that his brother, Horace, could figure out a way to "manufacture" any item for which a blueprint existed. But his use of the word "manufacture" goaded Baker and the visiting Frenchmen into a litany of protests and explanations.

"Two American companies already tried to produce the mechanism," a French delegate protested. "Both failed."

"There are no machines with the fine degree of precision necessary to turn out the gun apparatus," another explained. "We need trained craftsmen to hand-tool the mechanism. And that is what we want from Dodge Brothers."

In salty, earthy terms, John voiced irritation at the doubts expressed by the Frenchmen in Dodge Brothers' abilities—which actually meant in Horace's inventive talent. And the French delegates were equally irritated by John Dodge's swaggering assurance. They questioned, now, whether they wanted this American madman even to attempt to work with the mechanism.

Nonetheless, John Dodge returned to Detroit with a model of the apparatus. Horace carefully studied it, and declared that Dodge Brothers certainly could manufacture the recoil device. He set to work at once, designing a lapping machine which would be the most important of 129 pieces of equipment planned by Horace to produce the gun mechanism.

The machinery had to be operational by March 1, 1918—only four months from the date of the signed agreement with the government. Dodge Brothers, John boasted to government officials, would erect a $10 million munitions plant to produce the recoil mechanisms. They would equip the plant with newly designed machines, and begin manufacturing the gun parts by March 1 at the rate of 50 each day—ten times the number turned out in any French factory.

Both Henry Ford and the Dodges already had confrontations with the U.S. War Industries Board when the two auto manufacturers balked at cutting back their production of cars for civilian use, as a wartime measure. Now, the Dodges expressed their willingness to personally finance the building and equipping of their munitions factory, several miles northeast of their Hamtramck complex, with one reservation. They wanted assurance that government personnel would not supervise the day-to-day operation of their ordnance plant.

Matilda Dodge saw little of her husband from November 1, 1917, until after the ordnance factory moved into production at Mt. Elliot Avenue and Lynch on March 1, 1918. For Matilda, the winter months at East Boston Boulevard were unusually quiet—not only because of John's absence, but because Red Cross knitting teas substituted for regular society festivities in these wartime weeks of especially severe weather and "Heatless Mondays." At occasional theater or orchestra concerts, the atmosphere remained subdued—"demi-toilette" and even street clothes replaced the usual formal attire of attending socialites.

In the second-floor nursery at the John Dodge home, Matilda hired a separate nurse to care for her infant son, Daniel. Three-year-old Frances had her own nurse, or nanny, who always accompanied the child on the family's excursions out to Meadow Brook Farm. There, in the spring of 1918, Matilda bought a pony, named Freddie, for little Frances. As she carefully placed the child in a wicker basket on wheels, the nurse observed how eagerly Mrs. John Dodge tried to enkindle her own love for horses in her young daughter.

During the early weeks of work on their munitions plant, both Horace and John had slept in a temporary shelter erected on the vacant 11-acre site for their new 600-by-800-foot plant. From this shelter, they could oversee installation of gas and sewer lines, and a railway spur. With the arrival of heavy equipment to dig foundations, 1800 construction men had begun their work, warming themselves over open-drum fires as construction continued throughout the bitter winter months.

At the end of February, John exultantly boasted to Matilda that Dodge Brothers met its commitment to the U.S. government...that the ordnance plant could begin its operations on March 1, right on schedule. Despite John's delight, Matilda suspected that her husband surely must experience some apprehension that the machine-made recoil mechanisms might have an imperfection that would make them useless. Any such apprehensions vanished when munitions experts examined the first mechanisms produced by Dodge and rated them "perfect."

Although Dodge Brothers met its deadline with a perfect product, attaining quantity production so glibly promised by John Dodge—fifty per month—remained out of reach. Thirty recoil mechanisms a month continued to be Dodge Brothers' top production. And the brothers' dealings with the Office of Inspector of Ordnance, U.S.A., set up at the Dodge plant at the insistence of the government, were strained at best...often openly antagonistic.

The munitions plant operated more than a month when John and Matilda decided to enjoy a brief vacation at the popular golfing resort at French Lick, Indiana. This relaxing time together at the posh vacation spot ruptured abruptly when a newspaper caption, bearing the bold-lettered name of John Duval Dodge, impelled them to pack their valises and return to Detroit. Nineteen-year-old John Duval, the newspaper divulged, had disclosed his secret marriage, two weeks earlier, to 18-year-old Marie O'Connor.

"Who the hell is Marie O'Connor?" John demanded of Matilda, who was equally uninformed. Both of them feared the name indicated an Irish-Catholic background, and suspected that as the reason John Duval never mentioned the girl's name to them. The boy was too young for marriage, anyway, John and Matilda agreed. And to elope with the girl—then to calmly discuss the elopement with a newspaper reporter before telling his parents...an unforgiveable offense, John Dodge raged.

Matilda took up John Duval's defense many times in the past, but now she found it impossible to excuse the young man's irresponsible behavior, aggravated by his flow of dialogue with reporters as he confided details of his marriage. The couple had continued to live, separately, in their parents' homes until Marie became ill with pneumonia, John Duval told reporters. Then, as he moved into the O'Connor home to be with Marie, rumors of the marriage reached the press.

Swollen with expansiveness under the focus of the press, John Duval confessed to reporters that he and his father never had a good relationship. The papers quoted John Duval further as reluctant to discuss his future plans, except to say that he anticipated going into business for himself.

John Dodge's anger at his son's impetuous elopement could have been inflamed by the memory of his own earlier, indiscreet, and secret marriage. But the father recognized no resemblance to his own conduct in John Duval's swaggering behavior. He saw only defiance...total irresponsibility...deliberate disloyalty to the Dodge family.

In a brief confrontation between father and son at East Boston Boulevard, John Duval expressed no repentance. He seemed unintimidated by his father's threat to disown him. He was getting out of Detroit, John Duval retorted, and starting a new life, somewhere else, with his wife.

As soon as his bride recovered from her illness, John Duval took her to Texas where he went to work at a gas station. His father visited his attorney's office and instructed his lawyer to draw up a new will.

In May, 1918, Michigan became a "dry" state—more than one year before Prohibition took effect throughout the country by federal law, to the satisfaction of Henry Ford and growing numbers of prohibitionists. Like Ford, Matilda Dodge favored the new law, but she soon learned that the legislation would not deprive the Dodge brothers, nor other heavy drinkers, of liquor. The Detroit River became an illegal runway for rum-runners from Canada to Detroit. "Blind pigs" and beer flats flourished throughout the city as gangsters warred among themselves for control of the profitable bootleg-liquor trade.

Other changes occurred in 1918 that Matilda found even more pleasing than the Prohibition Amendment. While young American men trained for combat and sailed for European battlefields, the first women mail-carriers and streetcar-conductors appeared on Detroit's streets. As early as 1916, Detroit women could vote in local elections, and fashions soon reflected the dawning age of independence for women as "pegtop" skirts, full at waist and hips and narrow at the hems, rose to a daring mid-calf length.

Large hats remained popular. Della bought a variety of elegant hats, styled by her milliner in colors to match her dresses, and had the bills sent to her brother John. She wore her choice of the bulky hats, headbands level with her eyebrows, when she attended her meetings of the Detroit Federation of Women's Clubs, a 10,000 member league of 95 organizations. In support of Della's charities, John contributed generously to the American Red Cross and Salvation Army Auxiliary, provided an endowment to supply "penny lunches" to foreign-born school children, and gave $6000 annually for milk distributed to young students. In 1919, he donated the renovated clubhouse at Second and Hancock, valued at $100,000, to Della's federation.

Although he rarely attended church services, John Dodge was a major contributor to the First Presbyterian Church attended by his wife. On Sunday mornings, Matilda sat proudly in the Dodge pew, number 47. But unless she brought along her little daughter, Frances, the rest of the pew usually remained unoccupied.

Like John Dodge, Henry Ford was not a churchgoer. But unlike either of the Dodges, Ford did not contribute to organized charities. He supported only charities of his own conception and planning. Beginning in 1914 and continuing through the early 1920s, he spent more than $11 million constructing and supporting Henry Ford Hospital—an institution where wealthy industrialists and the poorest of laborers were to receive the same kind of prime-quality care, according to Ford's precepts.

In his fervor for reforming other people, Ford began another program in 1914 by employing ex-convicts in his factories where marine-corps discipline was enforced for all workers. Workmen were expected to run, not walk. Men who were slow to pick up a tool could expect to be kicked or cuffed by a superior. This tough discipline, Ford believed, also helped to shape new and better lives for the ex-convict workers. In his zeal for reform, Ford even hired a number of former prostitutes who went to work in departments off-limits to visitors.

The atmosphere at Dodge Brothers was much different—more relaxed, even convivial at times. Here, too, ex-convicts were at work. Horace, named an undersheriff by his buddy, Wayne County Sheriff Ed Stein, sported a glittering badge and relished the excitement of speeding down the highway with Sheriff Stein in pursuit of a thief or escaped prisoner. At the county jail, Horace talked with prisoners, brought them gifts at Christmas time, and offered the more industrious prisoners, when eligible for parole, opportunities to learn trades at the Dodge plant.

Strangely, Horace found the excitement of a Detroit Symphony Orchestra concert as stimulating as a police chase. Although the John Dodges made generous contributions to the orchestra, Horace Dodge remained its outstanding patron. Henry Ford was not remotely interested in the orchestra or the Detroit Institute of Arts or anything else that he equated, scornfully, with "high society."

Despite Horace Dodge's support, financial problems plagued the orchestra in the early months of 1918 as it became dependent on visiting conductors for its concerts. Then Horace personally financed a search for a conductor whose brilliance could attract the support of wealthy Detroiters. The search ended with the hiring of Russian conductor and concert pianist Ossip Salomonowitsch Gabrilowitsch.

Detroiters celebrated the announcement of the end of the war in November, 1918, with an outbreak of noisy clamoring in the streets. Gabrilowitsch immediately set up his own clamor for a new auditorium to permanently house the Detroit Symphony Orchestra, and Horace Dodge influenced other orchestra board members to approve "Gabby's" request. "We want this to be an enduring monument to Detroit's musical culture," Horace insisted as the board selected a site at Woodward and Parsons where the old Westminster Presbyterian Church would be razed and an auditorium, with the best of acoustics, built at a cost of $700,000.

By the time of the Armistice, the John Dodge family was expanding. John's daughter Winifred had given birth to her first daughter earlier in the year. And now, Matilda verified that, once again, she was pregnant. For the past year, John Dodge had been consulting with architects to design a home in Grosse Pointe splendid enough to eclipse any mansion in Michigan and equal the magnificence of any mansion in the country. A home to glorify the name Dodge and provide a lakeshore ancestral home that would be inherited by his younger son, Daniel. John committed himself to an expenditure of $4 million to erect a 110-room house with 24 baths, which would overshadow Horace's Rose Terrace where Mrs. Horace E. Dodge "received " on second Tuesdays, according to Dau's Blue Book.

Although John's plans for the palatial house excited Matilda, she retained some reservations about the degree of chill the John Dodges might expect to encounter from Grosse Pointe's aristocracy. She fretted, too, about sharing her magnificent new home with the sister-in-law she detested and with Della's companion, Helen Bovee. True, she might anticipate avoiding both women in a house with 110 rooms, but Matilda was agitated, nonetheless, at the thought of the two women moving into her Grosse Pointe home when it was completed.

In February, 1919, the Michigan Superior Court handed down its decision reinforcing the lower court ruling and ordering immediate payment of $19 million plus interest to stockholders by the Ford Motor Company. Horace and John Dodge collected $2,081,213.

Forced by court order to continue making annual dispersements of surplus profits in a similar manner, Ford now wanted to rid his company of other stockholders by purchasing the shares of the Dodges and other investors. Because he wanted to propel stockholders into eagerly selling their stock, without holding out to wait for a higher sale price, Ford already had a plan in mind.

Two months earlier, anticipating the decision by the higher court, Henry turned over the presidency of Ford Motor Company to Edsel Ford, who continued to be dominated by his father. At the same time, Henry left for California. Shortly after he lost his appeal in the higher court, Henry Ford followed through with his plan by calling a press conference. He announced that he was branching out from his production of tractors—a company separate from Ford Motor Company —to produce a new car to sell for $250. Since the new "better and cheaper" car, manufactured by the tractor company, would compete with the Model T, it was likely that Model T sales would decline.

The Ford strategy worked. Anticipating decreasing dividends from their Ford stock, John and Horace Dodge agreed to sell their shares (numbering 2000 since the 20-to-one split) for $25 million, although they had refused an offer of $36 million for their stock from S.K. Rothschild only one month before Ford called his press conference. Other stockholders, as fearful as the Dodges of Ford's rival company and new product, also unloaded their shares. The $250 Ford never was manufactured.

Automobile production soared in the months following the end of the war. The normal work force at Dodge Brothers factory reached 18,000 as car production rose from 300 a day in February, 1919, to 500 a day in June of that year. The brothers introduced a four-door

Dodge sedan in 1919, fitted with velvet upholstery and also sporting cream-colored wire wheels and a cream stripe to accent the blue and black machine.

In June, the John Dodges' third child was born—a girl named Anna Margaret. Anna—as part of Matilda's relentless campaign to strengthen her friendship with her sister-in-law. Margaret—for Matilda's mother.

Elated that the child, blond and blue-eyed like her older sister, Frances, appeared to be healthy, Matilda also was happy that construction of the Grosse Pointe home was progressing. The previous April, much to Matilda's surprise, Della had edged out from John's protective sheltering to take a position as superintendent of the Industrial Home for Girls at Adrian, Michigan. Helen Bovee accompanied Della, to serve as her secretary at the institution in supervising 450 wayward girls. Della, who previously served on the institute's board of directors, departed from Boston Boulevard in a flurry of excitement, talking of offering French lessons and art classes to the culturally deprived girls confined within the Industrial Home.

With Della's departure, with Winifred safely married and occupied with her own family, and John Duval living in a distant state, Isabel was the only remaining child of John Dodge's first marriage still at the East Boston Boulevard address. Even Isabel, caught up in a whirl of debutante parties and travels, rarely stayed at home. The Dodge business was firmly established and flourishing and Matilda began to feel, for the first time in 12 years of marriage, that her husband's attentions centered almost entirely on her and his three young children.

The previous winter, the John Dodges had made a first trip to Florida. They took Matilda's sister, Amelia, with them and rented a beach house where Matilda, still pregnant with her third child at the time, could have the kind of privacy that was not possible in the fashionable Palm Beach hotel—The Breakers—where Horace and Anna stayed for "the season."

Now, after the birth of her baby, Matilda contentedly filled her days by updating inventories of the contents of the East Boston Boulevard house—making lists of items to be moved into the Grosse Pointe home when completed the following year, and listing new items to purchase.

Still, the year 1919 brought its problems. A series of unsigned letters, delivered to the Dodge home, frightened Matilda. The letters, with crudely drawn pictures of time clocks attached to bombs and guns, threatened the entire family with death unless Dodge factory workers were paid a minimum $5-a-day wage.

A handwriting expert, acting on the assumption that the letter-writer was a foreign-born Dodge employee, carefully examined the signed employment cards in Dodge offices and traced the anonymous writer—a Polish resident in Hamtramck. The incident made an impact on the John Dodge family. Matilda became wary of leaving her children at home in the care of nurses for more than a couple of hours, and looked forward with impatience to the move to Grosse Pointe. The new home, she thought, would be less accessible to intruders. She was certain that her family would be safer there.

Her husband had already spent $2 million on the new mansion. Some 350 workmen, including 110 stonecutters who previously worked on Andrew Carnegie's castle in Scotland, erected the home's thick stone walls. Elaborate plans for the grounds included a children's playground, tennis courts, horse stables, gardens, and a huge greenhouse, with eleven temperature-controlled compartments, which was already completed in preparation for the return of botanists sent to the tropics to collect rare plants.

Newspaper reporters could see for themselves the size and magnificence of the Tudor mansion, for which Dodge had already ordered a pipe organ, as the owner took them on a tour of the building site. He pointed out 6000 square feet of servants' quarters and a basement that would contain a ballroom and a swimming pool. He was equally expansive in telling reporters what was yet to be done...Lake St. Clair filled in from its present shoreline to a distance of 500 feet to provide space for such luxuries as a bowling green and a boathouse from which would be operated a sprinkling system of 900 heads. A tunnel, already being dug under Lakeshore Drive, would connect the mansion with the boathouse and a pier.

One reporter who asked for permission to have a private visit to the lakeshore properties was permitted to come only if John Dodge were given censorship privileges before the writer's article was printed. John objected, first, to the statement that the home would cost $3 million, even though later estimates placed the cost at $4 million (an amount equal to a current cost of more than $120 million.)

"With all the unrest now, that would be an unwise thing to print," Dodge protested. He also objected to the description of the lake-fill as "a place for his children to play."

"It looks a little stingy," he parried, but was equally dissatisfied when the writer changed the statement to read "...a place for his children and their friends to play."

John had other grandiose ideas as well, once his court case with Ford was settled. He approached directors of the Hudson Motor Car

Company with an ambitious plan and a desire to put out a more expensive automobile. John's idea was for Hudson, Timken-Detroit Axle Company, and Continental Motor Company to merge with Dodge Brothers, under Dodge control. When the Hudson people would not agree to the merger, John had to put aside his plans, temporarily at least.

Matilda drew back from making personal comments to reporters about the magnificent new Dodge home in Grosse Pointe, but avoided criticizing her husband's swaggering. She preferred to wait and allow the great house to make its own impression on reporters when the mansion was completed.

On the evening of October 23, 1919, John and Matilda accompanied the Horace Dodge family to the opening performance of the Detroit Symphony Orchestra in the beautiful new Orchestra Hall built at Conductor Gabrilowitsch's request. The robust Dodge brothers, in black-tie attire, escorted their bejewelled wives into the Dodge box where they carefully settled themselves into their plush, plum-colored seats. Looking out from the circle of crescents in the blue and gold horseshoe of box seats, they watched as Gabrilowitsch conducted the 90-piece orchestra in the flourishing style so fervently admired by its major financial supporter, Horace E. Dodge.

Unlike Horace and Anna, John and Matilda were not innate music lovers. But they tried to develop their musical tastes by exposing themselves to classical music. At Meadow Brook, they accumulated a quality record collection that excluded such popular hits as "Alexander's Ragtime Band"—a brassy tune that set Amelia's toes tapping whenever she heard it.

But, Amelia did not hear the tune at Meadow Brook, where records were played on a large phonograph fitted with a hand crank. When John Dodge stayed at the farm, he assigned Amelia to crank the phonograph and set the needle on the individual records. He forbade her, or anyone else at Meadow Brook, to play ragtime music.

Before Christmas, the stock-purchase payment arrived from Henry Ford. Seventy years later—when, in 1989, the Dodge Division of Chrysler Corporation would celebrate the seventy-fifth anniversary of the debut of the first Dodge Motor Car—Detroit Monthly magazine would relate a story of John and Horace's celebration at receiving Ford's $25 million check. The two men swaggered into the Detroit Athletic Club—that bastion of respectibility and favorite retreat for its membership of wealthy businessmen, including the Dodges. There they announced their intention of paying for all the food and drink consumed on the club's four floors that night. Then, according to the magazine article, the brothers "tried to pay for it with a multimillion-dollar certified check from Ford."

The Dodge brothers used part of their $25 million for philanthropic purposes. Horace financed a new church, with a powerful organ, for the Jefferson Avenue Presbyterian congregation. John wrote a quarter-million-dollar check to the First Presbyterian Church and another to the Salvation Army for $135,000. He made Matilda happy with a gift of a million dollars for any personal baubles she might desire, and then piqued his wife's jealousy by giving Amelia a $5000 ring.

Although John never learned to share his brother's passion for boats, he wanted his new mansion on the lakeshore equipped with every possible luxury, including a cabin cruiser moored at his private dock. Unruffled by Horace's reminder that a 104-foot gasoline-powered cruiser could consume 160 gallons of gas per hour, John placed his order for the craft and planned to christen it _Frances_.

In the Robert Manzer household on Detroit's west side, where a $5000 ring—not to mention a cabin cruiser or a million dollars—was a treasure not even dreamed of, there was a good deal of excitement that year about the family's recently acquired automobile. A shiny new Dodge.

Neighbors watched enviously as Manzer and his wife, Minnie, got into the front seat of the Dodge to drive to the Port Huron area for a weekend of camping and fishing. Their young daughter, who quickly tired of long drives, sat on the back seat with a doll on her lap. The carpenter, Manzer, was not steadily employed, but there were rumors that he was planning to build a new home for his family. The neighbors talked among themselves as they watched the Dodge disappear around the corner, wondering how Manzer could afford a new home, his new automobile, and his camping trips.

True, the Manzers had only one child, but they dressed the little girl fashionably enough to attract attention when she accompanied her parents to church. In the wintertime, the child wore a fur coat, her blond curls fanning out over the collar from beneath a velvet hat trimmed with matching fur.

Robert and Minnie Manzer were not close friends with any of the neighbors, but their lively daughter played with many children in the Hogarth neighborhood of her early childhood. When bad weather kept her indoors, Lucille was never bored. Her father read stories to her in the same dramatic style in which he performed in plays at the Methodist Church. Often he took the little girl to the library for the children's story hour.

When left to her own devices, Lucille loved to play with paper dolls, weaving fanciful and exciting stories around the fragile manikins as she dressed them in their glamorous dresses and capes and slit hats. At Minnie's call to supper, Lucille carefully stacked the dolls and their wardrobes inside a large box—a box that opened the doors to a magic world created by her own imagination...a world quite different from the ordinariness of Hogarth Street.

Chapter 9

The Inseparable Dodge Brothers—Together for Eternity

On New Year's Eve, 1919, the Dodges' Boston Boulevard home glittered with the brilliance of crystal chandeliers, glowing lamps, and a huge, shimmering Christmas tree. To celebrate the arrival of 1920, John and Matilda followed their custom of inviting their closest friends to their home—Horace and Anna, of course. The Oakmans. The Marxes.

Not long after maids brought coffee and dessert to the dinner table, the men gathered in a separate room to relish drinks and jokes, leaving their wives to entertain themselves with "women talk." Since both Horace and John leaned to the extremes of belligerence or sentimentality when they drank, their friends were not particularly surprised when the brothers went into the library just before midnight, closing the door for complete privacy as they celebrated the arrival of 1920, toasting each other and their mutual success.

The women, clustered together in the sitting room and tiring of their own chatter by midnight, shared their hopes that the men would soon be ready to go home and get some rest before leaving for the National Automobile Show in New York. Both Anna and Matilda were miffed that John and Horace did not want their wives to accompany them to New York for this 20th annual event, expected to be a gala affair since the automobile business was now fully recovered from the effects of the war.

The Dodge brothers and their three close friends—Milton Oakman, Oscar Marx, and Ed Fitzgerald—arrived by train in New York on January third. The men checked into reserved suites at the Ritz-Carlton

Hotel where, newspapers reported with some awe, the charge for supper reservations on New Year's Eve amounted to an unprecedented $15 per person.

The Dodge party mixed with throngs of people, including visitors from the Orient, Africa and South America, viewing 350 models of 84 different makes of cars displayed in Grand Central Palace that afternoon. The Premier automobile with an aluminum motor. Three eight-cylinder cars—Peerless, Oldsmobile and Cadillac. And two powerful 12-cylinder cars—Packard and Haynes.

But Dodge Brothers' sturdy four-door sedan, exhibited in space A-20, still flaunted the "dependability" banner of its efficient four-cylinder engine. Their automobile also boasted wire wheels and 45-inch rear springs. At another building—the Eighth Coast Artillery Armory—Dodge motor trucks occupied space L-3, alongside trucks made by 68 manufacturers. Nationally, Dodge Brothers rated fourth in the industry in sales of cars.

Hotel managers and clerks kept watch for revenue agents who might search guests for possession of liquor, while drinking parties went on in private suites of conventioneers. Because serious problems plagued the automotive industry, manufacturers such as the Dodges were not simply playboy-conventioneers, but were concerned with topics of discussion at the Waldorf-Astoria dinner given the first evening by the Rubber Association of America.

At the Hotel Commodore dinner the next evening given by the National Automobile Chamber of Commerce, speeches and discussions centered on the problem of automobile theft in the United States, numbering 4,621 cars stolen within the last six months. And there was the problem of raising money to build improved highways when unpaved roads were ruining automobiles…while nearly two million more cars added to roadway traffic in 1919.

A luncheon for Dodge dealers went ahead as scheduled on Thursday noon at the Ritz-Carlton, although a sense of apprehension clouded the affair when the genial Dodge brothers did not make their expected appearances. An announcement that Horace Dodge was ill and his brother was at his side fueled rumors that both brothers had been poisoned by illegal "moonshine." Still another rumor circulated that Horace Dodge was stricken with influenza.

Both rumors frightened other automobile men, all of whom had lived through the killer Spanish influenza epidemic of a year ago when, in the winter of 1918-19, influenza swept across the country, spreading the sour smells of sickness and death and claiming the lives of more than a half-million Americans. No one could believe that another flu epidemic would strike again, so soon.

Most of the automotive men attending, who—exclusive of teetotalers such as Henry Ford—stocked illegal liquor in their rooms, had good reason to shudder at the rumors that the Dodge brothers were suffering the effects of drinking bootleg liquor. Although the auto tycoons and their associates were well aware that many Americans had been blinded or killed by drinking bootleg liquor brewed in stills operated by hoodlums in hideaways across the country, they knew, also, that the Dodges had brought their own liquor—illegally transported across the Detroit River by speedboats—from Canada. "Clean," expensive, imported whiskey brought to New York in a trunk.

In his posh Ritz-Carlton suite, the influenza-stricken Horace Dodge was very ill. When the attending physician would not permit John Dodge to remain at the bedside of his brother throughout the night, John then sat on a chair near the bedroom door, nodding off to sleep intermittently but determined to stay as close to his brother as possible while he waited for the doctor's reports.

When the physician emerged from the sickroom, he had bad news for John, advising him that his brother's wife should be notified of her husband's critical condition. As quickly as John's friends called Anna at Rose Terrace, a distraught Anna phoned Matilda who tried to calm her sister-in-law by promising that she would go with her to New York on the earliest possible train.

The two women left for New York on Friday and were met at the station by their husbands' friends, Marx and Oakman. The men tried to be encouraging, assuring the women that New York's finest doctors were treating Horace, who had a strong will to survive. But John also was ill, now, with the flu, the men added.

At the hotel, Matilda and Anna wore gauze face masks for protection as they hovered over their husbands while doctors and nurses moved in and out with hot water bottles, aspirin, quinine. Shaking with chills, breathing harshly and coughing, the brothers looked to their wives for help—their friends completely forgotten. By Monday, Dr. Hill spoke optimistically to Anna. Her husband had passed the crisis and could be expected to make slow progress within the next few weeks from his critical bout with pneumonia.

No such assurances were given Matilda. John Dodge was struggling for each breath as his lungs filled with fluid.

Matilda decided that her stepdaughters should be summoned to New York, even though Winifred was pregnant with a second child. And "Doc" Chittick, spending the winter months in California where he also heard of John's illness, immediately boarded a train headed for the East Coast.

By the time Winifred and Isabel reached New York, their father had slipped into unconsciousness. He died at 10:30 p.m. on Wednesday, January 14, 1920—hours before the arrival of Chittick who, upset at the loss of his friend, told Matilda of his deep regret that he had not arrived in time to "save John's life."

By the next morning, news of the death had reached the Dodge plant. When the foreman walked into the tool-room on Thursday morning, he held up his hands to indicate the men should leave their machines and gather at one end of the room. "Men," he said, "I have sad news. John Dodge died last night—in New York."

The workers stood there silently, unable to believe that the lusty, energetic Dodge would not be returning to the factory. "I guess that means you're all rich," the foreman added, referring to the million dollars that John Dodge said he was leaving, in his will, to the tool-room workers who numbered nearly a hundred.

Ten thousand dollars each. When he came home from work, Henry Batz excitedly told his family of the magnificent inheritance he expected to receive. A man could buy two very nice houses for that amount. And for months...for years, Batz would live in anticipation of receiving his inheritance until, in retirement after nearly 50 years with Dodge-Chrysler, the mention of the "inheritance" was enough to send him into a bitter tirade against false promises, or broken wills—he was never quite sure which was to blame.

It was impossible for Anna to keep the news of John's death from Horace. He continued to ask, weakly, about his brother, whose body already was being shipped west on the Wolverine as the steam train, battling huge snowdrifts, shuddered its way from New York City toward Detroit throughout the early morning hours of January 15.

In a private railroad car, Matilda endured the starts and fits of the panting train while her doctor and nurse prepared cold compresses to reduce the 36-year-old widow's flaming fever. In her concern for the needs of her three young children at home, Matilda refused to dwell on thoughts of the black-draped baggage car carrying the portly body of her 55-year-old husband, encased in a heavy casket with glass- windowed lid to prevent contamination to viewers. She was too ill to reflect on the fortune that the death of John F. Dodge had placed in the hands of his young wife, to whom control of money and power was a prime goal.

On Saturday morning, hundreds of people braved cold January weather and formed a line outside the Dodges' Boston Boulevard home. The line wound its way up the sidewalk and through the front entrance of the house where each visitor could glance quickly at the face of John Dodge beneath the glass viewer. The front door stood ajar for the convenience of the visitors, as Matilda ordered, and the furnace ran constantly, fighting off blasts of icy wind that penetrated the house while a feverish Matilda lay in her bed behind closed doors on the second floor...and while Horace still lay in his bed in his New York hotel suite.

Although John Duval Dodge was on his way to Detroit from Texas, Matilda decided that the funeral would be held on Saturday afternoon, January 17, without waiting for John Duval's arrival. Amelia and her mother came from Meadow Brook Farm and John's sister, Della, returned from Adrian to her third-floor quarters at Boston Boulevard, bringing her friend, Helen Bovee, with her. Hesitantly, Helen Bovee asked Amelia if she thought that Matilda would object if she— Helen—went downstairs to view the body. Fearful of being trapped at the center of controversy, Amelia replied only that she could not speak for her sister, who was so ill that even Amelia and Margaret Rausch were permitted to approach no closer than the doorway of Matilda's bedroom.

Sadly, Amelia clipped newspaper stories of John Dodge's life and death...of the strong ties that had bound the brothers together throughout their colorful lives...of the refusal of either man to respond to any letter that came into the Dodge office if the letter were addressed in any way other than to Dodge Brothers, the second word with a capital B... of their personal acts of kindness and financial aid to ailing employees and to widows of employees...of their generous support of civic projects and cultural events.

In his funeral address, the Reverend Dr. Vance spoke of the last ceremony he had performed at the Dodge home...the baptism of young Frances, and of how emotionally both Dodge brothers had reacted at the service...of John's "marvelous virility" and of his "indomitable will." The minister admitted that he had seen John Dodge in church for a religious service "only once"—but added that Dodge had professed an intention to "get around to it" (going to chuch) someday.

A throng of dignitaries, including Henry and Edsel Ford and James Couzens (now mayor of Detroit) among a legion of honorary pallbearers, swelled the ranks of mourners as the casket—still unsealed —was placed in the Dodges' great marble mausoleum guarded by two sculptured sphinxes at the pillared entrance. The casket would not be sealed until Horace returned home and could view his brother for the last time. For now, Horace continued a painfully slow recovery from the pneumonia that almost took his life...and from the blow of his brother's death. Nor could Matilda, still very sick, attend her husband's funeral.

Within ten days of John Dodge's death, New York officials recognized that an influenza epidemic had returned to the metropolis when the city's police force was decimated by illness and when courts could not function with so few judges and employees untouched by the flu. The epidemic was already spreading into other cities—Philadelphia, Chicage, Detroit.

Weakened by influenza and pneumonia that "had her life hanging by a thread," as Amelia told friends, Matilda began a slow recovery only to have to cope with a feverish, seven-month-old Anna Margaret as she, too, contracted the flu. From her bed, Matilda also coped with other problems, one of which included providing security against grave robbers at the mausoleum. In the early twenties, theft of corpses—and demands for ransom from wealthy families—rivaled the frequency of kidnapping children. Matilda decided to hire two watchmen for the mausoleum. The men sat, throughout long winter nights, in a car parked at the site of the cold, white edifice rising starkly against a shadowy background of pale moonlight and ice-sheathed tree branches snapping in the wind.

At the Manzer home in Detroit, five-year-old Lucille waited patiently as Minnie Manzer brushed the child's blond hair, buttoned her shiny patent leather shoes, and cautioned the little girl to mind her manners as she paid a visit to a lady she had never met previously. In childish acceptance of her mother's bidding, Lucille expressed no curiosity about the visit until a car stopped near the house and she realized she was expected to get into the car—without her mother.

Years later, an adult Lucille would recall the day she was taken, by a red-haired woman, to a great home with a sweeping expanse of lawn on Boston Boulevard, wondering whose home she had visited. And why. Fragmented memories of that day were chiseled into her memory. The street name. Recollections of walking up a winding walk and a curved stairway with tall carved posts that made her feel very tiny. Recollections of going into a bedroom, decorated in pink and gold, where a thin-faced woman, hair pulled severely back from her face, sat—propped up by pillows—on a large bed. Of heavy drapes at the windows and a richly upholstered chaise lounge. Of going back downstairs to a table where she was fed cookies and milk in a room with many windows and plants and a parquet floor. Remembrances of a kaleidoscope of colors and impressions, flashing into her mind, as elusive as dust motes in sunlight.

Impressed by the drapes she saw in the Boston Boulevard house, five-year-old Lucille made window drapes out of crepe paper to hang over the lace panels in her own bedroom. Her questions to Minnie Manzer about the house went unanswered. The child stopped asking when she realized that her mother retreated at such inquiries as if a gap were widening between mother and daughter. Lucille chose, then, to coexist with a sense of the unknown rather than to risk intensifying the coolness between them. Minnie Manzer was a good and conscientious mother, but, always, it was Robert Manzer who provided the warmth and closeness that fed the child's emotional needs.

When Matilda finally regained her strength, she penned a letter to her sister-in-law Della at the Industrial Home for Girls in Adrian. The letter requested Della to transfer the remainder of her belongings, and those of Helen Bovee, from their former third-floor quarters at Matilda's Boston Boulevard home to Della's present residence in Adrian.

It was doubtful that Della considered the Adrian institution her "home" but equally obvious that she would no longer be welcomed at her brother's former home. Della made a trip to Detroit to collect her belongings, and a permanent estrangement commenced between John Dodge's widow and his sister. To Matilda's consternation, the estrangement soon began to influence the closeness between Matilda and Horace's wife, Anna, who remained a firm friend of Della Dodge Eschbach.

In early February, while Matilda submitted to a fitting for mourning clothes, a pale and tremulous Horace returned from New York and made his sad visit to the mausoleum for a final look at the clay-like face of his brother. He turned away only after the coffin was sealed and placed into its niche. Then, assigning most of his responsibilities as company president to his assistant, Frederick Haynes, Horace permitted himself to be taken by Anna to Palm Beach in their private railroad car.

Dressed in a stylish black coat, with black ankle-length skirt showing beneath, and wearing black accessories that included a hat with long mourning veil, the widowed Matilda occasionally instructed her chauffeur to drive her to the Dodge plant where she conferred with Haynes. The obligatory mourning period for her husband allowed for no social affairs, so Matilda tried to keep occupied with her home and family, with Dodge business affairs, and with church activities.

Although Matilda regularly read Detroit newspapers, she tried to avoid them now. Since early February, a "Dodge Will Cuts off Son" headline preceded a series of similar headlines following the filing of the John Dodge will in probate court. John Duval, allotted only $150 monthly for life so he "would never be a public charge," was threatening to sue for what he called "a fair share" of his father's estate. Apparently having visualized the possibility of such a suit, the father had specified in his will that "no one should accuse my wife or any of my children" of having influenced John F. Dodge in regard to his provision for John Duval.

At this point in her life, while coping with her husband's death and her own physical weakness and that of baby Anna Margaret as they convalesced from influenza and pneumonia, Matilda felt too shattered to deal with the harassment and notoriety of a family battle over money. But as she regained strength of mind and body in the spring and began to conceive of the wealth now in her control, she assumed the protective armor typical of people of wealth—a determination to guard her fortune from erosion or incursion and to wrest as much power as could be extracted from the possession and manipulation of her assets.

John had left a number of bequests to extended-family members, including his half brother, a cousin, the two aunts in Decatur, plus $15,000 to his personal attorney and a $5000 bequest to his friend, "Doc" Chittick. John provided generously for his sister, Della, with a $5000 bequest and a yearly payment of $6000 for the remainder of her life.

This legacy relieved Della from financial worry at a time when the board of guardians of the Adrian Industrial Home was pressuring her. As superintendent at the home, the idealistic and childless Della was poorly equipped to deal with 450 "delinquent" girls in her care. Because of her own impoverished youth, she felt a great deal of sympathy for young people from deprived backgrounds, but could not cope with the ugliness and depravity exposed in the case histories of many young inmates. Incest. Prostitution. So-called "social diseases." Della, wrapped in her refinement, could find no words to discuss such problems with her charges. Instead, she tried to shift the entire operation of the institution to a higher plane which would swathe the corruption and frailities of the girls' earlier lives with an aesthetic veiling that would, in time, smother the memories of their earlier experiences and imperfections.

Della was horrified to learn that the girls had been punished for previous offenses at the institution with bread-and-water diets, by having their hair shaved, or with solitary confinement. She immediately discontinued all such punishments. Instead, unruly girls were lectured by Della on the merits of courtesy and self-respect, or, when necessary, were refused the privileges of attending one or more of the fine-arts classes.

To motivate the girls toward more ladylike behavior, Della authorized a rash of expenditures for beautifying the interior of the home, for extensive repairs to the buildings, and for supplies of music and painting and fine-arts materials to inspire the inmates to an appreciation of artistic values.

By early 1920, the guardians demanded an accounting from Della for expenditures considered out of control by the board. The home's inmates were also out of control, boldly defiant of authority.

When the board named a new superintendent for the industrial home in July, an embarrassed Della fled to California, anticipating prompt payment of the money left to her in John's will. Her friend, Helen Bovee, accompanied Della to California and the two women did not inform the board of guardians of their new address.

To her sister, Amelia, Matilda indicated no surprise at Della's unfortunate performance at the girls' home. It was Matilda's opinion that if John had not consistently pampered his sister by bankrolling her extravagances, Della might have become a more practical person.

John's will also provided a $5000 gift to Amelia, plus a lifetime annuity of $2500; a $5000 bequest to his mother-in-law, Margaret Rausch, plus $1000 a year. Deciding that her husband was more than generous to her sister and her mother, Matilda discontinued payment of the monthly salaries that John Dodge had paid them at the farm. But Matilda did not suspect that Amelia already planned to leave the farm, now that John Dodge was dead, and to move into the town of Rochester. Amelia waited to receive her bequest so that she could carry out her plans.

Because John gave a $250,000 Indian Village home to Winifred at the time of her marriage, he specified in his will that Winifred's sister, Isabel, should receive $50,000 each year for five years in addition to her share of his estate. The jointly-owned Boston Boulevard home, the unfinished Grosse Pointe home, and the farm at Meadow Brook automatically became Matilda's properties. John specified in his will that his wife was to be supplied with enough money to complete the Grosse Pointe home and to furnish it as she chose. In addition, Matilda would receive $15,000 a year for maintenance of the Grosse Pointe home, $10,000 annually for farm maintenance, plus money for taxes and insurance.

Because the will was executed in 1918, before the birth of Anna Margaret, the youngest child was not mentioned in John's papers. The law protected her interests, however, by granting her equal portions of the estate with her sister, Frances, and brother, Daniel.

Apart from the properties that now belonged to Matilda, the bulk of the $37 million estate was invested in 50,000 shares of company stock greatly under-valued at $460.375 a share. John had set up a trust for this money and specified that the annual income from the trust should be divided equally among his wife and each of his children. The minor children's income was to be held in trust for them until each one reached the age of 25 years, but Matilda would also receive thousands of dollars each year for the expenses of each minor child. The trust itself would remain operative until the death of the last child; then the money would be distributed among the children's heirs.

Indecisiveness played no part in Matilda's character. Yet, in the spring of 1920 when work on the Grosse Pointe mansion should have resumed, the young widow delayed issuing work-orders for the great house. She still felt that the Grosse Pointe environment would be more secure for her children. And she knew that the mansion was intended as John's monument to his success and power—a monument supposed to be passed on to young Daniel Dodge. But Matilda feared rejection from Grosse Pointe residents. Her two stepdaughters, spurred by Winifred's husband, Jack Gray, pressured her to simply sell the unfinished house rather than to invest millions more in the home and its furnishings and decor.

Matilda deferred making her decision, although she did not intend to place the house on the market at this point. On the contrary, she determined not to acquiesce to suggestions from Jack Gray, for whom she had acquired a definite distaste.

Before the Horace Dodges returned from Palm Beach in late April, Matilda's temper flared when she saw an announcement in the Detroit newspapers of the engagement of the Horace Dodges' daughter, Delphine, to James H.R. Cromwell of Philadelphia. Matilda had no doubts that Anna Dodge considered Delphine's fiance, son of socialite Mrs. Edward T. Stotesbury and the late Oliver Cromwell, as a notable acquisition. But Matilda felt that, in deference to the John Dodge family and its recent loss, the Horace Dodges should have delayed announcing the engagement. Because the announcement included no wedding date, Matilda took some solace in assuming that the marriage would not occur very soon.

At the same time, society columns carried items concerning Horace's preparations for building another steam-powered yacht, larger and more luxurious than the <u>Nokomis II</u>. The yacht was to be completed in 1921.

In this lonely and quiet period of her life, Matilda envied the pleasurable lives of Horace and Anna. Envy turned to resentment when Matilda learned, on the Horace Dodges' return to Detroit, that their daughter's wedding was planned for June 16, only six months from the date of John Dodge's death.

Matilda curbed any admonitions she might have given her brother-in-law on his return from Florida when she saw his lined face and hazy eyes, his slumped shoulders and drooping mouth. Clearly, Horace was not well; when he went into the plant, he had little interest in the work in progress. At home, he offered little resistance or opposition to the whims and aspirations of his wife and daughter.

Anna's aspirations were ambitious. She engaged the services of the haughty Sara Burnham, crusty mentor of Detroit and Grosse Pointe society, to plan and execute Delphine's wedding and to impress the East-Coast Stotesburys with the most lavish reception that money could achieve.

Influenced by Anna Dodge's willingness to put unlimited sums of money at her disposal, Sara Burnham began to mold and shape a wedding extravaganza that would dazzle local socialites, all of whom knew of the Dodges but few of whom had met the automotive family socially. Still, more than 2000 guests responded affirmatively to invitations addressed by Sara Burnham.

On the wedding day, guests filled Jefferson Avenue Presbyterian Church and swelled into a throng at Rose Terrace for the reception. Under the watchful eyes of private detectives and guards, Anna Dodge fingered her Catherine II, Empress of Russia, pearls as she greeted guests with Miss Burnham at her elbow.

Matilda Dodge decided to appear briefly at Rose Terrace for the sake of family harmony—and, especially, as a concession to Anna whose good will she wanted to retain. Even in her resentment of a wedding that she considered premature, the black-garbed and veiled Matilda recognized that Delphine and James H.R. Cromwell were picture-perfect participants in a storybook romance—the chestnut-haired bride, slim and graceful; the darkly handsome Cromwell, a former marine captain, tall and well built. Behind them, the Midwest millions of the Dodges; the Stotesbury prestige.

Matilda left Rose Terrace before a 100-piece band began to play for dancing on a lawn pavilion, but not before she heard the music of the pipe organ within the house and the medleys performed by the Detroit Symphony Orchestra on the side lawn, nor before she observed a swarm of waiters toting huge trays of glasses which were rapidly emptied by thirsty guests and replaced from an inexhaustible supply of illegal liquor. Soon after Matilda's departure, the newlyweds sailed away from the Rose Terrace pier aboard the Dodges' white and gold yacht.

A month later, Amelia clipped a photo from a Detroit newspaper society page. The photo showed the fashionable Cromwells boarding an ocean liner in San Francisco, for a trip to Honolulu and around the world. When Matilda and the children and their nurses came out to the farm the next weekend, Amelia displayed the clipping—dapper Jimmy

Cromwell wearing knickers and cuffed knee socks and sporting a cane under one arm as he mounted the gangplank with his bobbed-haired wife, in her stylish mid-calf dress.

Matilda had no interest in chatting with her sister about the Cromwells, or even about the Horace Dodges and their recent purchase of a Spanish villa along the Palm Beach ocean front. It was obvious, to Amelia, that Matilda was preoccupied with the problems that her stepson, John Duval, was bringing to the family.

When her stepdaughters wanted John Duval to have a job in the Dodge plant after John Dodge's death, Matilda posed no objections. But her stepson, often absent from his job, now revived his earlier threat to bring suit for a larger share of his father's fortune. Repelled by the possibility of a public fight over the money, Matilda did not oppose an adjustment of the will's provisions to provide more money for John Duval. Michigan law, however, would not permit the terms of the will to be changed by an agreement among heirs. The purpose of this restriction was to prevent the possibility of conspiracy among, or intimidation of, beneficiaries of an estate.

In early autumn, the stepdaughter Isabel offended Matilda with a disclosure that she intended to marry New Yorker George Sloane—soon. Matilda did not disapprove of Sloane, a Princeton graduate and offspring of a prominent family. But Isabel's choice of wedding date, the following February, appalled Matilda who would wear her mourning wardrobe until 1922.

Isabel flashed a brilliant diamond ring despite Matilda's reminders of the respect that the daughters should show for their deceased father. The widow Dodge had no choice, then, but to announce the engagement although she decreed that no wedding could be held at John Dodge's Boston Boulevard home until the end of the traditional two-year mourning period.

She would not accept Isabel's arguments that her Uncle Horace had given Delphine an elegant wedding only six months after John Dodge's death. Horace was not a well man, Matilda pointed out, and had no strength to resist his family in doing what was, clearly, inappropriate.

Still, Matilda did not realize the extent of Horace's illness. He suffered a serious relapse shortly after his daughter's wedding. In late November, when Anna and Dr. Haass of Detroit took Horace to the new villa in Palm Beach, Horace became so weak and melancholy that Delphine was notified, in Japan, of her father's declining health.

Less than two weeks from the date of the Horace Dodges' departure for Florida, Matilda learned that the critically ill Horace was hemorrhaging. He died in Palm Beach two days later—December 10—of cirrhosis of the liver.

Matilda phoned Amelia at the farm, telling her that despite Horace's weakness, he had visited the Woodlawn tomb of his brother the day before he left for Florida. Had Horace experienced a premonition that he would never again return to Detroit, the sisters wondered. Was it possible that the brothers, such close companions during their lives, were predestined to die within the same year—1920?

Amelia accompanied Matilda to the funeral services at Rose Terrace. Della Eschbach had arrived from California and she and Lucretia Stotesbury, along with Horace Junior and his fiancee, hovered near the distraught Anna.

"A mechanic with the soul of a poet," one journalist described Horace at the time of the mid-December funeral, during which the Detroit Symphony Orchestra performed in tribute to the orchestra's benefactor.

The Cromwells were still aboard ship, traveling toward home, but they did not arrive in time to take part in the long funeral procession that wound its way from Grosse Pointe past Dodge Brothers factory—its foundry fires stoked and its machines shrouded and muted—to Woodlawn Cemetery and the Dodge mausoleum...its large doors open; its silent interior waiting. The heavy bronze casket was carried up the steps into the mausoleum and the Dodge brothers were together again. Forever.

In 1920, the Robert Manzers sold their home on Hogarth and rented a house on McGraw while Manzer worked at building a new home for his family on Stanford. In the evenings, he sat in his comfortable Morris chair and read the newspapers, which carried many stories in 1920 and 1921 about the deaths of the Dodge brothers.

Before Christmas of 1921, the Manzers moved into the new house on Stanford. On Christmas Eve, Robert and Minnie Manzer warned Lucille not to look behind a sheet strung up in the archway between the dining room and living room. The sheet concealed her Christmas present, they told the child, and she could see it on Christmas morning.

The next morning, seven-year-old Lucille waited, in a glow of excitement, as her father removed the sheet. There, against the living room wall, was an upright piano, its walnut case polished to gleaming perfection.

Pleased with the gift of her "very own piano," Lucille soon sensed that her own excitement was outmatched by the intensity of pleasure exhibited by the usually phlegmatic Minnie Manzer. Minnie seated herself on the piano bench to demonstrate the tone and resonance of the instrument as she played a familiar Sunday School hymn, and Robert

Manzer began to sing in his off-key baritone. She had already arranged for piano lessons for Lucille, Minnie assured her young daughter, from Mrs. Curtiss—their church organist. Someday, Lucille, too, could be a church organist, Minnie rhapsodized.

Lucille's enthusiasm for the piano faded rapidly when she discovered that her mother expected her to sit at the piano for 45 minutes each day, practicing the scales and exercises assigned by Lena Curtiss. A few months later, while Minnie Manzer made a trip to the grocery store, Lucille's silent rebellion changed to noisy protest as she kicked at the piano with small flailing feet that could not quite reach the pedals. Startled by a harsh voice warning her to "stop kicking that piano," Lucille whirled around to see her grandfather—Minnie's irascible father, Marvin Fish—hobbling toward her, his cane upraised in a threatening motion. Giving a final burst of kicks at the piano, Lucille slid off the bench. "It's my piano!" she said defiantly as she scurried out of the room.

To no one but Grandfather Fish would she have dared been so impudent. But she did not like the old man because of the way he sometimes berated her mother. Lucille was always relieved when Grandfather Fish left, in the springtime, after spending the cold winter months with the Manzers. She sensed that her father was equally pleased when the old man departed.

By the summer of 1922, the Manzers took a red-haired, baby girl into their home as a foster child. Minnie Manzer, who rarely displayed any emotion toward her daughter, Lucille, became quite sentimental over baby Margaret as the Manzers began to discuss the possibility of adopting the child.

Minnie thought that a little sister would provide companionship for Lucille and help to keep the active, older child out of mischief. The presence of the younger child, however, did not restrain eight-year-old Lucille from pulling a stepladder in front of a closet one day, standing tip-toes on the ladder, and reaching up to a top shelf near the ceiling where the Manzers stored documents and papers. The little girl took down an old newspaper from the shelf and saw a caption in which the words "Boston Boulevard" caught her attention. Before she read further, she heard footsteps and whirled around to see her mother approaching, face flushed with anger.

"Don't you ever dare to get into things like this again!" Minnie Manzer warned, snatching the paper from the child's hand. "Not ever, do you hear?"

Loud threats and scolding frightened Lucille as much as more severe punishment might have frightened a child not reared in the quiet,

Christian home of people like the Manzers. Lucille never again dared to pry into the secret place where her parents kept their papers. But she did not forget the words on the newspaper, and wondered why her parents saved it. Was there some connection, she wondered, with the large home on Boston Boulevard where she was taken by the unknown woman?

Frank Upton and his wife, Viola, frequently visited the Manzer home on Stanford. Since both Upton and Manzer were stewards at Nardin Park Methodist Church, it seemed natural to little Lucille for the married couple to visit the home of their friends. The child had no idea that Upton, as a trustee for the Methodist Children's Home, may have been involved with the placement of the baby, Margaret, with the Manzers. And it was never mentioned, in Lucille's presence, that Frank Upton worked at Dodge Brothers office.

Chapter 10

Tragedy Strikes the Widowed Matilda

In his will, Horace also provided annuities for Della Eschbach and various Dodge relatives, as well as for his in-laws, the Thomsons. But Anna Dodge became a wealthier widow than Matilda, since the younger Dodge brother left almost 2/3 of his estate in the control of his wife. Another $13 million went into a trust fund.

Although Horace Dodge specified before his death that Frederick Haynes should succeed him as president of Dodge Brothers, the factory remained idle for three months following Horace's funeral. Matilda consulted with Haynes during this reorganization period, worrying that the automobile company, in which so much of Dodge wealth was invested, might languish without a Dodge in charge of the business. Neither John Duval nor Horace Junior exhibited any capabilities for managing the factory nor any interest in acquiring a knowledge of the business built by their fathers.

In February, the wedding of Matilda's younger stepdaughter, Isabel, took place in the home of Winifred, matron-of-honor for her sister. The sisters' close friend, Eleanor Clay (Mrs. Edsel) Ford, served as a bridesmaid. Because Isabel promised that the wedding would be a quiet and simple affair, Matilda bowed to convention and, wearing black chiffon, assumed what would have been John Dodge's obligation to give the bride away at the ceremony. Immediately following the newlyweds' departure for a European honeymoon, Matilda's attorney informed her that Winifred and Isabel had taken legal steps to prevent their stepmother from completing the Grosse Pointe mansion.

Since she had not yet decided to order work begun on the mansion, she could not understand why her stepdaughters acted so hastily.

Although Matilda had recently begun operating the 8000-square-foot greenhouse built on the Grosse Pointe properties, she thought of her investment in the greenhouse, with its honeycomb of rooms for exotic plants, as a practical business venture. Her horticulturists were already growing choice flowers for sale to florists and retail outlets.

Matilda instructed her attorney to protect her rights to make any decision she chose regarding the Grosse Pointe mansion. "That was my husband's wish," she justified her resolve to Amelia.

Because the Dodge sisters had planned their legal strategy at the same time that Matilda condescended to take part in the wedding in order to avoid fracturing family ties, the stepmother felt betrayed. With her three young children and their nurses, Matilda escaped Detroit's gloomy weather and her problems with her stepdaughters for two quiet weeks in the sun at Palm Beach in March. She returned in time to join Anna in early April at christening ceremonies for the $1.5 million yacht that Horace ordered shortly before his death.

When Matilda arrived at the River Rouge shipyard, crowds of people were already waiting to see the five-deck, 257-foot-long ship launched into the river. Escorted to a platform beneath the ship's bow, Matilda stood near Anna and Delphine, the faces of the three women obscured by dark veils through which they looked up at the elegant ship. The largest yacht ever built in America, the Delphine would retain its "largest" designation some forty years later, its opulent furnishings enhanced by a $60,000 pipe organ installed according to Horace's orders.

The gasoline-powered cruiser that John Dodge ordered prior to his death had not yet been delivered to the dock at the unfinished Grosse Pointe estate. But Matilda knew that the craft would soon arrive, and that she must make another decision—whether to keep the Frances.

For now, she reached one important resolution—to vacate the Boston Boulevard home and to move into Grosse Pointe, where she wanted to buy a comfortable and attractive home, but not the kind of palatial manor that even approached the size and magnificence of the unfinished Dodge showplace facing Lake St. Clair. In June, she bought the Muir family home on Lincoln Road in Grosse Pointe and hired a designer to carry out extensive remodeling plans for the house. In June, too, she attended the wedding of Horace Dodge, Jr., to Lois Knowlson—a quiet, family affair held in the Detroit home of the bride's parents.

When 21-year-old Horace Junior returned from a European honeymoon later that summer, Matilda took as much pleasure as did Anna with the change in his attitude...his eagerness to work in the plant and learn the business...his willingness to channel his mechanical abilities from powerboats and the glamor sport of speedboat racing to the operation of factory machines. Under Frederick Haynes' direction, the factory had reopened in March of 1921 with a reduced work force of 4000, but additional workmen steadily increased production to a point where, four months later, 600 cars rolled off the assembly line each day. The 1921 touring car was fitted with an oblong, plate-glass, rear window and beginning in July, the Dodge sedan looked less angular with a four-inch reduction in height.

In the same year, Haynes cooperated with the three Graham brothers to produce Graham motor trucks, using Dodge engines and transmissions and marketing the trucks through Dodge dealers. Matilda joined in business meetings with the Grahams and Haynes, entertained them at her home, and became a close friend of the Graham families.

In November, 1921, French war hero, Marshal Ferdinand Foch, arrived in Detroit, welcomed by the roar of 19 cannons as the Marshal's party moved up Woodward Avenue in military procession. After a visit to the Packard plant, the French war leader drove to Dodge Brothers factory to pay tribute to the memory of John and Horace and to view the special machinery that turned out the indispensable recoils for French guns.

Still, it seemed to Matilda that adversities outweighed this and every other bit of good news in the two years of mourning following her husband's death. Her stepson's threat became a reality in July, 1921, when newspapers reported that John Duval filed suit to break his father's will.

During those same summer months, Matilda heard the first scraps of gossip about the troubled Winifred-Jack Gray marriage. Matilda's distaste for Jack Gray was not nearly as strong as was her abhorrence for the unsavoriness of divorce. Her stepson was already providing more than enough unpleasant publicity for the family. She could scarcely imagine that her eldest stepdaughter soon would exhibit the same disregard for propriety.

In response to John Duval's suit, Matilda and her stepdaughters commissioned their attorneys to find a way to settle his claim out of court...to get the state law changed, if necessary. The attorneys did exactly that—pressuring legislators to alter the state's inheritance law to allow out-of-court settlements of will disputes among legatees. Before the end of 1921, the change became effective and the new ruling was informally tagged as the "Dodge Law."

This allowed for a quick settlement of John Duval's claim. Matilda and her stepdaughters agreed to a provision of $1.6 million for John

Duval with his promise that he would seek no further payments from the estate. Since the conditions of the will were already broken, Matilda's two stepdaughters determined to satisfy their personal appetites for a sizeable lump-sum of money out of the principal amount.

The sisters agreed to accept immediate distribution of a million dollars each. Fairness demanded, then, that each of Matilda's children should have the same amount, which would be held, gathering interest, until the three individual minor children reached the age of 21. Matilda received the largest bonanza as she rejected the 1/5 share of trust-money income willed to her by her husband, in addition to the properties, and elected instead to take half of what would have been hers legally if her husband had died without a will. This amounted to $5 million of automobile corporation stock.

The personal possession of so much money empowered Matilda to push nagging thoughts of her working-class background and the Rausch saloon further into the deep recesses of her mind. With the financial futures of her three children assured by the Dodge trust income, Matilda could freely enjoy her wealth as her two-year mourning cycle ended at the beginning of 1922.

John Duval was free, also, to enjoy his $1.6 million. He proceeded to leave his job at the Dodge factory, sailing for Europe with his wife for a tour of the continent.

His departure provided only a fleeting respite for Matilda from the problems of her stepchildren as her eldest stepdaughter's marital difficulties became a source of rumors linking Winifred's name with that of Wesson Seyburn—dashing horseman and real-estate business- man. The youthful Grays and their around-the-corner neighbors, the Seyburns, had made an attractive and lively foursome on the elegant Indian Village social scene. Now, it was whispered, Seyburn had left the home of his wife and young daughter; the Grays, parents of two small children, had separated and soon would be divorced.

Winifred fled to Europe when the Grays divorced in March, 1922. She was still in Europe when the John Duval Dodges returned and settled into a Grosse Pointe apartment. Recurring newspaper items concerning John Duval's traffic offenses annoyed Matilda, but annoy- ance changed to humiliation as John Duval's behavior set off a blitz of bad publicity. The notoriety erupted after her stepson picked up three girls from Kalamazoo College in a borrowed, high-powered car. As a reckless John Duval slowed the touring car to pass over a railroad track, one of the girls leaped to the highway. John Duval sped on down the road, leaving the girl to be found by another motorist who took her to a hospital. John Duval and a male friend spent the night in a jail cell.

In the next few days, newspapers published lawsuit threats from the injured girl's family, who claimed young Dodge was drunk when their daughter jumped from the car. There were photographs of a distraught Mrs. John Duval Dodge waiting at the jail for release of her husband on bond and plaintively telling reporters that her husband was "just unlucky." Photographs of a jaunty John Duval boasting that he "ought to run for president after all the publicity." Details of John, in prison garb, serving five days in the Detroit House of Correction on an earlier speeding charge.

When a Kalamazoo jury found John Duval guilty of "possessing, transporting, and distributing liquor," the judge sentenced him to one year's probation. The sentence contained the provision that young Dodge must go to work at a steady job in Detroit.

Thoroughly disgusted with her stepson, Matilda was grateful to Henry Ford who agreed to become John Duval's custodian for a year while young Dodge worked in the Ford factory. Matilda did not know whether Ford's interest in John Duval was part of the automotive titan's zeal for reforming people, or the result of some undefinable affinity on the part of Ford for the late John F. Dodge.

Whatever the motivation might have been for Ford's action, the gesture increased Matilda's liking for the industrialist whom she had always admired for his teetotaler views and his deference toward his wife, Clara. Matilda refused to believe persistent reports that circulated of Ford's cruelty to his only son, Edsel, despite lack of resistance from the soft-spoken young man to his father's needling. And she could scarcely believe current rumors of a love affair between Henry Ford and a much younger woman—an employee at the Ford Motor Company. No hint of this relationship crept into the newspapers, however, while it seemed to Matilda that every movement of the Dodges held a peculiar fascination for reporters.

When Winifred returned from Europe with a new wardrobe designed in Paris, Matilda learned of her beautiful stepdaughter's plans to marry Wesson Seyburn in September, 1922, at the Long Island home of her sister, Isabel. Scandalized, Matilda made a quick decision to separate herself from the troublesome behavior of her stepchildren by escaping to Europe.

She continued her struggle to shelter her own children from public scrutiny, not only because she feared kidnappers but also because she felt that her children could live more natural, unself-conscious lives if she, their mother, supervised their activities in the privacy of their comfortable home. It disturbed Matilda to hear of one persistent rumor regarding her carefully shielded daughters. One of the young, blue-eyed and blond Dodge sisters, Frances or Anna Margaret, had been burned in a fire ignited by a candle, according to the story. When asked by acquaintances about the accident, Matilda angrily denied that such a mishap occurred.

In late August, 1922, Matilda and her three children, accompanied by the maid, Mary Matthews, and the children's nurses, boarded the Aquitania for France where Matilda leased a villa in Nice. She planned to spend at least a year abroad—to be far away when Winifred re-married and to be free of the relentless notoriety given the Dodges in Detroit.

Correspondence from Amelia to Matilda at her Villa Les Falaises in Nice included clippings describing 627 acres of parklands, covering eleven separate sites, donated to Michigan by Dodge Brothers, Inc., as a memorial to John and Horace Dodge. Matilda also corresponded regularly with Frederick Haynes at the Dodge plant. She reacted with disappointment, but not surprise, when Haynes informed her that Horace Junior's flush of enthusiasm for the business had faded...that he reported to work infrequently...that the young man's life centered around parties and powerboats, even though Horace was now the father of a daughter. But with or without Horace Junior, production at Dodge Brothers remained high with 20,000 workers employed and with closed-car production climbing to 35% of total output.

Assured by Haynes' reports that the family's investments in Dodge Brothers stock were solid, Matilda stayed in France, hiring a French tutor for eight-year-old Frances. She took the child to art museums and concerts, and endeavored to steep her young family, and herself, in the traditions and culture of France. When at times, this cultivation of culture became burdensome, Matilda buoyed her spirits with shopping trips and fittings at the salon of a French designer who swathed Matilda's short, maturing figure in chiffon flounces and beaded trimmings, in brocaded panels and jeweled necklines—all in rich shades that colored her life with a new zest for whatever lay ahead.

After a couple of months at the French villa, Matilda arranged for Amelia and Margaret Rausch to board an ocean liner and to join the Dodges in France in time for Christmas holidays. She wanted the children to have their usual family-oriented observance of Christmas, Matilda explained. If she sometimes felt lonely, she never admitted it nor explained that her life in France with her children was not as eventful as it would have been in Detroit. To admit to loneliness was a weakness despised by Matilda.

She already had hired a housekeeper to replace Margaret Rausch at Meadow Brook after Amelia complained to Matilda that their mother could no longer physically meet the demands of this responsibility. When the new housekeeper arrived, Matilda ordered the Rausches' belongings moved into a nearby tenant house. Unhappy with the small tenant house and separation from affairs of daily life at the main farmhouse, Amelia reinforced her plans to own a home in the neighboring town of Rochester. Margaret Rausch demurred at the thought of risking her older daughter's displeasure, but Amelia lost none of the resolve to move from the farm—although, for now, she did not mention her plans to her sister as the Rausches sailed for Europe.

The children excitedly greeted their aunt and grandmother on their arrival in Nice. Although Frances and the brown-eyed Daniel soon settled down, three-year-old Anna Margaret, caught up in a tizzy of excitement and determined to be the center of attention, flared into a series of temper tantrums. The tantrums were not limited to the day of their arrival, with its attendant excitement, Amelia and Margaret soon discovered. The child frequently exhibited such violent episodes, holding her breath until her lips turned blue.

To Margaret Rausch, the fits of temper seemed to be replays of a young Matilda's similar rages years previously at the Princess Saloon flat. Margaret Rausch and her daughter Amelia agreed that Anna Margaret, with her broad face and fair complexion, was "the image of John Dodge." Both women also agreed that the child unfortunately inherited her irritable temper and moodiness from both Matilda and John.

To Amelia, Margaret confided her hopes that Anna Margaret would not be the same kind of shy and lonely schoolgirl that Matilda had been. Amelia, who still favored Daniel because of his resemblance to the Rausch side of the family, ventured the opinion that the stockily built Anna Margaret had an "adult-like" face—too old for her three years.

Because Matilda enjoyed Amelia's amiability as a traveling companion, she invited her sister and mother to go along with the family on a tour of Italy. There, they learned that Anna Dodge and her sister-in-law Della Eschbach were also in Rome, but Matilda avoided meeting with them because of her dislike for Della. Her distaste for the Catholic religion did not prevent Matilda from requesting, and receiving, an audience with the Pope, which was the popular thing to do, she conceded, when visiting in Rome.

Returning to Nice, Matilda prepared to take part in the Festival of Flowers parade on the eve of the Lenten season. Costumed in white by Worth of Paris, Matilda and her children rode in a carriage drawn by two white horses—the Cinderella-like coach draped with tiers of white lilacs and orange blossoms. From within the coach, the Dodge children tossed bunches of violets to crowds lining the avenue. Two hundred colorful floats competed in the parade for a "most striking" award, which was presented to Matilda—a most fortunate turn of events since she spent $20,000 on her entry.

The Rausches returned to Meadow Brook in April of 1923. In mid-summer, Matilda received a communication in Nice from Frederick Haynes, informing her that the new assembly building designed for the Dodge industrial complex was completed. This assembly plant would quickly move production of Dodge cars up to 1000 a day.

Matilda and her entourage returned to Detroit in December, the month when the one-millionth car emerged from the Dodge factory to establish a "World Record" in nine years and eleven days of production, according to newspaper accounts. Even more important to the image of Dodge Brothers motorcars and their reputation for dependability was the fact that ninety percent of all Dodge automobiles manufactured since the company's 1914 beginnings were still in service.

Soon after Christmas, Matilda moved her family and possessions, with masterful drill-sergeant efficiency, from Boston Boulevard into the smaller Lincoln Road home in Grosse Pointe. The Boston Boulevard home was listed for sale. Another Dodge possession—the 104-foot-long Frances, equipped with two 1200-gallon gas tanks —had been docked at the unfinished Grosse Pointe estate since its delivery in late 1921. Matilda decided to sell the cruiser, also. But she made no decision about the huge house facing Lake St. Clair. Matilda was not yet willing to fulfill her husband's expectations, made clear in his will—that if he did not survive to complete the palatial home, his widow should carry out his plans. Yet, she was unwilling to ignore John Dodge's last wishes.

In March, the nurse who cared for Daniel and Anna Margaret was confined, with her charges, to the nursery quarters of the Lincoln Road house when the two younger children became ill and were placed under quarantine for measles. Apparently recovered, the children came out into the yard with their nurse, for the first time since the quarantine began, on a Sunday afternoon in late March when the Rausches came to visit from the farm, bringing eggs and butter. As Amelia drove back to the farm in early evening, the conversation between the two Rausches focused on Matilda and her children. The women agreed that Anna Margaret looked unusually pale and tired...that her light blue eyes kept watering...that the nurse should have kept the little girl indoors, protected from the crisp March breeze.

In the following week, Anna Margaret, feverish and petulant, began to writhe in pain, despite frequent visits from the family physician, Dr. Lanning, who prescribed medications and brought a private nurse to the home. On April 8, the doctor ordered the four-year-old taken to Harper Hospital where physicians consulted among themselves while Matilda sat at the bedside of her delirious child.

For five days the child grew weaker. Dr. Lanning explained to Matillda, finally, that only emergency surgery could save her daughter's life...that infection, resulting from the measles, had spread into the little girl's intestines...that Dr. Max Ballin, an expert surgeon, would perform the operation.

As the surgery proceeded, the doctors discovered that inflammation had spread far beyond what they had expected. Anna Margaret rallied for a short time after the operation, then died at the age of four years and ten months on Palm Sunday, April 13, 1924, when her heart gave out under the strain.

Matilda's grief flared into resentment when she saw local accounts of her daughter's death. Victim of Heart Disease, the Detroit News captioned its story of the tragedy. "The child...had previous heart attacks," the article stated. A Detroit Free Press caption was similar. Heart Disease Fatal Following Attack of Measles and Operation. Within the article, the writer claimed that the little girl "had been subject to heart attacks."

Although Anna Margaret's death certificate listed the cause of death as acute infection of the intestines, colon and kidneys, with myocarditis as a contributing cause, Matilda wept over the newspaper stories. Obsessively concerned with a perfect physical and mental image of her children, Matilda became more distrustful of journalists than ever before.

Sitting with her two children—Frances, ten years old, and Daniel, six—Matilda struggled to control her grief as funeral services were conducted at the Lincoln Road home on the Tuesday before Easter. With her face concealed behind folds of a black veil, she watched, her shoulders erect, as the coffin of her small daughter was taken to Woodlawn Cemetery and placed in the family mausoleum beside John F. Dodge.

In the months following her youngest child's death, Matilda held herself aloof from family members who tried to console her. From Anna Dodge, whose son, Horace Junior, had taken care of such details as providing data for the death certificate. From Margaret Rausch and from Amelia, who sorrowfully confided to her mother that she understood, now, why Anna Margaret had such an adult-looking face. "Because the child had to live her entire life in less than five years," Amelia sighed, tears springing to her eyes.

The hard shell of Matilda's self-containment allowed for none of Amelia's sentimental indulgences. Her expressionless face permitted only perfunctory expressions of sympathy from family friends and acquaintances, after which Matilda tried to submerge her grief in a relentless pursuit of volunteer work for the church, the Salvation Army Auxiliary—of which she again became president that year, League of Women Voters, and Detroit Historic Memorials Society. She eagerly took up whatever worthy cause promised to occupy her mind and body to the exclusion of visions of the pale face and milky blue eyes that haunted her dreams and quiet moments.

Young Daniel was a comfort to her in those quiet times, his dark eyes softening as he came into her sitting room to sit quietly beside her, his head resting against her arm. In the summer and autumn months of 1924, she often took Frances with her when Compton, the chauffeur, drove her to church bazaars or teas or Salvation Army Auxiliary affairs. Even these mundane events seemed worthy of comment and speculation for newspaper readers as one reporter wrote of Matilda attending various functions, following the heart-attack death of the youngest Dodge child, while holding tightly to the hand of the blond-curled Frances. The burn-story rumors appeared again in this same article as the writer recalled that either Frances or Anna Margaret had been burned in a fire ignited by a candle.

Numbed since the death of her child by her own rigid suppression of emotions, Matilda ranted, now, about the article to friends and employees, insisting that Anna Margaret had always been a perfectly healthy child…that she had no heart attacks or other problems—until she contracted the measles. "Neither of my girls were ever burned," she asserted.

Matilda vehemently repeated these disclaimers later, year after year, to newly hired personal secretaries and business secretaries. In this way, the denials served to perpetuate stories that might otherwise have been forgotten.

Although 1924 was a sad and depressing period in Matilda's life, two gratifying occurrences lifted her spirits before the year ended. In October, she received a unique honor when officials of the Fidelity Bank and Trust Company in Detroit appointed Matilda Rausch Dodge to its board of directors. The directors publicly cited the "desirability" of having an outstanding woman on the board, adding that they selected Mrs. Dodge "because she combines intelligence and business sagacity with a very unusual experience not only in charitable, social, and religious organizations, but also in extensive business interests." Shortly after her appointment to the Fidelity board, she was pleasantly surprised when her minister, Dr. Vance, asked the distinguished looking bachelor and church deacon, Alfred G. Wilson, to escort Matilda to her home after a meeting. "It's part of the duties of deacons," the minister joked to Wilson, "to care for widows and orphans."

Matilda had been aware of Wilson for some time. The man's tall, straight figure, bachelor status, and moderate success in the lumber business made him a desirable male in the eyes of many widows of means who attended First Presbyterian Church.

By Christmas time, Matilda Dodge and Alfred Wilson appeared together frequently at church, but rarely at other public places. It was, of course, less than a year since the death of the youngest Dodge child. But Wilson often came to visit Matilda at the Dodge home, and her step was lighter now than it had been in the months since Anna Margaret's death...her dark eyes more luminous, her face more glowing.

The Robert Manzers sold their home on Stanford and moved again in 1924 to still another home built by Manzer himself at Woodside Avenue. Their daughter, Lucille, had enjoyed the presence of her red-haired baby "sister" only a short time at the family's former Stanford home when both children contracted the measles. While Lucille recuperated from the illness, the baby was taken to the hospital. A short time later, Minnie Manzer told Lucille that the baby died of a mastoid infection...that services would be held at a nearby funeral home to which Lucille was not taken. But years later, Lucille would learn that tuberculosis, the disease no one wanted to talk about, was the cause of the baby's death.

As on only child, Lucille spent much of her time in church with Minnie Manzer who occasionally played the organ for services when the regular organist, Lena Curtiss, could not be there. Mrs. Curtiss, who still gave piano lessons to Lucille, was also the child's Sunday School teacher. Lucille would have preferred dancing lessons to piano instructions, but was knowledgeable enough not to express such a preference. Dancing was sinful, according to the tenets of strict Methodists such as the Manzers. Card-playing, gambling, shopping on Sundays, drinking—all were equally evil according to Methodist precepts.

Near the end of 1924, the Manzers brought a baby boy into their home and introduced him to ten-year-old Lucille as her "brother." Named Robert Jr., the little boy thrived under Minnie Manzer's watchful attention. Lucille was so pleased to have a little brother that she asked no questions about his arrival.

The girl had already learned, without being told, that there were many topics her gentle, soft-spoken parents did not discuss. Money, for example. Family background. The only thing she knew about her father's background was that he was brought to Michigan as a young child from Kanakee, Illinois; that he had fallen from the wagon transporting his family to its new home and had been run over by a wagon wheel, leaving an indentation in his chest. Otherwise, Robert Manzer was a strong and energetic man who believed in the health value of standing on his head—an exercise he often practiced.

Although friends from church—the Curtisses, Uptons and other Methodists—frequently visited the Manzers, few relatives came to their home except for Robert's cousin, June Eschtruth. And Minnie's father, Marvin Fish, still came every winter to spend the coldest months with his daughter and her family. The stoical Minnie waited on the sharp-tongued old man without complaint until he left in early summer. He was her father, after all, and Minnie Manzer had a firm sense of duty.

Chapter 11

The Wilson Era Begins

Ever since the Dodge families recognized that neither John Duval nor Horace Junior could be groomed for management positions in the automobile corporation, Matilda and Anna Dodge began to consider selling the family business. When 1924 ended with record sales totalling almost $217 million for the year, the value of Dodge stock escalated and the company was in a position to command a maximum selling price.

General Motors made a bid of $124,500,000 to purchase Dodge Brothers in March, 1925. But a New York investment-banking firm—Dillon, Read and Company—offered a higher cash bid... $146,000,000. When the Dodge widows accepted the latter bid in late March, 1925, the biggest single cash transaction took place that had ever occurred within the realm of private business in the United States until that date.

The three stockholders in the original Dodge company—Matilda Dodge, the John Dodge estate (trust fund), and the Horace Dodge estate—were now assessed $12 million in federal taxes on an increase in value of more than $90 million in company properties, which had been valued at approximately $54 million when the Dodge brothers died in 1920.

With the sale of the business and the issuing of nearly three million shares of stock for public purchase, both Matilda and Anna prepared to buy sizeable blocks of common stock in the new Dodge Brothers, Inc. But Matilda could not afford to match Anna's purchase of 60,000 shares.

The John Dodge trust fund, set up originally only after inheritance taxes were paid and payments made to beneficiaries when the John Dodge will was broken, now increased by an additional $28 million.

John Duval, living in affluence ever since his earlier $1.6 million settlement, read accounts of the $146 million sale of his father's business and resented his exclusion from a share of the additional money. Coinciding with the announcement of the sale, John Duval filed suit in probate court, claiming one-fifth of the estate of his deceased half-sister, Anna Margaret—a child he had never seen.

Disheartened by another glut of newspaper articles featuring photos of Anna Margaret and repetitious accounts of her untimely death, Matilda resented John Duval more than ever before for bringing this notoriety to her family. She was comforted by Alfred Wilson who was also a source of "strength and encouragement," Matilda told friends, when her daughter, Frances, caught her hand in the wringer of the washing machine.

When Doctor Max Ballin suggested several forms of therapy for strengthening the damaged muscles of the girl's hand, horseback-riding therapy appealed to Matilda because of her own liking for horses. She traveled out to Meadow Brook more frequently, then, with the children, and began to seriously consider making the farm their permanent home. Still, Alfred Wilson was now a major figure in her life, and she was not willing to risk putting 40 miles between them. Instead, she bought a piece of property, with a riding stable, only a block from her Grosse Pointe home.

In April, Amelia and Margaret Rausch were shocked to read, in a Detroit newspaper delivered daily to Meadow Brook, an informal announcement of Matilda's engagement to lumberman Alfred Gaston Wilson. The next day, the New York Times carried a report of the engagement, including a background sketch of Wilson—bachelor son of a retired clergyman, the Reverend Samuel N. Wilson. The article also included a comment by Matilda Dodge, wearing a six-carat diamond engagement ring, that she was convinced that "my children need Alfred for a father."

Seven-year-old Daniel Dodge, a serene and even-tempered boy, displayed no resentment toward the new "father" coming into his life. But ten-year-old Frances, a moody child, did not hide her jealousy of her mother's fiance. In an effort to reassure the children of her love for them, Matilda took Frances and Daniel on a vacation to Hot Springs, Virginia, where "just the three of us," Matilda told the youngsters, could share a special closeness away from friends and family, including Wilson.

While the three Dodges vacationed in Virginia, Alfred Wilson carried out an assignment from Matilda. She wanted him to attend probate court proceedings when John Duval's attorney pleaded his client's case, asking to have Anna Margaret's $7.5 million divided among the five children of John Dodge.

Alfred folded his tall frame onto a bench in the courtroom on the morning that John Duval's attorney presented his arguments, pointing out his client's need for the money—to set up a business for the manufacture of his newly designed automobile, the Dodgeson, and to follow in his father's footsteps. As the judge took the matter under advisement, Wilson dutifully reported his version of the courtroom proceedings back to Matilda by telephone.

The Dodge-Wilson engagement, so quickly following the national publicity heralding the profitable sale of the Dodge automoblie business, fueled gossip and speculation among the First Presbyterian Church members and other Detroiters who knew the couple. Their speculations were inflamed by provocative newspaper articles similar to a Detroit Times item: "The Dodge widows today are classed among the wealthiest persons of the world, and possibly at the top rank among women, as far as ready money is concerned."

Matilda, sensitive enough to know that Wilson was perceived as a fortune-hunter, was beginning to learn to ignore rumor and innuendo as temporary vexations. More important, she glowed with the flush of love and desire for this man of erect bearing and impeccable manners. Dazzled by the suddenness of her own good fortune, the 41-year-old Matilda realized that Wilson, at 42, could have chosen a younger and virgin bride for himself. The realization intensified her eagerness to marry Wilson as soon as possible. Although only a year had passed since the death of her youngest child, Matilda agreed to set the wedding date for June 29.

Anna Dodge tried to repair her waning relationship with her sister-in-law, Matilda, at this time by honoring the engaged couple at a small party. One week before the wedding, 20 guests boarded the luxurious Delphine for the affair, cruising Lake St. Clair during the afternoon and returning to Rose Terrace for dinner.

On the following weekend, Sara Burnham came to Matilda's Lincoln Road home to manage the small wedding even though only family members would attend. Still, a crowd of spectators pressed against hedges surrounding the house, watching as the stepdaughter Winifred arrived with her husband, Wesson Seyburn. Winifred's sister, Isabel, and her husband,George Sloane, from Long Island. Wilson's mother and his father, who would assist Dr. Vance with the ceremony. Wilson's sister and brother, with their families. Margaret Rausch, her heavy figure draped in a dark dress. Amelia, her sister's maid-of-honor, emerging from the house after the ceremony in green chiffon and a flowing scarf aflutter with green ostrich feathers. Behind the hedges, the onlookers were rewarded when the bride, in cream chiffon with lacy sash and a hat with a lacy brim, came out from the house on the arm of the six-foot-tall Wilson.

Frances, in pale pink chiffon, and Daniel, in white linen short pants and blue coat, were generously supplied with confetti and serpentines which excited them to race around the yard, tossing their colorful ammunition indiscriminately at the wedding party and guests. The guests did not include John Duval, who was not invited to the ceremony. Although the judge's decision on John Duval's claim was still pending, Matilda managed to dismiss such painful thoughts from her mind as she was caught up in the intoxication of her delicious ardor for Alfred Wilson.

Amelia Rausch, accompanying her sister up to her second-floor bedroom suite, watched wistfully as a flushed-faced Matilda put aside her bouquet of orchids and slipped out of her wedding dress. "She's surely marrying for love this time," Amelia whispered to her mother as the bride, stylish in a dove-gray suit lavishly trimmed with platinum fox, joined Alfred to be driven by the Seyburns to the railroad station. There, Matilda's French maid waited with the couple's luggage.

Frances and Daniel were to remain in the care of their nurses while the newlyweds boarded the <u>Aquitania</u> for a four week honeymoon in England. As Amelia drove back to Meadow Brook with her mother, her small face drooped. Her mind whirled with thoughts of her bright-eyed, glowing sister, with an attentive and solicitious Alfred at her side, introducing her husband to the sights and sounds of London...traveling together throughout England's countryside where, Amelia knew, Matilda planned to study the great Tudor homes of English aristocracy...returning together in the evenings to the plushness of the finest hotel suites...

The Meadow Brook tenant house looked even smaller and more unappealing to Amelia on her return from the wedding. Margaret Rausch's suspicions were confirmed when Amelia issued her ultimatum. She had decided to move into Rochester, the younger daughter declared, just as soon as she could have a house built there.

Margaret Rausch protested nervously that there was nothing wrong with the tenant house...that it was big enough for just the two women. What would Matilda say, she asked Amelia, if they left the farm now—after 15 years?

Amelia brushed aside her mother's timid concerns for Matilda's reactions, reminding Margaret Rausch that she always wanted to live in town and that she hoped that Margaret would want to live with her in Rochester. "But if not—well, I'll live alone," she insisted.

The older woman's silence did not pacify Amelia. "Why should we always worry about 'what will Matilda say'?" she demanded. Matilda had her own privileged life, Amelia pointed out. And now the younger sister wanted a life of her own.

Words came freely, now, as she reminded her mother that Matilda had not done all that much for them compared to all the supportive things that Anna Dodge did for her family—the Thomsons. Providing them with homes, educations, Florida vacations...

"You've had the use of the Dodge sedan," Margaret defended her absent, older daughter. Amelia regarded this as unimportant, but was more impressed with her mother's reminder that they would miss the visits of John Cline to their home if they moved to Rochester. The farm manager, Cline, certainly could find transportation into Rochester if he wished to continue his visits to their home, Amelia finally replied. And the very next day, Amelia drove into town to see about buying some property where she could have a house built.

The Rausches had more tidbits to discuss when the newlywed Wilsons returned to Grosse Pointe later that summer and began consulting with architects on plans for a Tudor-style mansion they wanted built at Meadow Brook. To her mother, Amelia complained that Matilda was displaying little, if any, loyalty to John Dodge. She had married Alfred Wilson only a short time after starting to keep company with him, and a year after the death of her youngest child by John Dodge. Now she was planning a huge new home at Meadow Brook—"for Daniel," Matilda told the Rausches. But the unfinished house in Grosse Pointe was John Dodge's dream for Daniel, in Amelia's opinion.

It appeared to Amelia that Matilda simply had abandoned the unfinished Grosse Pointe mansion...that she had no concern for it, now, in her absorbing fascination for Alfred and in her eagerness to do everything to please him. When the Rausches visited in Grosse Pointe on Christmas Day that first year of the Wilsons' marriage, Matilda bubbled with happy excitement as she described her surprise gift to Alfred that morning—a new Lincoln automobile parked in front of the house so that her husband would catch sight of the gift when he looked out the bedroom window.

Matilda was decidedly unhappy when Amelia described her own Christmas gift to herself and her mother—a house she had ordered built in Rochester. They already had a place to live, Matilda protested.

Amelia gathered up her courage to say that she wanted her own home...a house with more space for mother and daughter. A house close to the downtown area.

Matilda launched into the matter of ingratitude, then, reminding Amelia of what the John Dodges had provided for the Rausches at the farm for so many years. "If it were not for John Dodge's legacy," she accused, "you wouldn't be able to afford a house."

It was true that John's money was paying for the house, Amelia reflected as Matilda flounced out of the room. It was true, also, that Matilda's gift of a Lincoln motorcar to Alfred resulted from John Dodge's legacy, Amelia reminded herself.

Amelia's house in Rochester was under construction before the end of the year, but the Rausches still were living in the tenant house in early January, 1926, when the National Automobile Show opened in New York. Journalists at the exposition were attracted to John Duval Dodge who stood near a model engine—an eight-cylinder, rotary-valve type—for his new Dodgeson automobile. John Duval exuded confidence as he distributed brochures stating that the Dodgeson was "designed and engineered by Mr. John Duval Dodge, son of John F. Dodge..."

John Duval, who had hired engineers and designers to draw the plans for his car, returned from the exposition with no commitments from investors to provide capital for the manufacture of his Dodgeson automobile. Gambling losses and bills for cars and jewelry and luxury vacations had steadily eroded his settlement money from the John Dodge estate. But, with irrepressible optimism, he anticipated receiving an award of some $1.5 million from the estate of Anna Margaret and using it to manufacture the Dodgeson.

His plans dissolved in that same bleak month of January when the court ruled that Anna Margaret's entire $7.5 million should be awarded to her mother. If Matilda thought the matter ended with this decision, she was mistaken. John Duval, joined by Winifred and Isabel, filed an appeal. Again, the John Dodges' money battles became subjects of countless newspaper stories that delved into the family's past, weaving it into the fabric of the current struggles for control of the fortune.

To separate herself from the Dodge name that she found so troublesome, while still carrying on the battle to claim as much of her husband's money as possible—this became Matilda's goal. Stung by every reference to herself as Matilda Dodge Wilson, she carefully signed her name, and presented it to journalists, as Matilda Rausch Wilson.

Early in the spring, Amelia and Margaret Rausch moved into the younger sister's new two-story home on West Fifth Street in Rochester. Regardless of Matilda's irritation, Amelia and her mother had just settled comfortably into the routine of small-town life in

Rochester when, to Amelia's surprise, Matilda asked her younger sister to accompany her on a shopping expedition to New York City in late April.

Amelia loved the excitement of New York...she enjoyed every minute of going along with Matilda to Tiffany's and to smart Fifth Avenue shops. The evening before they planned to return home, Matilda suddenly informed her sister that Anna Dodge was waiting for them, with a friend, in the hotel lobby. As the sisters emerged from the elevator on the first floor, Anna Dodge approached them. Amelia's eyes shifted in the direction of the handsome man, obviously younger than Anna, who also walked toward them. "That's the man Anna's going to marry," Matilda whispered.

Amelia scarcely had time to realize that another sudden marriage was pending when she was introduced to Hugh Dillman. The man's warm smile and charm quickly captivated the Rausch sisters as they talked briefly with Anna and Dillman, who were leaving for Detroit on the night train.

Matilda was snappish as the sisters returned to their hotel suite. Amelia checked the question that almost popped out of her mouth. Whatever did that good-looking young man see in Anna? She realized that her sister probably was reflecting on the same question, and that Matilda would not relish any analogy to her own marriage to Wilson.

In the quiet of the hotel sitting room, Matilda began to relax, finally matching opinions with Amelia regarding the age difference between the 54-year-old Anna and her fiance. At least a dozen years' difference, they agreed. They would learn, much later, that Anna was 14 years older than her husband. For now, Matilda shared with Amelia the scattered bits of information she had acquired...that Dillman was the real-estate salesman who sold a $3 million Palm Beach mansion to Anna this past winter. The man's real name was McGaughey, but he had taken Dillman as his name when he became a stock-company actor. His marriage to Anna would take place the following week, Matilda confided to her sister.

The Alfred Wilsons attended the Dodge-Dillman wedding held at Gray House—a 76-room manor, neighboring Rose Terrace on the west, purchased by Anna for the use of Horace Junior and his family. Amelia, who was not invited to the ceremony, clipped newspaper accounts describing the affair and the departure of the Dillmans for a European honeymoon.

Her collection of clippings pyramided beginning on May 31. On that date, the New York Times ran a front-page article exposing the financial mess that Anna Dodge's son-in-law, Jimmy Cromwell, generated in his attempt to build a luxury resort at Fort Lauderdale, Florida, and to pre-sell properties to celebrities and to people of blue-blood status. When his uncompleted "Floranada" extravaganza collapsed into bankruptcy, people as diverse as Major General Douglas MacArthur (Cromwell's brother-in-law) and ex-King George II of Greece charged Cromwell with unauthorized use of their names in lavish "Floranada" advertising.

Matilda was horrified by the implications of fraud, so closely associated with the Dodge name, reiterated in an avalanche of newspaper stories. Anna Dodge Dillman, still traveling in Europe with her new husband, avoided some of the embarrassment by her absence, but suffered the personal loss of some $4 million in her son-in-law's "Floranada" misadventure—both investment and "bail-out" money.

The land-development notoriety had not yet subsided when the name of Horace Junior and his marital difficulties hit gossip columns. Horace, it was reported, had left his wife and two children and joinied his current paramour in the casinos at Cannes. A divorce settlement of $1 million of Anna's money freed Horace for a quick second marriage and left Anna with the care of her two grandchildren. By this time, Anna's daughter, Delphine, had filed for divorce from Cromwell, charging that her only means of support since her marriage was a monthly allowance from her mother. A custody fight for the Cromwells' young daughter and a quick remarriage for Delphine provided notoriety that stiffened Matilda's resolve to sever ties with the Horace Dodge family...to separate herself from the Dodge name as far as possible, even though her two children were Dodges.

The Alfred Wilsons sold their Lincoln Road home and moved out to Meadow Brook in 1926—farther away from the bustling city of Detroit with its still growing population of 1,242,000 people and its increasing assortment of car showrooms and gas stations. The entire country panted with the process of rapid change, and Detroit was running in the fast track as the last Model T came off the assembly line in 1927 and the new, modern Model A replaced it. The structure for the 47-storied Penobscot Building rose skyward, and the first talking picture—"The Jazz Singer" with Al Jolson—played to Detroit audiences. Regular passenger airline service began that year, from Detroit to Cleveland, and soon to Chicago.

Across the country, people marvelled at Charles Lindbergh's 1927 solo plane flight to Paris, at marathon dances and flagpole sitters, and at the reputation of Detroit as a wide-open booze town and the home of the notorious "Purple Gang." The country's "wickedest city," a

Rockefeller Commission declared. Some 300,000 "blind pigs" and speakeasies, plus numerous brothels, enhanced the lusty reputation of the Midwest city, still afloat with illegal booze smuggled in from Canada.

Forty miles north of Detroit, Matilda, Alfred, the two children and their nurses, plus an assortment of maids, settled into the Dodge farmhouse to conduct the business of the farm and to oversee construction of a Tudor mansion of brick and sandstone. Matilda decided the splendid mansion should have 36 huge and individually designed chimneys similar to those of Hampton Court in England.

As giant shovels gouged the earth for the foundations for Meadow Brook Hall, Matilda had a $10,000 five-room playhouse of 3/4-sized bricks, complete with cedar-lined attic and full basement, built for Frances near the farmhouse. The reduced-scale playhouse, named Hilltop Lodge, was equipped with matching-sized furnishings and kitchen appliances so that 12-year-old Frances could practice the art of housekeeping with such accessories as a miniature sewing machine, Limoges china and a guest book which contained a notation of the family's first tea party at Hilltop Lodge on December 15, 1926.

"Hilltop Lodge—a beautiful and wonderful gift to Frances from her dear mother," Alfred Wilson recorded in a burst of sentimentality that the inhibited Matilda could not have expressed. He wrote that "Mother Daddy, Danny and Frances" enjoyed a sleigh ride "over lots of beautiful white snow with Black Boy drawing the cutter," before coming back to Hilltop Lodge for tea. Matilda reminded Frances that the young girl was expected to make similar entries each time she entertained.

For a while, the elaborate playhouse fascinated Frances, but soon the riding horses at Meadow Brook lured her from the playhouse back to the stables where she liked to help groom her own horse, Jewel. As the Wilsons prepared for horseback riding across the countryside, they were a patrician-looking family. Matilda—still not too stout to wear boots and breeches. Frances—a wide-brimmed hat set squarely on her head, her long blond hair gathered at the back of her neck and blowing in the breeze. Gray-haired Alfred Wilson—tall and lean in the saddle as he prodded his horse to a gallop. Young Daniel—riding-crop in hand, as he trailed the group on a smaller horse.

Unlike Frances, Daniel was not captivated by horses. Since her son liked working with his hands, Matilda built a log cabin workshop, equipped with tools sized for a boy, at the edge of the golf course. There, Daniel contentedly experimented with his tools while Frances rode her horse.

For a time, only Frances and Alfred went down to the stables. Matilda, who wanted to bear a child for Alfred, suffered a miscarriage, and began to realize that another pregnancy could be risky, since she was nearing her middle forties. As Alfred pressed for adoption, she brushed aside the nagging suspicion that her husband's desire for children might have evolved from a conviction that Wilson children could provide Alfred with a stronger claim to the Dodge fortune.

At the Rausch home near downtown Rochester, Margaret Rausch was now recovering from cancer surgery performed by Dr. Ballin at Harper Hospital in February, 1927. Amelia and her recuperating mother occasionally visited Meadow Brook, marveling at the magnificence of the L-shaped manor—the Tiffany stained-glass windows, originally ordered for the uncompleted John Dodge mansion in Grosse Pointe...the Christopher Wren-styled dining room with its carved ceiling...the main- floor gallery, its oak-panelled walls and interlaced wood-ribbed ceiling in the style of England's Knole House.

The great house was nearly completed when, in February of 1928, Matilda and Alfred went to Jacksonville, Florida, for the remainder of the winter. In the second week of March, Amelia tearfully interrupted their vacation with a telephone call from Rochester. Margaret Rausch had suffered a stroke, Amelia sobbed. Their mother was paralyzed—in critical condition.

The Wilsons arrived in Rochester shortly before Margaret's death on March 12, at age 69. The mother's will specified that some of her personal possessions should be given to a sister in Ontario and a sister-in-law in Detroit—the wife of Uncle Harry Glinz who had begun to speak with Margaret only after the death of John Dodge. The rest of the $30,000 estate was willed to Amelia, except for a $1000 bequest to Meadow Brook Farm manager, John Cline. Although Matilda would have turned over any financial bequest from the small estate to her sister, Amelia, the older sister felt rejected by her mother's failure to include her in the will. She begrudged the $1000 gift to John Cline which symbolized, in Matilda's mind, an affection expressed by her mother for the farm manager that had not been expressed for Margaret Rausch's elder daughter.

Matilda knew that the farm manager frequently visited the Rausch home in Rochester. The association, she felt, should no longer be cultivated by Amelia. The man was a Polish immigrant to this country, and although he had changed his name to Cline, the language of his native land flavored his speech. While her mother lived, Matilda remained silent about Cline's visits to the Rausch home, reasoning that the farm manager's handyman skills were useful to the two women in the upkeep of their home. Now that her mother had died, Matilda expected Cline's visits to the Rausch home to cease. Her sister was an unmarried woman who should not be entertaining men—particularly men of Cline's menial status—at her home.

Matilda's opinions influenced Amelia, but certain other considerations, by this time, became even more important. Companionship. Attention and deference from a male. For these reasons, Amelia continued welcoming Cline to her home, deciding that her sister was sufficiently absorbed in her own affairs—the completion of Meadow Brook Hall and the resolving of the court appeal filed by her step-children in the matter of Anna Margaret's estate.

When the court denied the appeal in the spring of 1928, Matilda's fortune fattened as she became the sole recipient of her deceased child's $7.5 million. In anticipation of receiving the money, Matilda had embarked on a budding career as a business entrepreneur by investing $3 million in a theater to be built in downtown Detroit. She planned to call it the Wilson Theater, flashing the Wilson name in brilliant lights and bringing classy stage entertainment to middle-class audiences.

While Matilda thrilled to the excitement of opening and managing her own theater, the Dodge company, source of dividends to Matilda and to the John Dodge trust fund, was currently choking on its banker-buyers' production of larger, more luxurious, six-cylinder cars sold at bloated prices. After the new owners also had purchased Graham Brothers Truck Company in 1925, the three Graham brothers became officials at Dodge. But this arrangement lasted only six months when the Grahams left to organize their own automobile company, Graham Paige Motor Corporation—on whose board of directors Matilda would begin to serve in 1931.

Without the Grahams, the banker owners of the Dodge company were struggling to meet their payroll by the spring of 1928. When Walter Chrysler offered to take over the Dodge business in that year by way of a $170 million deal, the owners agreed to the terms, even though no cash changed hands. Chrysler assumed the liability for $56 million in Dodge bonds, and issued stock in the Chrysler Corporation for the remainder of the money. The deal multiplied Chrysler's physical size by five and gave it access to 4600 Dodge dealers. One year later, Chrysler held third place in the automobile industry as one of the "Big Three." Years later, Walter Chrysler would say: "The greatest thing I ever did was to buy the Dodge."

As Matilda fussed with her business responsibilities, Alfred became accountable for the farm and its operations, spread over the larger part of 1400 acres. He carefully noted every expenditure and took pride in worksheets recording profits. His wife's horses and show ponies were not expected to make money, but Alfred wanted everything else to be profitable. When he was not satisfied with farm operations, he lashed out at workers or impulsively fired employees.

When John Cline was arbitrarily fired by an angry Alfred Wilson, the farm manager took his complaint of unfair treatment to Matilda. "John Dodge hired me back in 1910," he reminded her. "I worked under your father until he died. And this is the first time anybody's complained about my work."

In the few years since she had married Alfred, Matilda gradually assumed the dominant role in the husband-wife relationship, reinforced by the power of her fortune. Now, without conferring with Alfred, Matilda reinstated Cline, who returned to work—a constant reminder to Alfred of his subservience to his wife.

On visits to Meadow Brook, the sister, Amelia, observed the interactions of the Wilsons and decided that Matilda was certainly in love with Alfred, but that her domineering characteristics were even more pronounced since she came into possession of more money. Then, too, there was the matter of a $2 million loss of Matilda's money that Alfred incurred, playing the stock market. With his pride considerably injured by the memory of this failure, Alfred never confronted his wife with his resentment of her authoritive behavior. Instead, he measured out small retributions—dashing off for a ride on his horse when the maid had just begun to serve breakfast to an annoyed Matilda sitting across from Alfred's empty chair at the table; disappearing for hours on an unspecified errand when he knew that Matilda waited for him to return; pretending not to hear when his wife issued one of her edicts.

Matilda frequently flared into anger at her husband, but the episodes were brief and quickly forgotten when Alfred remained outwardly calm, despite his own quick temper. Matilda worried, though, about Frances' unremitting coldness to her stepfather, who made many attempts to win the girl's trust and confidence. Daniel reacted neither with hostility nor sullenness in his stepfather's presence, but since he was not an outgoing child, he tended to retreat out of shyness from Wilson's overtures. The Wilson relatives also tried to cultivate close relationships with the Dodge children. Alfred's father wrote a lengthy and sentimental poem in celebration of the completion of Frances' Tudor playhouse. Alfred's brother, Don, and his family, who moved into a new home—called Lawnridge—built by Matilda across the main road from Meadow Brook, also tried to be companionable with the children.

On December 10, 1928, the Wilsons invited Amelia to accompany them to the grand opening of the Wilson Theater which lured an assortment of photographers and press people to Madison Avenue and Randolph. Above their heads, a glittering marquee flashed the name of Marilyn Miller starring in "Rosalie" as a crowd gathered to watch the first-nighters parade into the plush lobby. It was a gala, standing-room -only night for the Wilsons who met with the gorgeous star of the musical after the performance in a mutual exchange of congratulations and lavish floral sprays.

"My heart is really in the business world," Matilda confided later to reporters from her private office, adjoining a similar office for Alfred, in Detroit's Fisher Building where she worked at magnifying her reputation as a successful businesswoman.

For Matilda, it was not enough to be, in her own cultured and restrained style, an ardent feminist at a time when women had been able to vote for less than ten years. Nor to be one of ten women delegates, of 66 Michigan members, who attended the 1928 Republican National Convention. Nor to be elected treasurer for the National Council of Women. She found her greatest satisfaction in managing her theatrical enterprise, in her board of directors' appointments, and, with Alfred, dabbling in real estate as they organized the Anchor Realty Company.

In June of 1929, Matilda opened the doors of Meadow Brook Hall for a meeting of First Presbyterian Women's Missionary Society, even though the oversized, wood-burning range that she had ordered was not yet installed in her otherwise modern kitchen. In happy anticipation of a spectacular official opening of her new home later in the year, Matilda tried to ignore the irritating string of current news items concerning John Duval and his public pursuit by process servers because of unpaid bills.

Other items, concerning the stepdaughter Isabel and her divorce from George Sloane, were also disturbing Matilda, while publicity surrounding the activities of Winifred and the Seyburns was of a different kind. These news items tracked the Seyburns' movements from their new lakeside home in Grosse Pointe to their East-Coast summer home and their glamorous social life which included hob-nobbing with European royalty. Although Matilda had social ambitions of her own, her aspirations also included a much wider range of interests—in business, in philanthropy, and in broadening her own scope of knowledge. She had little respect for dedicated socialites.

Long before the official opening of Meadow Brook Hall in November, 1929, copper eavestroughs and downspouts, cut-stonework window casements and wood paneling were taken from the unfinished mansion in Grosse Pointe and brought to Meadow Brook for installation at the new home. The great three-manual pipe-organ, originally ordered for the Grosse Pointe home, was also brought to Meadow Brook and installed. And despite Matilda's resolve to separate herself from the Dodge name, she felt compelled to bring the John Dodge bedroom furniture from Boston Boulevard, John's roll-top desk from the plant, John's first tool box and assorted items to third-floor storage quarters at the Hall.

A few other John Dodge possessions were used on the main floor of the house. A large, intricately-carved dragon-footed table, which few people knew had been a gift to John from the owner of Churchill's saloon. Two comfortable chairs in which John and Horace had customarily relaxed after a midday lunch at Boston Boulevard. And a large oil portrait of John Dodge, placed above the fireplace in the oak-panelled library. ·

This obeisance to the memory and uncompleted plans of John Dodge seemed to free Matilda from the bonds that had paralyzed her into procrastination, regarding the Grosse Pointe property, that was foreign to her usual decisive nature. In nine years of neglect, the Grosse Pointe homesite was overrun with weeds and molding leaves. The greenhouse, which failed to provide the expected revenue, was now abandoned, and flowers for the Wilsons' own use were grown at the farm-greenhouse. Still, another dozen years would pass before Matilda finally ordered the razing of the deteriorating buildings facing Lake St. Clair.

Through periodic newspaper reports, the Manzers, along with other Detroiters, shared the accounts of 12-year-old Frances Dodge's birthday gift—the fabulous playhouse...stories of Frances riding her horse, Jewel, to a third-place award at a local horse show...accounts of the building progress at palatial Meadow Brook Hall.

Society columns held no interest for young Lucille Manzer, however. The reports of Frances Dodge's playhouse might have fascinated Lucille if someone called her attention to the stories, but horseback riding and horse shows were entirely removed from her experience.

Lucille's experiences were those of an average, happy child of working-class parents. She was a Girl Scout. She occasionally went along with her father on camping or fishing trips, sitting patiently in the small boat while Robert Manzer rowed out to his favorite fishing spot...walking through the woods with her dad who showed her how to find clumps of arbutus beneath the moss and taught her to recognize species of trees and wild flowers.

There was no playhouse for Lucille's twelfth birthday, but her father bought her a pretty blue dress for the occasion. He liked to have her wear blue, he told her, because it brought out the clear blue of her eyes.

Even when Minnie sewed a blouse or dress for her daughter, the materials were usually blue, at Robert Manzer's insistence. Sometimes Lucille tired of wearing blue, but dared not complain about it to her mother who could become a tower of indignation at any suggestion of impertinence. Much worse, was Minnie's outrage on the day when, after sending Lucille to the basement to bring up a jar of tomatoes, she asked the girl to run down the stairs a second time for a jar of peaches.

"Why the devil didn't you ask me the first time?" Lucille complained.

Minnie's face registered shock. "We never want to hear that language in this house again!" she said, her voice rising loudly. "Never! Do you hear?"

Frightened, Lucille nodded quickly and ran downstairs to get the peaches.

Church and Sunday School, where Minnie taught a Sunday School class, continued to play an important part in Lucille's life. The young girl adored her two-year-old brother, Rob, and, as she grew into her early teen years, was always willing to take care of the boy when Minnie went to a Ladies Aid Society meeting at church. But Lucille's piano lessons, from church organist Lena Curtiss, had ceased after five years when the unwilling student skipped out of the house at practice time.

Apart from Girl Scout affairs, outings for Lucille were usually church-sponsored events with her Methodist Junior League friends and, as she grew into her teens, with Epworth League companions. On one Epworth League picnic at a lake where the young people went swimming, Lucille's wet hair clung to her scalp, soaked strands separating at the nape of her neck. A friend stared at her curiously. "Hey, Lucille," she said. "I never saw those scars before." She peered at the back of Lucille's head and base of her neck.

Lucille shrugged. She was scarcely aware of the scars, hidden, usually, by her hair and clothing. And she never asked her mother about them—she had always had the scars and she accepted them without questioning their origin. But when she returned from the lake that day, she decided to ask her mother what had caused the scarring.

Minnie Manzer simply continued peeling vegetables at the kitchen sink, without turning her head to look at Lucille. "You fell down the back steps when you were very small," she said curtly, "and cut your head."

Lucille had no reason to doubt her mother's explanation because she knew that Minnie Manzer, a devout Methodist, had a healthy respect for the virtue of honesty. And because the teenager was not given to introspection, she never tried to analyze the reasons for the feelings of guarded restraint that she received in her relationship with her mother.

She sensed the same feelings of constraint, on Minnie's part, the day her mother showed her a large black and white photograph. "I thought you might want to see a picture of yourself when you were a baby," Minnie said. Lucille stared at the photograph of two chubby babies, old enough to sit up, side by side, in a wide Victorian wicker chair. The little girls, each with a string of pearls around her neck, wore identical dresses and pouchy, soft shoes. Only their bonnets were different—one more bouffant than the other.

"You're the baby on the left," Minnie told Lucille. "But the other baby is wearing your bonnet."

"Why is she wearing my bonnet?" Lucille demanded, feeling an instant jealousy for the child in the frillier bonnet. "And who is she?"

Minnie ignored the first question. "Her name is Amy," she replied to the second as she replaced the photograph in its envelope.

It was the only explanation Lucille ever would receive. She wondered less about the unknown "Amy" at that time, however, than she would later in life when the photograph of the two twin-like baby girls began to take on new significance.

Chapter 12

Mistress of Meadow Brook

In 1929, when the Wilson family moved from the farmhouse into elegant Meadow Brook Hall, industrialists who built palatial homes, modeled after mansions of European aristocracy, were popularly referred to as "robber barons." At Meadow Brook, Matilda tried to set a modest tone of family attitudes by always calling the magnificent residence "the farm." Perversely, this deliberate unpretentiousness on the part of the Wilsons only served to magnify the magnificence of Meadow Brook Hall and its 80,000 square feet of living space.

Matilda was already addressing invitations to the official opening of Meadow Brook Hall, which she cozily termed a "housewarming," when Henry Ford staged his official opening for Greenfield Village—the 200-acre site in Dearborn where Ford collected tons of memorabilia from an earlier era. Lincoln's courthouse, moved to the village from Illinois. The home in which Stephen Foster was born. Longfellow's blacksmith shop. Thomas Edison's laboratories.

Prominent people mingled with the crowd attending the dedication ceremonies for Ford's Greenfield Village. The 82-year-old Thomas Edison. President Herbert Hoover. Walter Chrysler and other celebrated industrialists whose minds had been preoccupied, for days, with the troublesome and erratic performance of the stock market. Such concerns did not worry Henry Ford who despised Wall Street and its brokers and who frequently expressed his disparaging opinions on the subject. He had more opportunity to rage about money manipulators one week later with the "Big Crash" of Wall Street on "Black Tuesday," October 29, 1929.

One month later, the Wilsons' housewarming at Meadow Brook Hall went ahead as planned on a stormy November 29 when groundskeepers plowed and shoveled snow furiously along the stretch of curving driveway to clear the entrance for 800 guests. Silver-haired Alfred Wilson, a foot taller than his wife, stood at Matilda's side to greet the first arrivals. Matilda wore her dark hair parted at the center and marcelled into soft waves by her maid, Mary Matthews, in the third-floor room equipped as a beauty salon. Her figure, heavier and more matronly at age 46, was still firm enough to permit her to wear a sleeveless yellow dress embossed with velvet flowers and flaring into a short train. Her sister, Amelia, wore a $250 cocoa-chiffon dress, purchased with a check supplied by Matilda.

Guests poured through the low-passage entrance to the great hall, where a fire blazed in an open fireplace, its reflection flickering across stone arches and oak ceiling-beams. The visitors admired the fur- nishings—needlepointe draperies and chairs, and a long antique table from England at the center of the room, then moved on to view the rest of the house. On to the drawing room, which Matilda called the "living room," panelled in English oak in the style of the Bromley Room in Kensington Museum and decorated with a plaster cast ceiling like that of the Reynolds Room of England's Knole House. To the library with its expanse of oriental rug and its frieze of carved visages of writers and philosophers. To the Georgian dining room; its oak parquet floor and magnificent inlaid walnut table that could seat 36 people. And on and on—through the morning room, Alfred Wilson's study with its secret spiraling stairway of stone, the breakfast room, the lower-floor ("basement" in Matilda's modest terms) with its ballroom, fountain room and games room.

The second floor and its bedroom suites were off-limits to all but a select group of close friends who followed Matilda up the broad staircase for a personal view of her own Louis XIV-styled suite with its bed set regally on a dais. Of Alfred's adjoining room—its seven-foot- long bed accessorized, like Matilda's bed, with satin sheets bearing out- sized silver monograms. Frances' early-American suite with its pine- wood floors and its own secret staircase—the latter a small "extra" to placate the teenager's envy of her stepfather's private, almost magical, access to all floors of the great house. Daniel's medieval-styled suite outfitted with the kinds of modern accessories that fascinated the boy—lighting fixtures and drawer handles designed like automobile and airplane parts. The Italian Room, French Room, English Room, Adams Room—each contributing to the mosaic of impressions retained by visitors of gold-plated faucets...collections of antiques...paintings by Joshua Reynolds, Van Dyck, Gainsborough...assortments of smaller rooms including a secretary's suite, sewing and pressing rooms, a linen room holding 1295 tablecloths, and staff living quarters encompassing a butler's pantry. A grand total of 100 rooms.

Although Matilda employed both a butler and assistant butler, she would continue to have trouble keeping these positions filled. A well trained butler expected to have command of household operations and staff. But at Meadow Brook, Matilda would not delegate total control of her household. Recurring conflicts resulted in the departures of several butlers and in lengthy periods when a haughty butler was not in residence at Meadow Brook Hall. Nor was a housekeeper employed. Matilda still prided herself on her meticulous system of inventories and filing that kept her informed of the status of household supplies, menus, servants, and routines.

Within three months of the housewarming, a very sick 15-year-old Frances was taken to Harper Hospital where doctors diagnosed her illness as acute appendicitis. Ever since the death of four-year-old Anna Margaret following emergency surgery, Matilda feared losing another child in the same way. Still, there was no alternative but to allow the operation to proceed.

Frances recuperated rapidly following successful surgery. Several weeks later, Matilda and Alfred boarded a Miami-bound train for five weeks of relaxation in the Florida sun, after which they sailed to Europe. In May, 1930, they arrived in Vienna so that Matilda, as a delegate from the U.S. National Council of Women, could attend the Council's international meeting. Wherever she traveled, she bought postcards—two sets of them, always, so that Amelia could have the second set.

Amelia carefully saved the postcards, along with her newspaper clippings. But the vicarious thrills of European travels, via postcard perusal, were not sufficiently satisfying to the younger sister who retained vivid recollections of earlier exciting journeys abroad with Matilda. Those, of course, occurred in the pre-Alfred Wilson era, Amelia reminded herself. Now, since Alfred was more willing to travel than John Dodge had been, it was natural that her sister wanted her husband at her side, and equally conceivable that Amelia's presence could be a nuisance.

Although Amelia made new friends in Rochester since moving into town, she found that attending church teas and sewing circles and potluck suppers really could not be compared to her former European jaunts, yacht excursions and New York shopping trips in the company of Matilda. Still, Amelia tried not to nurture her jealousy of Alfred.

At the summer's end, Matilda and Alfred made their decision to adopt children to round out the Wilson family. In November, 1930, they traveled to The Cradle, a Chicago orphanage, to pick up a dark-eyed, fair-skinnned boy of 18 months. The child, Richard, was pale, scrawny and bow-legged, but staff people assured Matilda that a nutritious diet would rapidly correct such deficiencies. In three months' time, the child's health noticeably improved, and the Wilsons returned to Chicago for another child. This time, the parents took Frances with them, to foster a personal interest on Frances' part in the second adoptee—a blue-eyed, three-month-old girl. The Wilsons named her Barbara. In her brisk, efficient way, Matilda endowed both children with the same birthday—May 15.

The adopted children were ensconced in a second-floor nursery suite, complete with its own kitchen and a luxuriously furnished room for the children's nurse. By this time, Frances left for Ward-Belmont School in Nashville, shipping her favorite riding horse to the school's stables. Along with the horse, Frances' long-time governess accompanied the John Dodge daughter to the school, although her title changed from "governess" to "companion" at Frances' insistence.

In the first year following the children's adoption, Matilda kept a busy schedule. She had served as president of the Salvation Army Women's Auxiliary in Detroit for seven years, 1922-1929. Now, after a two-year respite, she became president of that organization again because of her singular success in promoting money-raising affairs for charitable causes such as financing the auxiliary's new Children's Home. Providing for orphaned or deserted children, both at Meadow Brook Hall and in institutions, yielded the most satisfaction to Matilda in her philanthropic ventures.

The grip of the Great Depression tightened throughout the country in 1931; the Wilson Theater marquee rarely glittered with lights and the Wilsons' real estate business stagnated. Still, Matilda went regularly to her Fisher Building office to deal with matters concerning her board of directors' appointments and the Salvation Army. In June of 1931, she was elated by her appointment to chairman of the board of directors of the Fidelity Bank and Trust Company, for which she previously served as a board member.

First U.S. woman to head the directors of a major bank, newspapers announced in front page stories in Detroit and in business sections of newspapers in other cities. Fidelity board members com- plimented Matilda in interviews with reporters, lauding her as "the best informed woman in high finance in the country."

This was heady stuff for a woman whose goal, in the business world where she craved status, was to become a successful woman-executive prototype for other women to emulate. Flattered when reporters sought appointments to ask her opinions on finance, Matilda responded by stressing her intense feelings of responsibility to the bank's stockholders and depositors. "...I hate waste of all kinds," she was quoted, adding that she felt she had no right "by unwise judgment" to waste other people's money.

The year, which began so auspiciously for Matilda, lapsed into sudden decline when, later in the summer, Amelia came to Meadow Brook Hall to talk with her older sister. Facing Matilda across the highly polished desk in the "morning room," Amelia nervously broached the subject of John Cline and her decision to marry the farm manager.

"You? And John Cline?" Matilda's voice was hard; brittle as the crystals in the dazzling Waterford chandelier above her head. Amelia certainly could not expect the Wilsons to take such an arrangement seriously, Matilda protested. Cline was a farm worker. Worse—a drinking man.

So had John Dodge been a drinking man, Amelia thought. But Matilda had been able to endure the drinking for a greater advantage. She dared not mention this to Matilda, though. Instead, she tried to placate her sister. "John Cline has never allowed his drinking to interfere with his work here on the farm," Amelia said. "He's a hard working man. He's trustworthy and..."

"If you marry him," Matilda cut in coldly, "it will be an embarrassment to the family—to all the Wilsons." With an angry thrust of her head, she opened the door and walked out.

A depressed Amelia drove home to Rochester. She had already considered the possibility of alienation from her sister, knowing how great were Matilda's pride and stubbornness. She often had seen how sensitive Matilda was to reporters' questions concerning her back- ground. "My father was a merchant," Matilda always replied to questions on these matters, determined to conceal any mention of George Rausch's saloon business. When asked about her schooling beyond eighth grade, Matilda invariably said, "I was privately tutored."

Matilda's pride had not allowed her to accept Amelia's pleas that the farm manager was aware of his subservient position and that he would not attempt to intrude into the family circle in any way. Cline had observed George and Margaret Rausch, years earlier, eating their meals with the hired help—never with the family...and was prepared to do the same. But marriage to Amelia was an unforgiveable intrusion by Cline, in Matilda's view. He would have to leave the farm, Matilda had said. And Amelia already knew that she would no longer be welcome at Meadow Brook.

Nonetheless, Amelia had no intentions of changing her mind about Cline. At age 44, she already had weighed the advantages and disadvantages of living alone, continuing to skirt the margins of her sister's glamorous life, versus having Cline's companionship and putting up with his occasional drinking binges. She had decided that companionship was of primary importance at this point in her solitary life.

Cline's separation from the farm turned out to be no problem. For 20 years, he had saved his money and was not averse to retirement at this point. Amelia already had sold the home she built in Rochester, at a tidy profit, after her mother's death. Her new, smaller, Rochester home would nicely accommodate the newlyweds. Amelia also had savings, her money from her mother, and her John Dodge annuity. Though not worried about finances, she worried about her estrangement from Matilda. Still, she did not imagine how long the estrangement would last—some 30 years.

Before the end of 1931, more than $4 million in additional income taxes were levied on the John Dodge estate—reaching back to the 1925 sale of the Dodge plant. Taxes continued to be a recurring issue of dispute for Dodge attorneys to handle. The heirs to the fortune resigned themselves to steady payments of large fees to lawyers protecting their interests.

The estrangement from Amelia was a greater irritation to Matilda, but the September wedding of the Clines turned out to be a small embarrassment compared to the crushing humiliation Matilda experienced the following month. In October, the Fidelity Bank and Trust Company failed—just four months after she became chairman of the board. Stunned by the quick takeover of the bank by state authorities, Matilda was devastated at the realization of her own naivete...her own enthrallment with business-leadership prestige that had stimulated her to buy blocks of Fidelity stock as they came on the market. A total of 8737 shares, making her Fidelity's largest stockholder. She realized, now, that other directors, who knew the bank was on the verge of collapse, had outwitted her by unloading their stock while they encouraged her to purchase the unwanted and depreciating shares.

In Rochester, mutual friends of the sisters confided to Amelia that the bank-failure notoriety "nearly killed" the older sister in her concern for Fidelity depositors who eventually would recover only 25% to 30 % of their savings. To the emotionally distraught Matilda, her personal money loss of $1 million did not compare to the shattering loss of her reputation as a financial genius.

The bank failure became the catalyst that changed the focus of Matilda's life from her office in the city back to the farmlands of Meadow Brook. In Detroit, repossession officers were moving furniture and refrigerators, bought on time payments during the booming years of the late 1920s, from the homes of laid-off automobile workers. People crowded the entrances to public welfare offices. And to fit the national mood of retrenchment, Matilda closed off sections of Meadow Brook Hall, including the west-wing suites of Frances and Daniel, who were away at school. Lavish entertaining seemed inappropriate to the melancholy spirit of the nation. So, Matilda only occasionally received guests at Meadow Brook Hall for such affairs as a garden party for 500 members of the Salvation Army on the south-end patio and lawns where walkways circled among varieties of colorful roses.

The tableau of cattle grazing in meadows and varieties of vegetables flourishing in carefully cultivated rows was as appealing to Matilda as the sight of the 1200 blooming rose bushes; more appealing, because of the basic practicality of her nature. In these years of economic depression, the perimeters of the farm became the perimeters of the major part of her life as she shared with Alfred the business of farm management. She took charge of the huge flocks of poultry, the dairy cattle, greenhouse, vegetables and orchards, but left the beef cattle, pigs and sheep under her husband's supervision. On horseback, they rode together across Meadow Brook acreage like English gentry surveying their properties within the shadows of the great chimneys of the Hall.

Away from the Hall, Matilda's circuit centered around her usual Salvation Army Auxiliary meetings and duties, occasional visits to her Fisher Building office, trips to Lansing for meetings of the State Agricultural Board, and visits to horse shows and sales where she added to her stable of show ponies and draft horses. The frenetic pace of her life had moderated, but she allotted little time for visits with the two adopted children tucked away in their nursery with a governess who kept the children in well scrubbed readiness for the sudden appearance of either of the Wilsons. Usually, it turned out to be Alfred Wilson who came to the nursery to spend a few minutes with the children.

With marriage to John Cline, the peripheries of Amelia's life expanded as rapidly as the boundaries of Matilda's life contracted after the Fidelity Bank failure. Immediately following their marriage, the Clines bought a Chrysler automobile in which they made numerous leisurely trips, eventually visiting every state in the country and collecting postcards and mementos at each point of interest.

Because of Cline's fondness for alcohol, Amelia kept her husband under close surveillance. With repeal of the 18th amendment in 1933, Cline was attracted to beer gardens that swiftly multiplied in towns and cities along the highways. It was not easy, however, for Cline to separate himself from Amelia's hovering presence. They soon reached a compromise of sorts. When Cline felt an overwhelming urge to stop at a bar, Amelia waited in the car while he went into the beer garden for a couple of drinks. His awareness of her presence in the car spurred him to finish his beer and to leave the bar without undue delay.

For Amelia, her husband's bar-stops were the only flaw in her marriage, but their shared fondness for travel compensated for this imperfection. Unlike Matilda, the younger sister had a distaste for housekeeping and cooking that reached back to her early life. Among her collections and clippings, recipes and cookbooks were noticeably absent. In her Rochester home, she did what she called "plain cooking" for Cline, but their travels provided her with the opportunity to enjoy "eating out" at hotels and restaurants.

Matilda possessed a thick and neatly filed collection of recipes with which she enjoyed experimenting on the cook's day off. Mostly, though, she relished carrying on the baked-beans tradition established by Margaret Rausch. Matilda cooked the beans on the wood-burning range and later washed her dishes by hand, since she did not want an automatic dishwasher. At Thanksgiving time, she insisted on preparing and baking her own large turkey for the family dinner at Meadow Brook Hall when the children returned home from their schools.

Whenever possible, Frances entered her Shetlands or Hackneys in horse shows during these school breaks. Her midget-sized, dapple-gray Shetlands—Sonny Boy and Sonny Girl—were a perfectly matched pair that won numerous ribbons as Frances drove them from an open four-wheeled carriage. She also favored a chestnut Hackney team, a championship winner in breeding classes in shows at Boston, New York, Chicago, and Toronto.

Frances frequently brought schoolmates to Meadow Brook when she came home for short visits. These private-school girls, daughters of wealthy families, were awed nonetheless by the magnificence of Meadow Brook Hall, the wide choice of riding horses, and the matter-of-fact manner in which Frances arranged a 40-guest dinner-dance at the Grosse Pointe Country Club as if she were simply taking them to the movies.

In June of 1933, Frances graduated from Mt. Vernon Seminary and returned home to a rush of plans for the summer horse show circuit, and longer-range plans for her "coming out" parties as a debutante in the fall. By the end of June, she swept the state horse show in Michigan by winning six first places, three seconds, and two third places. Her so-called "wonder horse," Rosalie Bonheur, was the star of the show. In mid-September, she still traveled the horse circuit, shipping her horses and their grooms and trainers on to Massachusetts for the Brockton show, then on to Springfield, regretful that she was then expected to return to Meadow Brook where her mother worked at arrangements for her debut.

Frances became the first Detroit-area debutante of the season when Matilda and Alfred formally presented her to society at a party given at Meadow Brook Hall on October 21. Music from the pipe organ and a harp floated through the mansion as guests arrived. Frances, in a silver-gray velvet dress with huge slit sleeves, greeted her guests in the drawing room. As she stretched her hand toward each guest, her long fingernails, boldly painted silver, helped establish the Dodge debutante's reputation as an innovator of new fashions.

Soon after the stuffy reception ceremonials ended, Frances and ten of the young women guests escaped the formalities to board the Tallyho—Frances' elegant horse-drawn coach with high seats. As Frances sat up front with the driver, the other girls tucked their expensive mid-calf dresses around their legs as they crowded onto the seats and were driven down the 3/4-mile driveway and back again. The noisy laughter of the debutantes did not disturb the sheep grazing on the slope of a nearby hill, but captive deer, peering through a fence near the entrance, bolted back among the trees.

Although most debutantes swung into a round of parties following the official announcement of their debuts, Frances was not as interested in parties as in horses. She left for Chicago the morning after the Meadow Brook party, accompanied by her mother. There, Frances showed her Hackneys at the World's Fair horse show before moving on to New York.

Frances returned to Detroit in mid-December with her junior five-gaited saddle horse, Anita Rose. With her three-gaited horse, Pendennis. With her harness horses and Hackney ponies and a stack of blue ribbons. On her return, she frantically wrapped Christmas gifts, in the personal tradition established by Matilda, for friends, for her horse-trainers, and secretary and maids, and for her family, including the young adopted sister and brother who rarely saw Frances.

The Dodge debutante's moody behavior intimidated the children when they came down to the drawing room on Christmas Day to join the family for traditional festivities and an exchange of gifts. But both Richard and Barbara enjoyed being with 16-year-old Daniel Dodge, who wore large glasses that overshadowed his thin and pale face and gave him a scholarly look. Daniel was not scholarly, though, any more than was Frances. Unlike his older sister, Daniel liked the company of the young Wilson children and the children returned his affection.

Two days later, the Wilsons staged a spectacular party for their daughter at the Book Cadillac Hotel. Although Frances specified that her parties were not to be stuffy and boring affairs, Matilda hired Sara Burnham to manage the December party for 700 guests. Still, the black and silver ice-palace motif carried the distinctive imprint of Frances Dodge's unconventional ideas. The "Bal Moderne" theme was revealed in silver canopies and silver-draped ceilings from which hung black and silver panels. In silver-bordered black tablecloths and tall standards twined with black eucalyptus leaves. In black and silver vases, an ice-carved horse, and a silver colt placed at the center of the main dining table.

Frances' silver lame' dress hung, tube-like, straight to her knees, then flared into tiers and a small train. She wore a black feathered tiera perched on her blond hair, adding height to her thin, bony frame. If she held a jeweled cigarette holder, she would have resembled movie vamp, Theda Bara. But since Frances, a couple of inches taller than Matilda, did not yet smoke or drink in the presence of her disapproving mother, she carried, instead, a single orchid—dyed black.

Away from her mother's presence, Frances observed no such restraints. Aware that her daughter both smoked and drank, but helpless to do much about it, Matilda concentrated on firmly curbing any inclination on Alfred's part to drink more than was proper according to the decree of his wife who accepted only a glass of sherry at a gala dinner or party. Even in the privacy of Alfred's study, where he drank from a well stocked bar concealed behind a wall panel, he had the sense of being watched by those pentrating dark eyes of the mistress of Meadow Brook.

On the night of Frances' "Ball Moderne," Matilda and Alfred greeted groups of media people arriving at the Book Cadillac, their jaded curiosity piqued by the expectation that the esoteric aura of the $25,000 affair would not conform with the propriety of most "coming out" parties supervised by the classicist, Sara Burnham. A superabundance of money, it seemed, could purchase the allegiance of even the most conservative social mentor by a sulky debutante with a peculiar fascination for the color black. And if Sara Burnham could defer to Frances' eccentric fancies, so, too, could the fastidious Matilda—short, plump, and less than seductive in a black, beaded gown.

The ice-palace ball was only one newsworthy display in the high-roller style of life that Frances launched at the time of her debut. As the new year, 1934, began, Matilda completely closed Meadow Brook Hall and moved the two small Wilson children and their governess, with a small staff, into the farmhouse. Then Matilda and Alfred left, with Frances, for a Mediterranean cruise as the first part of a six-months' world tour, all expenses paid by Frances. Traveling on to Morocco and North Africa, they went next to India and then to big-game country in South Africa before sailing for England for a two months' tour of polo tournaments and horse shows and races.

Their return, in July, sparked a series of newspaper items that disturbed Matilda much more than they bothered Frances. The Wilsons took their daughter around the world to snare an Arabian sheik for her, the gossip columns reported. The Dodge heiress returned with an entourage of exotic animals and a selection of English-bred dogs complete with an English kennelmaid.

Photos of Frances accompanied the articles, her hair cut short and curled close to her head. Her eyebrows thinned and finely pencilled into elongated lines above heavy-lidded eyes. Her wide mouth escaping sulkiness only when she smiled, which was not often.

Although Arabian horses and donkeys roamed about the farm at Meadow Brook, courtesy of Frances' extended shopping trips, a few tiger-skin rugs were the only "exotic" items in her collection. The two white Pekinese dogs that she purchased in England, along with several other dogs and blooded horses, were a rare variety of animal—the only Pekinese of their kind in the United States.

On her return to Meadow Brook, Frances hatched a plan for spending more of her annual income, which now amounted to an approximate $400,000, from the Dodge trust fund. She decided to build a 200-foot-long stable to house her most valuable horses and their silver-encrusted saddles. She also ordered her elaborate mini-sized cottage, Hilltop Lodge, moved westward from its site near the original farmhouse past Meadow Brook Hall to a wooded location near a bridle path. The lodge was moved and renamed Knole House as more fitting to its English architectural features. Frances then began to use Knole House as a retreat for some of her smaller parties while, at the former site of the playhouse, construction began on an elaborate Tudor-styled kennel, ordered by Frances to lodge her precious Pekinese, with adjoining living quarters for the kennelmaid.

Kennel construction continued when Frances left in September for the Marian Coates Graves School in New York to study interior decorating—a skill she would use, she said, in beautifying the interior of the handsome kennel.

Society publicists, enamored of the maverick heiress, wrote tirelessly of Frances' kennels and of the English "canine-nurse" who bred, reared, fed, groomed, and trained the dogs. Of the Hollywood stars who vied to purchase offspring of the Dodge Pekinese pair. Of Frances' weekend trips away from school when she entered her two-pound Pekinese dogs in various shows. Of rail shipments from the town of Rochester of two dozen of Frances' horses, with one dozen attendants, in four express cars to horse shows. Of the costly saddles, the maroon and gray Dodge stable colors, the attractive costumes worn by Frances—gray carucal jacket and maroon skirt and perky maroon hat—as she drove her Hackneys from a carriage lined in mulberry.

"Maintenance, education, and clothing expenditures" for Frances Dodge amounted to a quarter-million dollars in 1935, a Detroit Times article reported. Some of this money paid for operating expenses at Meadow Brook Hall, since Frances chose to keep the Hall open after Matilda decided to close it. Frances' decision was not opposed by her mother, even though the high operating expenses for the Hall were an embarrassment to Matilda when the country's ecomonic depression continued.

The sight of Frances in the show ring, an image of poise and self-confidence as she sat tall in her saddle in perfect control of her high-stepping horse, stirred Matilda to pride and pleasure. If spending money made Frances happy, Matilda cheerfully supported such expenditures. Happiness certainly was preferable to sullenness.

While the country languished in the clutch of the early-thirties' depression, Lucille Manzer attended Detroit's Northwestern High School—one of the largest schools in the city. Boarding schools, to Lucille, were dream-like institutions referred to only in teen novels such as the "Ruth Fielding" series that she borrowed from the public library.

The Manzers, who encouraged their daughter to limit her close friendships to the young Methodist members of the Epworth League, unwillingly surrendered their hope that Lucille would become a church organist when the teenager resisted renewing her piano lessons. Per- haps art, rather than music, was Lucille's forte, the Manzers speculated when their daughter became absorbed in art classes at school.

Although Lucille's friendly personality made it unnecessary for her to work at popularity, she found it difficult to separate herself from her circle of school friends when they wanted to play cards or attend Sunday afternoon movies which were forbidden for Lucille. When some of her closest friends decided to skip classes one day and to meet at the corner drugstore, Lucille went along with the plan.

Sitting at the drugstore counter, chatting with her friends and sipping a soda, she heard a male voice call her name. She raised her head to see Robert Manzer standing in the doorway, beckoning for her to come outside. Her cheeks burned as she left the store, walked at her father's side to the corner, and began to cross Grand River Avenue, heading toward home. When he asked why she was in the drugstore, she admitted she had skipped school. "Then you had better write a letter of explanation to your teacher," he said quietly.

At home, Lucille went into her room and carefully worded a letter of apology to her teacher, confessing her truancy. She took the letter to her father who read it as she nervously watched. "I'm proud of you, Lucille," he said gently. "It's always best to tell the truth."

Lucille felt a warm glow of love and pride at his words—the kind of glow that never was inspired by the austere Minnie Manzer. Nonetheless, the teenager was roused to outrage on behalf of her mother when, one early spring morning, she overheard Grandpa Fish venting his explosive temper on his daughter, Minnie. Complaining loudly, he swore at his daughter because his breakfast-oatmeal was not hot enough by the time he sat at the kitchen table.

When Robert Manzer returned home from fishing later that day, Lucille greeted him with a report of Grandpa Fish's angry outburst—of the way he cursed his daughter because his oatmeal was cold.

Before suppertime, Manzer collected his father-in-law's belongings and suitcase and set them out on the front porch. Grandpa Fish departed without his evening meal, vowing never to return.   Lucille was sure, however, that he would return by November or December. He always had, in previous years. In the meantime, it was much more peaceful at the Manzer home without the presence of the irritable grandfather.

Lucille's senior class was scheduled to graduate from Northwestern High School in June, 1933. Her brother, Rob, was now a handsome eight-year-old boy, and, despite the difference in their ages, the brother and sister were very close and affectionate.

Without waiting for high school graduation, Lucille went to work for $12.50 a week as a receptionist in the office of a dentist who was a Methodist friend of Robert Manzer. Jobs were scarce in the early 1930s, and Lucille was happy to get office work so she could buy her own clothes and have her own spending money.

The J.L. Hudson department store attracted Lucille and her friend Virginia to its stylish misses' clothing displays in downtown Detroit in their after-work hours. In November, 1933, as the two friends strolled among the garment racks in Hudson's coat department,Lucille slipped a leopard skin coat from its hanger and admired her reflection in a full-length mirror as she buttoned and unbuttoned, belted and unbelted, the handsome coat. Virginia whirled about in a gray kidskin garment that she coveted as much as Lucille wanted the leopard skin.

When she learned, on Monday, that Virginia was going to buy the kidskin coat, Lucille phoned her father from the dentist's office and asked if he would buy the leopard skin coat for her, promising she would pay him two dollars a week until he was paid back. "Today?" Lucille begged, when it seemed her father did not object to lending her the money. "Before someone else buys it?"

At her father's suggestion, they met for lunch at Hudson's. After lunch, Lucille modeled the coat for her dad and observed the soft, admiring look on his face as she tightened the belt around her slim waist and flipped her smooth hair over the collar. "Well?" she asked, then kissed his cheek as he nodded his head, agreeing to buy the coat.

Although the tiny Virginia was a few inches shorter than the five-foot, six-inch Lucille, the two girls traded coats for a week that winter. But Lucille quickly tired of the novelty of wearing the gray kidskin which was tight across the shoulders and short in the sleeves. She happily retrieved the leopard skin, making three two-dollar payments to her dad—after which the remainder was forgotten.

By springtime, Lucille began dating a young college student who worked in a bakery to earn money for school expenses. As the two dated more frequently, Robert and Minnie Manzer objected to their daughter continuing her relationship with the young man, who was not a Methodist.

In the Manzer household, confrontations among family members never occurred. This time was no exception. Lucille simply stopped dating the young man to whom her parents objected, and her life resumed its usual family-oriented, church-centered pace.

Even when many banks failed in the early 1930s, the Manzers were not impoverished. Robert Manzer had stashed a considerable amount of cash in a hollow place at the back of a closet behind the doorjamb where he also kept the documents that Lucille had never seen.

For Detroiters, generally, the Great Depression of the early thirties was a disaster because the economy of the city swelled or ebbed in direct proportion to the numbers of cars spewing or trickling, depending on financial tides, from assembly-tributaries of the city's automobile plants. No Detroit suburb was more thoroughly drained by the fiscal drought than Hamtramck, as production at Chrysler Corporation's Dodge Main plant sank to a low point of only 28,111 cars in all of 1932.

Soup kitchens proliferated. City employees collected payments in scrip. The government distributed white margarine with packets of yellow food coloring, flour, rice, and canned milk to hungry families. Although these were the stigmata of the times, Hamtramck people prayed that with the inauguration of a new president, Franklin Delano Roosevelt, the great chimneys of Dodge Main once again would belch clouds of dark smoke over the city.

Despite the economic stagnation, Hamtramck's Joseph Campau Avenue and its collection of ethnic shops—bakeries with trays of pierogi and nalesniki in the windows, and meat markets with fat loops of kielbasa hanging from the ceilings—attracted many visitors from nearby Detroit neighborhoods. Young Mabel Burgett, who lived with her husband, Andrew, in the home of her mother-in-law in one such neighborhood, often walked to Hamtramck to shop or window-shop on Joseph Campau.

Mabel's mother-in-law, Ida, accompanied her one cold winter day in 1931 as the younger woman, expecting her first child in June, stopped at a Joseph Campau news stand to stare at a front page Detroit Free Press photograph and story of newborn Siamese twins. Since many people believed that a baby in the womb could be unfavorably affected by the pregnant woman's viewing of such photos, Ida Burgett quickly steered the young woman away from the news stand.

"Siamese twins—what does that mean?" 17-year-old Mabel asked her mother-in-law.

"It means twins who are joined in some way," Ida Burgett explained.

Mabel shivered, thinking of her own pregnancy and hoping that she carried a normal child. "Can't Siamese twins be separated?" she asked.

"Not if their vital organs are connected," Ida said.

As the two women walked home, Mabel pulled the collar of her heavy, black coat tighter around her neck against the force of a brisk wind. "I hope I don't have Siamese twins," she said.

"It's very uncommon," Ida assured her. "You shouldn't worry about it." Ida was silent, then, as they trudged along. "But I did hear of one pair of Siamese twins who were separated," she finally said.

When Mabel barraged her mother-in-law with questions, Ida protested that she had promised her husband not to repeat the story. "Promise not to mention this to anyone," she warned, then told of the time that Silas Burgett had gone with John Dodge to a saloon after work, and said he'd been told by Dodge that his wife had given birth to Siamese twins. Both girls. Silas also claimed to have been told by his employer that the baby girls had been separated and that the Dodges kept one of the babies.

"But what happened to the other child?" Mabel asked.

Ida Burgett could not answer that. Perhaps it had died, or perhaps it had been given away. Her husband did not know and had not asked. But despite Silas Burgett's impression that his employer spoke to no other Dodge Main employee about the twin birth, the mother-in-law confided to the younger woman, her husband had come home from work with still another story. Rumors were circulating in the shop, Silas had told her...rumors that "John Dodge's wife gave birth to a litter."

The mother-in-law's disclosure made an unforgettable impression on the pregnant Mabel Burgett because of her own desire to bear a healthy baby. Was the discarded Dodge twin still living, she won- dered. If so, would the twin ever discover her heritage?

The Dodge brothers (John at left, Horace at right). Courtesy of Amelia (Rausch) Cline Collection.

Early photo of Matilda Dodge. Courtesy of
Amelia (Rausch) Cline Collection.

Early photo of Amelia Rausch. Courtesy of
George McCall Collection.

1936 photo of Matilda and Alfred Wilson at the
front entrance of Meadow Brook Hall.
Courtesy of Meadow Brook Hall Archives.

John F. Dodge's East Boston Boulevard home.
Photo by: Manning Brothers.

John Dodge's Farmhouse and Club House at
Meadow Brook near Rochester, Michigan.
Courtesy of George McCall Collection.

The unfinished John F. Dodge mansion in
Grosse Pointe (1920). House was demolished
in the 1940s. Photo by: Manning Brothers.

Aerial view of Meadow Brook Hall. Courtesy
of Meadow Brook Hall.

1903 Model A—First car produced by Ford
Motor Co. (This is the Tonneau version due to
the bolt-on rear compartment). The Dodge
brothers manufactured the complete car, except
for wheels and body. Courtesy of George
McCall Collection.

With the Dodge brothers and Henry Ford,
Alexander Malcomson—seated at center in his
coal stove office—sought financial help from his
uncle, banker John S. Gray, seated at left near
the stove. Malcomson's bookkeeper, James
Couzens, stands at right. Courtesy of George
McCall Collection.

The first auto produced at Dodge Main, 1914. Photographed in front of the John F. Dodge estate on East Boston Boulevard in Detroit (Horace Dodge, left rear and John Dodge, right rear). Courtesy of Chrysler Historical Collection.

John Dodge's last car (1919 Dodge Sedan) parked at Meadow Brook Hall (on right) during a Dodge Brothers Club Meet in 1987. This car had a tilt-steering wheel to accommodate Dodge's bulk. Car at left is Hedger's 1920 Dodge touring car manufactured in Windsor, Canada. Courtesy of D.L. Hedger of Dodge Brothers Club.

1908 photo of John Dodge with (left to right)
Matilda, John Duval, Isabel and Winifred on a
west coast vacation.   Courtesy of Meadow
Brook Hall Archives.

John Dodge at the Farmhouse at
Meadow Brook near Rochester, Michigan.
Courtesy of Meadow Brook Hall Archives.

Baby picture of Frances Lucille Manzer (Mealbach). Courtesy of Frances Lucille Mealbach.

Little heiress, Frances Matilda Dodge. Courtesy of George McCall Collection.

Photo of Frances (Dodge) Van Lennep and her husband, Frederick L. Van Lennep. Courtesy of Mr. & Mrs. Henry Johnson.

1985 photo of Frances L. (Manzer) Mealbach. Photo by: P. Charles Rossi.

Photo of Frances Lucille Manzer (Mealbach)
with mystery baby on right (Twin?
Half-sister?).

Francis Matilda Dodge on her 2nd birthday, November 27, 1916. Courtesy of Meadow Brook Hall Archives.

A young Frances Dodge. Photo by: John Henderson Studios, © 1948. Courtesy of Richard Wilson.

At wedding of Frances Dodge and Jimmy
Johnson, Henry Ford (in light suit) shakes
hands with Johnson. Daniel Dodge (wearing
glasses) stands next to Ford. Matilda is at far
right with the Wilson children, Richard and
Barbara. Courtesy of George McCall
Collection.

Photo of (left to right): Amelia Rausch (Cline),
Mrs. George (Margaret) Rausch, Doris
Haynes and the widowed Matilda Dodge at the
Riviera in France (1923). Courtesy of Amelia
(Rausch) Cline Collection.

1964 photo of (left to right) Matilda (Dodge)
Wilson, and Frances (Dodge) Van Lennep,
Barbara Wilson and Richard Wilson. Courtesy
of Richard Wilson.

Frances Dodge in a familiar pose at the horse
stables.   Photo by: Freudy Photos, Inc.
Courtesy of Richard Wilson.

1922 photo of Matilda Dodge and her children: Daniel, Frances and Anna Margaret. Courtesy of Amelia (Rausch) Cline Collection.

John Dodge and baby Frances. Courtesy of Amelia (Rausch) Cline Collection.

Aerial view of Dodge Main.　　Courtesy of
Chrysler Historical Collection.

Production at Dodge Main, circa 1915.
Courtesy of Chrysler Historical Collection.

Chapter 13

Romances of the Unwelcomed Kind

In the spring of 1936, Frances and the Wilsons boarded the S.S. Manhattan and sailed, again, for England. "Franny" Dodge's costume, the long-stemmed roses she carried, her plans to buy more horses—all were a part of the steady stream of printed drivel pumped into newspapers about the lives of the super-rich.

"Franny" was not the only member of the flamboyant Dodge clan to attract the scrutiny of the press in the 1930s. Although Matilda deliberately shrank from the observations of reporters in these years, society and sports pages ran frequent accounts of Isabel Dodge Sloane and her Brookmeade Stables in Virginia. Ever since Isabel's divorce in 1929, Matilda expected to hear or read of a second marriage for this attractive and wealthy stepdaughter. It did not happen. Instead, Matilda read of new thoroughbreds Isabel added to her stables, amounting to a total 140 horses in 1934.

At the close of that year, Brookmeade thoroughbreds had won a series of races and purses adding up to more than a quarter-million dollars. Isabel's three-year-old colt, Cavalcade, starred by winning the Kentucky Derby, and her High Quest won the Preakness.

John Duval's problems edged back into the news in the early thirties when his wife filed for divorce, claiming desertion. A property settlement of $325,000 to his wife and a trust fund of $108,000 for his young daughter exhausted John Duval's finances, but not his attraction to marriage. He remarried immediately, then plunged into still another business—the manufacture of oil burners.

The concessions of Winifred and Isabel in financing their younger brother's ventures helped sustain John Duval's unfading optimism. Still Winifred, who had four daughters, and the childless Isabel continued their close, sisterly intimacy that did not include John Duval. The sisters gave fashionable parties in their winter homes at Palm Beach, they visited back and forth at Isabel's home in Virginia and Winifred's East Coast and Grosse Pointe homes, and they retained close ties with their friends of teenage days—Josephine and Eleanor Clay, now Mrs. Ernest Kanzler and Mrs. Edsel Ford.

One year after Winifred and Wesson Seyburn built their handsome lakeshore home in Grosse Pointe, Eleanor and Edsel Ford followed the Seyburns from Indian Village to Grosse Pointe where the Fords built their own $3 million Cotswolds-styled lakeshore home on 87 acres of property.

Henry Ford, frequently quoted on his expressions of contempt for Grosse Pointe's "Four Hundred Set," regarded Edsel's move into this bastion of country-club society as a personal affront. Although Edsel may have thought that, by moving to Grosse Pointe, he further distanced his home life and that of his family from his father, Henry Ford employed enough spies and undercover men to keep close surveillance of Edsel, inside and outside the plant. Both Henry and Clara Ford blamed the evil influence of Edsel's Grosse Pointe friends when the parents learned that their son served cocktails at social gatherings in his home.

Henry Ford also resented his son and daughter-in-law's interest in art collecting, as dedicated patrons of the Detroit Institute of Art. The senior Ford was riled by rave notices of Edsel's purchase of paintings by Cezanne, Matisse, and Diego Rivera for his home. He was irritated by reports that Matilda Dodge Wilson decorated her home with Dutch masterpieces. . .that Anna Dodge Dillman commissioned Lord Duveen, well-known art connoisseur, to travel the world with her and her second husband to advise them in their selection of objets d'art for the new mansion they were building in Grosse Pointe.

At Ford's Fair Lane, only a few family portraits relieved the bare expanse of walls. Lord Duveen, whose services were reputedly in demand by people of great wealth, came uninvited to Fair Lane to try to entice Henry Ford to purchase the works of master artists for his large home. Although the sight of Fair Lane's unadorned walls tantalized Duveen with visions of the commissions he could pocket by selling a houseful of paintings to the billionaire industrialist, Ford speedily dispatched the art connoisseur. Ford boasted that he had no intention of hanging works of foreigners on his walls. Eventually, because Clara decided she wanted paintings to decorate her home, Ford permitted the purchase of several soft-toned English landscapes—but not from Duveen.

Lord Duveen, however, collected generous commissions from the Horace Dodge widow for an assortment of treasures selected as they traveled the world. Ming vases. Boushetti tapestries. Exquisite porcelains and jardenieres. Candelabra from the palace at Versailles. Wall sconces once owned by Marie Antoinette. A piano from the castle of King George III. And a collection of sculptures, paintings, and bric-a-brac, bought in Europe and the Far East, to grace the interior of Anna's new French chateau.

Several years before the construction of the chateau commenced, Anna purchased additional lakeshore property, adjoining Rose Terrace on the east, where the Grosse Pointe Country Club was located. Anna paid $625,000 for ownership of the vacated country club in which she and Horace once were denied membership by "old-family" Grosse Pointers who prided themselves on their exclusivity.

Workmen dug foundations for Anna's new chateau, which would retain the name Rose Terrace while the original house was razed, on the former country club property. When the Dillmans held a formal party and reception in the new Rose Terrace in January, 1936, reporters described the magnificent chateau as "a miniature Versailles." But the term "miniature" seemed inappropriate to the vastness and museum-like quality of elegant Rose Terrace.

On the evening of the Rose Terrace party, Anna's daughter, Delphine, stood in the reception line with her third husband. Her first husband, Cromwell, had recently married Doris Duke, known as the "richest girl in the world." And by this time, Delphine's brother, Horace Junior, already had been divorced twice and now pursued a blond showgirl—whenever he was not pursuing another trophy by racing one or more of the expensive powerboats in his personal fleet.

The publicity surrounding the opening of Anna's chateau over-shadowed Meadow Brook in the mid-thirties. Matilda, whose wariness of publicity intensified following the Fidelity Bank and Trust collapse, did not resent the focus of the press on the Dodge-Dillman family. But Matilda took every opportunity to contrast the formality of Rose Terrace with the "lived-in" atmosphere of Meadow Brook by pointing out that the architectural design of Meadow Brook Hall was "Tudor inspiration modified to fit present day living." The Hall was, she said proudly, "faithful" in every detail to traditional Tudor homes in England, but "all the materials, save that of one room, and all of the work performed by artisans and sculptors are native to America."

The "one room" exception was Alfred Wilson's study, for which he imported logs of burled wood from England. In this room, a series of wall panels with wood carvings protrayed events in Alfred's life, including his Beloit College days and his marriage to Matilda.

Matilda openly disparaged the trendy zeal of affluent Americans for bulk importation of entire sections of European buildings. But her criticism did not directly include mention of Anna Dodge's importation of an antique inn and its contents from the French countryside to Grosse Pointe where the inn became a barroom in Rose Terrace.

The quaintness of the barroom charmed visitors to Rose Terrace, but Anna kept the contents of the room locked away from Horace Junior's explorations when he was in Grosse Pointe. She also assigned Frank Upton to surveillance of her capricious son, who had a weakness for women and alcohol.

At the time the Dodge automobile company was sold, Upton continued working as an officer for Dodge Estates Corporation, and also became Anna's personal employee and financial advisor. Horace Junior already had a bodyguard assigned by his mother, but Anna also wanted the services of Frank Upton as a trouble-shooter for her son. Upton, trusted with the secrets of both sides of the Dodge family for many years, now found that he was subject to Anna's summons at any hour of the day or night—whenever and wherever Horace Junior acquired problems.

Because many of Horace Junior's escapades were graphically detailed in newspapers along with reports of a quarter-million-dollar settlement by Anna of an alienation-of-affections suit filed by the cast-off wife of Delphine's latest husband, Matilda separated herself even more rigidly from "the other side" of the Dodge family. When the sister-in-law, Della Dodge Eschbach, died in Santa Monica, California, in 1936, no communications regarding the death passed between Matilda and Anna. Matilda did not know that Della's body was cremated, and did not know that Della's long-time companion, Helen Bovee, returned the ashes to Anna who promptly hired Bovee as a secretary. The woman's secretarial duties, however, became secondary to her spiraling powers as spiritual advisor to Anna in the study of reincarnation.

For Matilda, life ran smoothly now as the country began its recovery from the economic depression. By 1937, she abandoned all attempts to live more frugally in the farmhouse, and once again made use of the entire capacity of Meadow Brook Hall. Throughout the thirties, the Wilsons made purchases of additional farmlands, to a total tenure of 2600 acres at the end of the decade.

"Franny" Dodge's comings and goings in 1936 and 1937 continued providing palatable ingredients that were whipped into spun-sugar newspaper stories for the consumption of readers bored by the tedium of their own lives and tired of reading about conflicts between the UAW and Henry Ford. They read, instead, of the Dodge heiress' so-called "thousand-dollar-a-day" expenditures for journeys to dog shows with her fluffy white Pekinese in their wicker travel-baskets and with her uniformed kennelmaid; for journeys to exhibitions with her prancing showhorses, grooms, landaus, and her velvet-draped "tack" room; for her furs, jeweled cigarette holders and diamond-studded cigarette cases.

Frances' stint at the New York school for interior decorating ended in less than one year, but Madison Square Garden horse and dog shows still drew her to the East Coast metropolis. Her Pekinese dogs now numbered 18, and two of them won blue ribbons at the Westminster Dog Show in New York in February, 1937. But Frances thought her prized dogs should have won more honors. And although she had recently purchased a $20,000 showhorse, King of the Plains, to add to more than 80 already in her stables, Frances decided not to enter her horses in the National Horse Show later that year, but to concentrate on putting together a new and more select Dodge Stables for a debut in 1938.

When "Miss Frances" was in residence at Meadow Brook Hall during the late thirties, the duties of the guard at the mansion's gate- house entrance became more demanding. A stream of flashy roadsters, crammed with young people, periodically sped up Adams Road, squealing to a stop at the gatehouse for a check by the Meadow Brook guard and admisson to "Franny's" popular pool-parties at the handsome poolhouse the young heiress recently built. To simplify the guard's job of identification, Frances issued guest cards for use by the young people invited to her regular "Sunday Nights" at the poolhouse or in Meadow Brook's ballroom or in the "trophy" rooms above Frances' indoor riding ring.

Frances' parties held no more appeal for her brother, Daniel, than did her showdogs and horses. During Daniel's schooldays at Choate, one of the essays he wrote complained of his dislike of the "two-penny tricks that dogs are taught." At age 16, Daniel had been accused of setting out poisoned meat and causing the death of a valuable English setter, a championship dog owned by an Adams Road neighbor who sued for $10,000 in damages. When Daniel confessed to his mother that he set out chunks of meat to poison "wild dogs" that roamed the area, Matilda settled the neighbor's claim out of court. She excused her 16-year-old son's behavior as part of his restless search for the kind of excitement that he had not previously experienced in his sheltered life.

Daniel was not fond of Ming, the fist-sized, fluffy-furred Pekinese that his mother adopted as a house pet from Frances' kennels, but he enjoyed rough-housing with the friendly St. Bernard lodged in an oversized doghouse near the rear entrance to Meadow Brook Hall.

Daniel's small adopted sister, Barbara, liked to put Ming into her doll carriage and to wheel the button-nosed Pekinese about on the patio, while Richard, like Daniel, preferred to wrestle with the patient St. Bernard. The adopted children's governess hovered nearby, watching the youngsters as they played.

Although the Wilson children lived lives of splendid isolation from their peers, they amused themselves not only with dogs, but with two other family pets that Matilda loved. The pets included two African tortoises, one of which came to an untimely death in the jaws of a tractor-lawnmower. The other, bathed regularly in a foot-bath in Matilda's spacious bathroom—replete with marble and draped with a lavender and sea-green decor, suffered a couple of misadventures. The first, when the silent tortoise narrowly avoided becoming turtle soup by hissing when the foot-bath water was too hot. The second, when it grew to a weight of nearly 50 unwieldly pounds and was finally given to the Detroit Zoo.

Matilda gave orders that both adopted children must be taught to ride Shetland ponies. The blond Barbara was only two years old when her governess placed the child on the broad back of Little Babs, her special pony. Outdoors or indoors, the young children were immaculately dressed, often in English wools, Scotch plaids, and imported angora sweaters. Since they could not go outside without their governess, they stayed indoors much of the time, confined to their own suite. Except for breakfast, when their governess brought the two children downstairs to the breakfast room, meals for three were served in the nursery suite where the governess coached her charges in dining etiquette.

When Daniel Dodge finished his studies at Choate preparatory school, he divided his time between his Model Development Company in Detroit, where he experimented with engines including a diesel mechanism, and his Canadian hunting lodge on thickly wooded Manitoulin Island in northern Ontario. To Daniel, who bought the six-bedroom, rustic lodge, built of logs, in 1935, his summers spent on the remote island were wonderful, free-spirited times when he enjoyed the natural splendor of quiet forests and sunrises over the cold, often treacherous, waters of Lake Huron and Georgian Bay.

Matilda did not object to Daniel's absences when he stayed at the lodge because she knew that he felt restless at Meadow Brook. She was relieved, however, when Heath Ballagh, a long-time family employee who was companionable with Daniel, accompanied the boy on his hunting and fishing expeditions. When Ballagh did not go with Daniel, Matilda relied on the lodge caretaker, Dick Drolet, to watch over her son.

At age 18, Daniel disliked the constant surveillance of Drolet. To get away by himself, he often drove his car over 20 miles of narrow, twisting road into the nearest town, Gore Bay. In search of a place to stay overnight in the small town, Daniel was directed to a 1 1/2 story frame house badly in need of a scraping and paint job—the home of tugboat captain John MacDonald. Everyone in Gore Bay had heard of the wealthy Dodge heir and his Kagawong Lodge. And when the young millionaire came, in early evening, to the MacDonald home for a night's lodging, the tugboat captain recognized the youth and tried to hide his surprise at Dodge's request. The captain's wife was both surprised at Dan Dodge's arrival and nervously concerned about the plain and shabby appearance of her home.

Mrs. MacDonald's nervousness gradually faded when young Dodge returned to the house frequently in the months that followed, saying that he appreciated her home-cooked meals. She soon discovered that his basic shyness matched her own diffidence. She learned, too, that home-cooked meals were not the prevailing reason for Dodge's visits. Daniel was obviously attracted to the MacDonald's 16-year-old daughter, the auburn-haired, blue-eyed Annie Laurine.

The two were often seen together in the year that followed. The girl intrigued Daniel with her quick smile, her slim but sturdy figure, and her love for outdoor life. He warmed to her friendly personality and to what he saw as her sensitivity to other people. Laurine liked to swim in the sparkling waters of Georgian Bay as much as Daniel relished racing across the bay waters in his motorboat. And in 17 years of Gore Bay's long, snowy winters, Laurine had become an expert skier whose skills Daniel could not match, although he patiently followed her cross-country on skiis. At intervals, when she waited as he hurried to catch up with her, he loved the sight of her rosy cheeks and her long eyelashes fringed with snowflakes.

In his distaste for his sister's parties, Daniel had never learned to dance. Because rhythm was as natural to Laurine as was engine-repair to Daniel, he escorted her without complaint to local dances where he quietly watched her whirl about the dance floor with other partners.

The senior MacDonalds were undecided what their reactions should be to the couple's increasing preoccupation with each other. Did youthful heirs to multi-million-dollar fortunes actually marry 17-year -old Cinderellas, they wondered. Would the wealthy Mrs. Wilson permit her young son to marry a $17-a-week telephone operator from an isolated small-town background? Was Laurine letting herself in for hurt and disappointment? And if marriage did take place, would Daniel Dodge follow the pattern of the Dodges and later file for divorce from his unsophisticated bride?

In the autumn of 1937, a large diamond glittered on the fourth finger, left hand of Laurine MacDonald as she adjusted her headset in the Gore Bay telephone office. The hardy and laconic residents of Gore Bay expressed little surprise at either the valuable ring or the sight of Laurine dashing about the island at the wheel of Dodge's powerful Graham-Paige convertible. She had been known to Gore Bay people as "Dan Dodge's girl" for some time, now. To the islanders, Dan Dodge was a "regular guy"—a view reinforced by Laurine's insistence that Daniel enjoyed the simple life away from the formal atmosphere of Meadow Brook Hall and its staff of servants; that he hated life in the fast lane and the demands placed on young men sucked into the role of escorts to pampered girls on the debutante-party circuit.

Rumors of Daniel Dodge's liaison with a young telephone operator circulated in Detroit, to the astonishment of Frances Dodge's friends who regarded Daniel as decidely immature. When Daniel attempted to speak of Laurine to his mother, Matilda brushed away his timid explanations as if he were speaking of a schoolboy crush too fanciful for serious consideration.

Her young son would have lots of time, later, to think seriously of marriage, she told him. He would meet lovely girls from good families, educated in the best finishing schools. After all, she reminded him, he and his future wife would inherit Meadow Brook Hall some- day, and would be expected to carry on family traditions.

Daniel sulked at the firm response, but Matilda ignored the sulking. Her own perception of her son's immaturity blinded her to recognition of the quiet determination that already motivated Daniel to find a speedier mode of transportation from Meadow Brook to his Ontario lodge. And to Laurine.

He settled on the purchase of a twin-engined, four-passenger, amphibian airplane that could make the trip in less than three hours and could land on the lake near his lodge. Daniel hired a pilot for the the Sikorsky S-38, which formerly belonged to famed explorer Martin Johnson, and rented hangar space at Detroit City Airport.

Laurine experienced her first plane ride when Daniel and his pilot flew the Sikorsky to Gore Bay in mid-winter. By this time, a spate of newspaper reports and conjectures, concerning Daniel's engagement to the Gore Bay telephone operator, infuriated Matilda. "I don't know anything about any engagement," she replied huffily to the questions of a reporter who came to Meadow Brook. The same reporter, pursuing the engagement-rumor to Gore Bay, was told by Laurine's father that the announcement of the engagement was premature, and that it was "given out by some society woman who wants to see the affair broken up."

When the reporter questioned Laurine personally, the girl refused to waver. She admitted that her diamond ring was a gift from Daniel. "Our affair is just like any other love affair between a boy and a girl," she said. The quote appeared in the <u>Detroit</u> <u>News</u> along with Laurine's denial that her fiance's $10 million fortune meant very much to either Daniel or her. Nonetheless, Daniel's wealth made it possible for him to buy a high-speed, twin-engined Lockheed "12" in June, that could make an even faster trip to Manitoulin Island—one hour and ten minutes.

It did not seem unnatural that any mother should be concerned about a 20-year-old son making such an early commitment to marriage. But Matilda's unhappy absorption in her son's engagement to a young backwoods girl was bisected when her 23-year-old daughter, Frances, became romantically involved, at the same time, with a New Jersey man she met at a New York horse show. James Johnson, in his early thirties, was a horse show promoter with ambitions to become a magazine publisher.

Matilda took no pleasure in the Dodge-Johnson romance. Her own life had been carefully channeled to reap great financial rewards which benefitted her children and gave them access to friends who led similarly privileged lives. Yet both Daniel and Frances were choosing to marry into mediocrity, in Matilda's view. Into family backgrounds with neither money nor patrician pedigree.

After 23 years of indulgent cultivating of the moody Frances' whims as a way of encouraging her introverted daughter to become more self-confident, Matilda now confronted a strong-willed eldest child made financially independent by John Dodge's fortune. By the time popular syndicated columnist Walter Winchell wrote, in a May 10 column, that Frances Dodge would soon announce her engagement to James Johnson of New Jersey, Matilda faced the dilemma of how to respond to the intensifying Daniel-Laurine relationship.

Young Daniel was ill, suffering from a mastoid infection that required surgery. He demanded to have Laurine at his side as he went into the hospital. In her concern for her son's health, Matilda relented sufficiently to allow Laurine to come from Windsor, Canada, where the girl was visiting with her married sister, to stay at Meadow Brook Hall during Daniel's hospitalization and recuperation.

Despite the increased publicity given the Frances Dodge-James Johnson engagement rumors, Matilda refused to affirm or deny the engagement when reporters besieged her with questions, even though Frances had already installed Johnson in a section of the Wilsons' Detroit office-suite in the Fisher Building. Reporters traced Johnson there, surrounded by stacks of the first issue of his swing-music magazine, The Cats Meow, written and edited by the versatile Johnson and backed financially by Frances. Johnson's questioners found him voluble on plans for his magazine, which featured Tommy Dorsey on the front cover of the first issue, but much less talkative about wedding plans. "Don't know when we'll be married," he admitted, adding that he was busily planning for a 20,000-copy issue of the second edition of his magazine.

Reporters persisted with questions. Was it romance at first sight when he'd met Frances at a 1933 horse show, they wanted to know. "No, it wasn't anything like that," Johnson replied. "We just kept running into each other at horse shows around the country."

Frances encouraged subscriptions to The Cats Meow by throwing a party in her trophy rooms above the indoor riding ring, inviting friends whom she frequently entertained at Meadow Brook, and placing copies of the magazine and subscription blanks at strategic points in the rooms. But there was no mention of an engagement; no diamond sparkling on Frances' left hand.

Eight days later, 18-year-old telephone operator, Laurine MacDonald, made her first social appearance as a Dodge-Wilson appendage when close family friends came to Meadow Brook Hall for a Sunday evening supper party. Previous publicity and rumor made it highly unlikely that the visitors would be surprised by hearing the Dodge-Johnson engagement announced at the party. The guests were surprised, however, at the unexpected appearance of the young MacDonald girl at the side of a pale Daniel, his neck and jaw still wrapped in bandages.

Guests noticed that the quiet-spoken Canadian girl wore a beige street-length dress similar in design to the black dress worn by Frances Dodge. The natural assumption was that the 18-year-old girl was being shaped into a more sophisticated mold by Daniel's sister, Frances.

Any such assumption was incorrect, as Matilda learned in the short time that Laurine had been staying at Meadow Brook Hall. The girl from Manitoulin Island displayed a quiet assurance that made an impact on Matilda, despite her disappointment with her 20-year-old son's willful behavior. Daniel, who would be 21 years old on July 23, made it clear that he planned to marry Laurine soon after that date, despite his mother's protests. And the strong bond between Daniel and Frances impelled the sister to side with her brother and, even, to extend herself to try to make friends with the reserved Laurine.

Reluctantly, Matilda sensed it was time to bow to the inevitable. Her children were so closely aligned at this point that the supper-party was hastily arranged to announce a double engagement. Frances and Jimmy. Daniel and Laurine. Only the wedding dates remained unannounced. Certainly not before late summer, the party guests surmised. Matilda Dodge Wilson, the perfectionist, surely would need time to plan and produce perfectly executed weddings.

In the mid-thirties, a variety of public ballrooms flourished in Detroit as the motor-city gained a reputation as "a dancing town" even while labor unrest and sit-down strikes plagued the city's faltering recovery from the worst of the Great Depression. The most popular big bands—those of Woody Herman, Glenn Miller, the Dorseys, Benny Goodman, Duke Ellington—came to perform at Detroit's ballrooms. At the Vanity on Jefferson Avenue. At the west-side Grande. And at Woodward Avenue's Graystone, among others. In the opinions of performers such as Count Basie, the brilliant Graystone, with its art-deco interior, was matched in magnificence only by Chicago's Aragon Ballroom.

To the vivacious Lucille Manzer, who began to go on weekend-night jaunts with her girl friends to the Grande...later to the Graystone, the ballrooms were glamorous pleasure-palaces where shopgirl Cinderellas could be a pseudo-Ruby Keeler or Ginger Rogers or Joan Blondell for the evening. The broad oaken stairway at Meadow Brook Hall could not have been more impressive to Lucille than was the grand stairway, with ornate iron railings, at the Graystone. The Waterford chandeliers at Meadow Brook could have been no more glittering than the Graystone's revolving mirrored chandelier, casting its shimmering beams over a floor designed to hold 3000 dancers, but often crowded with 5000...over a plush mezzanine lounge with carpeted and candlelit alcoves.

In the Manzer home, where Lucille often danced across the kitchen floor to the tune of a "Hit Parade" melody played on the radio, unspoken concessions were granted by Robert and Minnie whose religious precepts opposed the sinful pleasures of dancing. Realizing that younger Methodists of the thirties were not as rigorously hostile to some of the lesser evils of fleshly pleasures such as dancing and attending movies (apart from Sundays), the Manzers did not prevent their lively daughter from going downtown to the Graystone.

This concession did not entirely appease Lucille's growing impatience with Minnie Manzer's unwillingness to give her daughter a doorkey so that she could come home at night without disturbing her parents. "There's no need for a key," Minnie declared. "I never get any sleep until you're safely in the house."

Lucille knew this was true. Minnie was always waiting at the door in silent reproach when her daughter returned at night to the house on Woodside. Chafing at the expectation that her mother, in her long nightgown, would be watching and listening for her footsteps as she walked from the bus stop, Lucille began to consider moving in with a girl friend who lived in a small, rented apartment. Like her friend, Lucille recently had begun to smoke cigarettes, and she feared that Minnie surely would notice the smoke-smell of her clothing and might not attribute it solely to an odor picked up in a smoke-filled dance hall.

When she finally gathered up enough courage to tell her father that she planned to move into her girl friend's apartment, she was overcome with guilt at the distressed look on his face. She already knew her parents' opinion of young, single women who left home—such females were "fast," they said. But now, there were no recriminations from Robert Manzer. "Your mother will give you a key to the house," he said quickly. "You needn't worry, after this, about her waiting up when you come home at night."

That evening, Minnie handed her a key. "Your father told me to give this to you," she said. "We don't want you to leave home." When Lucille came home late the following Saturday night, she did not know if her mother was awake or asleep—Minnie Manzer could not be seen or heard.

There were advantages for Lucille in continuing to live at home—largely financial. Because she loved pretty clothes, she spent her money on dresses and matching hats and shoes, regardless of the disapproving look on Minnie's face when her daughter arrived home with another J.L. Hudson box or shopping bag. The day she bought a beige linen suit, Minnie watched closely as Lucille looked at herself in the bedroom mirror. "You think you're a rich girl," the older woman said suddenly, "but you're not."

The suit wrinkled so easily that Lucille hung it in the back of her friend's car the next night when several girls drove out to the ballroom at Walled Lake. Changing in the ladies' room, Lucille emerged in her unwrinkled suit for a night of dancing—never sitting down during intermissions.

Even Minnie Manzer thoroughly approved of the young man whom Lucille began to date steadily in 1936. Both Minnie and Robert nodded approvingly when their daughter's date parked his red roadster in front of the house and came up the walk.

Lucille's plans for a Memorial Day outing in 1937, however, did not include her "steady" boy friend. She looked forward to spending the day with another girl at the popular Lake Erie resort, Estral Beach. Since the other girl's parents were accompanying the two young women, the Manzers were not worried about sinful temptations that the Estral Beach dance floor might present.

The dance floor was crowded that holiday evening, but not so crowded that Lucille's luminous blue eyes could not quickly focus on a well dressed, dark haired man—one of the smoothest, most graceful dancers she had ever seen. When he approached Lucille and politely asked her for the next dance, she placed one white-gloved hand on his shoulder and they moved together across the floor, whirling, hesitating, bending, gliding in perfect unison.

His name, he told her in a deep and vibrant baritone, was Bill Mealbach and, although he was staying at the Estral Beach hotel through the weekend, he lived in Detroit. Lucille felt a happy sense of anticipation at his disclosure that he was a Detroiter. Already attracted to this tall man of impeccable manners, she was pleased to learn that he, too, often went to the Graystone Ballroom on Woodward Avenue.

The couple met at the Graystone several times after Memorial Day. Then, because Mealbach had no car, the two began meeting at a Grand River corner and boarding a bus to one of the downtown theaters. To various restaurants. And, most of all, to the Woodward Avenue ballroom where they wanted to dance with no one but each other.

Bill Mealbach was, she soon learned, in his early thirties. Ten years older than Lucille. He was articulate and entertaining and she loved going out to dinner with him at the better restaurants where he ordered before-dinner and after-dinner drinks for her and for himself. At other times,too, she noticed the faint odor of liquor on her escort, partly concealed by the pleasant scent of cologne or chewing gum. Lucille knew, by this time, that many people's lives were not bound by the kind of restrictions that the Manzers observed.

When her parents learned that she was seriously interested in this older man with a marriage and divorce in his early background, their objections were of great concern to Lucille. Nonetheless, she could not bring herself to stop seeing Mealbach—a foreman for the Detroit-Michigan Stove Company where, he said, "lots of Italian immigrants, fresh off the boat," were employed. When the couple went, together, to Belle Isle on a Sunday afternoon, they could see, just east of the bridge to the island, the 15-ton "world's largest stove"—built by the Detroit-Michigan Stove Company to represent Detroit at the 1893 Chicago World's Fair.

"What has he got that I don't?" her younger—and plainly jealous—former boy friend asked as he implored Lucille to resume their relationship. It was a question she really could not answer...a question she herself pondered as she faced the fact that the younger man owned a car, had a better job, attended church, and was approved by her parents. "You can't get serious with a man just because he's a good dancer!" he protested.

"Don't talk to me like that'" Lucille snapped back. Yet she found it impossible to explain, even to herself, why she preferred Bill Mealbach.

She continued dating Mealbach despite Robert Manzer's warnings that his daughter would not find happiness with the dapper older man who was not a Methodist, nor affiliated with any other church; despite the tight and disapproving set of Minnie Manzer's mouth each time she suspected that Lucille was leaving the house to meet her new escort.

Lucille hated hurting the younger man the Manzers liked...hated, even more, hurting her parents—particularly her father. But she could not resist the urge to be with Bill Mealbach...to slip into his arms and feel the symmetry of their movements in response to the beat of the music at the Graystone...to feel his arms tighten around her as they spun across the dance floor.

Chapter 14

Tragic Honeymoon

Five weeks after the small engagement party at the Dodge-Wilson mansion, more than 500 guests came to Meadow Brook Hall on Friday evening, July 1, for the wedding of Frances Matilda Dodge and James Johnson. Amelia Rausch Cline, still estranged from her sister, Matilda, was not among the guests, although she came to the Hall earlier in the day for a visit with her niece and a view of the wedding gifts, at Frances' personal invitation. Amelia, who yearned to re-establish her ties with her stubbornly resistant sister, swallowed her pride and accepted Frances' offer.

Amelia did not see Matilda that afternoon. Instead, she followed Frances down to the games room where gifts of crystal, silver, and china gleamed on white satin-draped tables...past masses of white flower arrangements and up to the second floor to see the display of gift-linens. For Amelia, it was a thrill to once again move through the familiar interior of the elegant home. Although she would have enjoyed meticulously examining the array of expensive wedding gifts, she did not indulge her inclination to dawdle. In her gratitude at Frances' thoughtful overture, she scrupulously determined not to take too much of her only niece's time on such an eventful day.

Matilda, caught up in a maelstrom of arrangements and details in the few weeks preceding Frances' hurriedly planned wedding, presented her usual self-contained image that evening. Wearing a rose taffeta creation, a serene Matilda slowly led the way down the grand stairway with Alfred at her side. Five bridesmaids, including Laurine MacDonald, and a maid-of-honor followed the senior Wilsons. An organist pushed the crescendo pedal of the great organ, swelling into the processional march as Frances, swathed in pale blue satin with a train more than four yards long, appeared at the staircase landing on the arm of her brother, Daniel.

Guests filled the drawing room where the Reverend Dr. Vance waited in front of the fireplace to conduct the marriage ceremony at 8:30. Other guests jammed the Great Hall and spilled outside near umbrella-shaded tables and a platform erected on the lawn for dancing. Among the guests, Henry Ford, lean as ever in a white linen suit, complained about the crush of people as he edged forward to offer congratulations to the wedding couple. In grudging compliance with family obligations, Matilda had included Anna Dodge Dillman on the guest list. Bride-like in white satin with a train rivaling that of Frances, Anna swept into Meadow Brook Hall where her immediate concern was for the protection of her train and her corsage of white orchids from the press of the assemblage. Minus her husband, who spent most of his time at the elite Everglades Club in Palm Beach, Anna was accompanied by the social secretary on whose guidance and finesse she depended during Hugh Dillman's ever increasing absences.

For the Wilson children, nine and seven years old, the party was a wonderland into which they could peek from vantage points on the stairway, since they had permission to stay up until midnight for the event. They made only short excursions, with their governess, into the drawing room and dining room, looking up at huge silver trays filled with delicacies and carried high by a flock of waiters circulating among the guests. And they were allowed, briefly, to venture to the outdoor dance floor where couples whirled about to the rhythm of a six-piece swing band.

Matilda's keen-eyed attention focused, periodically, on her new son-in-law, whose smile never faded as he chatted with guests and playfully teased the bridesmaids. She began to catch sight of the charm and geniality that might have entranced her daughter. If the insecure and moody side of Frances' nature could be lightened by marriage to the confident-appearing Johnson, Matilda conceded that something worthwhile might come out of the relationship, after all. She soon could assess this possibility for herself; on returning from a honeymoon trip to England, the newlyweds would move into the John Dodge farmhouse on Meadow Brook properties.

Although Frances' wedding reception progressed with no evidence of accelerated planning, her hastily arranged travel plans teetered into chaos later that evening when a thunderstorm and rising winds created precarious weather conditions for the use of Daniel's plane in a flight to

New York City. Instead, the newlyweds left Meadow Brook Hall in a flurry of paper rose petals, tossed by guests, to go to a Detroit hotel and wait for a train to Buffalo.

Accustomed to having her orders and wishes rapidly carried out by underlings hired to smooth her path of irritations, Frances was unnerved by a 4:25 a.m. train trip to Buffalo, where an American Airlines plane waited for the Johnsons' arrival before taking off for New York City. There, they could not board the Bremen because of Jimmy's passport difficulties. The passport office had already closed for the weekend.

Johnson then received a preview of money-power when, by way of cable communications with Washington, the couple was permitted to board ship with the agreement that necessary documents would be issued by a U.S. consul when the Johnsons reached the port of disembarkment. Photographers, who waited for hours to get pictures of the newlyweds at the New York pier, reported that the bride was in tears as she came aboard the ship.

A week after Frances' wedding, Daniel and Laurine returned to Gore Bay where they attended the usual Friday-night dance at the Community Hall. Laurine's closest friends clustered around the former telephone operator as she confided that she and Dan would be married on August 14, immediately following the sister's return from England.

When news of this wedding date drifted back to Detroit, reporters rushed out to Meadow Brook where Matilda denied knowing anything about the arrangements. Pressed further, she replied firmly that her son and Miss MacDonald had left Meadow Brook for Gore Bay the previous Friday and without discussing their wedding plans with her. "Arrangements for the wedding will be made by Miss MacDonald's family," she concluded icily.

Regardless of Matilda's denial of knowledge of wedding plans, a small item appeared in a Detroit newspaper column on July 31. Daniel Dodge and Laurine MacDonald, it predicted, will soon be married quietly at Meadow Brook Hall.

The report turned out to be true, although Matilda struggled to keep the plans secret. She attempted, first, to stall the wedding as long as possible, then was pressured into agreeing to a late-August date, after Frances' return from England. But Daniel, as he celebrated his 21st birthday in mid-July, proved to be surprisingly impetuous and obdurate for a young man who had previously been tractable and compliant. Matilda attributed the change in her son's attitude to one person—the youthful Miss Laurine MacDonald.

When Daniel insisted that the date must be advanced to Friday, August 2, to allow the young couple to be together at Manitoulin Islamd for the peak weeks of summer, Matilda blamed Laurine for refusing to wait for Frances' return. But Matilda had no choice but to comply with her son's wishes—with one reservation. Before Laurine could become a Dodge, Matilda insisted, family attorneys should draw up a will for Daniel. And a pre-nuptial agreement would have to be signed by Laurine, agreeing to the provisions of the will.

Neither Daniel nor Laurine objected to signing what they thought of as a legal formality. On July 25, Laurine affixed her signature to the pre-nuptial agreement and Daniel met with family lawyers to execute the will. The documents provided that the young Mrs. Dodge would receive a quarter-million-dollar settlement, plus certain properties, in the unlikely event of Daniel's death, attorneys explained. Daniel specified that $25,000 should be willed to his friend and family employee, Heath Ballagh. Various sums, none of them great, were willed to family members, with the remainder of his fortune going to his mother, Matilda.

Matilda's careful management of her own fortune, with meticulous detailing of finances, left an indelible impression on her children—money management was an awesome responsibility, never to be taken lightly. Still, at age 21, Daniel could expect to have a lifetime ahead of him in which to concern himself with his fortune and its management and the likelihood of changing his will. When he signed the document, his mother consented to the August 2 date for marriage to the girl he loved—Annie Laurine.

On the afternoon of August 2, Alfred Wilson and Heath Ballagh assisted the Reverend Joseph A. Vance, D.D., in moving a few chairs around in the living room before the ceremony. "These were the only arrangements there were," Dr. Vance later admitted to journalists.

The half-dozen wedding guests included Mr. and Mrs. Frederick Holmes of Windsor—the brother-in-law and sister of the bride, who served as the bridal couple's best man and matron-of-honor. The bride's parents did not come from Gore Bay. "Mrs. MacDonald is ill," Matilda explained to those who inquired. So there were few to admire the bride's full-skirted French gown of Chantilly lace nor to offer congratulations at the conclusion of the quiet ceremony.

Shortly afterwards, the bride and groom climbed into Daniel's roadster, with a trailer hitched behind, and roared up Adams Road toward Sault Ste. Marie for an overnight stay on their way to Manitoulin Island. After the couple's departure, the wedding was announced to newspapers. The newlywed Dodges would return to Rochester, Matilda told reporters, to live in a large home on the opposite side of Adams Road, facing Meadow Brook Hall.

In another strange parallel, the year of marriage, 1938, for both Frances Dodge and Daniel Dodge was also the year in which Lucille Manzer married William Mealbach. Like Matilda Dodge Wilson, the Manzers disapproved of their daughter's fiance. They remained firm in their quiet-spoken disapproval even when it became clear that Lucille was determined to marry Mealbach despite her parents' refusal to give the couple their blessing.

There were no threats; the Manzers' Methodist consciences excluded any kind of blustering or wrathful behavior. But Lucille realized that her parents were deeply hurt by her rejection of their values. This knowledge burdened Lucille with a sense of betrayal, despite assurances from her friends that there should be no guilt attached to the decision of a 23-year-old woman to marry the man of her choice. Still, Lucille expected that after the wedding took place, her parents would accept the inevitable. They did not hold grudges. And they were kind-hearted people.

Since the Manzers refused to attend their daughter's wedding, the young couple made a quick trip to Bowling Green, Ohio, in January of 1938 to make their vows. As Lucille walked out of her parents' home to leave for Bowling Green, her father could not resist expressing his disappointment. "This feels more like the day of a funeral than a wedding," he said sadly.

The newlyweds returned from Ohio to set up housekeeping in the Shirley Manor Apartments in Detroit. Lucille quit her job, as did most brides at that time. And as she expected, her parents concealed their disappointment after their daughter's wedding. In their minds, marriage was an unchangeable lifetime commitment, so they had no choice but to recognize and accept Lucille's husband as a son-in-law.

The Manzers occasionally visited their daughter at her apartment, usually in the daytime when the husband was at work, but sometimes on a weekend or evening when Bill Mealbach was at home. At such times, Lucille hid her husband's beer bottles so that the Manzers would not catch sight of them, and warned Bill not to drink before her parents arrived—nor, of course, while they visited. Within a short time, Bill was unable or unwilling to continue with this facade. Then the Manzers pretended not to notice when their son-in-law opened the icebox, grabbed a bottle of beer and popped off the cap.

More often, Lucille stopped in at her parents' home to help with the care of Grandpa Fish, now frail and ailing as he lived out the last months of his life with the Manzers. Although his deteriorating physical condition did not reduce the acidity of his tongue, Minnie never lost patience as she cared for the father who, in earlier years, had sometimes used his horsewhip on his wife—Minnie's mother.

The mother gratefully accepted Lucille's help in staying with the old man while Minnie went to church or to the grocery store. On her return from one of these brief absences, Minnie put a large envelope into Lucille's hand as the daughter walked toward the front door. "I thought you might like to have this baby picture," Minnie said quietly. The younger woman opened the envelope and looked inside to see the photo of the two chubby and identically dressed baby girls—Lucille herself and the unknown "Amy"—seated in the large wicker chair.

A few weeks later, Marvin Fish died at the home of his daughter. After his death, Robert Manzer's cousin, June Eschtruth, visited more often at the Woodside address. When Lucille stopped in at her parents' home, she often found June, who managed a real estate business, talking with the Manzers. But occasionally, when Lucille arrived, only her brother Rob, now entering high school, was at home. His insistent questions, at such times, bewildered Lucille as he reminded her that she was ten years old when her parents had brought Rob into their home. Hadn't Lucille wondered where he had come from, he asked. Why was it that all his records showed he was born in the town of Lake Orion, when the Manzers never lived there? Was he adopted, he wondered. And if he was adopted, he wanted to find out who his real parents were. "Didn't you ask any questions when they brought me here?" he prodded. "Don't you know anything about it?"

She hadn't asked questions. She could remember only her happiness at having a baby brother to love and help care for. And although the teenaged Rob was so curious about his background, it was clear he had not asked these questions of the senior Manzers…that he was not willing to risk hurting their feelings by trying to break down the wall of reserve that his parents always maintained on such subjects.

There remained a close bond of affection between Lucille and Rob, even though his questions gave the sister an uneasy, almost guilty, feeling—as if she always had been too accepting of the silence that enveloped her parents concerning family matters…finances, their early lives, or family background. She had never known her parents to celebrate their wedding anniversary—did not even know the date. Nor was she sure how old they were, nor the dates of their birthdays.

But her father always had been loving and generous to her; her mother was a good and concerned parent. There was no reason for her to question anything, she told herself. No reason to feel any deficiency in her own complacent acceptance of her life—past and present. She determined not to permit Rob's speculations to unsettle her own agreeable accommodation with a life that was both comfortable and, it seemed, secure.

When Dan Dodge arrived at Kagawong Lodge with his bride that first week of August, he resolved, in his new spirit of independence, to discharge the man employed as caretaker at the lodge. At age 21, Daniel decided he no longer needed nor wanted an older man on the premises; Dick Drolet, young Dodge felt, was too authoritative...too quick to tell him what to do and how to do it. In Daniel's mind, Kagawong was his very own Eden—his and Laurine's—and he resented any interference from Drolet.

As soon as he discharged Drolet, he replaced the man with a younger caretaker, Lloyd Bryant, who promptly moved, with his wife, into the caretaker's house neighboring the main lodge. To assist Bryant, Daniel hired 20-year-old Frank Valiquette. With Drolet's removal, both Dan and Laurine were freed of the sense of restraint they had felt with the older man on the premises.

The five young people enjoyed a free and easy exchange of conversation and companionship. Young Dodge, dark eyes gleaming behind silver-rimmed glasses, issued only one rule. No one was to call him "Danny," he commanded. "Daniel" or simply "Dan" were fine. But not "Danny;" he considered the name childish. At age 21, the slight-figured Dan Dodge was determined to be a man—to make his own decisions and take control of his own destiny.

On Monday, 13 days after their marriage, the young Dodges decided to cross the bay in Dan's powerboat and to head for the town of Little Current. There, they intended to buy enough provisions to stock the lodge for a few more days, after which Dan and Laurine would leave, reluctantly, to drive back to Longview—the 20-room house, across from Meadow Brook Hall, formerly occupied by the Don Wilsons who recently moved to Illinois. Daniel had already arranged to buy an additional 250 acres of land adjoining Longview. He planned to convert the additional property into a landing field for the two airplanes he now kept at Detroit City Airport.

By the time Dan and Laurine got into the boat—named Mac for Laurine—to cross the bay to Little Current, a brisk wind whipped across the water. Although Laurine was a vigorous swimmer, she was not an avid boater who enjoyed battling the powerful forces of nature. But her husband, eager to challenge wind and waves, relished maneuvering the bouncing powerboat on its journey across the roughened bay.

The newlyweds spent a couple of hours in town, shopping for groceries and supplies and packing the provisions into the boat. They wandered up and down the main street, stopping for ice cream before returning to their boat. As soon as Daniel started up the motor and edged the craft away from the dock and out into open water, Laurine realized that the wind had picked up speed. Spray doused the couple as Daniel headed the craft directly into the whitecaps. The trip back to the lodge became a leaping battle with waves that smashed hard against the bottom of the boat.

Frightened by the force of the waves, Laurine released her tense grip on the seat only when Daniel steered the craft toward the Kagawong dock. "I'm never going to ride in this boat again!" she said as, with relief, she leaped on to the dock. A moment later, knowing how much Daniel prized his boat, she regretted her hasty words. She knew, too, how great was Daniel's admiration for the sleek powerboats owned by his older cousin, Horace Junior—a fleet of them, each named Delphine and numbered consecutively as Horace entered them in Harmsworth and Gold Cup races.

Laurine was grateful that, in every other way, the serious-minded Daniel differed greatly from Horace Junior—the playboy who drank too much and chased beautiful women. Daniel's quiet life at his remote lodge would have been an unbearable kind of existence for the gregarious Horace.

From the kitchen of the lodge, the savory smell of dinner cooking drifted toward the young Dodges as they came up the path. Then, as Laurine set up the ironing board to press some clothes, Daniel talked briefly with a reporter waiting to see him after driving up from Detroit. He and Laurine were extremely happy, Daniel told the reporter, just being together in the setting they both loved. When the reporter left, Daniel headed for the garage, calling back to Laurine that he was going to work on a marine motor with Bryant and Valiquette.

When the caretaker's wife said that dinner was ready, Laurine disconnected the iron and walked toward the garage. For one brief second, as she approached the side-window of the building, she saw, framed inside, a tableau that stamped itself into her mind in a spasmodic fraction of time. Daniel—holding a rod or stick in his hand. Frank Valiquette—flicking a cigarette lighter and touching the small yellow flame to the stick. Dynamite! The realization rocketed through her mind as she watched her husband swing his arm in the direction of the door. A trail of sparks instantly flared into flames and a deafening explosion blew out the garage windows and parts of the building itself.

Dazed by the impact of flying glass and pieces of wood, Laurine screamed and fled to the house, feeling that she was on fire. She turned on the cold water faucet, splashing water on her face and arms before realizing that Dan and the other two men were inside the garage. Badly injured, she was certain. Perhaps dead.

She turned and ran back to the garage, catching sight of Lloyd Bryant stumbling outside and collapsing into the arms of his wife, who had run to the garage at the sound of the explosion and screams. Valiquette, already climbing outside from a window, was bleeding and confused but not as badly injured as Daniel, who lay, stuporous, in a pool of blood on the floor of the wrecked building.

Calling Bryant's wife to help carry Daniel out of the garage, Laurine found that she had no strength in her limp and throbbing right arm. Blood, from a gash in her leg, soaked the hem of her dress. She could not phone for help; the lodge had no telephone. Half-dragging Daniel outside, the two women managed to get him into a car. Then, gritting her teeth against the pain pulsing through her body, Laurine tried to decide what to do next. With Daniel lying in the back seat of the car, there was not enough room to fit all five people into the automobile for the hour's drive, over twisting roadway, into town. But everyone could fit into the boat, and the 14-mile trip across the bay would be 20 minutes shorter.

With the help of Valiquette, who was regaining his awareness of what needed to be done, Laurine and Bryant's wife also got the caretaker into the car for the drive down to the boathouse. At the dock, Valiquette helped to place Daniel on cushions in the rear cockpit of the boat. Then he tried to stop the flow of blood from his employer's wounds.

As Valiquette tended to Daniel, Bryant's wife also sat at the back of the boat, holding her unconscious husband and applying a tourniquet to his bleeding arm. Laurine knew she must force herself to take over the controls, holding to the wheel with her left arm while the other arm hung helplessly at her side. Blood trickled from cuts in her face as she pulled the throttle and drove into the waves as Daniel had tried to teach her. Tears of pain stung her eyes as she reminded herself that only two hours earlier, the boat had made this same trip. Safely.

But now the wind, coming from behind, seemed even more powerful, sweeping the waves into four-foot-high crests...pounding the plunging boat with a force that threatened to rip the wheel from her grip. Still, she clung to the controls with a desperate tenacity, keeping the speed at 20 knots and knowing that all of them could drown in the surging waters if she relaxed her numbed grasp of the wheel. She could not surrender to pain and exhaustion and fear for even a moment.

Willing strength into her hand and arm, she stared, trancelike, into the relentlessly pounding waves of the bay's north channel while the sounds of her husband's moans dissolved into the shuddering of the boat and crashing of water. Laurine steeled herself to endure the pain, knowing that she must hold on for another 20 to 25 minutes...an eternity, it seemed.

When she saw Rabbit Island ahead, to the right, she recognized it and knew they were passing the halfway mark, with almost 20 minutes to go. And she could not make it! The wheel was slipping out of her weakly clutching, deadened fingers. "Frank!" she screamed to Valiquette.

Valiquette scrambled toward the front of the boat. At the same time, Dan Dodge sat up, then struggled to his feet as if in response to Laurine's screams. Bryant's wife was the only one who saw young Dodge rise as Laurine surrendered the wheel to Valiquette. As Dan swayed, Bryant's wife shrieked a warning. Laurine turned her head toward the rear of the boat in time to see her husband plunge over the side and disappear under the surface of the waves.

If Valiquette had tried to turn too swiftly, the powerboat could have tipped. He cut the speed and circled wide to return to where Dan had been swallowed by the waves. Laurine, weeping hysterically, caught sight of her husband's head briefly bobbing up above the water's surface in the boat's wake before disappearing a second time. But as Valiquette circled and re-circled the area, there was no further sight of Dodge. Valiquette had no choice but to pull the throttle and cut through the waves once again toward Little Current.

Stunned by the quick sequence of horrors in the past hour, Laurine scrambled onto the pier at Little Current and dashed up the street, calling for help, even before Valiquette finished securing the boat to the wharf. A local doctor gave first aid, then provided transportation to the Red Cross Hospital at nearby Mindemoya. Laurine agreed to be taken to Mindemoya, with Bryant and Valiquette, only after she was reassured that a searching party—planes and six fishing boats—had already set out to look for Daniel.

At the Mindemoya hospital, Laurine protested when a nurse tried to remove the young woman's wedding and engagement rings before wheeling the patient into the operating room. At Laurine's insistence, the rings remained on her fourth finger, the large diamond sparkling under operating room lights as surgeons removed fragments of glass and wood splinters from her face, arms, and legs.

Like Laurine, Valiquette and Bryant had been cut and pierced by glass and wood fragments, and were treated for burns. Although doctors released Valiquette the next day, Laurine's mother came from Gore Bay to stay with her daughter, who was expected to be hospitalized for a couple of weeks. After just 13 days of marriage, Annie Laurine MacDonald Dodge had to face the reality that she was a widow—a very young widow, with a confused and uncertain future.

Shortly after the drowning, authorities notified the Wilsons at Meadow Brook of Daniel's death. In his concern for his distraught wife, Alfred Wilson summoned two doctors to come to Meadow Brook to care for Matilda. The unexpectedness of the tragedy was compounded for Matilda by her own tormented questioning; had her son fallen from the boat, or had he leaped out?

This same question was reflected in newspaper stories of Daniel's death. Amelia Rausch Cline, traveling with her husband in Manitoba when she read about the drowning, immediately asked John Cline to drive to Manitoulin Island.

When the Clines arrived on Wednesday, a dismal rain fell steadily and a heavy fog kept its death watch over the channel. The Clines learned that Daniel's body had not yet been found…that bad weather hampered the search but that, whenever weather conditions permitted, boats went out on the bay with weighted nets to continue dragging operations over an area of twelve square miles of choppy waters.

The Clines learned, too, that Alfred Wilson had already arrived at Little Current to oversee the search for his stepson's body. Gar Wood, famed inventor and race-boat driver, had piloted Daniel's amphibian plane from Detroit to the Canadian town, bringing Alfred, a private nurse for Laurine, two policemen from Detroit's harbormaster division, and specially designed grappling hooks and equipment for recovering the body after the actual drowning site was determined.

The Clines made no attempt to meet with Alfred in Little Current. Instead, they drove to Daniel's Kagawong Lodge and talked to an employee who took them to the garage where the explosion occurred. He told the Clines that Dan Dodge was fascinated by explosives and, particularly, by a cache of dynamite sticks that former caretaker Dick Drolet kept hidden in the brush—remnants of a supply of explosives used, years earlier, to blast out tree trunks when the lodge was built. Curious about the dynamite, Dodge had wanted to test it and see if it was still operative. But Drolet, saying that it was old but still dangerous, had repeatedly warned young Dodge not to touch it. Soon after firing Drolet, Daniel tried to satify his curiosity about the dynamite—with appalling results.

Like her sister, Amelia always thought of Daniel as a docile, agreeable youngster. Yet, as she sadly reflected on her nephew's tragically short life, she remembered the year—1931—that she went to Palm Beach with the Wilsons. Even then, 13-year-old Dan was infatuated with boats. To please her son, Matilda had rented a motor launch for the season. Dan, looking forward to navigating the launch on the canal that ran behind their rented house, was crushed when the family boarded the launch for a first ride and the boy learned that the launch arrived complete with a captain-navigator. Dan sulked throughout the ride, then refused to go aboard a second time.

Now, in discharging Drolet and trying to test the dynamite, Daniel again had stubbornly asserted himself and inadvertently fueled the catastrophe that claimed his young life.

Amelia, who always felt especially close to Daniel, brooded over the tragedy as her husband drove back to their Rochester home. How would her sister be able to cope with the loss of her only son, Amelia fretted. And should she—did she dare—go to Meadow Brook and try to help console the sister who had coldly closed the great doors of the Hall to her?

Chapter 15

The Known and the Unknown

Frances and Jimmy Johnson, already back in New York, boarded a plane as soon as they received news of Daniel's death. Arriving in Detroit at 4:50 a.m. on Wednesday, they drove out to Meadow Brook to be with the distraught Matilda as Alfred left for Little Current. Despite Frances' efforts to keep her mother from seeing newspapers—all containing vivid stories of Daniel's death and the search for his body—some of the stories came into Matilda's possession.

An article captioned <u>Girl Heroine of Bay Tragedy</u> lauded the bravery of the 18-year-old Dodge bride in navigating the boat and attempting to bring the injured young people to Little Current. The account quoted the opinion of the doctor who had administered first aid to the survivors at Little Current. "Young Dodge," the doctor surmised, "probably was temporarily insane from the agony of a shattered arm and lacerations on the face and head when he plunged from the speedboat..." And, beginning with newspapers dated only one day after Daniel's death, headlines predicted that <u>Widow Will Share in Trust Income</u>.

While Frances hid or destroyed newspapers, and ordered family maids to do the same, Matilda tuned into radio reports in the privacy of her bedroom suite. She listened as commentators probed the circumstances of the drowning and told of the search for the body in the north channel's 90-feet-deep waters. Resentment tinged Matilda's anguish as she heard each newscaster's speculations concerning how much wealth the 18-year-old Laurine would collect. Only one private solace remained for Matilda at this time—to go, alone, into Daniel's room in the west wing and to seek comfort, among his possessions, in quiet communion with her memories of her son.

Each time she came out of the room, she locked the door so no one else could enter and disturb any of the contents. She wanted everything kept just as Daniel had left it. The room would be her personal memorial to her only son, enshrined—eternally young—among the collections and possessions of his teenage years...as if Matilda's own prescience of the fading and blurring generated by time's relentless passage were already pressing her to preserve for herself this cocoon of infinity.

Two weeks after Daniel Dodge drowned, doctors allowed Laurine to leave the hospital. Her husband's body had not been found and her mother-in-law wanted the young widow brought, by plane, to Meadow Brook Hall.

Although Matilda presented her usual exterior of controlled endurance by this time, the anxiety that troubled her could not be calmed until she heard Laurine's own account of the tragedy. Why had Laurine not driven the car, with the two more seriously injured men, into town? Surely she knew the terrible risks of trying to make the boat trip across the turbulent bay under such conditions. Why was Daniel not watched more closely—or why was he not secured to the boat in some way? Why were life preservers not used? Why? Why?

Laurine's arrival at Meadow Brook and her explanations to Matilda did little to soothe the mother-in-law's anxiety. The two women did not draw together in the pain of mutual sorrow. Rather, each withdrew within the accommodating vastness of Meadow Brook Hall to nurse her grief in seclusion.

Amelia Rausch Cline finally mustered enough courage to drive to Meadow Brook Hall to express her sympathy to her sister. Once again, she was disappointed and depressed by the brevity of her visit as Matilda ordered a maid to call Laurine to come down and meet Daniel's aunt. Offering her condolences to the soft-spoken girl whose facial abrasions were not yet healed, Amelia had the disquieting feeling her that own words were too formal. Even superficial. But because Matilda screened her face and emotions so carefully, Amelia found no way to be more expressive...to convey any more warmth to the newly introduced Laurine than to her only sister, with whom she had shared so much of her earlier life.

Driving back to Rochester, Amelia's dark eyes blurred with tears. She realized, again, that Matilda felt no need of emotional support from the younger sister—any more than she felt any need for closeness with her only son's youthful widow. Frances and Alfred, especially Alfred, were the only two whose compassion aroused any depth of response from Matilda. Amelia suspected that her sister loved and appreciated Alfred more than ever before at this traumatic point in her life when her husband immediately went to Little Current to oversee the search for Daniel's body.

When planes and boats were unsuccessful in their search, Alfred ordered the use of an 11-ton diving bell, equipped with powerfully beamed undersea lamps. The diving bell, already being shipped from Connecticut to Little Current, would be guided in its underwater search by electrical controls from another ship on the bay's surface.

By telephone, Alfred kept in close touch with his wife who could not share her distress with anyone else. And yet she was unable, even with Alfred, to unburden herself of the core of her pain—her deeply supressed sense of guilt for what she must have felt was the terrible transgression of her youth—for having married a divorced man...a man who put aside his wife to wed his secretary, Matilda Rausch. Guilt surely had troubled her at the time of her small daughter's death, even as she tried to put thoughts of God's retribution out of her mind. Now, with Daniel's death, the same, barely submerged guilt would have seared her even more strongly as it became the cross she would bear, silently, throughout her life. Even Alfred, reared in the ministerial home of his father, knew nothing of John Dodge's secret second marriage and divorce.

In Little Current, a tired and discouraged Alfred Wilson observed preparations made for use of the diving bell, fitted with flotation devices so it could be towed out to the north channel on Wednesday, September 7, three weeks after the drowning. Very early that Wednesday morning, dawn faintly blushed across the horizon when a small boat carrying two fishermen moved out on the bay from the mainland. Sighting a flock of gulls screeching as the birds spiraled and dipped down to the choppy waters some five miles from the mainland, the fishermen headed their boat in the direction of Rabbit Island and the gulls.

As they approached the object that excited the gulls, they saw a body, covered in mud, that had only recently drifted up close to the surface. The men immediately suspected that the expensive and carefully outfitted diving bell would not be utilized after all...that they could claim the $1500 reward offered by the Wilsons for recovery of Daniel Dodge's body.

Screaming their protests, the gulls soared into the air and hovered as waves rocked the fishing boat and washed over the dark torso bobbing in the water. Grimly, the fishermen set about their grisly task, roping the bloated, battered body and tying it to their boat for the trip to Little Current where Alfred Wilson kept his vigil.

Arriving at Little Current, the two men delivered the corpse to officials for a postmortem examination. When the coroner completed his work, Alfred accompanied his stepson's body on its last trip in the amphibian plane that Daniel owned—back to Detroit and to Smith Undertaking Parlors.

On Friday afternoon, Dr. Vance came to Meadow Brook Hall where, only one month earlier, the minister performed Daniel and Laurine's wedding ceremony. As the minister gave the funeral eulogy, the family sat quietly on the staircase landing. The young widow, Laurine. Matilda and Alfred. Frances and Jimmy. The Donald Wilsons from Illinois. And Daniel's Aunt Amelia—accompanied by John Cline who, in his years as Meadow Brook's farm manager, shared some of Daniel's boyhood experimentations in his child-sized machine shop.

The cast bronze coffin stood in the reception hall at the foot of the staircase. Next to a six-foot cross, covered with red rosebuds and white orchids, Dr. Vance spoke briefly of Daniel's short, but happy, life. Then, as the family and guests filed from the Hall for the ride to Woodlawn Cemetery, the organist played a hymn requested by the family. "Onward Christian Soldiers"—the resounding chords and familiar words echoing Matilda's credo as she walked at Alfred's side out to the waiting car to escort her only son to the marble tomb bearing the name <u>Dodge</u>.

Two weeks after the funeral, newspapers carried headlines stating that Annie Laurine MacDonald Dodge was not satisfied with the quarter-million dollars, plus properties, allocated as her share of her husband's estate according to terms of the pre-nuptial agreement. Her lawyer informed Dodge family lawyers that the young widow would contest the will unless the parties worked out a satisfactory settlement before October 10—the date scheduled for a probate court hearing.

As rumors circulated that Laurine was willing to accept two million dollars in settlement, lawyers representing Daniel's two half-sisters, Winifred and Isabel, appeared in court to plead their clients' claims that the three sisters, including Frances, should inherit Daniel's estate. Because Daniel had not lived to age 25, when he would have inherited his share of income accumulated from his father's trust fund, the sisters' attorneys argued that this income should remain in the trust fund for the siblings.

Laurine's lawyer already had petitioned the court to appoint someone other than Matilda Dodge Wilson as administrator of Daniel's estate, since Dan's will named his mother as principal beneficiary.

When Laurine's lawyer won this concession from the court, Matilda tried to be objective, not only about this setback but about the entire will contest. But it was difficult for her to restrain her anger when newspapers made public the financial sparring within the family. A headline, Dodge Widow Opens Battle, initiated another series of news items featuring Laurine's request for a $33,000 monthly widow's allowance until the estate dispute was settled. Matilda's attorneys attacked this request, trying to slash Laurine's allowance to a fraction of the $33,000 figure.

To Matilda's dismay, John Duval complicated the money squabbles by filing still another suit in circuit court. This suit pointed out certain legal technicalities which John Duval's lawyer stated were previously overlooked in the original John F. Dodge will, disinheriting the son from his share of the trust income.

The battle for Daniel's fortune was only a part of the difficulties facing Matilda. The attorney general's office in Toronto, Canada, had already announced that young Dodge's death would be investigated and an inquest held. The inquest proceeded simultaneously with the filing of the court suit.

On October 22, Matilda's problems intensified as Laurine's lawyer petitioned probate court to seek a "full and proper accounting" from Matilda Wilson of funds she had received, as guardian of her minor son, for Daniel's expenses through the years. The charge, "conceal- ment of assets," was filed on the same day that Laurine MacDonald Dodge arrived in Little Current to testify at the inquest into her husband's death.

In earlier inquest proceedings, which the hospitalized Laurine could not attend, the doctor who performed the autopsy on Daniel's body testified that the deceased youth's wounds—a shattered hand, penetration of the upper arm by a piece of steel, and face and head injuries—would not have proven fatal if Daniel had not plunged from the boat and drowned. The discharged caretaker, Dick Drolet, testified that the boat was fully equipped with lifebelts.

The interest shown by the inquest jury in the witnesses and testimonials abruptly changed to apprehension when an overeager constable seized the opportunity to stage his own pageant in the small, overcrowded courtroom. Holding a stick of dynamite in his hand, he tipped the 14-inch fuse with a lighted match. He then allowed the fuse to burn for a brief time before extinguishing it, to demonstrate at least part of the few minutes of sputtering that occurred before dynamite would explode.

The appearance of the young Dodge widow, dressed in black and accompanied by her parents, injected a different kind of excitement into the courtroom on October 22. Bryant's wife and Frank Valiquette also testified on this same day. Valiquette described events leading to the explosion, recalling Daniel's insistence on experimenting to see if the dynamite was "still good." He told of fitting one stick of dynamite with a 14-inch fuse which, Valiquette estimated, should have burned for nearly three minutes before exploding. He went on to describe Daniel's effort to toss the dynamite stick outside the garage and the immediate explosion as sparks from the fuse ignited caps and other sticks of dynamite left on the window sill.

Laurine's quiet and demure demeanor did not diminish the inquest jury's keen interest in the young widow's recital of events on the day of the accident. Despite unpleasant connotations that arose during the course of the inquest, suggesting that neither the explosion nor the drowning was accidental, there was little doubt of the outcome of the hearings after Laurine's brief testimony. Ten minutes later, the jury of area residents returned its verdict, ruling that Daniel Dodge's death was an accident.

The outcome of the series of court battles regarding the distribution of Daniel's estate, however, remained unpredictable. The sparring continued to seesaw, spurred by the filing of suits and countersuits involving a battery of gladiator-attorneys, paid well for their efforts. In the meantime, Laurine began collecting a monthly $5000 widow's allotment, later raised to $7500 by court edict. The amount, Laurine's lawyers pointed out, was paltry compared to the annual $350,000 or more that Daniel's sister Frances and his two half-sisters each collected as their shares of the John Dodge trust-fund income.

When the probate court hearing finally took place before Judge Thomas C. Murphy in late October, 1939, attorneys pleaded their clients' respective cases day after day. If the Daniel Dodge trust-fund income were awarded to the widow and Daniel's mother, the federal government and state would claim more than $5 million of the $10 million estate for inheritance taxes, attorneys for the three sisters pointed out. These lawyers also claimed that, by the specific wording of John F. Dodge's will, the share of any deceased child was to be divided among the remaining children until all children-inheritors were dead, when the fund itself would be divided among the children's heirs—meaning those who directly succeeded John F. Dodge by birth. The sisters' lawyers strongly stressed that "proper" return of Daniel's trust-fund income to the fund itself would eliminate the heavy inheritance taxes.

While Judge Murphy's decision was pending, life for Matilda and Frances took on a nearly normal complexion. From Frances' new stable, Jimmy Johnson had sent 26 saddle and harness horses to the

National Horse Show at Madison Square Garden two months after Daniel's death. When Frances' bay gelding was runner-up in the three-gaited saddle class, and her chestnut mare, Sunday Swing, won the saddle pony stake, the family hoped that Frances, still depressed after her brother's death, would regain her enthusiam for her show horses.

The door to Daniel's room remained locked as Matilda tried to bury her own grief in a flurry of philanthropic enterprises to occupy her mind and body. Her Salvation Army and church work, above all. An active membership in Friends of the Detroit Public Library. In the Founders Society of the Detroit Institute of Arts. The Society of Arts and Crafts. The Detroit Historical Society. And a lengthy listing of other organizations, including those offering care to orphans and to tubercular children.

Although she prided herself on careful, even stringent, money management in the operation of the farm and Meadow Brook Hall, Matilda could be surprisingly generous at unexpected times. When a young man, who formerly delivered newspapers to Meadow Brook, came unannounced to the Hall to talk to Alfred Wilson, Matilda called out from the next room. "Who is it, Alfred?"

Explaining that it was their former paperboy seeking a donation to an organization sponsoring a playground and basketball court for underprivileged children, Alfred saw Matilda whip out her checkbook. Pen in hand, she went into the hallway. "How much money are you trying to raise?" she asked, as she filled out the check.

"$72,000," the young man answered. Murmuring thanks for the donation, the caller took the check and left. Only then did he look at the figure. $72,000.

In their mutual struggle to pick up the pieces of their lives, Matilda and Frances drew closer together as they planned various trips with Alfred and Jimmy. The foursome went to Los Angeles in March, 1939, spent a few days at the Ambassador Hotel, and then sailed for Honolulu. The following July, Frances and Jimmy were, once more, in California where Frances rode her five-gaited Harmony Lane to victory in the stake event at the Coronado Horse Show. By mid-November, the Wilsons and Johnsons were together in Manhattan, sharing adjoining suites at the Sherry-Netherland Hotel.

Probate Court Judge Thomas Murphy had not yet ruled on the dis- tribution of Daniel's trust-fund income when, on November 27, 1939, Frances reached the age of 25 years and became eligible to receive her own fortune—$9.5 million in accumulated interest from the John F. Dodge trust fund. Frances knew that her mother planned a formal dinner party for 20 guests to celebrate the birthday. But as the guests ate dinner from what one newspaper described as "solid gold place-settings" in the stately dining room, a startled look crossed Frances' face as she heard the clear strains of dance music, played by a trombone and accompanying orchestra.

The formality of the dinner party dissolved into an informal evening of enjoying, and dancing to, the music of Tommy Dorsey and his orchestra—imported to Meadow Brook's ballroom where another 150 guests quietly gathered to surprise the birthday-girl. Because of John Duval's circuit court suit, seeking to break his father's will, the 25-year-old Frances could not yet collect her inheritance, however.

In early December, Judge Murphy prepared to read his ruling on final distribution of the Daniel Dodge estate when Dodge attorneys requested an adjournment. Because an out-of-court settlement of the dispute now seemed possible, the opposing lawyers asked for a postponement of the decision until January 10, 1940.

"That possibility should have been thought of long ago and not after the case has been dragged through the courts," Judge Murphy scolded. Nettled by the last-minute request, the judge went on to warn the lawyers not to conduct any "fishing expeditions" nor to attempt to "play horse" with the court. At the same time, he admitted that a settlement might benefit all parties.

Notoriety surrounding the tragedies and conflicts of the contentious Dodges provided absorbing newspaper stories read by householders as they drank their morning coffee, and by factory and office workers jolting along on streetcars and buses. But for Lucille Manzer Mealbach, the fairy-tale lives of the Dodges held only mild interest compared to exciting changes in her own life as she began to suspect that she might be pregnant.

Lucille still had no realization of Frank Upton's involvement with the Dodge family—no idea, certainly, that Upton, with no legal background, served as the court-appointed Guardian ad Litem for the Dodge estate, beginning in the 1930s. She had no way of knowing that, as Guardian ad Litem, Upton took responsibility for representing those "known and unknown" likely heirs to the John Dodge fortune during the litigation over Daniel Dodge's estate. Although the Uptons often saw the Robert Manzers at church affairs, they no longer visited so frequently at the Manzers' Woodside address as they had visited at the family's former homes when Lucille was a young girl.

Before their first child's birth in 1939, Lucille and her husband moved from their apartment into a rented upstairs flat on Lawndale. Somewhat shyly, Lucille told her mother that she was "expecting." The term was a generally accepted euphemism, as was "in the family way" or "with child." But in the Manzer household, even such euphemisms were rarely spoken.

So, in many ways, Lucille's increasingly obvious pregnancy took on a mythical quality as the childless Minnie Manzer kept her eyes fixed on her daughter's plump and lovely face when the two women talked. . .as if the older woman were too embarrassed to glance at the swollen abdomen which, within a few months, assumed an activity of its own with precipitous bulging and rippling.

Lucille's choice of physician was a young Methodist doctor whose schooling had received some financial help from Robert Manzer. Her visits to the doctor's office were routine affairs. On each visit, the doctor tested her blood pressure and gently scolded her for gaining too much weight. He gave her a diet instruction chart and she tried to follow the rules on the sheet. But by the time she went to bed at night, her dreams were permeated with visions of freshly baked bread, chocolate cake with fudge icing, strawberry sodas...

Mystified by some of the medical terms the doctor occasionally mentioned, Lucille did not concern herself with them. After all, having a baby was a natural function, she told herself, even though she had never discussed the birth process with her mother or anyone else. An expectant mother went into the hospital, the baby was extracted in some sterile way by the doctors, and the new mother had an adorable infant to love and cuddle. No more dieting. No more weight problems. She could scarcely wait to go into the hospital, which, in itself, would be an entirely new experience for her since she had no memories of ever before being hospitalized.

When at the end of nine months of pregnancy, a mild cramping and discharge signaled it was time to go to the hospital, Lucille bathed and then carefully set her blonde hair in curlers. Next she raided the refrigerator, feasting on all the foods, including a large piece of coconut cake, for which she yearned while she was dieting. She brushed her hair into its usual attractive coiffure, applied make-up, and attached her prettiest earrings. She squeezed her feet into high-heeled shoes and completed her costume with her newest hat and matching gloves.

Attributing curious stares from the admitting clerk to bad manners, Lucille followed a nurse up to a room with two beds, referred to by the nurse as the "labor room." Disrobing in the small adjoining washroom as directed by the nurse, Lucille thoughtfully fastened the ties for the short, wrinkled "gown" the nurse supplied. Where, she wondered, had the nurse taken the suitcase that she had packed carefully with her own ruffled gowns?

Deciding to ask the nurse for her own nightgown, Lucille came out of the washroom. Clutching at the gaps in the round-necked hospital wrapper, she was struck by her first premonition of impending distress when she saw, beneath the partly drawn curtain that separated the two beds, a pair of men's shoes. Lucille's heart pounded. She decided to forget about asking for her own nightgown and to ask, instead, to move to a different room—with a female roommate.

Cautiously, Lucille peeked around the edge of the curtain to see another swollen-bellied woman sliding her feet into the large shoes, alternately groaning and wailing as she walked, in a bent-over position, alongside the bed. Totally absorbed in her own misery, the woman seemed unaware of the new arrival's presence.

Disturbed by the other woman's suffering, Lucille got into bed and pulled the sheet up around her chin. She hoped the nurse would take the other woman into the delivery room very soon. For the first time, too, she began to wonder about the delivery room...how it looked...what the birth of her baby would be like. Perhaps she wouldn't know much about it, she thought—they probably would put her to sleep.

When the nurses took the other woman out of the labor room later that day, it made no difference to Lucille. By this time, she was struggling with her own relentless pain—pain that tore at every part of her body, as if she were being stretched on a medieval torture rack. Terrified by what was happening to her, she clutched the headboard of the bed and tried to draw herself up and away from the spasms that gripped her, only to hear the nurse scolding. "Bear down," the nurse ordered. "Fighting like that will only make it worse."

Worse! The pain couldn't possibly get worse, Lucille despaired. But it did worsen as the hours wore on toward evening and as she cried and vomited repeatedly, emptying her stomach of the food she ate before coming to the hospital.

Suddenly, she understood what it meant to "bear down" as the racking pain changed to a thrusting, pushing kind of encompassing pain when, finally, a nurse took her into the delivery room. With arms and legs strapped to the table, she screamed and battled the pain until a nurse clamped an ether cone over her nose. Lucille breathed deeply and sank into oblivion just as the doctor delivered her baby, a healthy girl.

Thirty minutes later, orderlies wheeled Lucille down the hallway to her room and lifted her from the stretcher to the bed. She lay there, totally exhausted, scarcely aware of the muted early-morning sounds of the hospital, when she heard Minnie Manzer's soft voice next to her ear. Lucille half-opened her unwilling eyes to squint into Minnie's face. "I've brought you a present," Minnie said cheerfully, opening a rectangular box she set on the bed.

From the box, Minnie drew out a filmy lavender negligee with creamy lace inserts and a small train. The kind of negligee, Lucille knew, that Minnie had never worn. The kind of nightwear that would have brought expressions of rapturous delight from Lucille, had she not just undergone what she would always recall as "the worst shock of my life—childbirth," of which she had been totally ignorant.

Now as she looked, with a strange mixture of sadness and pity, at the childless Minnie—equally ignorant of such matters—she croaked an almost unintelligible "thank you" for the gift, breathing in the lingering smell of ether. Her throat was raw from screaming. Her eyes swollen shut from crying. Her blond hair matted with sweat and vomit and stuck to the pillow.

But she had a baby girl of her very own to love and care for. She decided to name the baby Brenda.

As much as she dreaded bearing another child, Lucille became pregnant again soon after Brenda's birth. "Everyone has a hard time with a first baby," Bill's sister, Clara, told her. "Having a second baby is much easier."

Lucille, always an optimist, began to lose some of her fears as other friends told her the same thing. But when she went into the hospital for the birth of her second child, she became hysterical with fear when hard labor pains tore at her body hour after hour. Doctors tried to turn the baby from its breech position, but without success.

When Lucille emerged from a hazy fog of pain and ether fumes, she smiled weakly as her husband told her they were parents of a son, William, Junior—a healthy child despite the trauma of a breech birth.

Two children were enough, Lucille determined as she left the hospital ten days later with her son. Never again did she want to endure the misery of childbirth.

Chapter 16

Evidence of Origin

Detroit's economy boomed in 1940 when factories began turning out steel, rubber, and other essential supplies to support the British in the war against Germany. Racial tensions rose in the Motor City as Detroit's black population increased by an additional 60,000 people between 1940 and 1942. At the same time, an influx of white Southern workers helped generate an acute housing shortage.

The housing shortage compelled working-class families to move into moldering two-room apartments rented to them at inflated rates by landlords who had partitioned comfortable flats into cubby-hole living quarters. The plight of families of newly arrived workers, frantically searching for housing, was portrayed in news stories read by affluent householders in Grosse Pointe and Birmingham who forgot such problems as quickly as they tossed aside their newspapers.

Wealthy suburbanites were much more captivated by published details of the marriage of Edsel Ford's eldest son, in mid-June of 1940, to Anne McDonnell—slim and aristocratic daughter of Wall Street financeer William McDonnell. Edsel and Eleanor Ford gave the young couple a substantial wedding gift—a luxurious home in Grosse Pointe and 25,000 shares of Ford Motor Company stock. Middle-class Detroiters, reading of the marriage of the 22-year-old Henry II, viewed the wedding in New York as a fabulous affair of almost royal dimensions.

For Matilda Dodge Wilson, news accounts of the wedding created a rising sympathy for the bridegroom's grandparents, Henry Ford I and Clara. She knew that the senior Henry's distaste for Wall Street barons surely was exacerbated by the fact that the McDonnells were Roman

Catholics and close friends of the Joseph P. Kennedy family. Matilda could imagine Henry's repugnance when he learned that his namesake grandson "took instructions" from Monsignor Fulton J. Sheen and converted to Catholicism previous to the wedding.

Vast sums of money did not exclude young Henry Ford II from the company of a half-million Detroiters required to register for the first selective service in October of 1940. And even if Ford money and business responsibilities could have commanded a privileged status for young Henry at home in Detroit, his father, Edsel, did not want his sons sheltered from military service. The memory of his own exemption in 1917, at the insistence of Henry I, still pained the sensitive Edsel who now suffered from stomach ulcers.

Between visits to the hospital, Edsel was aggravated by the behavior of his perverse and dictatorial father. Henry I continued countermanding the son's orders and decisions, even though the president's door at Ford Motor Company still displayed Edsel's name-plate.

If Daniel Dodge had lived, Matilda Wilson surely would have been preoccupied with concerns for the safety of her son in serving his country. Because of his untimely death, she mourned because her son was not alive to be included in the mobilization of strong young men preparing to defend their country if the United States became involved in the worsening European conflict. Daniel had loved boats, and Matilda was certain that he would have chosen to serve in the Navy. Or perhaps the Air Force. But she tried not to brood unduly on what might have been. There were significant events shaping in her own life to bolster her determination to live each day to its fullest despite disappointments and wounds to the spirit.

Her daughter, Frances, adjusted to Daniel's death by spending more time with the horses that both she and Matilda loved. In October of 1940, Matilda felt a thrill of pride in her daughter's skills as Frances saddled her champion trotting horse, Grayhound, and rode the eight-year-old gelding one mile at Lexington, Kentucky, to a world's record—2:01 1/4. In sports columns, horsemen applauded Frances' feat, in recognition of the tough challenge in riding a trotter, at speed, for any distance.

Two weeks later, Frances exhibited the largest stable entered at Madison Square Garden in the National Horse Show. There, her three-gaited and five-gaited horses, saddle horses, harness horses, and harness ponies won a collection of ribbons and $1845 in prize money—a source of gratification to the horsewoman who willingly spent her money to assure a top rating for her stable.

Because of John Duval's suit, claiming that the $1,350,000 annual income from the John Dodge trust fund should be shared among the four surviving children because the original Dodge will had been broken, Frances had not yet received the $9-plus million due on her previous birthday. And with the settlement of Daniel's estate, she also expected a portion of her brother's fortune.

Before the end of 1940, when Frances learned that her first child would be born the following July, she permitted her husband and their trainers to do all the riding and driving for her stable. Delighted with the expectation of having a first grandchild, Matilda was equally delighted with an unexpected honor bestowed on her in November, 1940. On that date, Michigan's Governor Luren Dickinson announced his intention of appointing Matilda Wilson to fill his own unexpired term of lieutenant-governor after Dickinson moved up to the state's highest office at the death of the elected governor. Although the appointment was largely symbolic, lasting only until January 1, 1941, Matilda eagerly anticipated breaking the discriminatory custom that excluded women from the office of governor or lieutenant-governor, not only in Michigan but in most other states.

She did not anticipate the furor that erupted at Dickinson's announcement. The 81-year-old Dickinson, a puritannical Methodist who promoted a return to Prohibitionist days of the 1920s, met with strong opposition to many of his proposals which were, he said, a result of his "spiritual pipeline to God." The state's solidly male administrative board now bucked the appointment of Matilda Wilson, particularly after Michigan's attorney-general gave his opinion that Dickinson was both lieutenant-governor and acting-governor—that no appointment should be made.

Elegantly wrapped in silver fox fur, Matilda traveled by plane from a shopping trip in Chicago to Lansing where she calmly made an entrance into the board room at the Lansing Capitol on the morning of December second. The other board members, shuffling about uneasily as they waited her arrival, bowed their heads and smiled stiffly as the governor escorted Matilda into the room and introduced her as the new lieutenant-governor.

Matilda sat down next to Dickinson, and the others also sat, obviously relieved at concluding the introductory rites for the intruder into their masculine domain. As they proceeded with their agenda, the men carefully averted their eyes from the small and tidy feminine figure of the new lieutenant-governor.

Matilda was not accustomed to being ignored. But it was not her nature to display her emotions in public, however often close family members might have experienced her flashes of temper. Now, as she sat demurely in her assigned chair, her sharp brown eyes moved carefully from one man to the next, her gaze reflecting her own composure and sense of intactness.

As if abashed by her self-assured presence, the board members quickly decided on matters on the agenda. They voted unanimously in each instance, Matilda assenting in her soft but firm voice to each vote. Before noon, the newest board member was whisked away to Grand Rapids to attend a meeting of the Michigan Horticultural Society.

Attorney General Read, refusing to appear at the first December meeting, could not avoid attending a second board meeting two weeks later when he sat uncomfortably close to Matilda Wilson—at her immediate right. Matilda seemed unfazed by Read's presence despite his previous prediction that, in the event of Governor Dickinson's death and the rise to power of Matilda Wilson, "...the state would be in a fine mess."

In published statements, Matilda offered quiet reproof to detractors, saying that she would "adequately discharge any duties that might be required" of her as a result of her appointment. She made it clear to reporters that she considered her appointment "a symbol" of the rightful place of women in public service.

Shortly after Matilda's appointment expired in January, 1941, Judge Murphy of the Wayne County Probate Court gave his final order settling the Daniel Dodge estate. He mandated five percent of the estate returned to the John Dodge trust fund principal for the benefit of "undetermined heirs." The three sisters received nearly half the remaining 95%. The widow, Laurine, now taking business classes at Alma College, was awarded $1 1/2 million in addition to the previous $1/2 million in monthly allowance and the Canadian properties. The remaining chunk would go to Matilda. But since John Duval's suit was still pending, Daniel's heirs could not collect their money.

Throughout 1941, the spread of the war in Europe overshadowed the world with horror as Hitler's armies attacked Yugoslavia and Greece, then invaded Russia. In a last fling at retaining their carefree ways, Americans went about singing lively popular songs. "Chattanooga Choo Choo." "The Hut-Sut Song." Still, "The White Cliffs of Dover," best selling novel, became a movie with a title song that struck a response from most Americans hoping for a brighter future.

The birth of a healthy granddaughter—Judith Frances Johnson—brightened Matilda's life in July, 1941. It pleased her that, by this time, her daughter, Frances, was no longer as painfully thin as she had been in her post-debutante years. And as Dick and Barbara Wilson approached adolescence in the early 1940s, Matilda took a more active part in the lives of her adopted children, permitting them to help decorate Meadow Brook's huge Christmas trees—towering firs set up in the drawing room and in the huge entrance hall, plus a tree in the servants' quarters.

Dick enjoyed accompanying the chauffeur on his rounds at Christmas, delivering beautifully wrapped packages sent out by his mother. He noticed that none of the packages went to Rose Terrace, the lavish Grosse Pointe residence of Anna Dodge. When he asked about this, Matilda emphasized to young Dick and Barbara that she wanted nothing to do with the Horace Dodges because of their penchant for notoriety and divorces. Critical of the ostentatious spending by Anna and her children, Matilda tried to instill her own values in Dick and Barbara by taking them along when she carted baskets of Christmas gifts to orphans' homes, encouraging her adopted children to help distribute presents to the orphans.

Alfred Wilson often took his young son to football games at Michigan State University, and Matilda expected Barbara to help in the kitchen when her mother gratified her own yen for cooking. In the fall, as mother and daughter peeled and canned tomatoes, Matilda's admonitions to Barbara frequently echoed the slogan "Waste Not, Want Not" lettered in blue on white wall-tiles. Matilda also taught Barbara the housewifely arts of knitting and crocheting as they made mittens and scarves for donation to the Salvation Army.

When Dick was 12 years old, Matilda relaxed the rules confining the two children to their own quarters at Meadow Brook Hall. There remained only a few "off-limits" places such as Knole House, Frances' unused and locked playhouse that always enticed the children to look longingly through the casement windows to see the miniature furnishings.

When, occasionally, Dick got into trouble for breaking a rule, Matilda prodded Alfred to apply a willow stick to the seat of the boy's trousers. He applied the willow stick rigorously on the day that Dick set off a large firecracker at Frances' kennels, sending one of the high-strung dogs into fits. Ruby Watson, the kennelmaid, was so incensed by the boy's prank that she would not speak to Dick for many months afterward.

At age 13, Dick was sent to Culver Military Academy; later to Wesleyan University. When Dick left for Culver, Barbara departed for a boarding school in the East.

Soon after the Japanese bombed the United States fleet at Pearl Harbor on December 7, 1941, followed by declarations of war by the United States against the Axis powers, Edsel Ford underwent an operation for stomach ulcers. In accordance with Edsel's wishes, his eldest son, Henry II, enlisted in the navy and went to Great Lakes Naval Training Station. Henry's younger brother Benson also enlisted, but both young men worried about their father's failing health.

The concerns of their grandfather, Henry I, were quite different. Edsel's deteriorating health, the senior Henry expostulated, was simply a manifestation of his failure to "toughen up." If Edsel developed some backbone, Henry insisted, he also would develop a healthy resistance to physical ailments. The stubborn Henry applied the same unenlightened philosophy to his own health problems—denial of their existence. He had a stroke in 1938 which, his family recognized, left his judgment impaired. But Henry pridefully attributed his increased irascibility and unreasonable tyranny to manifestation of his own backbone.

In February, 1942, when the court ruled negatively on John Duval's appeal to acquire more money from the Dodge estate, Frances' accumulated trust-fund income, now some $10 million, was released. So, too, was the Daniel Dodge estate of $13 million. By this time, Daniel's widow, Laurine, had shucked the navy-serge and black-bloomered uniform of Alma College, where she had enrolled to learn money-management, and deserted the campus to marry the doctor who performed cosmetic surgery on her facial scars incurred in the dynamite explosion.

It did not surprise Matilda that Laurine remarried. But she resented the fact that the girl, made wealthy by Dodge money, chose to marry a divorced man. Laurine's marriage to the divorced physician cemented a permanent estrangement between the two women who had been closest to Daniel. By June of 1943, Laurine had divorced the plastic surgeon and married for a third time.

Bewildered Detroiters read the maze of figures published in newspapers before, and during, the distribution of Daniel Dodge's millions. At the same time, Minnie Manzer gave her daughter, Lucille, an envelope containing a document—a registration of Lucille's birth. Lucille accepted it without question, aware that, in recent years, the issuing of social security numbers to workers required presentation of birth-date documentation. She looked at the registration, filed with the state, and found that it contained only her name—Frances Lucille Manzer, date of birth—November 23, 1914, and place of birth—Detroit, Michigan.

Only one word on the registration form aroused her curiosity—the listing of Frances as her first name. Minnie Manzer curtly dismissed her daughter's questions about the name. Lots of people always used their second names, Minnie pointed out. The Manzers simply preferred the name <u>Lucille</u>—that was all.

"Then why didn't you call me Lucille Frances?" the daughter persisted.

"Because Frances Lucille sounds better," Minnie snapped.

Lucille did not wonder why the registration form did not list her parents' names. Nor did she question the date of registration with the state—September 2, 1941. Twenty-seven years after her birth. Lucille was totally unaware that a delayed filing of birth documentation required an explanation for the delay. Nor did she have any reason to link the 1941 filing of the registration with Judge Murphy's order, given that year, to settle the Daniel Dodge estate. She had no knowledge that her father's friend, Frank Upton, had any connections with the Dodge family—nor that he served as an appointed "officer" of the court, charged with serious responsibilities to represent unknown heirs during the court litigations over the estate of Daniel Dodge.

Seven months after the court denied John Duval's appeal, his name catapulted back into newspapers when he died, ignominiously, in a Detroit hospital in August, 1942. Events leading up to his critical injury, his death, and the following inquest, played out their own sordid story before an audience of readers fascinated by a series of repeat performances in the pages of newspapers, day after day. The scenes flashed back to an intoxicated John Duval fighting with his wife at the home of an acquaintance...returning to the same house and trying to force his way into a young woman's bedroom through a window... becoming belligerent with police officers in the station until they forced him into a sitting position on the terrazzo floor whereupon he flopped backward, his head thudding against the terrazzo.

The unconscious 44-year-old John Duval, suffering a severe skull fracture, was taken to the hospital and placed in an oxygen tent where he died a day later. But his death did not end the nightmare of publicity so humiliating to Matilda. Newspapers also reported details of the inquest, which determined that policemen were not to blame for Dodge's death. Unhappy highlights of John Duval's life were exposed again in print, along with accounts of other tragedies endured by the Dodge family.

Matilda did not attend her stepson's funeral and did not meet John Duval's teenaged daughter, who was among the mourners at the service. Matilda had no interest in the girl; had no intention of ever meeting her. But, at the request of her stepdaughters, she reluctantly agreed to permit John Duval's coffin to be deposited in the Dodge mausoleum—near the remains of his father and mother, his Uncle Horace, and Matilda's own two children.

A large floral arrangement from John Duval's cousin, Delphine, added to the profusion of flowers heaped at the bier. Ten months later, in June, 1943, Anna Dodge's daughter, Delphine, died at age 44. From pneumonia, newspapers said. But friends knew that alcoholism ruined her health.

The strange parallel between the Dodge and Ford families emerged again after Edsel Ford was hospitalized in serious condition with undulant fever in November, 1942. His father, Henry, whose food fetishes included drinking unpasteurized milk from his own dairy cows, had regularly sent containers of milk directly to Edsel's home and insisted that his son, too, must drink pure milk from the farm. Pasteurization, Henry pontificated, was a process that destroyed milk's natural goodness.

When physicians identified Edsel's illness as undulant fever acquired from drinking unpasteurized milk, Henry Ford refused to accept the diagnosis. Edsel's illness resulted from his living habits, the father raged. His son must change these habits in order to get well. Quit reading so many books. Become a vegetarian. Stiffen his will to be strong.

In May, 1943, doctors performed a second operation on the critically ill Edsel. When the doctors discovered stomach cancer, they told Henry his son was dying. Incredulous at this horrifying news, Henry demanded the impossible of Ford Hospital physicians—that they restore his son's health. Quickly. Permanently.

When Edsel died on May 26, 1943, at age 49, Matilda felt a great sympathy for the embittered Henry in the loss of his son. The grandson, Henry II, soon was released from the navy to take an active part in the Ford business in its production of tanks and bombers. The death of Edsel Ford marked the rapid rise of Henry II to head the company, and accelerated the mental and physical decline of Edsel's father until his death four years later.

One month after Edsel Ford's death, a race riot erupted in Detroit. On the day that Delphine Dodge's funeral cortege moved out to the Dodge mausoleum, army troops took command of the central city. Eleven people were killed and hundreds injured before troops restored order and factories could operate again at full capacity to supply war materials. The Dodge Division of Chrysler Corporation then returned to its manufacture of four-wheel-drive vehicles—400,000 of them used as weapon carriers, ambulances, and command cars because of their serviceability in off-the-road operations.

By this time, Jimmy Johnson joined the Army Air Corps and was serving in Panama. Frances and her small daughter, Judith, spent most of their time at the Meadow Brook farmhouse, and Matilda closed off part of Meadow Brook Hall to conserve fuel. Recently, she had given orders to raze the unsold and unfinished Grosse Pointe mansion, built more than 20 years previously by her husband, John F. Dodge. She donated the steel girders for conversion into war materials; then sold the cleared property. Soon afterwards, Matilda also sold her unprofitable Wilson Theater.

With the fall of Mussolini in 1943 and the capture of Rome and the Allied landings in Normandy in 1944, the war took on a favorable outlook for the Allies. Ever since Jimmy Johnson had joined the Air Force, Frances went regularly to the USO center in Detroit where she served coffee and doughnuts and chatted with lonely servicemen to the throbbing melodies of a jukebox flashing its rainbow lights. When Matilda decided to accompany her daughter to the USO center, the older woman made herself useful in the kitchen. But Frances chafed at Matilda's regular presence, suspecting that her domineering mother was motivated by her resolve to keep her daughter under close surveillance...to make sure that Jimmy Johnson would return to a dutifully waiting wife.

Resisting suggestions from her family to have an automatic dishwasher installed, Matilda sometimes washed dishes at home, too. When help was scarce at the Hall, she did the laundry or, even, scrubbed floors. She carefully checked functions of her reduced staff in these years, enforcing conservation measures as fitting to her personality as to wartime demands.

A maid—Veronica Sullivan—hired by Frances at the farmhouse, provided a variety of personal services for Frances, including preparing meals for her child, Judy Johnson. Although life at the farmhouse, working for "Mrs. Johnson," was leisurely and relaxing, Veronica frequently found her services commandeered by the more demanding Matilda Wilson. At such times, Veronica went willingly over to the "big house" to help the cook or waitresses prepare for a special dinner party. After one such affair, Veronica questioned another maid who busily scraped butter remnants from bread-and-butter plates and combined the remnants in a larger bowl.

"Why are you saving that?" Veronica wanted to know. She was startled by the response that Mrs. Wilson ordered the butter remnants collected—for serving at the "help's" table.

"It's not sanitary," Veronica sniffed. "I'm not going to eat it."

In those early and middle 1940s of gas rationing and fuel shortages, Matilda had more time for reading. The best selling novel of 1945, Forever Amber, held no interest for her because she remained dedicated to self-improvement. She read Bible-study books, English usage books, foreign-language studies, history books, and biographies in her quest for knowledge.

Matilda also grew more attached to her granddaughter, Judy, in those years as the small child took her first pony rides, helped her grandmother bake cookies, and begged to help wrap packages at Christmas time when Matilda and Frances shopped for stacks of gifts for friends and servants. Although snow blanketed Meadow Brook Farm that winter of 1944-45, shopping excursions into Detroit were not curtailed—neither for Matilda and Frances, nor for the maids on their once-a-week day off.

Veronica Sullivan's boy friend picked her up on a free day and drove her into Detroit as snow sifted down from a gray and cloudy February sky. By the time they drove back to Meadow Brook that evening, snow whirled furiously and piled into drifts across the farmlands. As Veronica's friend tried to steer his car along the winding roadway leading to the farmhouse, the automobile ran into a fence completely covered by snow.

Making timid explanations about the damaged fence the next morning, Veronica was relieved when Matilda Wilson seemed unperturbed. "Don't worry about it," she assured the maid. "The road wasn't plowed, and you couldn't see the fence."

Mrs. Wilson wasn't so bad after all, Veronica decided.

On Jimmy Johnson's release from military service in 1945, he joined Frances in setting up a new stable of harness horses—this one located in Lexington, Kentucky. There, Frances had purchased Castleton Farms, an historic estate in the choicest of bluegrass country-side where horse breeding was big business. As the Johnsons left for Lexington, the maid, Veronica, transferred to the "big house" to work for the Wilsons. When the Wilsons prepared to leave for Florida that winter, they asked Veronica to go south with them. But Veronica, who did not want to leave Detroit, took another job at that point. . .and was promptly sent a bill, by Matilda Wilson, for repair of the fence that was knocked down a year earlier.

At the war's end, Matilda kept busy with the renovation of the west wing of Meadow Brook Hall. Dodge Stables' show horses brought a 1946 world championship in pony competition to Frances' King Commando and a world championship award to Matilda's six-horse team of Belgian draft horses.

By 1947, Frances' stable at Castleton Farms acquired national recognition. Her stallion, Victory Song, set a world record in Illinois and was named "Harness Horse of the Year." Her $5000 colt, Hoot Mon, won the Hambletonian, earning $56,810 that year.

Matilda also received national recognition when the national commander of the Salvation Army came to Detroit to present her with the Distinguished Auxiliary Service Cross for 28 years of work, including 21 years as president of the Auxiliary. Only 60 years previously, the commander pointed out, the Salvation Army was declared "a public nuisance" when it first began beating drums and blowing bugles at Detroit street corners.

Matilda was pleased with the honor...pleased, too, with the smooth flow of family life at Meadow Brook in these early post-war years. When, in the spring of 1947, she learned of her sister-in-law Anna's divorce from Hugh Dillman, Matilda severed the remaining links of minimal civilities that she had grudgingly retained with the Horace Dodge side of the family.

Frances Dodge Johnson must have interpreted Matilda's bitter reaction to the Dodge-Dillman divorce as a warning, but it was a warning that the heiress chose to ignore. Although Castleton Farms' horses were winning prizes and plaudits, Frances' marriage was not running smoothly. In January, 1948, the press revealed that horsewoman Frances Dodge Johnson filed for divorce on charges of extreme cruelty and desertion.

At the April divorce hearing, only Frances came before the judge. A private agreement on a property settlement and custody rights had already been arranged after Jimmy Johnson withdrew his plans to fight the divorce and to claim custody of the couple's daughter. The judge awarded Frances an uncontested divorce.

For Matilda, the divorce was an ugly scar to be endured in her attachment to her daughter and granddaughter. But when, soon after the divorce, Matilda heard rumors that her daughter planned to marry, the older woman was infuriated by the possibility of such a precipitous remarriage. Her fury exploded when she discovered that the man Frances planned to marry was also divorced, and the father of a son.

To Matilda, it mattered little that Frederick Van Lennep came from a family of well bred New Englanders, that he was distinguished—both in appearance and manners, and had attended prestigious eastern schools including Princeton University. His divorce was the unforgivable factor that inflamed Matilda into confronting Frances. "Either give up Van Lennep, or get your things off the farm!" she raged at her daughter.

Frances did not remove her possessions from the farm, but she left for Kentucky, taking Judy with her. Despite Matilda's mandate, Frances returned to Meadow Brook at intervals. At such times, Matilda tolerated her daughter's presence, but there was no warmth and little communication between the two women.

When Dick Wilson came back to Meadow Brook from college that summer, Matilda surprised him by offering him the use of Daniel's room. Since she had already given him the car that Daniel had owned, Dick interpreted these actions as an unusual expression of affection.

Frances married Van Lennep in January, 1949. Under pressure from Alfred "to do the proper thing," Matilda decided that she and her husband would attend the quiet ceremony in the drawing room of Castleton Farms manor. Immediately afterwards, the Wilsons left to fly by private plane to Arizona where they had recently bought a winter home in Scottsdale. The couple became so attached to the mountainside ranch-style house, with its glorious view of Paradise Valley, that they planned to spend every winter in Arizona. On their return to Meadow Brook Hall, Alfred frequently expressed his opinion that he and Matilda rattled around in the Tudor mansion where a whisper or cough reverberated with eerie persistence through the vaulted hallways. To Alfred, a house the size of their western residence in Arizona seemed much more homelike.

The outbreak of the war had no direct effect on the Mealbach family at first. Bill Mealbach, in his late thirties and the father of two children at the time of the Pearl Harbor attack, was not called into service. Lucille's brother, Rob, however, received his induction orders soon after graduation from high school. Rob was newly married when he was sent overseas to serve in the European conflict. Lucille worried about her young, handsome brother and saved the letters she received from him, although he could tell her little about his reconnaissance intelligence assignments.

When Rob left for Europe, Minnie Manzer's health failed rapidly. Although she rarely complained, she finally went to a doctor who diagnosed the illness as cancer. For the stoic Minnie to submit to medical examination and treatments was tacit admission of the pain she endured. When, finally, she complied with her doctor's recommendation for hospitalization, her husband and daughter took her to the hospital. As they tried to help her up the approach to the entrance doors, the frail Minnie shook herself free of their support. "I might not walk out of here by myself," she said as she tottered up the steps, "but I'm going into this place on my own."

Minnie's condition quickly deteriorated in the hospital where she spent her last days. On the night she died, Lucille came, earlier in the evening, to visit her nearly comotose mother. Minnie's sunken eyes shifted about, her gaze following her daughter as the younger woman busied herself with straightening the paraphenalia on the bedside table, arranging fresh flowers in a vase, walking from one side of the room to the other while she told her mother of the latest news from Rob.

Anything, Lucille thought, to shield herself from the anguish mirrored in Minnie Manzer's dark-circled eyes and from the terrifying feeling that her mother, who could scarcely talk, desperately wanted to tell her something. Lucille could not bring herself to press her face to the quivering lips of the woman who lay helpless in the bed...to try to hear and understand whatever it was that her mother, who always had been so dispassionate and aloof, now wanted to confide. Whatever it might be, Lucille was afraid to hear.

As she stood there, undecided, her father came into the room and the spell was broken. Robert Manzer still sat at his wife's bedside when Lucille left the hospital room to return to her family.

When she learned, in the early morning hours, that her mother had died, Lucille felt a twinge of guilt. Why hadn't she tried to find out what her mother wanted to say? But that was nonsense, Lucille scolded herself. Very likely she only imagined that Minnie Manzer wanted to tell her something. Still, she could not then—or later—erase the remembrance from her mind.

The funeral took place without Rob's presence as the war in Europe continued. After the funeral, Robert Manzer asked Lucille to sort out Minnie's personal belongings—mostly clothing. Since a Woodside neighbor, Mrs. Kischenheider, was a good friend of the Manzers, Lucille invited her to come and choose any items of clothing she might want for herself, because the neighbor-woman's height and weight were similar to Minnie's. Lucille packed everything else for donation to Good Will Industries.

As she removed clothing from the closet, then wiped down the closet walls and mopped the floor, wisps of blond hair hung limply on Lucille's forehead. She brushed them back impatiently. "My hair is so fine!" she complained to Mrs. Kischeneider. "It just won't stay in place. I wish I had thick hair like my mother."

The neighbor looked inquiringly at Lucille. "Oh, so you _knew_ your mother," she said.

A strange feeling, like a hot shiver, flashed through Lucille's body. What a peculiar thing for Mrs. Kischeneider to say, she thought, but made no reply. It seemed disloyal to Minnie, somehow, to ask more questions—right after her mother's death.

For the first time, Lucille wondered if she might be an adopted child. But she had never been curious about family background in earlier years, and now, very quickly, her flash of curiosity faded. There were so many current family matters to keep her attention fastened on the present...not the past, or even the future, except for looking ahead to Rob's return—and hoping that he would return.

The war had not yet ended when Rob was shipped back to the States. Wounded in the legs by shrapnel, he was discharged with a 50% disability.

Lucille's concern for Rob's well-being meshed with fear for herself when she found that, once again, she was pregnant. Burdened with anxiety that she might have to undergo a second breech-birth delivery, she went to another doctor recommended by a friend who had given birth to her first baby without difficulty. But when the Mealbachs' third child, Linda, was born in 1945, Lucille had to endure another long and difficult delivery that left her more fearful than ever before of another pregnancy.

She mentioned none of her fears, however, to her brother's wife, Lillian, when the young woman became pregnant. After months of recuperation in a veteran's hospital, Rob now worked for Ford Motor Company. Deciding to buy a house, the young couple ordered new furniture. As they prepared to move into their new home, Rob fell from a scaffold at work and was killed. His distraught young widow stayed with Lucille during the funeral and until Lillian went into the hospital for the birth of her infant son two weeks later.

Despite his strong Methodist faith, Robert Manzer was devastated by Rob's tragic death. Lucille grieved, also, but the demands of her lively children kept her from sinking into self-pity and despair.

In the Mealbach home, responsibilities for the children rested entirely on Lucille. While Minnie Manzer had lived, she helped, without being asked,when the babies were sick. But now, Lucille could expect to deal, alone, with such emergencies. Her husband worked steadily at the stove manufacturing company, going off to his supervisory job each day in a handsomely fitted suit. He supplied money for necessary family expenses, but he rarely stayed at home in the evenings. He preferred the conviviality of his friends in neighborhood bars.

Lucille's objections to these nightly excursions were ignored, as were her requests for Easter outfits and white shoes for the children. Her husband's personal expenditures were more important to him than providing money for unessential items for his wife and offspring. Lucille, who was not a worrier by nature, was concerned about saving money for a down payment on a house. But because her quick smile gave no indication of her problems, her father never suspected his daughter was unhappy. To Lucille, it was important to protect her own pride...to avoid pity from her parents who had not approved her marriage to Mealbach. And after her mother's death, she continued hiding her personal difficulties from her father.

It became harder for Lucille to be cheerful when she suspected she might be pregnant again, while Linda was still in diapers. Obsessed with the idea of finding a doctor who could ease the terrible suffering she feared, Lucille listened as her sister-in-law, Clara, talked about a doctor who used caudal anesthesia to minimize the pain of his obstetrical patients in giving birth.

Although the use of caudal anesthesia was still a relatively new technique, Lucille went to the physician mentioned by Clara. When her labor pains began, months later, she went into the hospital with feelings of apprehension mixed with confidence that the spinal anesthesia would take care of her problems. As the terrible, wracking pains went on for hours, Lucille begged the nurses and doctor for the anesthetic. When, finally, the doctor injected the anesthetic into her lower spine, the pain stopped—for a while. And then the real nightmare began as the doctor used instruments to deliver a very large baby.

Lucille's ten-pound baby boy was lifeless, his neck broken, when the infant was extracted from his mother's pelvis, which was too small to accommodate passage of such a large baby. The doctor explained this to Lucille the next day. He kept her in the hospital for the usual ten days, and asked if she would have someone to help out at home if he allowed her to leave. Tired of lying in bed for so long and anxious to return to the children, Lucille nodded.

The doctor stood at the foot of the bed, looking intently at her, promising to send her home in an ambulance the next afternoon. But if she became pregnant again, he warned, it was important for her to go to a top-flight obstetrician. "Only the very best. Someone like Dr. Henderson. Most important," he emphasized.

Lucille did not want to even think about another pregnancy...only about getting home to care for the children so her sister-in-law, Clara, and the neighbor girl could stop sharing the responsibility for baby-sitting the Mealbach youngsters. When the ambulance brought her to Lawndale the next afternoon, the attendants followed the doctor's orders and carried Lucille, on a stretcher, up the stairs to the Mealbachs' second-floor flat and into the bedroom. By the time the two men reached the bottom of the stairs with the empty stretcher, Lucille walked into her kitchen, planning what to cook for supper.

Before Christmas, that year, Lucille shopped for toys and gifts for the children, warning her husband that she would need extra money to get her purchases out of layaway before the holidays. When, a week before Christmas, the gifts remained in layaway, Bill Mealbach waved away his wife's anxious reminders about extra money. "Christmas Eve is payday," he said impatiently. "I'll be home early with the money."

By supper time on Christmas Eve, he had not yet come home. The children left for church to take part in a Christmas program, reminding their mother that the program would start at 7:30. And Lucille sat down by the front window, gazing out at patches of swirling snow in the glare of the street light, disheartened at the thought of the children's disappointment when they looked under the tree on Christmas morning. At seven o'clock, she saw her husband walking carefully across the street toward the house, and then heard his heavy footsteps on the stairs. Lucille grabbed her coat and hat and, as soon as her husband opened the door and flopped on the couch, she reached into his pocket to retrieve his billfold. Quickly she removed several bills from the wallet and hurried downstairs to the bus stop.

She went from one store to the next, collecting the gifts from layaway before the nine p.m. closing, with no time for regrets that she could not attend the children's Christmas program. Her children would find their gifts from Santa under the tree the next morning—and, for now, nothing else mattered.

In January, 1949, Lucille began a series of pre-natal visits to Dr. Henderson at his downtown Detroit office. On the first visit, Dr. Henderson examined her, verifying that her pelvis was, indeed, too small to risk a natural delivery and that this baby would be delivered by cesarean section.

Then, feeling the glands in her neck, he frowned as his fingers touched the shoulder scar near the base of her neck. Lucille quickly told him about the childhood fall that caused the scar, as well as the other scar at the base of her skull.

"Do you get headaches?" the doctor asked.

Lucille shook her head. No, she did not get headaches.

The doctor was quiet for a moment. "These scars aren't from a fall," he said firmly. "These are surgical scars. Like the kind that might come from the separation of Siamese twins."

What a strange idea, Lucille thought, quickly dismissing his words from her mind. Dr. Henderson might be the best of obstetricians, but he was wrong about her being a freak! Still, after her first visit to the obstetrician, she was no longer as frightened by the expectation of having another baby and did not brood about the surgical procedure as she went about her usual routine.

In August, on the date scheduled for the delivery of her baby, Lucille waited as long as she dared for her husband to come home, early, from work and take her to Providence Hospital as he had promised. When he did not arrive, she and her husband's sister, Clara, left by taxi for West Grand Boulevard and the large brick building

Chapter 17

Struggles for Independence

In June, 1950, florists delivered masses of great yellow orchids to decorate Meadow Brook Hall for the debut of Barbara Wilson, recently graduated from a private school in New Jersey. Since Matilda expected that the coming-out party for her adopted daughter would be the last of its kind held at the mansion, she wanted the occasion to be a splendid and memorable affair.

Matilda and her secretary addressed hundreds of party invitations, including one mailed to Mrs. John Cline, Matilda's sister in Rochester. Thrilled at her inclusion as one of the "family," Amelia dressed with care for the late afternoon reception—a second reception was to follow in the evening. The last time Amelia had traveled Adams Road to the main gate of Meadow Brook was in 1938 when her husband accompanied her to Daniel's funeral. This time she came alone, displaying her invitation to a gatehouse guard and driving on past rows of dahlias, snapdragons, and larkspur.

To Amelia, the mile of curving road from the gatehouse to the Hall was a sensual, nostalgic flashback to an earlier time when she had selected flower arrangements from the greenhouse, now in view on the left. A time when she had lived in the rambling white farmhouse, visited the stables, and supervised maintenance of the tenant houses beyond the curve in the drive.

The clarity of the flashback dimmed as Amelia entered the Hall and joined the reception line. Slowly she approached Matilda, wearing a buttercup yellow designer gown, who greeted her politely. Impassively. As if she were an obscure acquaintance, Amelia thought.

Barbara, a pretty girl in a white marquisette frock with a bouffant skirt, greeted her newly introduced "Aunt Amelia" with a look of surprise mirrored in her blue eyes. Until the debut, neither Barbara nor Dick Wilson had ever heard Aunt Amelia's name mentioned.

Within seconds of the introduction, the reception line pressed ahead and Barbara and Matilda turned their attention to the next guest. Amelia found herself isolated among party guests, few of whom she recognized, who clustered in animated groups oblivious to anyone but themselves. As soon as she could make an inconspicuous exit, Amelia left the house and retrieved her car from the meadow where a driver had parked it among numbers of sleek automobiles guarded by private detectives.

John Cline knew that his wife had no plans to stay for the evening reception when the popular Dick Jurgen's Orchestra would play for dancing. Still, Amelia's prompt return surprised Cline. "Back so soon?" he asked. Amelia's small face drooped with disappointment as she told him of her sister's indifferent attitude. For 19 years, she had lived with hopes that Matilda would mellow and seek to reestablish ties with her only sister. Now, Amelia's hopes for a reunion crumbled as she faced the hard fact that Matilda was approaching her 67th birthday with little change in her rigidity.

Few, if any, of Matilda's attitudes had altered in her late years, including her faith in the value of discipline and work. Dick Wilson, enrolled to begin his senior year of college with the 1950 fall semester, had been encouraged by his parents each summer throughout high school and college to take a job—one of which was selling Fuller brushes. Matilda helped with this venture by purchasing an overkill supply of brooms and mops and cleaning solutions and stockpiling them in a third floor storeroom. $10,000 worth of cleaning supplies bought, in two weeks' time, by Matilda and Frances, according to a Detroit Free Press article which quoted Wilson.

But in the summer of 1950, Dick worked with his father on the farm. At Matilda's urging, Dick recently had switched colleges to attend Michigan State University, majoring in agriculture economics. This education, he felt, would prepare him to begin managing the farm for his aging father.

Alfred, who had known poverty in his childhood and frequently boasted that he was a "self-made" man, took pleasure in having his son work closely with him that summer as the two took companionable jaunts around the countryside to barter for dairy cattle or other livestock. Dick realized, too, that he was establishing a closer rapport with his mother during these, his young-adult, years. Matilda clearly relished her adopted son's interest in her show horses and his proficiency at training Meadow Brook's high-stepping ponies. Dick hesitated to risk rupturing this increasingly pleasant relationship by telling his parents that he wanted to marry the young woman he was dating at school—Elinor Baldwin. He knew that Elinor's religion, Roman Catholic, posed a difficult problem to acceptance of his fiancee by his parents.

When Dick finally told the Wilsons of his plans to marry, his parents' reactions were even more disapproving than he imagined. Horrified by the realization that her adopted son was determined to be married in the Catholic Church, Matilda bitterly recalled her sympathy for Henry Ford when his grandson, Henry II, married a Catholic. Now, as Matilda faced a similar predicament, her response was more implacable than Henry Ford's had been.

Matilda gave her ultimatum to Richard with such deliberate calm that it took on an even more ominous cast. She pointed out that his choice was an affront to the personal values of his father, son of a Presbyterian minister...an affront, also, to his mother, active in her church and in the Salvation Army. She made it clear that by turning away from these values, Richard was severing his ties to the Wilson family.

Since Dick's earliest teenage years, Matilda had warned him that, as an adopted son, he could expect to receive every educational and cultural advantage the Wilsons could offer, but that, as an adult, he should expect to reflect Alfred's "self-made" image. Dick realized that, unlike Frances and the deceased Daniel, neither he nor Barbara held claim to the Dodge fortune.

As much as he wanted to remain in his parents' good graces, Dick was not willing to surrender all independence. Nor, certainly, to give up Elinor. In December, 1950, the two were married in a Catholic ceremony in a suburban Detroit church. The Alfred Wilsons did not attend the wedding. The farm at Meadow Brook and the horses that Dick trained were no longer a part of the young man's life. Dick returned to college, graduating in 1951 with a degree in business administration, then went to work for the Ford Motor Company Tractor Division.

His sister, Barbara, continued doing all the right things, remaining at the center of the shrinking family circle dominated by her mother. Sent off to junior college in the East, Barbara dutifully studied homemaking arts.

By this time, Detroit Historical Museum directors approached both the John and Horace Dodge widows for financial assistance to expand the museum's building program with construction of a Dodge Memorial

Hall of Industry. Although both families responded with a combined $135,000 gift, the only Dodge attending the October, 1952, dedication program was Matilda, a speaker at the ceremonies. Parts of her speech were quoted frequently in later years. "I believe in history," she told her listeners, "if knowledge of the past helps face the challenge of the future."

Privately, Matilda continued refusing interviews to writers who tried to probe deeper into her life, although she responded cautiously to those who wrote articles focused on her philanthropic activities. The responses to personal questions were always the same kind of programmed replies...her father had been a Detroit merchant; private tutors had provided her with an education.

In December, 1952, she willingly discusssed the engagement of her daughter, Barbara Jean Wilson, to Lieutenant Thomas Eccles of Suffern, New York. The couple would be married the following June, Matilda informed the press. At Meadow Brook, of course. It was apparent that, for Matilda, this wedding was unencumbered with bothersome apprehensions about the suitability of the match.

It also became apparent to Matilda that, with Barbara away at school, the senior Wilsons rattled around in the spaciousness of their baronial home. For Matilda, this was not a problem. But Alfred seemed uncomfortable when he was alone in the huge manor.

Before the Wilsons announced Barbara's engagement in December, they ordered a smaller contemporary home, which could be managed by two servants, built on their Meadow Brook properties. They planned to occupy the home, Sunset Terrace, on their return from Arizona in the spring of 1953, and to reserve the use of Meadow Brook Hall for large parties, including Barbara's wedding in June, and fund-raising events for charities.

Barbara's "Aunt Amelia" did not attend the June wedding. Her pride would not allow her to risk another display of indifference, which Amelia interpreted as rejection, from her sister. Instead, she bought copies of Detroit and suburban papers and repeatedly read details of the Wilson-Eccles marriage before adding the clippings to her accumulation of Dodge data.

Barbara's wedding was similar to the ceremony that united Frances Dodge to Jimmy Johnson in 1938. The adopted daughter, in white satin and lace, swept down the grand staircase to a full-toned wedding processional echoing from the chambers of the great organ. Unlike Frances, Barbara clung to the arm of her father, Alfred Wilson, until they approached the fireplace in the drawing room where the bride and groom took their vows.

In one important matter, Barbara made an independent decision, choosing Dick Wilson to serve as an usher at the ceremony. Knowing how close Barbara and Dick had always been, Matilda reluctantly accepted this decision, even though it meant that Dick's wife, Elinor, would be present at the wedding. Matilda customarily observed only minimal amenities in such cases, and this encounter with a previously unrecognized daughter-in-law was no different.

At the newlyweds' departure for a Hawaiian honeymoon, the Wilsons' lives took on a different contour as they settled into Sunset Terrace. In planning the senior Wilsons' $300,000 curvilinear home, architects opted for openness that provided a mirage of interior space to accommodate the couple's transition from huge Meadow Brook Hall. The result was a circular house boasting a looping, brushed-aluminum stairway with glass panels etched with images of Matilda's favorite dogs and horses, and a 50-foot living room fronted with a curved wall of windows and a panoramic view of Meadow Brook's pastures and grazing horses. In the evening glow of the sun dipping down to the horizon, the pink brick exterior of Sunset Terrace flooded with a rosy hue that delighted the Wilsons when they were in residence.

Very often, though, they were not home. Matilda had purchased her own plane—the Bluebird—and hired two pilots to fly the Wilsons on business trips, to summer home in Maine, and to their winter home in Arizona.

The separate organizations in which Matilda and Alfred held memberships took husband and wife in different directions much of the time. Like Matilda, Alfred served on the boards of directors of several businesses, including the Clark Equipment Company of Buchanen (near Niles), Michigan, of which Frederick Upton of St. Joseph was also a director. Matilda and Alfred owned some $2 million of stock in the company.

Because the Wilsons occupied themselves with meetings and travels, little opportunity remained for speculations on how different their lives might be if their son, Dick, were not barred from their home. If Amelia still were included in the family circle. Above all, if they kept closer ties with Frances and Frederick Van Lennep, who had their first child, Fredericka, in 1951; their second, John Francis, in 1952.

The Van Lenneps began spending more time in the Detroit area in the early 1950s, after investing $800,000 in Wolverine Raceway, west of Detroit. The purchase brought Frances and her husband to Michigan anually for the harness racing season, at which time they lived in a large home purchased by Frances in Indian Village. Frances visited Meadow Brook infrequently. Van Lennep's visits were even fewer.

Matilda's admiration for horses did not extend to the ticket-littered grounds and mutuel machines of commercial racetracks. Still, she respected the fine reputation of Castleton Farms in the siring and breeding of champion harness horses. She respected, too, the public admission of Fred Van Lennep to "give Frances all the credit—it belongs to her." But the withdrawn Frances preferred to have her husband deal with the strategies of the horse business and with the press. Her own gratification came from working with her prized three-gaited and five-gaited show horses—particularly with the famed champion, Wing Commander.

In the 1950s, Dick Wilson also moved into the horse business when the Van Lenneps hired him to manage their Michigan raceway. Frances had felt an increasing attachment to her adopted brother ever since he grew into his early teens. She admired his genial, outgoing personality and trusted him to carefully handle the Van Lenneps' racetrack interests. Dick, now the father of two children with a third expected, was eager to prove himself worthy of Frances' faith in his abilities.

By this time, Dick began visiting Meadow Brook and Sunset Terrace at regular intervals. No invitation arrived from Matilda; he simply came, with some trepidation at first. When his mother did not refuse him admittance nor forbid him to return, he came again—and again. Alone, in the beginning. Later, he brought his young son with him. Then his daughter. And gradually, Matilda thawed, although she never invited them to dinner or mentioned Dick's wife. She sometimes gave trinkets to the visiting children, but did not remember them at Christmas time with personal gifts. Still, Dick persevered, thinking that as Matilda aged, she might wish to be closer to her family.

Age did not bring loneliness to Matilda; too many interesting events sparked her life. At the 97th commencement exercises held at Michigan State University in 1955, she proudly accepted an honorary degree—Doctor of Laws. She felt that the university conferred the degree in good faith, in recognition of her years of service on its governing board, the State Board of Agriculture.

When, in 1956, the Ford family donated the deceased Henry Ford's manor, Fair Lane, and its surrounding acreage to the University of Michigan for construction of a branch campus in Dearborn, the gift fueled Matilda's imagination. Now approaching age 73, she still enjoyed good health, although Alfred had some health problems. But she became aware of her mortality at this point in her life and often considered what the future of Meadow Brook should be. Because of her own respect for education, she began to entertain the idea of donating her beloved Meadow Brook to Michigan State University.

In late December, she arranged to discuss this idea with the president and vice president of the university. The matter was quickly settled. Except for the two homes—Sunset Terrace and Meadow Brook

Hall—plus 127 acres reserved for the Wilsons' use, the university would take over Meadow Brook's 1600 acres for an Oakland County branch campus. At the death of the Wilsons, the homes also would become properties of the university.

When Matilda asked how soon the building program could begin, Dr. Hannah, university president, replied that if enough money became available, construction could begin in 1957 or 1958. Matilda looked carefully at Hannah, her friend for the past 30 years. "We'll need $2 million for the first two buildings," he explained. With hardly a pause, Matilda offered to supply the $2 million, escalating the value of the total endowment to an estimated $10 million.

She also had made a recent money-gift to the Walkerton Lutheran Church in which her father, George Rausch, was a charter member. In March of 1956, the Wilsons traveled up to Walkerton, Ontario— Matilda's birthplace—for the dedication of carillons funded by Matilda in memory of her father.

Groundbreaking ceremonies for the first building on the new campus took place in May of 1958. Holding a silver shovel, Matilda bent to stab the blade into the earth with surprising energy for a 74-year-old woman. Her mind stirred with excitement at the thought of splendid pavillions of higher learning rising around Sunset Terrace and Meadow Brook Hall, with the Wilsons ensconced regally in the midst of the principality.

In October of that year, Matilda reached her 75th birthday, honored on the occasion by the Detroit Federation of Women's Clubs at the clubhouse which John Dodge donated some 40 years previously. The federation feted Matilda as its honorary president, with special mention of a recent tribute paid by the Women's Auxiliary to the Salvation Army in naming Matilda Wilson its president emeritus. Her generous gifts to Michigan State University and to other charities were acclaimed. Nothing was said of that curious ambivalence in Matilda's personality that prompted her to take satisfaction in selling cream from her dairy cows to the Salvation Army Auxiliary for a tea; then presenting the organization with a sizeable check a short time later.

The first undergraduate classes began at the new Oakland County University in September, 1959. But, a year earlier, a former chicken house was converted into a classroom for an adult education class. Matilda's intense interest in the progress of her "god-child" university prompted her to enroll in this early adult program; one of 43 students in the rapid reading class.

At age 77, Matilda seemed to be reinvigorated, rather than exhausted, by the press of responsibilities that she eagerly accepted.

Robert Manzer, who still practiced headstands to promote healthy circulation of the blood, became increasingly depressed and forgetful in the years following the deaths of his wife and his son. When his dog broke its leash and ran into the street where a car struck and killed the animal, Manzer cried for days. To Lucille, it was apparent that her father suffered from a great deal of mental stress.

On days when his mood changed to a more cheerful outlook, Manzer often got into his Dodge automobile and drove to Lucille's house where he invited the children to climb into the car for a ride. Aware that her father was no longer an alert driver, Lucille warned the older children to make excuses so they would not have to ride with Grandpa Manzer. But the Mealbachs still did not own a car, and the children could not resist the chance to ride to a store or an ice-cream parlor with their grandfather who wheeled in and out of traffic without regard for other vehicles.

Even when the Mealbachs moved to the Detroit suburb of Dearborn in 1951 and rented a pleasant house on Ternes Street, Grandpa Manzer continued driving out to see the grandchildren. In the summertime, he liked to drive up to the farming community of Peck, north of Port Huron, where he visited his cousin, June Eschtruth, who had moved north to the small town some years previously with her children.

When the three oldest Mealbach children were enrolled in Dearborn schools and only two-year-old Sharon remained at home, Lucille enjoyed taking her small daughter to the park to play while the mother set up an easel and painted landscapes. When the youngsters returned home from school, the eldest child, 12-year-old Brenda, helped out with the younger ones while her mother fixed supper.

On a rare evening out with her husband on a pleasant October night, Lucille left her twelve-year-old daughter in charge of the three smaller children for a few hours. While the youngsters sat in front of a ten-inch, black and white television screen in the living room, someone knocked at the front door. Brenda peered out the window to see a woman, wearing a suit and a matching hat, standing on the porch. Hesitating for a moment, she decided it was safe to open the door to such a nicely dressed lady.

With apologies for the interruption, the woman asked if she might use the bathroom. It was quite necessary, she explained. "I didn't know where to stop, but your house looked so pleasant and well lighted..."

Not knowing what else to do, the Mealbach daughter opened the door wider and the woman walked inside. The girl directed the stranger to the bathroom, noticing that the woman was not as tall as her mother, and then stood protectively near her younger brother and sisters, still absorbed in the television program.

As the woman returned from the hallway to the living room, she smiled as she looked at the children. She stood there, as if undecided what to say, then left even more quickly than she had come, murmuring "thank you very much." From the window , the girl watched as the unknown woman walked down the block to a large, dark automobile parked in front of a neighbor's house. She got into the passenger side of the front seat and the car moved away into the evening shadows.

When the parents returned, their daughter told them of the woman's visit. Bill Mealbach, greatly excited, rushed into the bathroom and began looking behind the toilet and into the corners of the small room.

"She could've hidden a bomb somewhere!" he fumed. "Don't ever let a stranger into the house again," he warned his thoroughly frightened daughter who had not known that the stove company was having union trouble as organizers tried to sign up workers. Even Lucille knew little of the union troubles that plagued her husband, now a company superintendent, as the Detroit-Michigan Stove Company was accused by the UAW-CIO of conspiring with racketeers to intimidate employees and union organizers.

There was no bomb in the Mealbach home. Nor were there any answers about why the unknown woman came to the house, unless she actually did have to use the bathroom. Lucille thought no more about the visitor, but, years later, her eldest daughter clearly remembered the woman and wondered who she could have been.

The following spring, when Lucille learned that her father planned to move up to Peck, she worried that he might be lonely, especially for the grandchildren. She could not go to visit him often—she had no car and, at 38 years of age, underwent another cesarean section as her child, Thomas, was born. Although suburban life in Dearborn was much more tranquil than living in their former Detroit neighborhood, Lucille's marriage remained unimproved.

By 1953, however, Mealbach's job as superintendent enabled him to accumulate a down payment on a two-story, aluminum-sided home on Calhoun Street, close to Dearborn's shopping district. Although the rooms were small, the house had four bedrooms to accommodate the family of seven, plus a basement with attractive recreation room and fireplace. A narrow side-drive led to a garage at the back which provided storage for the lawnmower, Lucille's garden tools, and the children's bicycles.

The family liked the security of life in Dearborn—the domain of an autocratic but popular Mayor Orville Hubbard who kept the streets clean, the parks orderly, and the neighborhoods safe. The Mealbach children could walk to schools of the highest quality and Lucille could walk to large department stores—Montgomery Ward and Federal—within blocks of her home. Most of all, she enjoyed working in her yard—cultivating her tomato plants, watering her rose bushes and flowers, and trimming her shrubs.

For the Mealbachs, life at the Calhoun address became much more precarious when the Detroit-Michigan Stove Company announced that it was moving its operations to Long Island, New York, in 1957. The UAW-CIO finally had won bargaining rights for the stove company's workers, boosting the pay for unskilled workers to $1.75 an hour at a time when unskilled laborers in New York were paid $1.07. When the stove company, which dated back to the 1850s in Detroit, moved out of Michigan in June, 1957, the 25-foot-high, carved oak cookstove-landmark remained on East Jefferson Avenue to mark the passage of an era when the manufacture of wood-burning stoves was a leading industry.

The passage of an era meant little to 50-year-old Bill Mealbach. But the loss of a job and a regular paycheck meant disaster when he discovered it was not a simple thing for a man of his age to find employment.

With no money coming in, Lucille no longer concerned herself with the "little luxuries" she wanted for her family. She was concerned, now, with grocery expenses, meeting monthly mortgage payments,and paying utility bills. Even when the gas bill was overdue, Lucille never considered letting her father know that her husband had no job, nor asking her father for financial help.

Instead, she called a friend whose husband owned a small metal-stamping plant in Dearborn. "The stove company closed and we're getting desperate," Lucille told her friend as she asked if the friend's husband might have an opening in his factory for Bill.

The response was reassuring as the friend urged Lucille to send Bill to the plant to talk with her husband.

"Well," Lucille hedged, "I don't want to let Bill know that I've asked for help. He has a lot of pride, you know."

Between the women, arrangements were made to have the friend's husband phone Bill—to tell him that he'd heard the stove company closed and wondered if Bill might want to come to work at the metal-stamping shop. Within days, Bill began working as a press operator at the shop, with no suspicions—then or later—that his wife appealed for help.

Bill no longer needed to take the bus into Detroit, but could walk the several blocks to the small shop. He rarely missed a day at his machine and was well paid for his work, so he could afford to pick up his usual pattern of heading for a favorite bar each evening to enjoy the company of his buddies.

Lucille's diversions were home-centered. While the older children were in school and the youngest napped, she painted with oils and experimented with colors. Yet, she felt this kind of self-gratification could be put aside when her youngest child would enter school; she would find a job, then, so she could buy some of the extras that might make life more pleasant for the children and herself.

In the meantime, Lucille tried to make her family's Dearborn home as comfortable and pleasant as possible. Each springtime she got out her roller and brushes and paint cans and painted several rooms of the house with fresh colors. For holiday meals, the Mealbachs always gathered around a festive table, with snowy-white or ecru-lace cloth set with the Havilland china that had been Minnie Manzer's—even when, as sometimes happened, the husband and father was not at home to appreciate the meal.

Because the children's schools were nearby, Lucille wanted her youngsters to come home each day for lunch—often hot soup and sandwiches. Each evening, she placed a cooked meal on the table and, if Bill Mealbach did not come to eat, Lucille uncomplainingly fixed him a sandwich when he arrived much later...sometimes as late as one or two a.m.

Even Bill's sister, Clara, scolded Lucille for her refusal to demand that her husband spend more time at home...stop wasting money at bars... help with the care of the children.

"Clara, it's just not in me to fight," Lucille protested. "Yes, I want Bill to change, but I can't turn this house into a battlefield. I try to keep things as nice and peaceful for the children as I possibly can."

She recognized her mistake in marrying Bill, but she felt compelled to live up to her share of the bargain—to be a good wife and mother and homemaker, even if her husband did not live up to his share. Such were the principles instilled by her parents—the conscientious, Christian Manzers.

When Lucille's oldest daughter got her first job, part-time work in a dime store after school, the girl declared her intention of setting aside some of her wages for a week's vacation the following summer. Lucille cooperated by managing to keep a few dollars out of the household money to put together with her daughter's savings for rental of a cabin at Estral Beach.

Although Bill Mealbach indicated he had no intention of accompanying his family on this first vacation, he changed his mind on the morning of departure and joined his wife and five children, including two-year-old Tommy, as friends drove them to the lake.

Lucille brought along a stroller for the baby, but soon discovered that pushing a stroller through the deep sand of the beach was not an easy feat. She abandoned the stroller and carried the child under her arm, along with assorted gear needed at the lakeside, while the children cavorted in the water. She washed diapers by hand in the cabin, and cooked meals that were hungrily devoured by her offspring and by one of the children's friends who had accompanied them on vacation.

As Lucille fought flies and mosquitos, treated sunburns, and tried to keep the baby's milk from spoiling, she looked forward to the week's end and a return to her comfortable home on Calhoun. Bill had done the disappearing act as soon as they had arrived at the beach. Dressed in neatly pressed trousers and crisp shirts, he spent most of the vacation time sitting in the cool comfort of the nearby hotel bar, making new friends under the hum of whirling fans.

For the first time, Lucille began to think seriously of divorce. Yet, she realized the financial hazards of divorcing a husband who did, after all, provide a home and the necessities of life for a family of five children. She readily conceded that her husband, even when drinking, never abused her or the children. And she was certain that he did not pursue other women. Still, she deplored his expensive personal habits that deprived the family of both his companionship and the extra money that could have enriched all their lives.

"You can fight another woman, but you can't fight drink," she sometimes said to family members—Bill's own sister, Clara, for one—when they criticized her accepting attitude toward her husband's excesses. She knew that her peace-at-any-price temperament might be considered weakness. But she simply could not bear quarreling or fighting.

Even Lucille's threat of divorce did not impel Bill Mealbach to promise to change in any way. "I love you and the children, and I don't want a divorce," he said. That was all. No pleading. No pledging to moderate his drinking nor to spend more time with his family.

When the youngest child, Thomas, entered school, Lucille told both her husband and her father, visiting from Peck, that she was going to look for a job. For once, the reaction from both men was the same. "You won't be able to get a job. You don't have any skills or training," they discouraged her.

Perhaps not, but Lucille knew that she always had a flair for color and style and fabric. The first day that she searched for a job in Dearborn, she found one close to home—at Winkleman's.

Working at the women's clothing store, Lucille found, to her delight, that she could quickly establish a rapport with customers, resulting in good commissions on sales. When her sales topped those of the other clerks, she won first prize offered as part of the store's incentive program. At home, she modeled the prize—a sequined cocktail dress—for her admiring children. But because cocktail parties were not part of Lucille's life, the fancy dress hung in her closet for years—unworn.

Lucille's rapport with customers did not extend to the female store-manager who intimidated employees with her domineering and sarcastic attitude. Lucille had worked at this first job for a few months when she walked into the store on a Friday night to pick up her paycheck.

"Well, girls, it must be payday," the manager snapped loudly as Lucille approached. "Mealbach's here."

"Yes, I'm here," Lucille responded levelly. "And if I didn't need the money, I wouldn't work for you for one more minute."

She took her paycheck and left the building, walking across the street to another women's clothing store—Albert's. Because of the proximity of the two stores, Lucille was no stranger to the manager at Albert's, who promptly hired her.

Working conditions at Albert's were pleasant, but Lucille was fascinated by another store on busy Michigan Avenue in the heart of Dearborn's shopping district. Ray's Bridal Shop. A few months later, she switched to a job in bridal consulting at Ray's, where customers responded to her friendly personality and generous smile.

She saw little of her father in these years because of the demands of her five children and her job. Occasionally, Manzer drove to Dearborn to visit. On one such visit in the early fifties, he had told Lucille of his plans to marry June Eschtruth's former housekeeper, a widow and mother of three adult children.

"You needn't worry about me," he assured Lucille. "Florence is a good homemaker. And I sure will like having companionship." As far as finances were concerned, he boasted to Lucille that he had "enough money to last me if I live to be 199 years old."

Robert Manzer had never spoken of finances in earlier years. In these later years, his seventies, he had changed, Lucille observed. She felt relieved, though, that her father would no longer be lonely, because many of his old friends, including Frank Upton, had died. When, shortly after Manzer remarried, he and Florence came to visit at the Mealbach home, Lucille packed the Havilland chine that her father gave her after Minnie's death, and insisted that her father and his new wife take the china with them.

To Lucille's daughters, the Havilland china represented a rare touch of elegance in their mother's life. The girls, who appreciated the skirts and blouses their mother sewed for them and the sweaters she bought for them with her earnings, decided to try to do something special for Lucille by sending in her name to the Detroit Free Press for a drawing in a "makeover" contest. The winner would receive a week of beauty treatments at the Virginia Farrell Salon in downtown Detroit.

Now in her forties, Lucille Mealbach was an attractive, fair-skinned woman who wore her blond hair in the sophisticated upsweep style popular in the 1950s. When the newspaper announced the contest winner's name—Lucille Mealbach—the daughters met their mother with squeals of delight at the front door when she returned from work at the store.

The following day, Lucille took time off from work to go down to the newspaper office and have "before" photos taken; then rode the bus into downtown Detroit each morning of the following week. For seven days, her photos appeared in the daily newspaper. Wearing an exercise suit as she stretched and strained through a series of calisthenics. Clad in towels for a massage. Her head wrapped in a turban as a mudpack covered her face.

At the end of the week, beauticians cut her hair and created a new hairstyle in preparation for a photography session. Forty-two photos. When the newspaper published the best of the 42 as "after" photos along with the "before" shot, the Mealbach girls fussed about the display. "Mom, the 'before' shot is better," they complained. Lucille laughed, admitting that she agreed with them. She went to work the next day, chuckling when her co-workers and customers made similar comments.

Lucille's eldest daughter had a personality as attractive and upbeat as her mother's. Soon after high school graduation in 1957, Brenda married a young college student working for a degree in architecture. Her daughter was very young—Lucille was concerned about that, but pleased that Ken was such a fine young man. The young couple usually picked up Lucille in their car on Sunday mornings and went to church, returning to the Mealbach home for dinner with the family.

A letter from June Eschtruth in 1959 made it more difficult for Lucille to be cheerful. Her father's wife, she learned, had placed Manzer in a nursing-care facility, claiming that she could no longer care for him at home.

Brenda occasionally drove her mother up to Peck to visit the ailing man. There, they found an emaciated Robert Manzer lying on a thin mattress in a dark attic room of the nursing home, converted from an old farmhouse.

Depressed by the poor condition of the nursing home, Lucille tried to arrange to have her father transferred back to Dearborn and into more modern facilities. But her father's wife refused to cooperate. And Manzer's senility worsened rapidly during his confinement. When Lucille and her daughter visited, he recognized the women, but could scarcely communicate with them. "Grandpa, do you still stand on your head?" the granddaughter asked in an attempt to get a response. Manzer looked sadly at her, saying nothing.

Shortly after this visit, the Mealbachs learned of Robert Manzer's death when June Eschtruth phoned them. "You mean you weren't notified?" June asked in disbelief, although she, too, had not learned of her cousin's death until she saw the obituary notice in the local paper. "The funeral is scheduled for tomorrow."

Lucille's employer at Ray's Bridal Salon gave her an advance from her next paycheck, and her daughter drove her up to Peck that evening. When Lucille and Brenda, accompanied by June Eschtruth, came into the funeral home before the service began and occupied front-row seats, the funeral director politely asked them to move farther back. "The front seats are reserved for 'family'," he said. The women remained in their seats. "We are his family," they insisted.

Upset by the sudden appearance of three determined women, whose names were not listed in the death notices, the director retreated to the safety of his office to await the appearance of the widow and stepchildren. The widow, on her arrival, was equally upset by the front-row presence of Manzer's daughter, granddaughter, and cousin. In icy silence, the two sets of relatives sat through the service, then went their separate ways.

Chapter 18

Epitaphs and Testaments

Amelia's husband, John Cline, died in 1960. Soon afterwards, Amelia sold her home in Rochester and moved into an apartment. The diminutive widow's close friends in Rochester, concerned that the 73-year-old Amelia was alone, urged her to make an attempt at reconciliation with her sister. When Amelia's pride prevented her from approaching Matilda, the friends decided to act as emissaries by talking to people who had access to the older sister.

Since the death of Cline permanently removed him as an obstacle to communication between the sisters, Matilda had no reason to resist the peacemaking efforts of friends and the urging of Alfred to end 30 years of estrangement from her sister. In 1961, Amelia gratefully accepted the opportunity to become a part—even a peripheral part—of the family once again. She did not ask for details of how Matilda had been persuaded to relent. If her friends had portrayed the widowed sister to Matilda as a solitary and lonely figure, Amelia did not wish to know.

The reconciliation was only one of a series of changes in Matilda's life in the early 1960s. Because Meadow Brook acreage now belonged to the university, Matilda moved her powerful Belgian draft horses west to 500 acres she had purchased near Howell. She sent a trusted Meadow Brook employee to care for the 30 horses and their valuable harnesses, the latter stored in temperature-controlled glass cases. When the Wilsons visited the horse farm, they stayed in a comfortable apartment above the farm's business offices.

Although Matilda had announced that Barbara Wilson's debut party was to be the last one given at Meadow Brook Hall, she now made plans to open the Hall in 1960 for a similar party—this one for her granddaughter Judy Johnson. She retained a special warmth for Judy, reaching back to earlier years when the child lived at Meadow Brook. The Van Lenneps were planning a December debut for Judy at their Lexington home, but this did not dampen Matilda's eagerness to honor her granddaughter with a reception and ball at Meadow Brook.

At a summons from Matilda to a press conference at her Fisher Building offices in the spring of 1960, society editors scurried to the lofty gold-domed building. With her secretary at her side, Matilda conducted the "conference" as crisply as if she were presiding at a board meeting of industrialists.

She informed the press that there would be two receptions, like those for the debuts of Frances and Barbara, for one thousand guests. Decorations and gowns would complement a Sterling Rose theme.

Only the forces of nature dared refuse to genuflect in obeisance to a prospectus decreed by Matilda. A deluge of rain washed out a bridge on the approach to Meadow Brook and threatened to continue soaking the lawns and flower gardens. But the thunderstorms dissipated in time for the afternoon affair, and stars emerged from the overcast sky at night to enhance the display of sparkling colored lights for outdoor dancing as Judy bowed to Detroit society.

In May of 1961, a rain-dampened Matilda stood ready with her silver shovel to take part in ground-breaking ceremonies for the first two dormitory buildings on campus, planned to house 192 students. Many other traditions, such as the freshman dinner and dance held annually at Meadow Brook Hall in October, were being established as Matilda retained close ties with the university which soon would have its own identity as Oakland University.

Amelia Cline, who never lost interest in clipping published items about both Dodge families, removed still another clipping from the newspaper when she read that the 90-year-old Horace Dodge widow had broken her hip while at Palm Beach. Amelia wondered if Matilda would visit her sister-in-law at Rose Terrace when Anna Dodge returned to her Grosse Pointe chateau in the spring. Amelia would have liked to accompany Matilda to Grosse Pointe and to talk about old times with Anna Dodge. But Matilda, Amelia soon discovered, had nothing to say about Anna's unfortunate accident...had no intention of renewing their ties in these, the late years, of their lives. A caustic Matilda was more likely to express her criticisms of the scandals that still stigmatized the lives of Anna's son, Horace Junior, and two of Anna's granddaughters who had accrued several divorces.

At approximately the same time of Anna's accident, Matilda asked Dick Wilson to drive her out to the Dodge mausoleum at Woodlawn Cemetery. There, Dick and his mother unlocked the heavy door and went inside. Matilda stood silently for a moment, slowly viewing the interior where the heavy caskets were entombed. Whatever thoughts of her own mortality Matilda might have had were abruptly dissipated when her sharp eyes caught sight of a small box set on a low shelf. It was apparent to Matilda and Dick that the box had been there for a considerable time. It was also apparent, from an examination of one crushed corner of the box, that it contained ashes.

Immediately, Matilda sensed whose ashes they were. When she learned that cemetery clerks had no records indicating the depositing of the ashes, Matilda felt that her suspicions were verified—Anna Dodge had deposited the remains of Della Dodge Eschbach to rest beside the bodies of Della's brothers, John and Horace. Even in death and reduced to ashes, Della remained unforgiven by Matilda who also felt betrayed by Anna Dodge.

The discovery of the ashes increased Matilda's determination to proceed with plans stirring in her mind for a long while. She said nothing to Dick of her reasons for coming to the mausoleum; he would find out when the time was right.

At Christmas time that year, only the Eccles family—Barbara and her husband and children—came to Sunset Terrace to share Christmas dinner and a gift exchange. Since the Eccles' offspring already numbered five, the circular rooms of Sunset Terrace pulsed with the frisky children's rotary excursions throughout the day. The Van Lenneps were spending the holidays in Florida where they were now owners of Pompano Park raceway. Dick Wilson moved back and forth between the Van Lenneps' tracks—at Pompano Park in the wintertime and at the raceway in suburban Detroit, where Dick and his wife maintained their home for their four children, the rest of the year.

The Wilsons flew out to Arizona right after Christmas and had not yet returned in March when they received news of the death of Isabel Dodge Sloane at age 66. In recent years, the well known horsewoman Isabel had become equally well known for her lavish poolside parties in Palm Beach and for her generous hospitality to pretentious parasites who lived off the largesse of the wealthy. At her death, the body was shipped to Detroit and placed in the Dodge mausoleum, now as crowded with family members as had been the John Dodge home on Boston Boulevard when Matilda had come there as a bride in 1907. Of the three children born to John Dodge and his first wife, Ivy, only the eldest, Winifred Dodge Seyburn, was still alive. Only Frances Dodge Van Lennep, eldest daughter of John and Matilda, was still alive of the acknowledged three children of the marriage to Matilda.

Matilda posed no objection to having Isabel placed in the family mausoleum. It made no difference to her plans. Moreover, Matilda had other pressing concerns of her own that winter. Alfred had a serious heart attack in Arizona; so serious that Dick Wilson flew west to be with his parents. As Alfred recovered in the hospital, he appeared to be rapidly regaining strength in late March. At that time, Matilda and Dick flew to Detroit where Matilda attended to some business affairs and prepared to reopen Sunset Terrace, after which she planned to go back to Arizona and return home with Alfred.

A telephone call from Arizona on April 6 changed her plans. Alfred, she was told, had suffered a second heart attack. This one was fatal.

Dick Wilson volunteered to fly out to Arizona and to return with the body. Matilda gratefully accepted his help as she made funeral arrangements for her husband of 37 years at Detroit's First Presbyterian Church where the Matilda-Alfred romance had first bloomed. The final resting place for Alfred—a pink stone mausoleum overshadowed by its huge granite neighbor, the Dodge sepulcher—awaited its first occupant.

In this habitat of the dead, Matilda had not felt constrained to build a Wilson crypt of sufficient size and magnificence to surpass the splendor of the Dodge tomb, nor to have the Wilson crypt erected on a plot far removed from the Dodge memorial. But in the dominion of the living, she had long been motivated by an urgency to disassociate herself from the name Dodge and to be recognized only as Matilda Rausch Wilson. She achieved this recognition so successfully that most Detroit-area residents were unaware, by this time, that Mrs. Alfred Wilson had ever been a Dodge.

After Alfred's death, Matilda quickly moved back into Meadow Brook Hall, explaining to surprised friends and family members that she never liked living at Sunset Terrace. Locating there had been merely a concession to Alfred.

The widowed Matilda felt abundantly comfortable in Meadow Brook Hall, the home she had planned and watched throughout every stage of its construction; the home in which she was familiar with every hallway and closet and cupboard. Outside, a guard was always on duty, but a manservant and maid were the only employees within the mansion. The Eccles family, Barbara and her husband and five children, had recently moved to Arizona where the husband ventured into the real estate business. So Matilda stayed alone on weekends, with only her dogs for companionship inside the great house. She prepared her own meals, making her favorite soups on an electric range she finally installed for convenience.

Although Amelia lived alone in an apartment, the older sister did not invite the younger to move into Meadow Brook Hall for companionship. But Matilda did invite Amelia to accompany her on certain excursions, including a visit across the state to Niles, Michigan. Despite Matilda's determined strategy to separate herself from the Dodge name, she retained a secret reservoir of interest in Dodge family background that was openly shared by Amelia. The visit gleaned few, if any, revelations as the two women prowled about the small cemetery where John's parents, grandparents, and assorted relatives were buried.

Soon, Matilda made another suggestion to Amelia. How wonderful it would be, she urged, for the younger sister to move out to Sun City, Arizona, close to Matilda's mountainside winter home. Into a new retirement city with people her own age—new friends to associate with. Where everything was close at hand—recreation center, restaurants, and stores. And the sun—no more need to endure Michigan's gray and dreary winters and to risk icy sidewalks and roads.

Amelia had enjoyed her previous travels with her husband, but, always, the Detroit area was home to her. For Amelia, Sun City held no appeal.

When Matilda persisted in urging Amelia to move to Sun City, the younger sister capitulated. She and Matilda would become much closer companions in Arizona, Amelia surmised. There could be no other reason, except that of companionship, that Matilda would want her to live there.

In 1963, the sisters flew to Phoenix. With $17,500 loaned to her by Matilda, the younger sister bought a home in the 8900-acre tract where the first home in Sun City had been built only two years previously. Although it was still a small community in 1963, Amelia felt isolated in her new, air-conditioned home. She looked forward to visits from Matilda that winter, only to be disappointed when Matilda came only once to Sun City. Dick and Elinor Wilson drove Amelia's car out to Arizona so that she could have the use of her automobile, but Amelia used it only for a few necessary errands. Barbara Eccles, living nearby in Phoenix, was given to understand by her mother that Amelia chose to "keep to herself" in Sun City and that Matilda could not persuade her sister to be more outgoing.

It was unlikely that Barbara, now encountering her own problems with Matilda as the adopted daughter went through a divorce from Thomas Eccles, had either the time or resources to concern herself with the problems of a nearly unknown "Aunt Amelia." Caring for her five children and investing her money in a nightclub business presented Barbara with all the energy-draining challenges she could manage.

The nightclub investment added another source of alienation between Barbara and Matilda. The older woman felt that insurance money, plus stock holdings, willed to Barbara by Alfred, should not be invested in the kind of business that Matilda considered distasteful.

In the summertime, Matilda began her practice of inviting Amelia to spend several weeks at Meadow Brook Hall. At these times, Matilda took her sister along on trips to county or state fairs where the Wilson draft horses were being shown or where Matilda drove her hackney ponies. Even her 80th birthday on October 19, 1963, and the onset of heart trouble had not curbed Matilda's zeal for activity. When the first class of 175 students graduated from Oakland University in June of 1962, Matilda celebrated the occasion by inviting her "family," the graduates, to a dinner-dance at Meadow Brook Hall where she gave each student a gold class ring centered with a full-cut diamond.

The Van Lenneps, bringing 12-year-old Fredericka and her 11-year-old brother, John, came up from Florida to be with Matilda for her 80th birthday and again for the Christmas holidays. The conversation at the holiday dinner table revolved around the Van Lenneps' colt, Speedy Scot, and his recent title award—Harness Horse of the Year, after the three-year-old colt clocked 1.56 4/5 for the mile.

No one mentioned the recent death of Anna Dodge's son, 63-year-old Horace Junior, of cirrhosis of the liver and heart disease. Nor the funeral, scheduled for the day after Christmas, which would end at the Dodge mausoleum in Woodlawn Cemetery. If Matilda felt any compassion for the 92-year-old wheelchair-bound Anna Dodge in the loss of her adored son and only remaining child, there was no hint of such compassion reflected in the face of the resolute mistress of Meadow Brook Hall.

For weeks and months after the funeral, the Horace Dodge family chronicles were detailed in a multiplicity of newspapers after it was discovered that the late Horace Junior had filed eleven separate wills, none of which was effective because he had been outlived by his mother, Anna. Throughout her son's lifetime, the doting Anna had dribbled out millions of dollars to her profligate son who, in turn, squandered the money in doomed business ventures. In supporting a fleet of powerboats in his lifetime quest for racing trophies. In the pursuit of women with expensive tastes. In lavish settlements on his four divorced wives and in court battles with his fifth wife, gorgeous blond showgirl Gregg Sherwood Dodge.

The death of Horace Junior also unleashed a flurry of sensational reports of two lawsuits filed against Anna Dodge by Horace Junior's widow, Gregg. A $1 million suit for payment of a prenuptial money agreement. And a suit for $11 million which charged the 92-year-old Anna with alienation of her son's affections. Anna settled out of court for a total $9 million payment to Gregg, who soon would marry a policeman and proceed to squander her millions in Palm Beach.

The well publicized Horace Dodge money fracases stiffened Matilda's resolve not to permit similar occurrences within her own family. Frances, of course, was well provided for by the John Dodge trust fund. And Matilda had done her best to impress all her children with a high regard for the value of money and an appreciation for the frugal management of assets. She had made it clear to the two adopted children that her only obligation to them was to rear them to be self-sufficient adults. Her own self-reliant behavior, she felt, had always contrasted favorably with the clinging behavior of her sister, Amelia—a contrast established early in childhood; a contrast totally independent, therefore, of the fact that an individual did, or did not, have a great deal of money.

The self-reliant Matilda was pleased, nonetheless, that her favorite grandchild, Judy Johnson, began spending most of her time with her grandmother at Meadow Brook Hall after the girl left the Kentucky college she attended. Thrilled with Judy's interest in horses, Matilda set up a stable of thoroughbreds—eight horses—for her granddaughter, and ordered construction of a racetrack at the edge of her property.

Matilda's verve for travel continued to be as keen as in earlier years. Just prior to her 82nd birthday, she boarded a plane headed for Ireland where, in Dublin, she attended a conference of the Associated Country Women of the World. Returning in early October, she left for New York in mid-month to conduct fall council meetings for the Women's National Farm and Garden Association as president of the organization personally established by Clara (Mrs. Henry) Ford several decades earlier. Matilda made a quick trip back to Michigan on her own twin-engine Beechcraft to observe birthday ceremonies at Oakland University and to lay the cornerstone for the Matilda R. Wilson Hall on October 19 before flying back to New York and entertaining council delegates at a dinner party in the Essex House.

By this time, there were 2000 students on campus, registered in nearly 100 courses. The university had expanded to include many modern buildings. A Kettering Magnetics Laboratory. A $1.5 million Kresge Library. And a year later, the first Matilda R. Wilson Scholarship was set up by Friends of Oakland in observance of Matilda's 83rd birthday.

While Amelia visited at Meadow Brook Hall during the summer just previous to Matilda's 83rd birthday, the younger woman happily agreed when her sister suggested that they should pay a visit to Woodlawn Cemetery. Although Amelia retained a sharp interest in current events and the changing mores of the modern world, her role was that of a spectator as she read newspapers and watched television newscasts. The real world for Amelia centered around people who had lived in the Victorian Age and in the quarter-century following World War I...by her memories of the past as she leafed through her photo albums, sifted through her accumulation of newspaper clippings, and lovingly handled her cache of souvenirs and mementos. A visit to the cemetery, where she could stand at the graves of her parents and check whether the Rausch gravestones had been properly washed and the flowers carefully tended, was the kind of outing that nourished her spirit and rekindled her sentimental attachment to earlier times.

To Matilda, who bustled about in an excess of energetic preparations for tomorrow, the younger sister's affection for yesterday seemed an extravagant waste of vigor and creativity. The cemetery visit was planned by Matilda with a definite purpose that she disclosed to Amelia only after the two sisters were sitting in Matilda's car, parked near the Dodge Mausoleum.

She was having the coffins of her children, Daniel and Anna Margaret, taken from the Dodge mausoleum and placed in the Wilson memorial, Matilda quietly told Amelia. Ignoring the younger sister's murmured protests, Matilda explained that she had planned the Wilson crypt with spaces for four coffins—Alfred's, Daniel's, Anna Margaret's, and her own. Now she was carrying out that plan.

A trace of justification crept into Matilda's voice as the sisters walked toward the mausoleum to watch the workmen begin removing the two coffins from their resting places. "I spent only 12 years with John Dodge," Matilda reminded Amelia. "But I lived with Alfred for 37 years and feel that my rightful place is beside him. And with my two children."

Amelia dared say nothing of her feelings that Anna Margaret and Daniel were children of John Dodge...that the family fortune and Meadow Brook properties were John Dodge legacies. She knew that the huge Dodge tomb was filled almost to capacity with Dodge relatives for whom Matilda felt very little, if any, affection. Plus the ashes of Della. And Anna Dodge, now 95 years old, would be carried into this same Dodge sepulcher at her death. Perhaps, after all, the only surprising thing about the transferring of the coffins of Daniel and Anna Margaret was that the decisive Matilda waited until now to have it done.

Amelia wiped tears from her eyes and followed Matilda back to the car when the older sister finally relocked the door to the Wilson mausoleum and the workmen left. The two women rode back to Meadow Brook in silence, each lost in her own thoughts.

Matilda was not yet ready to confide to Amelia that she was troubled by her granddaughter Judy's romantic attachment to the veterinarian who gave medical care to the girl's horses. Not only was the man older than Judy, but he had been divorced. Matilda already had warned her granddaughter that the man was not an acceptable choice.

In early August, Judy abruptly left her grandmother's home to marry the veterinarian. Matilda immediately severed her ties with the girl. She had no intention of following the pattern of her sister-in-law, Anna Dodge, who had managed to maintain close relationships with her grandchildren no matter how offensively some of them behaved... bankrolling the free-spending habits of those of her intemperate descendants who lived pampered lives...forgiving even the most contentious of family members who resorted to court suits to wrest control of the fortune from the aged Anna who had outlived her son and daughter.

On returning to Meadow Brook in the spring, Matilda found a variety of matters awaitng her attention as she accepted the honorary chairmanship of the Salvation Army building fund campaign. The campaign goal was to raise $1.8 million; the first time in 25 years that the organization had undertaken such an ambitious capital-funds project in Detroit. Matilda personally pledged $200,000 to ensure the success of the fund.

She was unwilling, though, to make the slightest concession to repair the damaged relationship with her granddaughter Judy. In nearly 84 years of life, Matilda had become more unyielding as she aged, and more concerned than ever before to fill each day with a progression of events, as if a lull in activity, even in the heat of summer, might reveal a decline of energy...a surrender to the debilities of old age.

Since the 1963 inception of the Meadow Brook Music Festival, Matilda had become involved with kick-off teas and subsequent affairs promoting outdoor concerts on campus by the Detroit Symphony Orchestra. And this summer, she prepared for an "Afternoon at Meadow Brook Hall"—a tea and tour of the manor house by 300 members of the Detroit Historical Society in late July.

In September, Matilda left for Brussels, Belgium, asking her Howell farm manager and his wife, the Clarks, to accompany her on the tour of Belgian horse-breeding farms to select and purchase draft horses for the farm at Howell. By mid-September, the Clarks had spent several days with their employer in Brussels when Matilda complained of an upset stomach and was taken to a nearby hospital. She died at the Belgian hospital of a heart attack the next morning, Tuesday, September 19, 1967.

In preparation for the funeral on Saturday at the First Presbyterian Church in Detroit, family members came from Kentucky and Arizona to Meadow Brook Hall. In the confusion, the sister, Amelia, was not notified of Matilda's death. When she read the obituary notice in a

Phoenix newspaper, Amelia immediately made arrangements to fly to Detroit where she found that her sister's body would not lie in state at Meadow Brook Hall. Instead, Matilda's coffin was taken to a Detroit funeral parlor, then to her Woodward Avenue church for services highlighted with musical selections by the Oakland University Chorus.

At the university, a mourning period began and a memorial service was prepared even as Matilda's funeral procession moved out Woodward Avenue to Woodlawn Cemetery. The procession ended at the Wilson mausoleum as Matilda had planned, with entombment at the side of Alfred and her two deceased children.

Amelia flew back to Arizona the next day. Stunned by the sudden death of her sister and depressed by a realization of being totally alone in the world, she was aware, nonetheless, that she could and must make her own decisions for the first time in her life. She already knew what the first decision would be—to sell her Arizona home, for which she still owed $7500 to Matilda, and to return to the Detroit area.

Amelia had never liked the Sun Belt retirement city, even though it had mushroomed into a thriving community with choice shopping centers, a fine hospital, churches, and a glut of recreational facilities. Of one thing she was certain; Matilda surely would not leave her only sister unprovided for in her old age...unprotected in case of catastrophic illness.

That certainty shattered when, a few days later, official verification of Amelia's inclusion in Matilda's will reached the younger sister's Sun City home. Matilda had cancelled the $7500 debt, Amelia learned, and willed the younger sister an additional $7500 from her multi-million dollar fortune, as if the older woman had little concern for the care and health of her only sister. It did not soothe the 80-year-old Amelia to learn that Matilda willed only $10,000 to each of her adopted children, Barbara and Dick, plus a write-off of their minor debts which matched the $7500 owed by Amelia. To the younger sister, it seemed as if Matilda had evened out the lesser apportionments for these family members in the same measured and unemotional way in which she might have leveled off three tins of batter for a layer cake.

At least for Barbara and Dick there was icing on the cake in the form of $200,000 for Dick's children in acquiring college educations; another $200,000 for Barbara's children for the same purpose.

Unable to totally manipulate her family by bestowing or withholding money during her lifetime, Matilda did not attempt, posthumously, to purchase the allegiance of family members by awarding huge sums in her will. She had already given a $10 million gift of Meadow Brook properties to Oakland University, and had provided various pledges—$250,000 to Choate School, $150,000 to the United Presbyterian Church, $300,000 to Michigan State University among others. Her will also designated bequests to friends and employees. But the bulk of the estate was intended for her own foundation—the Matilda R. Wilson Fund.

Although Matilda stated her wishes that Meadow Brook Hall should be used as a conference center, she had not provided any money for the upkeep of the mansion. Oakland University officials now were seriously concerned about turning the manor into a self-supporting unit.

The adopted children, Dick and Barbara, had not expected to receive millions from Matilda's estate, but they were not pleased with the paltry amounts their mother elected to give them. Frances, too, was affronted by provisions of her mother's will, even though her own fortune had been assured by her father's legacy which would distribute still more assets to Frances' children at the final division of the fund.

According to terms of Matilda's will, Frances could take possession of any pieces of jewelry that had been her mother's during the years of her marriage to John Dodge, but not from the collection of jewelry from Matilda's years as a Wilson. Frances also was given a choice of family photographs and articles from Meadow Brook, excluding the furnishings, the silver, and the paintings. For Frances, the choice of assorted objects—a horse ashtray, a bronze elephant, several furs—amounted to approximately $100,000.

By the time Frances conferred with Dick and Barbara and they decided to contest the will, a year had passed. In May of 1969, the judge ruled against the children. Mrs. Wilson had expressed "clear intent, " the judge said, that her $16 million fortune should be turned over to the Matilda R. Wilson Fund.

The first major grant from the fund already had been made the previous December when Oakland University received $150,000 for an endowed John F. Dodge Chair in the School of Engineering, thereby resurrecting the John Dodge legend as the Wilson image gradually blurred and faded. Meadow Brook properties once again became known as Dodge ancestral lands...the deceased Mrs. Alfred Wilson was spoken of with increasing frequency as the John Dodge widow.

The 1960s brought major changes to Lucille Mealbach's life. Her oldest son, William Junior, married in 1962 and her middle daughter, Linda, married shortly thereafter. Brenda's son, the Mealbachs' first grandchild, was born in 1960, followed by the births of several other grandchildren in that decade.

Soon after her father's death in 1959, Lucille learned that Manzer's wife had taken control of all his assets during the late years of his life when he could no longer manage his own affairs. Eventually, after an extended period of probate maneuverings, Lucille received a copy of her father's will in which he specified a $2000 bequest "to my beloved adopted daughter, Frances Lucille Mealbach."

Her father's admission that she was adopted stunned Lucille, despite her knowledge that her younger brother had been adopted. To the Mealbach children, the revelation was an intriguing puzzle to be put together. The problem was that they had none of the puzzle-parts and very little conception of how to begin searching for clues.

For the daughter Brenda, who had great faith in the powers of the mind to communicate with a higher level of intelligence and spirituality, there was a series of visits to a Detroit psychic known to cooperate with Detroit Police in attempts to solve crimes of murder or kidnapping. On one of her visits to the psychic, Brenda convinced her mother to go along. "The people you thought were your parents are not your parents," the psychic told her. To Lucille, this was an impressive statement, but the information was no longer a revelation. "Your natural parents were people of wealth," the psychic added.

Spurred by the relentless pressure of her daughters to learn the facts about her adoption, Lucille finally asked her sister-in-law, Clara, to accompany her on a bus trip to downtown Detroit and to the new county courthouse. When she asked for information on her adoption papers at the courthouse, she was directed up to the office of Judge O'Brien. A clerk in the judge's outer office informed Lucille that she would telephone the old county courthouse and have a messenger deliver the file.

Lucille and Clara waited patiently in the hallway until the clerk summoned them into the office, again. The clerk put a large file, face down, on the desk as they entered, then told Lucille that no information could be released from the papers. When the clerk left the desk to go into the next room for a moment, Lucille impulsively lifted the back page of the file and saw a name printed there. Emma Nelson.

The name burned itself into her memory as the clerk returned and removed the file. With Clara, Lucille left the courthouse and walked to the bus stop. Who, she wondered, was Emma Nelson? Her mother, perhaps? The question became a refrain in her mind, blending with the hum and squeal and whine of the bus trip back to Dearborn.

Lucille's daughter still met occasionally with the psychic—a small, bird-like woman who, Brenda later said, had spoken of someone named "John," and, of someone else named "Amelia."

Lucille, with a daughter and a son still at home, kept busy with her family and her bridal shop job. Although she earned her own money, she retained her displeasure with her husband's personal extravagances.

When, rarely, she complained about his nightly excursions to bars, he became annoyed. "You don't even know who you are," he would say in sarcastic dismissal of her complaints.

"I know exactly who I am," she always replied. It was true that she did not know her parentage, but true, also, that Lucille Mealbach had a very real sense of self-identity stemming from her acute awareness of what she considered were priority values of life, centering around her five children.

On a trip with her daughters to the mountainside chalet of friends—Ken and Roberta Porter—vacationing in Gatlinburg, Tennessee, Lucille admired the attractive resort-home as she sipped at a glass of wine. She suddenly confided to the Porters that she recalled "being inside of only one home more beautiful than this." At the urging of her friends and daughters, she went on to tell them of her childhood memories of visiting a mansion on Boston Boulevard in Detroit.

As Lucille and her daughters drove back to Dearborn, the girls insisted on hearing the details of their mother's childhood visit to Boston Boulevard, over and over. The day after their return home, Brenda drove her mother and Sharon to West Boston Boulevard and moved slowly down several blocks on one side of the avenue, and up the other side. "You said you could remember the house," the daughters prodded their mother when Lucille seemed to be confused. She shook her head. "I just can't find it. Can't recognize it," she admitted. Giving up the search with disappointment, they returned to Dearborn. But Lucille's nebulous memories had triggered an obsession on the part of the daughters to learn more about their mother's parentage.

The younger son, Tom, was more interested in the automobile that Lucille bought in the mid-1960s, and in teaching her to operate the car. Like most brash teenagers, both Tom and Sharon teased their mother about her driving, even though they admired the spirit of independence that motivated Lucille, now in her early fifties, to get a driver's license.

Sharon, blond and blue-eyed like her mother, inherited none of Lucille's even temperament. Strong willed and independent, she was a high school student when she began dating youthful Larry Stajda. When 17-year-old Sharon decided to get married, Lucille had no choice but to help with wedding arrangements, hoping that the impetuous Sharon's marriage would work out as happily as had that of her sister, Brenda.

In 1968, Brenda and Sharon urged their mother to make another attempt to see the court file on her adoption. The two daughters accompanied Lucille to the courthouse where they were sent up to the probate court offices. This time, instead of being relegated to the ministrations of a clerk, they were ushered into the chambers of Probate Judge Thomas Murphy who looked up from his study of a thick file of papers as the women entered his office. The judge's name meant nothing to the Mealbachs. They did not know that Murphy was the probate judge assigned to earlier litigations involving the Dodge family, including the battle for the Daniel Dodge fortune which had concluded with Murphy setting aside more than a half-million dollars in 1941 for "undetermined heirs." And even if the Mealbachs had known this, they would not have suspected there might be a connection between Murphy's judicial interest in Dodge-family litigations and his interest in the adoption records of Lucille Manzer Mealbach.

Reminding the women that information could be released from adoption records only for good reason, the judge asked why they wanted the information.

The obviously pregnant Sharon answered quickly. "For medical reasons," she asserted. "I'm expecting my first baby and I think it's important to know what kind of genetic background I'm passing on to my child."

The mother and daughters waited nervously as the judge continued examining the adoption file. "I can tell you only this much," he said finally, looking at Lucille. "Your father was unknown. Your mother was from Jackson, Michigan, and you were born in Jackson. Your background is Scotch."

Disappointed that the judge would offer no more information, Lucille left the room at Murphy's request while he spoke briefly with her daughters. His advice to Brenda and Sharon, they later told Lucille, startled them with its bluntness. It would be unwise, the judge warned, for their mother to pursue the subject further. "You and your mother should consider the matter closed," he said sternly.

The judge's response both intimidated and thoroughly confused the Mealbachs. From his warning, Lucille and her daughters inferred that the adoption records held confidential information that, if disclosed, might be detrimental to Lucille's health. Their confusion stemmed from the conflicting data provided in the probate court file—that Lucille had been born in Jackson—and in the birth registration that she had received from the state in 1941, stating that she had been born in Detroit. They suspected it would not be an easy matter to clear up this confusion.

Chapter 19

A Link is Discovered

In early June, 1970, Matilda's sister-in-law, Anna (Mrs. Horace) Dodge, died in her 90-room Grosse Pointe chateau shortly before her 99th birthday. A flurry of airport-limousine arrivals delivered grandchildren, great-grandchildren, and assorted relatives to Rose Terrace as a prelude to the battle for Anna's fortune, reported at various sums approaching $100 million. Fueled by the demands of a few grandchildren who already had borrowed heavily and at exorbitant finance charges on inheritances they had expected to receive years earlier, legal conflicts erupted immediately among Horace Dodge heirs.

Matilda's daughter, Frances Van Lennep, did not live to perceive the scope of the Horace Dodge family's legal wrangles. Shortly after admission to a hospital in Boca Raton, Florida, where the Van Lenneps were spending the 1970-71 winter, Frances died of an "acute diffuse hemorrhagic disorder" as had her Uncle Horace a half-century pre- viously. Like her father, she died in her mid-fifties. The only known remaining child of John Dodge, now, was 76-year-old Winifred Dodge Seyburn, eldest of John's three children by his first wife, Ivy. At Winifred's death, the John Dodge trust fund would be distributed to his children's heirs.

Because, at Frances' death, no squabbling arose among the heirs to her personal fortune, there was little mention of money in published accounts of her demise. Frances willed her fortune to her husband of 22 years and to their son and daughter. A trust fund had been set up earlier for Judy—the daughter of Frances' first marriage. And Judy would also collect a share of the John Dodge trust fund after Winifred Seyburn's death, as would the two Van Lennep children.

Most of the publicity about the deceased Frances dealt with the only public part of her life since her marriage to Van Lennep—the domain of the horse show ring, horse racing, and horse breeding. In July, 1971, she was elected, posthumously, to the Hall of Fame of the Trotter and was acclaimed in The Horseman as having generated an unequalled "two-sport dynasty" at Castleton Farms.

At the time of Frances' death, the lawyer-executor of Matilda's will and foundation was still separating out the accumulations of a lifetime of collecting on the part of the former mistress of Meadow Brook. Sevres bowls and urns. A Louis XIV Boule table. Flemish tapestries. And a hodgepodge of other collectible items, some chosen impetuously by Matilda only because she was attracted to them. In her typically understated fashion, Matilda had called the miscellanea an assortment of "thing things."

Although the executor left enough of the paintings and objets d'art at Meadow Brook Hall to complement the furnishings and decor of the manor, crates of crystal, silver, Oriental accessories, china, vases, and other items were removed to be sold at auction. Paintings went on the auction block first, including a Rembrandt which was later donated to the Detroit Institute of Arts when bidding did not rise to expected heights. Accompanied by a gift of $80,000 from the Matilda R. Wilson Fund, the Rembrandt dominated a newly established Wilson Memorial Gallery at the Detroit museum. Matilda's paintings by Sir Joshua Reynolds also were auctioned. Reynolds' works, described by some modern critics as an odd mixture of "grandeur and tattiness" had served as appropriate embellishment to Meadow Brook's mixture of exquisite furnishings and Matilda's "thing things."

For four days in December, 1971, auctioneers at Detroit's DuMouchelle Art Galleries sold Matilda's Venetian stemware, Waterford vases, Sheffield desk sets, Wedgewood teapots, Sterling candlesticks, Limoges dinner service, and hundreds of other items. The auctioned treasures included a silver baby cup that once belonged to the ill-fated Daniel Dodge.

The DuMouchelle auction was dwarfed, though, when Anna Dodge's possessions were cleared from Rose Terrace and auctioned by Christie's of London, England. Christie's shipped some 700 pieces of the most valuable of furnishings and art treasures from Rose Terrace to London where they sold for $5 million in June, 1972. The remaining contents of Rose Terrace were auctioned in Grosse Pointe during a three day, giant tent sale on the lakeside grounds of the Dodge chateau.

With Rose Terrace emptied of its contents, the Horace Dodge heirs faced the decision of what to do about the mansion. None of the grandchildren could afford the heavy taxes and upkeep on the cavernous chateau. Nor were taxpayers in Grosse Pointe willing to pay maintenance expenses for preserving the great house.

The thick stone walls of Rose Terrace finally shuddered and fell to the onslaught of the wrecking ball in 1976. At the vanquishing of Rose Terrace, the destruction of the great mansions built along Grosse Pointe's Lakeshore Road, known as the "Gold Coast," progressed in a pattern of persistent mutation as plush estates were subdivided into condominiums and smaller, though expensive, homes.

Although the Dodge-Wilson manor, Meadow Brook Hall, officially became the property of Oakland University in 1971 when Matilda's estate was settled, officials in charge of the manor still faced the challenge of making Meadow Brook Hall self sufficient...of meeting rising maintenance costs and renovating expenses from manor income. Society women from neighboring Bloomfield Hills and Birmingham were inveigled into forming a volunteer corps to serve as patrons and guides and hostesses as the mansion opened to tour groups in the autumn of 1971. The society women acquired such an attachment to the manor that they became proprietary about it, even risking their manicured fingernails to participate in special "cleaning days" as they wielded mops and feather dusters and vacuum cleaners.

Growing numbers of visitors toured the mansion, following the well trained docents and marveling at their personal glimpses into the lives of the John Dodges and the Wilsons. Peeking into the Alfred Wilson study into which John Dodge's mahogany desk,used in the Hamtramck factory, had been moved. Admiring the drawing room with its one-piece red velvet rug, its inlaid Egyptian table, its English tapestry sofa. Mounting the grand stairway and peering into Matilda's suite with its silken wall-coverings, chaise lounge, and, over a marble fireplace, the large picture of Matilda's little girl, Anna Margaret, who died before age five.

Special groups came—senior citizens, church groups, Girl Scouts. At Christmas time, when the rooms were decorated with towering trees, holiday trimmings, and masses of poinsettias and holly, thousands of visitors came to Meadow Brook in a single week to participate in a Christmas Walk through the manor. The women's guild worked relentlessly to promote fashion-show luncheons, gourmet dinners, garden tours, celebrity teas, and a host of activities that raised enough money annually for the expenses and maintenance of Meadow Brook Hall, including replacement of all of the frugal Matilda's low-watt bulbs in the lighting fixtures.

When, in 1979, Amelia Cline read a newspaper item concerning the placement of Meadow Brook Hall on the National Register of Historic Places, she knew that Matilda would have been pleased with this recognition of her home as a national treasure. Throughout the 1970s, Amelia continued to live in a comfortable suburban apartment above a nursing home just north of Detroit. Occasionally she made brief visits to Meadow Brook Hall, but as she observed her 90th birthday in 1977, she became more reclusive and more worried that her savings might be insufficient to provide for an extended period of hospitalization if she became ill.

Apart from the visits of a younger cousin, daughter of Uncle Harry Glinz, Amelia had only her memories and her television programs— including her favorite, the Johnny Carson Show—and newspapers for companionship. Her curiosity was aroused in 1978 when newspapers and television carried reports of the publication of a new book, The Secret Life of Henry Ford. Written by John Dahlinger, who set out convincing data that he was an illegitimate son of the automotive pioneer, the book disclosed the so-called "open secret" of the love affair between Ford and his personal assistant at the Ford Motor Company, Evelyn Dahlinger, who lived in luxury, supported by Ford, throughout her adult life.

Amelia knew that her sister, Matilda, if still alive, would have been shocked by the revelations in the Dahlinger book, but would have taken satisfaction, nonetheless, that the senior Ford finally had been touched by personal scandal of this type—even posthumously. Not the slightest suspicion entered Amelia's mind that a similar, but much more sensational, challenge soon would erupt, baring the lives of John and Matilda Dodge to the scrutiny of a curious public.

Even before the Mealbachs' daughter Sharon was married, Bill Mealbach collapsed, at home, for the first time on a Saturday morning. Lucille, already at the bus stop where she waited for transportation to work, knew something was wrong when she saw her youngest daughter running down the street toward her.

"Run back to the house and call the firemen!" Lucille ordered as a breathless Sharon told her what happened, then turned and raced back to the house, Lucille following.

Within five minutes, firemen carried Bill Mealbach out of the house and, with ambulance lights flashing, roared off to Oakwood Hospital. Much later, when a doctor approached Lucille as she waited in the hallway at Oakwood, the report was encouraging. Her husband had suffered a heart attack, the doctor told her, but his condition had stabilized and he was now expected to make a good recovery. "But he'll have to lay off the drinking when he gets out of here," the physician warned.

Several weeks later, Bill Mealbach reported back to work. Coinciding with his return to work, he also resumed his usual pattern of visiting bars each evening. When he ignored Lucille's reminders about the doctor's warning, she realized her protests were useless.

Always a pragmatist, Lucille refused to brood on her husband's reckless disregard for his own health while she tried to make her own life as pleasant and fulfilling as possible. The requirements of her home and family became much less demanding in this period of her life when only the senior Mealbachs and their son Tom remained in the house on Calhoun, which seemed to take on spacious dimensions to accommo- date so few people.

When Bill Mealbach reached age 65 and became eligible for social security benefits shortly before the end of the 1960s, he retired from his job. Lucille, ten years younger than her husband, continued working as a bridal consultant. Her earnings were not the only motivating factor. She loved the stimulation of sharing wedding plans with young, engaged girls flushed with the excitement of selecting wedding dresses from racks of vinyl-sheathed gowns...of choosing among pristine white or soft-toned off-white or ivory creations trimmed with miniature pearls or rosettes or embroidered panels. With infinite patience and good humor, Lucille removed plastic wrappings and hangers, carried endless yards of lace and satin and tulle into dressing rooms where she tugged at zippers, adjusted panels, nipped at waistlines, lifted hemlines, and then eased the bouffant garments back into their plastic casings to the apologetic cadences of "I can't quite make up my mind," or "I'm going to look around first." Many of the undecided returned, drawn by the reassuring warmth of Lucille Mealbach in her romantic world of brides and bridesmaids and mothers-of-brides.

At home, life for Lucille held little romance, although she found occasional moments to relax with her oil paints and easel. She displayed her favorite paintings—one of swans at Greenfield Village, another of the Smoky Mountains, and a third, birch-tree landscape—in wide gilt frames on the walls of her green and gold living room.

There was even more time for painting when she decided to retire from her job at the bridal shop. Although she expected that adjusting to retirement would require patience, Lucille found that, with Bill in and out of the house at odd hours of the day and night, her at-home adjust- ment was a difficult one.

Retirement provided more time, too, for Lucille to worry about the failing marriages of some of her children. Linda's divorce, leaving her with three children to rear. Lucille's son's divorce, with custody of his child awarded to his ex-wife. And her youngest, Tom, leaving home for marriage and the quick escalation of marital difficulties.

Lucille decided that going back to work was better than dwelling on problems that she was helpless to solve. Again, she managed to find work near home, at the Cameo Bridal Shop, where she was once more caught up in the extravagant silk and satin world of bridal consulting.

Lucille's daughters had not forgotten their search for their mother's heritage. Since they knew that Rob Manzer, Lucille's younger brother, had come to the Manzers through the Methodist Children's Home, they decided to call that agency to inquire if its file on the Manzers held any information about the family's previous adoption of Lucille.

The response from an agency supervisor only added to the confusion. Yes, Rob Manzer had been adopted from the agency, the woman assured them. According to information in the file, the Manzers wanted to adopt Rob as a brother for their only child, Lucille. According to the records, the supervisor informed them, Minnie Manzer had told the agency that, after giving birth to Lucille, she could no longer have any more natural children.

This response puzzled the women. Lucille's earlier feeling of apprehension, inspired by Judge Murphy's warning not to look further into the matter, returned now as she wondered why Minnie Manzer, who had no natural children, would have lied to officials of the Methodist Children's Home. Minnie—to whom lying was a grave sin. What terrible secret motivated Minnie to choose to lie rather than to risk exposing any details of her daughter's adoption?

Lucille and her daughters had reached another blockage in their investigation. They had no idea what their next maneuver should be.

By this time, Bill Mealbach only rarely—when irritated by any interruption in his nightly excursions about town—reminded Lucille that she didn't even know who she was. A couple of years after his retirement, he had collapsed, for a second time, on the bathroom floor. As he hemorrhaged from the nose, firemen again responded to Lucille's call and rushed her husband to Oakwood Hospital where doctors stopped the bleeding twice, only to have the hemorrhaging begin again. This time, emergency surgery saved the patient from bleeding to death as a surgeon made an incision into the gullet and tied off the ruptured veins. But even this brush with death did not stop Mealbach from returning to his former habits after he came out of the hospital.

Near the end of the 1970s, Mealbach returned, voluntarily, to Oakwood Hospital for an operation when he could no longer put up with increasing discomfort from a troublesome hernia. Since no beds were available on the day of his hospital admission, he was temporarily placed in a small cubicle with several windows as hospital personnel rescheduled the operation for the following day.

Deprived of his customary nightly excursions, the patient began to hallucinate and had to be placed in restraints. From that point, his condition rapidly deteriorated as he suffered a seizure and lapsed into a coma. A doctor warned Lucille that her husband's condition was critical.

For one month, Bill Mealbach lay in a coma, totally dependent on a life-support machine. After a doctor finally admitted to Lucille that "it will be a miracle if your husband survives," the family was surprised when the patient emerged from his coma. Although the severe seizure and coma had extracted their penalties from the energy and independence that had marked Mealbach's earlier life, his body began to function independently of the supportive machinery and he gained enough strength to undergo the hernia operation.

Knowing that her husband was still kept in restraints at night, Lucille began to worry when she learned the hospital was ready to discharge her husband soon after the operation. Irreversible brain damage had left him with a clouded mind, so that he often failed to recognize his wife and family and surroundings. He seemed withdrawn into a quiet and remote world of confusion on the day that Lucille and her son drove to the hospital to bring Bill home. As his wife and son helped him into the house, his eyes were blank and uncomprehending.

"You're home now, Bill," Lucille said as she guided his shuffling feet toward the living room and settled him into a comfortable chair by the fireplace. Nervously, she switched on the television and went into the kitchen to fix lunch. When she returned to the living room, her husband's eyes were following the scenes flashing on the television screen. He seemed to be relaxing in the large chair. For the first time, Lucille dared hope that he might realize that he was home and might react favorably. That night, she helped him to bed at 11:30 and tucked him in like a child. He slept until eight o'clock the next morning.

Once at home on Calhoun, Bill Mealbach began to take care of some of his own needs. But he rarely left the house except to be taken by Lucille to the doctor's office or to go into the fenced yard on a nice day. He no longer read the Detroit newspapers, so neither he nor Lucille, who kept busy with her bridal consultant work and caring for her husband, read the newspaper reports when the John Dodge family was propelled back into the news at the death of Winifred Dodge Seyburn in early January of 1980—at age 85, the last of the acknowledged John Dodge children to die.

Church bells tolling in Grosse Pointe at the funeral of Winifred Dodge Seyburn also marked the death knell for the manufacturing com- plex built up by Dodge Brothers in Hamtramck. Although the Dodge Division of Chrysler Corporation still turned out the popular

Dodge automobile, the original Hamtramck factory—the landmark known as "Old Dodge Main"—was smashed by a wrecking ball in 1980.

The bell-dirge functioned as an assault signal, goading more than a dozen aspiring John Dodge heirs—of both likely and unlikely varieties—into adversary positions as they commissioned lawyers to stake out their claims to shares of the trust fund. After stock reissues and years of various court challenges, plus millions spent in attorneys' fees, the fund still amounted to at least $40 million.

The meaning of John Dodge's stipulation, that his trust fund should be divided among the "heirs of my said children," already was stirring debate. A lawyer for the former Laurine MacDonald, married for 13 days in 1938 to young Daniel Dodge, claimed his client was an "heir." Trustees for the Matilda R. Wilson Fund, set up to perpetuate Matilda's name and Wilson image, claimed a portion of the money; the deceased Matilda was, they asserted, an heir to Daniel's share of the trust. The two adopted children of Matilda Dodge Wilson filed claims as "heirs." The remarried Frederick Van Lennep asserted his claim as an "heir" to the share of the fortune accruing to his deceased wife, Frances. The attorney for John Duval's long ignored daughter affirmed his client's rights to share in the trust fund through her childless and deceased Aunt Isabel. All these—in addition to obvious heirs, Frances' three children and Winifred's four children.

Had John Dodge meant only issue of his own children—bloodline decendants—when he specified "heirs?" The battle over the meaning of the terminology, "heirs," was openly anticipated by zealous Dodge lawyers to continue for years.

"This family is a very litigious bunch," one Dodge attorney observed to a reporter. The attorney for the Seyburn grandchildren put it more pungently. "It's a zoo," he admitted. "But it always is when there's big money involved."

The court-appointed Guardian Ad Litem for the Dodge estate, Attorney Frederick G. Buesser, Jr., was not unwilling to comment for the press. His words implied another angle might be involved. "Little bastards have rights, too," he was quoted.

Attorneys for the numerous contenders expected that the court battles might drag along for years. But they did not expect that the tangled court case would be further complicated by a bold intrusion from another source. An intrusion in the person of Lucille Manzer Mealbach.

Although more than fifty biographies of automotive pioneer Henry Ford lined library shelves, not a single book on John and Horace Dodge was published until the end of 1981. Despite the flamboyant lives of the Dodges, John and Horace and their long lived widows had managed to shroud parts of their lives with a dark veil that successfully obscured their secrets from writers who had launched, but not completed, biographies of the Dodges.

Court battles to determine the "heirs" to the John Dodge trust fund were intensifying in November of 1981 when the first biography of the Horace and John Dodge families was released by Icarus Press. The Dodges: The Auto Family Fortune and Misfortune by Jean M. Pitrone and Joan P. Elwart. Soon after bookstores stocked the biography, Lucille Mealbach's eldest daughter, Brenda, visited the Grosse Ile, Michigan, home of her friends, Ken and Roberta Porter, for a Christmas holiday cocktail party.

Guests wandered about the Porters' gracious home, converted from a carriage house, as they admired the collection of grandfather clocks, antiques, and a glowing peacock lamp—a former possession of Anna Dodge, that the Porters purchased at the Rose Terrace auction. Brenda was admiring the peacock lamp when Ken Porter walked toward her, holding a book in his hand. "You'd like this book, Brenda," he said. "It's a fascinating story of the entire Dodge clan."

Porter opened the book to a page where he had placed a marker. "Could be that you own a Dodge lamp, too," he teased as Brenda reached out for the book, then read the passage to which he pointed—a description of a statue...a statue of a naked woman covered with a cloak. A statue that had belonged to John Dodge and which reminded Brenda of a lamp she had bought at an auction. The base of the lamp was a nude woman, wearing only a cloak.

Brenda laughed, then riffled through the book to a central section of photographs. A tremor passed through her body as she stared at a profile view of the broad-faced, firm-jawed John Dodge. "Ken," she said, her voice trembling. "This man looks like my mother!"

Aware that Brenda was an artist with a keen eye for bone structure and detail, Porter took another look at the photograph of the automotive pioneer as Brenda remarked on the amazing similarity to her mother's face in John Dodge's forehead, cheekbones, and jaw line. Quickly, she turned to another photo—this one of Dodge's blond granddaughter, Fredericka Van Lennep in her pre-teens. Brenda thought the young girl's picture bore an eerie resemblance to her sister Sharon at the same age.

She whipped through the photographs to one captioned as the early Dodge home on East Boston Boulevard. East! She remembered how persistently she had driven her car up and down several blocks of West Boston Boulevard in a futile search for the great home of her mother's memories.

East Boston Boulevard. How strange, Brenda told the Porters, that they had neglected to cross the jog on Woodward Avenue that would have brought them from the west to the east side of the boulevard and the city. The world didn't stop at Woodward Avenue—not even for people who had always been "west-siders."

Aware that someone was looking over her shoulder, Brenda turned to see another guest studying the photograph of the mansion. The man, who worked as a floral designer, told Brenda that he had decorated the Boulevard home several times for Christmas seasons. "The Catholic Archdiocese of Detroit owns the house," he added.

His remark triggered a barrage of questions as Brenda asked the floral designer about some of the details recounted earlier by her mother. Was there a huge staircase at the center of the house facing the front door, she wanted to know. Was the master bedroom at the front of the house, overlooking the boulevard? When the florist corroborated these details, Brenda described the multi-windowed, plant-filled room in which her mother recalled being given "cookies and milk." When Brenda identified the room as having a parquet floor, the man remembered only that the floor was carpeted.

The next morning, Brenda picked up her sister Sharon and her mother as she drove, again, in the direction of Boston Boulevard. This time, Brenda turned east from Woodward Avenue into the wide, divided street lined with great stone houses with porches stretched across the bay-windowed fronts and sides, with stained glass fanlights and protusions of towers and turrets. The houses, in various states of repair and disrepair, were now occupied by missionary societies or minority-race families and their relatives.

"That's it!" Lucille Mealbach cried out almost immediately, pointing at the first, large, three-story home off Woodward on the north side of the divided street.

"Oh, sure thing," Sharon said in disbelief. "After all our earlier searching, now the first house you see—'that's it,'" she mimicked her mother.

"It is! That's the house," Lucille insisted, overcome with a sense of deja vu as Brenda pulled the car to the curb. The three women stared at the house, now numbered 75 East Boston Boulevard and situated only a short distance from the corner, on property adjoining that of Blessed Sacrament Cathedral on Woodward Avenue.

Lucille Mealbach already was reciting the litany of details she had often described to her daughters—the great winding staircase, the bedroom with heavy draperies and a chaise lounge and huge bed that had dwarfed its occupant...a thin, pale-faced woman who had seemed to be very ill. Each detail soothed the sisters with its familiarity, like another bead in a rosary worn smooth with the repetition of tantalizing memories and romantic aspirations.

By the time the florist called to verify that, yes, there was a parquet floor beneath the carpeting in the room Lucille had described, Brenda had gone to a bookstore and bought her own copy of the Dodge family biography. As she read, the story exploded into her mind, enthralling her with possibilities she had not previously imagined.

On March 2, 1982, Brenda dialed the telephone number of biographer Jean Pitrone. Pitrone's accessibility—a home address less than three miles from Brenda's Grosse Ile home—seemed to be another in the series of strange coincidences that seemed to link the life of Lucille Manzer Mealbach with the lives of John Dodge heirs.

A biographer becomes accustomed to telephone calls from unknown individuals, each of whom is convinced that his or her life would "make a wonderful book," and learns to quickly and politely terminate such calls. But when Brenda Eilers phoned, the sincerity in her voice and in her "Please don't hang up until you've heard what I have to say," convinced this author to listen to her explanations of why she thought her mother might be an illegitimate child of John Dodge. The explanations were not entirely unreasonable, even if largely dependent on coincidences.

The Dodge book and its photographs, Brenda pointed out, focused her family's search for its heritage on John Dodge after she and her sisters had attempted to track down state and adoption-agency records with little success. She recounted their experiences in trying to get information...being turned away from Judge O'Brien's office after catching sight of only one bit of data—the name Emma Nelson, possibly listed as Lucille's mother. Brenda told of their bewilderment at the discrepancies between the meager bits of information given them at Judge Murphy's office and the information provided on the birth registration filed with the state by an unknown party in 1941—almost 27 years after Lucille's birth.

Then Brenda told of still another, and recent, visit to the courthouse in 1980, after the Mealbachs learned that laws concerning adoption information had been modified. This time, the mother and daughters were told by Probate Court personnel that Lucille's adoption records were "missing," although the file had been in the office of the now deceased Judge Murphy at the time of the previous visit of the Mealbachs to the courthouse.

Every experienced author knows that coincidences can lead the biographical writer along a flawed and winding trail of extensive investigation that may lead nowhere. Deciding to keep an open mind on the possible Mealbach-Dodge linkage, I answered Brenda's questions with whatever information was available and assured her she was wel- come to telephone me at any time. I notated the name, Emma Nelson, and decided to do some research at the Detroit Public Library.

The research, in Detroit City Directories, yielded interesting results. In 1914, the year of Lucille's birth, Emma Nelson lived on 4th Street in Detroit and worked as a domestic. In 1915, Emma Nelson apparently left Detroit—her name was no longer listed in the directory.

A check of the 1910 census later revealed that Emma Nelson had been employed that year as a domestic at 43 East Boston Boulevard. Further research clarified that the John Dodge residence at East Boston had been numbered in various years of Detroit's growth as 33 and then 43 before finally being numbered as 75. Emma Nelson—a maid at the John Dodge home, impregnated by her employer in 1914 and leaving the Dodge household before the birth of her baby; well paid, doubtless, to leave the city and to give the baby up for adoption. An assumption, of course. Only an assumption.

At Brenda's next phone call, she inquired about a source interviewed for the Dodge family biography and listed as Mrs. Frank Upton at the back of the book. "Who is Mrs. Upton?" Brenda asked. "Would her name possibly have been Viola?"

Viola Upton, yes, I verified. Wife of the deceased accountant and trusted employee of the Dodges—in their factory and, after the deaths of the brothers, in managing the financial and personal affairs of the widows.

Brenda's excitement vibrated along the telephone wire. We had found the link. Lucille Mealbach had recalled that Frank and Viola Upton were regular visitors at the Manzer household...Upton had been a trustee of the Methodist Children's Home, Brenda had now discovered, and had arranged for the Manzers to take foster children from that organization into their home.

Another assumption shaped itself—that Dodge employee Upton masterminded the adoption of the illegitimate Dodge child, Lucille, by the Manzers. And that the adoption was not handled through the Methodist Children's Home because the Dodges did not want Upton's friends and associates in that agency to have access to information about the child's adoption by the Manzers. Upton, we speculated, could have been the liaison to provide financing for the Manzer family so that Lucille would be adequately cared for.

I am now sufficiently involved with the Mealbachs to agree to a lunch-meeting with Lucille and two of her daughters, Brenda and Sharon. At lunch, the Mealbachs allow me to inspect family photographs which provide more compelling reasons, they insist, to suspect a Dodge-Mealbach linkage. There are likenesses, it appears, between their photos and the photos in the book plus others in my possession.

Lucille smiles tolerantly as her daughters chatter about their mother's right to knowledge of her background...to a share of the inheritance which may be hers. "I've had a good life," Lucille insists. "I've felt no need to pry into the past. But my children feel the need to know their roots...to benefit from the privileges their rightful background might supply. For their sakes, I want to make sure they have that opportunity."

There is something so practical in the words of this attractive woman, who dresses with such good taste and flair, that it is difficult to suspect her of being an opportunist...an imposter. And it is apparent that the daughters are much more caught up than is their mother in attempting to untangle the web of intrigue surrounding Lucille's birth and adoption.

In the weeks that follow, there are many telephone discussions with Brenda. She asks about the possibility of talking with Matilda Dodge's sister, Amelia Cline, who supplied a great deal of personal information about the Dodge family. If Lucille Mealbach is a John Dodge daughter, surely Amelia—in her years of close attachment to the family—would have some knowledge of that.

Regretfully, I tell Brenda that Amelia Cline died on Valentine's Day, just three months after the publication of the Dodge family biography...that she had a copy of the book on a nightstand at her bedside when death occurred. The Mealbachs have come to me with their story only several weeks too late to talk with Amelia.

Chapter 20

The Second Frances

When Brenda phones again, she inquires about Viola Upton—if she is still living and if they can get in touch with her. Soon afterwards, Brenda and her mother go to the Detroit nursing home where Mrs. Upton is now a resident.

Viola Upton, frail and in her nineties, still has a keen mind and is pleased to learn that her unexpected visitor is the former Lucille Manzer. She clearly remembers her visits, with her husband Frank, to the Manzer home more than 60 years previously, she says. Carefully, Lucille and Brenda channel the conversation to the matter they want to discuss. They tell Viola that Lucille knows she was adopted by the Manzers—of her suspicions that she is a daughter of John Dodge. Can Viola help them discover the truth, they ask.

The aged woman looks at them with concern. She can tell them nothing, she says. "You've had a good life," she reminds Lucille, echoing the younger woman's own admission. "Why don't you leave the past alone?"

Lucille and Brenda are disappointed, but they visit the nursing home again at a later date. Viola Upton acknowledges that her husband was a confidant of the Dodge brothers and of their widows...that he was deeply involved in their business, finances, and personal affairs, but that he could not, and did not, confide certain Dodge family secrets to his wife. Still, Viola is roused to enough excitement to introduce Lucille Mealbach to other nursing home residents as "a Dodge daughter" and to remark that "the secret is finally coming out." But further visits to Viola Upton end when the aged woman dies.

Brenda's sister Sharon continues trying to find the agency through which Lucille was adopted, since they know the adoption did not take place through the Methodist Children's Home. Sharon phones a number of agencies until she receives verification from the Brighton office—now the headquarters—of Child and Family Services of Michigan that Lucille's adoption by the Manzers was processed by that agency.

In June, 1982, Lucille and her daughters visit the Brighton office where they ask for information from Lucille's adoption records. They explain that since Lucille's adoptive parents are deceased and since it is likely that her natural parents are also deceased, there should be no obstacle to releasing the requested information.

The supervisor, Helen Cornell, agrees there should be no problem in supplying information, and gives them a form to fill out. They can expect to receive a letter very soon from the agency, she tells them.

When the letter arrives at the Mealbach home, Lucille learns that privacy restrictions prevent the agency from supplying the names of the natural parents. The agency offers only a brief background—informing Lucille that she was born in Detroit to young and unmarried parents...a 17-year-old Methodist father and an 18-year-old mother of German ancestry. The letter also says that Lucille was sent to a home near St. Joseph, Michigan, immediately after her birth; that she remained there, in the home's infirmary, for more than three months before being taken to a foster home and then to the home of her adoptive parents, the Manzers.

Because of the different versions of her mother's birth given by various agencies, Brenda is no longer bound to the "Emma Nelson—illegitimate birth" concept. Brenda now entertains thoughts of a possible love affair between John Dodge and his sister-in-law Amelia... a love affair that could have resulted in the birth of an unwanted child.

Again, Brenda's suspicions seem to have considerable validity. We consider Matilda's pliable younger sister, Amelia Rausch, and her admiration of the powerful John Dodge who often came alone to his beloved Meadow Brook. We know that the tiny sister, 27 years old in 1914—the year of Lucille's birth, had looked forward with pleasure to John's arrival on weekends. But what about the name, Emma Nelson—the domestic in the Dodge home? We remind ourselves of this, trying to control any flights of fancy. The name came from a court document . Such documents are supposed to be accurate, are they not?

For someone like Brenda, who always relies on her instincts, it is difficult to restrain her imagination as she points out that the Dodge biography states that 1914 was also the year that Amelia left the Dodge office to live at the farm. That later, John Dodge incurred his wife's jealousy by giving Amelia an expensive ring. That Amelia continued to wear her hair "the way Mr. Dodge liked it" for more than a half-century after Dodge's death. Was it really Amelia's marriage that caused the estrangement between the two sisters?

Brenda wants to know about the physical arrangements at the Meadow Brook farmhouse. I tell her that John Dodge's bedroom was on the second floor at the southeast end; that Amelia's bedroom was next to John's with a connecting door. Amelia had smiled coyly when she volunteered this information, and I clearly remembered the arch look on her face at this disclosure.

Brenda asks for the telephone number of Amelia's only living relative—the younger cousin who cared for Amelia in the last few months of the ailing woman's life. I give her the number and Brenda phones to find answers to her questions. The cousin is kind, but firm. "Amelia," she says, "definitely never gave birth to a child."

Still, Brenda is not convinced that Amelia is not her grandmother. She compares the November 23, 1914 birthdate recorded as that of her mother, Lucille, with the birthdate of John and Matilda's daughter on November 27, 1914. What strained relations this would have created between the two sisters if both were pregnant at the same time... inpregnated by the same man. Yet, if Amelia actually had a daughter, I point out, would she not have been compelled in her late years of great loneliness to seek out the child?

We waver back and forth between the possibilities. We have no luck in tracing Emma Nelson past 1915, but since Emma was a domestic in the John Dodge household in 1914, there is the possibility that she may have been well paid for the use of her name as the birth-mother of an unwanted Dodge child born of another mother.

No longer do such assumptions seem strange to us; so much that is unusual has already taken place in the Dodge saga. What we cannot yet imagine is the startling turn events will take as we go on pursuing one lead, then another, with undetermined or even negative results.

Since Lucille has never received a copy of her actual birth certificate in response to earlier requests, Brenda now tries to get the certificate by writing to Michigan Public Health Records in Lansing and requesting a certificate for the November, 1914, birth of Frances Dodge. Frances, after all, is the first name given on the registration of Lucille's birth filed in 1941—the first name mentioned in her adoptive father's will, as well.

The birth certificate that arrives in the mail in response to this request is that of Frances Dodge, born November 27, 1914, to John and Matilda Dodge. Since Lucille's birth is registered with a November 23, 1914, date, the Mealbachs assume they received the wrong certificate—that of John and Matilda's acknowledged child.

A new twist presents itself as the Mealbachs interpret markings on Frances' birth certificate as indications that the Dodge heiress might have been the first born of twins. Brenda points out the numeral 1 written in the box indicating "order of birth"...the line drawn through the word <u>Twin</u> in the box indicating <u>Twin</u>, <u>Triplet</u>, or <u>Other</u>.

The Mealbachs write back to Lansing, informing the records department of their receipt of the the wrong certificate—that of the twin, Frances. A letter from Lansing arrives promptly at the Mealbach home, requesting the return of the certificate sent by mistake. The most surprising part of the brief letter is the salutation. "Dear Margaret Frances," it reads. Never before has Lucille suspected her name might be Margaret...the name of Matilda Dodge's mother. The Mealbachs return the certificate to Lansing, as requested. The Lansing office never sends Lucille the birth certificate for "Margaret Frances."

My next telephone summons from Brenda startles me even more than the first call, months earlier. "You're not going to believe this," she says, and I detect uncontrolled excitement in her voice. "But we think my mother may be a Siamese twin of Frances Dodge Van Lennep."

She is right. It is difficult to imagine, much less to believe. Still, my mind flashes back to one of the photographs the Mealbachs showed me on the day we first met—the picture of two plump baby girls, from six to eight months old, sitting in a elaborately designed wicker chair. I remember the identical dresses with eyelet petticoats peeking out beneath the hems...the pearls around the chubby cheeks. Twins—very possibly. But Siamese twins?

Nonetheless, the Siamese-twin theory begins to take on believeable aspects to the Mealbachs, despite the four days' difference in recorded birth dates. We already know that Dr. Chittick—who supposedly delivered John and Matilda's first-born before the physician moved to California—was left $5000 in John Dodge's will...a substantial sum in 1920. And who could know how much money he was paid at the time of the delivery? Somewhere along the linkage of people charged with legal responsibilities, had records been filled out improperly?

The Mealbachs' supposition that Frances Matilda Dodge and Margaret Frances Dodge were Siamese twins is strengthened by Lucille's recollections of her obstetrician telling her, years earlier, that the scars on her head and near the base of her neck were surgical scars, resembling scars incurred in the separation of Siamese twins. Child and Family Services had confirmed, Lucille says, that she had not been well for the first three months of her life. And the fact that the very moral Minnie Manzer had lied about her adopted daughter's scars, as well as about her adoption, appears to corroborate suspicions that the origin of the scarring was intended to remain a deep and dark secret.

The Siamese-twin supposition spurs us to investigate the medical and genetic aspects of such births, which occur at a ratio of one in two million. Physicians state that Siamese twins always develop from a single egg and, so, must be identical babies. In appearance, Frances Matilda and Margaret Frances (Lucille) were not identical , although there were similarities between them. But the Mealbachs have seized on what they feel is another explanation—that Frances Matilda and Margaret Frances may have been fraternal twins...fetuses which were joined together at an early stage of gestation.

When I ask Dr. Angelo Stoyanovich—obstetrician and gynecologist in suburban Detroit—for an opinion regarding this explanation, he refers the question to Dr. Mark Evans, of the Division of Obstetrics and Gynecology at Hutzel Hospital and genetics expert at Wayne State University. Dr. Stoyanovich then reports that "...it has never been written, in any study of fraternal twins, that there is any evidence of attachment—be it superficial or otherwise."

There is still another question of deep concern to the Mealbachs. Did the late Frances Matilda Dodge Van Lennep have scars matching those of Margaret Frances (Lucille) Mealbach? The Mealbachs expect that an answer to this question will be difficult to acquire. Very difficult, indeed, they soon learn as Lucille Mealbach begins to use the name Frances—her rightful name according to three separate records. Frances Lucille Mealbach—it is like taking on a new identity.

She is not sure she wants a new identity. She has been comfortable, she keeps insisting, with herself and her children. But those same children are determined to know their heritage; to receive their rightful shares of the wealth for which other Dodge descendants are now sparring. And their mother is the only living child of John Dodge, the Mealbach daughters point out.

The daughters decide to drive to St. Joseph and Niles with their mother on a scouting expedition which elicits no new information, but brings them to Silver Brook Cemetery in Niles to search for Dodge-family graves. When they cannot find a caretaker, they wander among tombstones until they can no longer see their car, parked near the entrance and behind fringes of tall grasses and trees. The three women stand there, undecided in which direction to move and lost in a strange world of crumbling grave markers, until Sharon begins to walk ahead decisively.

She leads them, eventually, to tombstones bearing the name Dodge—to the graves of John and Horace's parents, Daniel Rugg Dodge and Maria Casto Dodge. And to the markers for other Castos...

the grandmother, Indie Duval Casto, and several relatives and in-laws. The Mealbach women leave Silver Brook Cemetery and Niles with no proof of their roots, but with an intense feeling of having stood at the side of their forebears' graves.

At age 68, Frances Lucille still works five days a week, at least five or six hours a day, and cares for her enfeebled 78-year-old husband. Her "golden years" are the same kind of work-filled and pressed-for-money years as those of her early life. And although she emphasizes that she enjoys her bridal-salon work, her children tell her how much more she will enjoy the Dodge "pot of gold" that is, they are becoming more and more certain, her birthright.

Frances Lucille continues to have ambivalent feelings about this. She knows that so much money has brought what she calls, "blight" to many of the Dodges. "While I," she says with justifiable pride, "who have worked for and earned everything I have, take great pleasure in my family." Any alienation, she thinks, between herself and her family would be too great a price to pay for a "pot of gold." No matter how valuable and glittering its contents.

Despite the coincidences pointing to the possibility of a Siamese-twin birth to Matilda Dodge in November, 1914, the theory is so bizarre that it seems practical for the Mealbachs not to ignore the possibility that Frances Matilda and Margaret Frances might have been twins of a more ordinary variety. In an era when even the birth of normal twins was looked on by prudish patricians as something less than human, the perfectionist Matilda could be expected to react with horror and shame to an imperfect baby. Suppose, we consider, that twins were born to Matilda in 1914, and that one twin was not perfect. Even when a caul covered a baby's head at birth, the caul was seen as an ominous sign—a curse signifying disaster or early death for the newborn. People unfortunate enough to give birth to more seriously handicapped children often kept them in the recesses of their homes, hidden from view.

This suggests another possibility. Suppose the scars on Frances Lucille's skull and at the base of her neck resulted from surgical removal of a sac that might have covered the back of her head and neck at birth. Such sacs may indicate various degrees of physical and (or) mental impairment, depending on how much of the spine is entrapped within the sac. Matilda's reaction to the birth of a twin daughter disfigured with a sac, called "the mark of the devil," could have been shock and guilt at this evidence of retribution imposed by God; punishment for her own sin in marrying a divorced man.

Frances Lucille believes she understands, too, why Minnie Manzer was unable to bridge the emotional coolness between mother and adoptive daughter. Minnie was a controlled and unemotional woman, yet Lucille remembered that, to the foster child Margaret, Minnie was able to express endearments and affection lacking in Lucille's early life. Frances Lucille is sure that Minnie's guilt in concealing, and even lying about, the adoption plagued her mother's conscience...caused Minnie to shield herself, for self-protection, from the adoptive child who was the prick to her parents' strong Methodist scruples.

Sharon decides to make a second telephone call of inquiry to the same agency called years previously—the Methodist Children's Home. She reports that an agency official informed her that the file on the adoption of Rob Manzer contains no background on the Robert Manzer family...that only a note is attached, which states that the family records were burned in a fire in 1945.

This response is a puzzling one. At the time of the earlier phone call to the same agency in the 1970s, Sharon says she was told the file disclosed Minnie Manzer's claim that Lucille was her own, natural child.

Several weeks later, the Mealbach daughters pay a visit to the office of the Methodist Children's Home. They ask to see the same official to whom they had recently talked, but are told he is out of town. A clerk gets out a file and then gives them some information which, the daughters later indicate, is similar to data provided in the first phone call...that there are old letters in the file recommending the Manzers as adoptive parents for Rob. When the clerk sees, near the back of the file, a notation of Sharon's earlier phone call, he supplies no further information.

The daughters decide to drive their mother out to Meadow Brook Hall, where docents regularly lead tour groups through the mansion and give well rehearsed spiels on the lives of the wealthy Dodge-Wilsons. The Mealbachs have encountered resistance to their quest for information on other occasions, but never before has the resistance been so well mannered, yet so inflexibly firm. At the sisters' insistence, a docent brings forth a mentor from the recesses of an inner chamber. The mentor's calm and polite manner does not change as she glances at the photographs the visitors have brought with them to prove family likenesses.

There are many visitors, with unusual stories, who have approached the people at Meadow Brook, she tells them. She is sure, she adds, they must understand how it is when a large estate is involved.

Even the photograph of the twin-like baby girls, which the Mealbachs have brought with them, fails to arouse any interest at Meadow Brook Hall.

As the Mealbachs drive back to Dearborn, Frances Lucille is very quiet. To her, the resistance encountered at Meadow Brook Hall signifies the hopelessness of their search for information. But the daughters' determination is unchanged.

While the probing for clues continues, the Dodge family dispute regarding the trust fund money has moved through the court of appeals and on to the state supreme court. More than three years of battling end when the high court finally upholds the original ruling that Frances Van Lennep's husband and eight Dodge grandchildren—Frances' three children, Winifred's four daughters, and John Duval's only daughter— should share the bulk of the John Dodge trust. A much smaller amount is appropriated for the Matilda R. Wilson Foundation.

As the money is prepared for distribution in 1984, Brenda, who has moved with her husband and children to Florida, telephones regularly with questions and suggestions. She reminds her mother that the supervisor at Child and Family Services seemed to want to be helpful. "Why don't you see her again?" Brenda asks. "Maybe you can learn something more."

Frances Lucille obediently returns to the Brighton, Michigan, office, where Helen Cornell checks the records, then regretfully says she has given out all the information she can legally provide. When Brenda visits in Dearborn that summer, Frances Lucille listens benignly as her daughters playfully fantasize about snatching their mother's files from the adoption agency office. One sister, they say, laughing hysterically, can ask to see the records. As soon as the file is in reach, Frances Lucille should pretend to collapse right near the desk, and while everyone's attention is focused on the fainting woman, one daughter will grab the file and start to leave the office. They giggle as they go on with the pretense. The one with the file will pretend to pass the papers to another daughter, who will be standing there with a briefcase. But, actually, the file will be hidden inside the jacket of the one who grabbed the papers.

The sisters are hilarious, imagining how frustrated the agency people will be when they check out the briefcase to find it empty. And in the meantime, the daughter carrying the file will have taken off in her car.

Frances Lucille thinks the joke has gone far enough. "That's enough foolishness," she protests. "If there's any more talk like that, I'm going to forget the whole thing."

The daughters know that their mother's commitment to tracking their roots is not as firm as their own determination. They are kidding, they tell her. But they feel a deep frustration as they envy the daring spirit of television's "Cagney & Lacey" and of "Charlie's Angels" reruns.

In that same summer of 1984, the daughters find a young lawyer who agrees to take Frances Lucille's case. The lawyer gets his client an appointment with Frederick Buesser, III—counsel to the Guardian Ad Litem for the John Dodge estate. Accompanied by Sharon, Frances Lucille goes to a northern suburb of Detroit to keep her appointment with Buesser. There, she is put at ease by the attorney's cordiality as they shake hands in his plush offices, and as he remarks on her strong resemblance to John Dodge.

Buesser listens carefully, nodding and asking occasional questions as Frances Lucille tells her story. He then explains the legal procedures necessary to establish her claim as a John Dodge heir.

Despite Buesser's encouragement, Frances Lucille is overwhelmed by a crushing sense of being trapped at the center of a controversy that can turn her snug little world upside-down. "At this point, I'd rather forget the whole thing," she tells Buesser as she and Sharon leave his office. "I'm not greedy for money. And I'm not really a fighter," she adds, ignoring her daughter's protests.

She watches television that night, feet resting on a hassock, her mind at ease with her decision to abandon her search for her roots, when her daughter phones.

"I've just talked to Mr. Buesser, again," the daughter says breathlessly. "Mom, you've got to go ahead with this...it isn't just a $20,000 amount we're talking about. And we've all got a stake in it."

An hour later, Frances Lucille receives a phone call from Florida. "Mom, you can't back out now. We've got to learn the truth—for all our sakes."

Frances Lucille, always supportive of her children, cannot separate her own desires from those of her offspring, now. The next morning, she allows her young attorney to take the first step in filing a brief, seeking access to his client's adoption records, with the juvenile division of Wayne County Probate Court.

The brief points out that his client's adoptive parents are deceased; that it can be assumed that the biological parents also are deceased. There should be no objections to Frances Lucille Mealbach being given the facts concerning her birth, thereby acquiring genetical information valuable to her and for her family's medical records. The birth information also would make it possible for her to claim her rightful share of the John Dodge trust fund, if the facts proved that she is a Dodge daughter.

The September hearing, in the juvenile court of Judge Y. Gladys Barsamian, is a disappointment to Frances Lucille. A 15-page brief, filed by an attorney representing Frances Lucille's "anonymous biological parents," opposes release of the birth information. Attorney Gail Mazey, appointed as Guardian ad Litem by the State to represent the interests of the birth-parents, points out that there is "a clear distinction between adoptions that took place prior to 1980 and those taking place after 1980 in terms of access to identifying information." She goes on to speak of laws protecting "confidentiality and the reputation of the dead."

Frances Lucille's attorney brings up his client's need for medical information, but the judge remains unconvinced. The Mealbachs are discouraged but not too surprised when Judge Barsamian rules against them, pointing out that "financial gain" is not a reason for violating the confidentiality of which biological parents are assured by sealed adoption papers.

The medical-problem reasons advanced by the Mealbach attorney are not strong enough to support his arguments for opening records, Judge Barsamian asserts. She adds that, in 1914, it was possible for parents to directly arrange for adoption, without going through an agency. The fact that Frances Lucille's parents chose to have an agency take care of the adoption was further proof of their desire to remain anonymous.

The setback inflames the Mealbach daughters' sense of being victimized and betrayed by what they refer to as "The System." They will not permit their mother to concede failure at this point. Instead, they manage to persuade a prestigious law firm to listen to their story and are successful in convincing the firm—Williams, Schaefer, Ruby & Williams—to represent Frances Lucille on a contingency basis. Near the end of October, the law firm asks Frances Lucille to sign a petition asking for a hearing in probate court to determine her status as a John Dodge heir…to restrain the distribution of Dodge-estate assets pending such a hearing.

On October 30, 1984, Frederick Buesser—Guardian Ad Litem—appears in probate court to request information regarding his obligations to Frances Lucille Mealbach. Buesser asserts his opinion that if Mrs. Mealbach is a biological daughter of John Dodge, her claim to a share of the estate should be adjudicated. For this reason, Buesser requests the court's permission to review Frances Lucille's adoption records.

The adoption records, Buesser informs the court, do exist and will disclose information which, in itself, will be evidence of the Mealbach-Dodge relationship or will lead to such evidence.

The court rules six days later, giving its opinion that the Guardian Ad Litem has "no fiduciary obligations" to Mealbach, since Mealbach has now become a "known" person. Buesser's services are discharged by the court. The question of reviewing adoption records remains unanswered. A hearing is scheduled for November on the petition to halt distribution of the estate until Mrs. Mealbach's status as a Dodge heir is resolved.

Francis Lucille is distressed by the court's discharge of Buesser, who supported her claim. She is distressed, too, when, the day after the court's ruling, Detroit newspapers carry front-page stories revealing the quest of "Siamese twin," Frances Mealbach. Photos of both Frances Lucille and the deceased Frances Dodge Van Lennep accompany the stories.

Frances Lucille is shrewd enough to realize that media exposure will bring the risk of public ridicule...of possible threats from the crazies who prey on the celebrated or notorious...of scorn from those who will consider her a fortune hunter. "It's too late to back down now, Mom," her children remind her when she tells them of her concerns.

Before the November hearing occurs, this writer meets with James Cunningham, the attorney selected by his firm to handle the Mealbach case. As we discuss the possible Mealbach-Dodge relationship, he tells me there is a good possibility that a jury trial, to determine whether his client is a Dodge heir, will be held within a few months.

We talk of many things as Cunningham verifies that different accounts of Frances Lucille's birth have been given by separate agencies. He has asked the Mealbachs for names of people who were close to Frances Lucille's adoptive parents during her early life. They have told him that Robert Manzer's cousin, June Eschtruth, was close to the Manzers, but that there was never any discussion of adoption between June and Francis Lucille before or after Manzer's death. Although June Eschtruth is deceased, Cunningham learned that there is an Eschtruth daughter, and that it is possible that June might have confided information to the daughter, regarding Frances Lucille's adoption. Since the daughter, Mary Henneman, lives in Utah, the attorney boarded a west-bound airplane.

Cunningham tells me, now, that Henneman informed him that her mother, June, confided to her that Robert Manzer spoke of Frances Lucille being adopted...that June had, on several occasions, asked Manzer why he did not disclose the facts about his adopted daughter's parentage to Frances Lucille. Manzer's unwillingness to do this had irritated June, who repeated to Mary what she knew of the adoption...

that Frances Lucille was the daughter of a prominent Detroit man and that the family name was on an automobile. Both Mary and June had assumed that Manzer referred to the Fords.

More important, Cunningham has tried to obtain information about possible scars on Frances Van Lennep's head and back to reinforce the Siamese-twin theory. Although Van Lennep family doctors would disclose no information, Cunningham has had a telephone conversation with the mother of a nurse who cared for Frances Van Lennep in her late years. The mother disclosed that her nurse-daughter had asked Mrs. Van Lennep about scars that the nurse observed on her patient's back and was told that they were "burn scars." Cunningham has been unable to talk with the nurse, herself, because she is suddenly un- available for comment as she moves to an unknown address.

Cunningham's mention of "burn scars" triggers my memory of an old newspaper clipping in my collection. In the clipping, a reporter informed readers that one of the Dodge sisters—either Frances or Anna Margaret—had been burned as a youngster in a fire ignited by a candle. I recall, for Cunningham, that this news story had upset Matilda Dodge to the point that she still protested the story, decades later.

We wonder if Matilda, after Frances' birth in 1914, had attributed scars on her first child to injuries from a fire, just as Minnie Manzer had attributed Frances Lucille's scars to a fall. We wonder if Matilda might have told this to a nurse or nanny who cared for the child. Could that have been the source of rumors that, later, Matilda tried to deny?

When the November pre-trial hearing takes place, I arrive at the courtroom of Judge J. Robert Gragg to listen and observe. Two Mealbach daughters also arrive at the courtroom—dark-haired Linda and very blonde Sharon. Their mother has not come, they tell me, because her blood pressure has climbed since the court jousting has begun. Her interests are represented by only one attorney—the mild-mannered but tenacious Jim Cunningham who studies his sheaf of papers as the ten Dodge attorneys politely await their turn to try to shred Frances Lucille's case with scathing rebukes and an arsenal of cliches.

Cunningham speaks first, pointing out that this is not a lawsuit; that he requests only a four-month injunction against the distribution of money from the Dodge trust fund so he will have time to prove that Mrs. Mealbach is a Dodge heir. He speaks softly, earnestly, hands clasped behind his back at times as he states that there have been problems of "misrepresentation by a court officer"...of discrepancies between the two birth certificates—state and city—for Frances Dodge. "All copies are supposed to be the same," he emphasizes. "Whoever did this, broke the law." He goes on to tell of the registration of birth, filed 27 years after Frances Lucille was born, which gave no names of parents nor any reason for omission of such names, nor reason for late filing.

The soft voice continues, narrating other unusual aspects of the case...that Robert Manzer had lost a home to foreclosure previous to adopting Frances Lucille, but had built, and then paid off all debts for, a new home in Detroit coinciding with the adoption of the child. That Francis Lucille has childhood memories of being taken to the Dodges' Boston Boulevard home. That she has surgical scars at the back of her head and base of her neck—scars of the kind resulting from separation of Siamese twins. That Frances Dodge Van Lennep had scars...

Cunningham's flow of words are obliterated, at this point, by audible snickering from opposing lawyers. He continues talking, undisturbed by their smirking, to tell of getting in touch with Frances Dodge Van Lennep's last physician...of the physician saying he could not be of any help because Mrs. Van Lennep's records had been destroyed according to the prescribed period of limitations.

There is no change of expression on Judge J. Robert Gragg's face as Cunningham concludes with a strong appeal for the court to issue the four-month stay on distribution of the trust fund. He stresses that "Mrs. Mealbach is the only surviving daughter of John Dodge." He remarks on "all she's lost" and points out that although the Dodge son, John Duval, was cut off from the fortune according to his father's will, John Duval was awarded money later, nonetheless. "And John Duval's daughter is going to receive a share of the trust fund," he adds. When he speaks of Frances Lucille, his client, he says, "I have no problems representing her; I am sure of my authority. She is entitled to her day in court."

Opposition lawyers respond in more dramatic style. Cunningham's arguments "are unsubstantiated by affidavits," the first Dodge-family attorney claims. He repeats this charge concerning the lack of affidavits intermittently throughout his arguments. He insists that Cunningham's only source are "the book, newspapers, and conjecture."

The arguments continue, as does Judge Gragg's impassivity. Or can it be apathy on the judge's part, I wonder, when this astonishing drama pulses within the drabness of the courtroom.

Hard-nosed Dodge attorneys toss cliches to make their points. No distribution-of-assets stay is in order, one claims, while Cunningham "fishes around" for a legal theory "to foul up the proceedings" that have already dragged on "in probate for 64 years and over four years in final distribution." In mixed metaphor, he adds that "the loaded gun is four months to go fishing."

Another Dodge attorney speaks sarcastically of "inferences and guesswork." He accuses Cunningham of coming before the court eleven or twelve months after "the petitioner sees a couple of pictures," and adds that the petitioner "has the fantasy of sharing in a large estate." Charles Dickens, himself, could not have "conjured up such a scenario," the attorney insists.

I begin to suspect that if sharp sarcasm prevails, the ten caustic defenders of the Dodge family and fortune will emerge victorious. And there is more to come as a Dodge attorney compares Cunningham's arguments to Churchill's description of Russian foreign policy. "...an enigma wrapped in a mystery surrounded by puzzles..."

The same lawyer insists that Cunningham is saying: "Wait—stop the distribution. It could be that I have a claim." He points out that the court-determined heirs to the Dodge fortune have "a right to invest that money in these changing times, and a right to its use."

In rebuttal, Cunningham seizes on the previous lawyer's assertion about depriving people of money to which they are entitled. But Cunningham refers, with obvious relish, to Mrs. Mealbach's lifelong deprivation. As I listen, I think of the five percent of Daniel Dodge's $13 million fortune ordered returned—by Judge Murphy in the early 1940s—to the John Dodge trust fund for the "benefit of undetermined heirs." Even that amount, some 45 years later, would have compiled to a very large sum. Would not Frances Lucille Mealbach—if her records were opened and a Dodge relationship proved—be entitled, at least, to that amount?

The lawyers debate, on and on, until Judge Gragg warns a Dodge attorney to condense his remarks and avoid repetition. The hearing winds down with the judge saying he will take the matter under advisement and will let both sides know his decision in writing.

He orders the courtroom cleared except for the attorneys. That same night, television newscasters announce that the Mealbach case will be tried by a jury in March, 1985.

Chapter 21

Probate Limbo

Frances Lucille is encountering difficulties by this time in evading Detroit and out-of-town newspaper reporters. They knock at her door and at the doors of Calhoun Street neighbors in their search for information. They crowd into her small front yard as she leaves for work, and try, again, to question her as she arrives home in late afternoon. When she will not talk to reporters, they telephone this writer's suburban home. They track down her attorney. They manage to acquire the Mealbachs' unlisted telephone number and her phone rings, insistently.

Inside Story of $40 Million Dynasty-Style Battle headlines a Star story. Similar stories appear in newspapers from San Diego to New York...in London and Paris.

Dodge family members are inveigled into making statements to the press. Each scoffs at the idea of the late Frances Dodge Van Lennep having a secret Siamese twin. The adopted brother, Richard Wilson, issues a denial that there were any scars on Frances Van Lennep's body. "I went swimming with her many times, and I zipped up many of her strapless party dresses," he is quoted in a news feature. The same feature quotes comments by Frances Van Lennep's first husband and her eldest daughter. "The silliest thing I ever heard." "Pre- posterous."

Officials for the Office of Vital and Health Statistics in Lansing knock down the claim of a "cover-up" regarding the two birth certificates, adding that "cover-ups don't occur in the state office." They explain to reporters that copies of any person's birth certificate, obtained from different places, might be recorded on different forms and, previous to the arrival of modern copy-machines, might not contain identical information...that it appeared, simply, that "somebody didn't do a very good job of filling it out." That, normally, the word "twin" would be written instead of being indicated by a diagonal line.

Cunningham is back in court on December 10 when the hearing is concerned with possible dismissal of the case, as requested by John Dodge grandchildren, on the basis that Frances Lucille Mealbach had failed to appear for interrogation as requested by Dodge lawyers. Cunningham has filed a protective order to inform the court that he is more than pleased to "produce" his client, but only after "reasonable notice." He cannot produce his client "literally overnight," he says. "It is unheard of," he insists, in a rebuke to Dodge attorneys, "to ask to speak to the most important witness on three days' notice."

The glasses slip more frequently down Cunningham's nose, now, as he and opposing attorneys argue about Mrs. Mealbach's availability. The Mealbach lawyer whips out a notebook to prove that he already is scheduled to be in court, on various matters, on many different dates suggested by the opposition for the interrogation of Mealbach.

Dodge lawyers are given permission to confer in the hallway, but they return to continue the dispute. Judge Gragg leaves the courtroom, removing himself from the arguments until both sides agree on a date for taking a deposition from Mrs. Mealbach by Dodge lawyers. The push-and-shove continues. Dodge attorneys are available, they say, even on Saturdays, Sundays and evenings for the next two weeks. A perspiring Cunningham resists, holding out for a January date. Every extra day gives him more time to chase down clues and hunt for witnesses.

Twice, a court clerk points out that "the judge is ready when you are." But when the judge re-enters, no date has been agreed upon. Attorney Joseph A. Sullivan complains to the judge that one date after another has been rejected by Cunningham. "Because of the vast notoriety of this case, it is best to quickly lay to rest the unpleasant innuendos appearing in the press," Sullivan insists.

Judge Gragg expresses annoyance with Cunningham. "How long has this case been going on?" the judge demands.

A surprised Cunningham supplies the date. October 29. "Of what year?" Gragg presses. "1983?"

When Cunningham reminds the judge that the date was 1984—only six weeks previously, Gragg glares at the attorney. Gragg then suggests that Cunningham should adjourn his other December court appointments in favor of these hearings.

"When I am supposed to be in court, your Honor, I am there," Cunningham mildly reproaches Gragg. The judge gives him a chance to prove this by arbitrarily setting a date for Mrs. Mealbach's private interrogation by Dodge attorneys. December 17—only one week from today, and earlier than even Dodge lawyers had anticipated.

Three days before the interrogation date, we are back in the courtroom at ten a.m. Frances Lucille, who has been told that her presence in court may help indicate her personal interest in the case, sits near the front. The fine lines at the corners of her clear blue eyes are deeper, the strain on her clear-complexioned face more evident, as she looks straight ahead, her lips drawn into a straight line. Her daughter Sharon and her very blond and blue-eyed grandson, Mark, are with her. They know that Frances Lucille is nervous about today's hearing; even more nervous about the upcoming interrogation by Dodge attorneys. And the daughter and grandson lean toward Frances Lucille in a protective manner as they wait for the attorneys to begin their harangues.

We rise to our feet as Judge Gragg comes into the courtroom. The judge says that the counsel for the appellant (Frances Lucille) has filed a petition for production and inspection of her adoption records and for her original birth certificate.

Cunningham then cites reasons why the records should be produced for his client, giving the same explanations presented at earlier court sessions. He puts particular emphasis on his client's scars, and the discrepancies between the two birth certificates issued for Frances Dodge Van Lennep. His client, he says, has a "psychological need to know" the truth of her heritage now that the matter has been "elevated to enormous public interest" through stories published "in every major newspaper in the country."

Again, he insists that the "right of privacy" no longer exists when both adoptive parents and biological parents are dead. He goes on to cite various cases, with numbers and statistics, to support his arguments that there is "good cause" for his client to have access to her records.

Dodge lawyers cite case numbers and statistics to support the opposite view, even as they piously respond that they and their clients have no personal objections to the petitioner's request for her birth records—it is simply a matter of observing the law.

The opposition attorneys take exception, however, to Cunningham's interpretation of the markings on Frances Dodge Van Lennep's birth certificate from the state. One of the lawyers points out that the media are interested in the case only because of the $40 million involved. "If the decimal point were moved so that the amount were $400,000, there would be no such interest," he asserts. Another emphasizes that when the petitioner's biological parents adopted her out in 1915, they purposely cut all ties, making her ineligible to share in a parental will.

Dodge attorneys are asking for "accelerated judgment" based on the doctrine of laches—unreasonable delay on the part of Frances Lucille Mealbach in filing her claim. Not for the first time, one lawyer reiterates that "Mrs. Mealbach sat idly by and then comes out of the woodwork."

Again, the hearing ends with no ruling by the judge. Reporters crowd around Frances Lucille as she leaves the courtroom. The next day's newspaper reports that Dodge "twin" loses estate bid.

What Frances Lucille really has lost is her solicitation to halt distribution of the remainder of the $40 million John Dodge trust fund, of which $28 million already had been distributed in the past six months. In this, his first significant written opinion on the Mealbach-Dodge matter, Judge Gragg states that the claimant had not proved that distribution of the remaining money would irreparably harm her. If she were proved to be an "issue" of John Dodge, and due any reparations, she could then sue the other heirs to recoup her share of the fortune.

Equally threatening are eleven counts for "summary judgment," filed by Dodge lawyers, detailing reasons why Mealbach's claim should be dismissed. Cunningham, who "produces" Frances Lucille for questioning at the office of Dodge attorneys on December 17, is aware that if Judge Gragg rules that any one of these eleven reasons is valid, the Mealbach claim may be dismissed.

Because of their mother's elevated blood pressure, the Mealbach daughters worry about Lucille Frances undergoing hours of questioning by opposition attorneys. "Five hours," she tells her daughters on her return. "And the Dodge lawyers were very nice," she says, her voice still echoing her surprise at this. She feels she did well under the intense questioning because, she says, "I simply told the truth about my life."

I learn that Cunningham's colleague has gone down to Fort Lauder- dale to take a deposition from Frances Van Lennep's first husband, Jimmy Johnson, who states that "there was not a mark on Frances' body." Cunningham points out, however, that we know Frances had an appendectomy scar.

Newspaper publicity has recently brought a welcome discovery to Cunningham with a telephone call from Mabel Burgett of Brighton, Michigan. Mrs. Burgett, a bright-eyed and alert woman of 72, had been visiting in Florida in November, 1984, she told Cunningham, when she went into a 7-Eleven store to buy tea. At the checkout counter, a front-page article in the Globe attracted her attention, she added. When she opened the paper to an inner page and saw an article about a Dodge Siamese-twin heiress, her heart began to pound. "I want to leave for home right now," she told her son-in-law.

On November 24, she was back at home in Brighton where she searched a Detroit telephone book for the name of the attorney mentioned in the Globe article; then phoned the lawyer to tell her story.

Her father-in-law, Silas Burgett, had been a employee and drinking buddy of the Dodge brothers, she said. Silas talked, often, of John and Horace Dodge, and annoyed his wife, Ida, by taking off with the brothers on fishing or hunting excursions. After the deaths of the Dodge brothers and, later, of Silas, the Burgetts still told stories at family gatherings about Dodge brothers' escapades.

When Mabel married Andrew Burgett, son of Silas and Ida, in 1930, the newlyweds lived with their mother-in-law on Andrus Street, just south of the Hamtramck border. In 1931, "when you couldn't buy a job," Mabel recalled for Cunningham, Andrew got work as a laborer in the Dodge plant—hired by his cousin, and long-time Dodge employee, Fred Lamborn. The young Burgetts were grateful for the job because 17-year-old Mabel was pregnant with her first child.

Mabel went on to tell Cunningham of the cold winter day when she and Ida walked down Joseph Campau Street, Hamtramck's main thoroughfare, and saw a pile of newspapers in front of the local theater. She told of seeing a headline about newborn Siamese twins and of asking her mother-in-law what Siamese twins were.

She still remembered her fearful feelings at Ida's explanations as Mabel felt the movement of her own unborn child. She recalled her worries, to Cunningham, that she, too, might have twins—joined together. The thought of little babies having to be cut apart made her shudder.

Mabel related her shocked reactions when, more than 50 years ago, Ida Burgett told her that Siamese twins had been born to Mrs. John Dodge...that John Dodge had confided this to Ida's husband, Silas, while the two men drank together in a Hamtramck saloon. And that Dodge also had confided that he and his wife kept one twin. The other, apparently, had been given away.

On a stormy day in January, 1985, Mabel Burgett arranges for a neighbor to drive her car along the snowy highway from Brighton to Detroit to have her deposition taken. She looks with disdain at Dodge attorneys who express doubts that she can recall a story after so many years. "Triple hearsay," they disparage her testimony.

Mabel is insulted. "The story left a deep impression on me because of my own pregnancy," she tells them, adding that she could remember the color of the dress she wore under her dark coat at the time she saw the newspaper headline. She reveals that she prayed, every night after her mother-in-law's disclosure, that her child would be healthy...that she would not deliver Siamese twins. "And I continued wondering, over the years, if I would ever learn what happened to the other Dodge twin," she adds firmly.

Mabel goes on to tell the attorneys that when she finally sold her home, she discarded an accumulation of possessions collected during her lifetime. But, inexplicably, she kept photographs of John and Horace Dodge, plus a copy of John Dodge's funeral eulogy.

The lawyers interrupt her flow of words to ask if her mother-in-law had confided the Siamese-twin story to any other person.

For the first time, Mabel is reluctant to answer a question. "One other person," she finally admits.

When they press for the name of the other person, Mabel refuses to tell them. She cannot, and will not, reveal the name, she insists under intense questioning. The attorneys eventually yield to her determination.

In early January, I visit Frances Lucille's eldest daughter, Brenda, in the Orlando, Florida, area.

As we talk, Brenda speaks of the Dodge family's refusal to cooperate in determining if her mother is a relative. Can all of them be unfeeling, she asks, caring only about the money? Can all of them be determined to resist finding out if there are ties of blood, especially with a twin?

She says doctors have found "a Mediterranean element" in her blood. She wonders if this can be traced to John Dodge's maternal ancestors, the Castos. She adds that even if "nothing comes from this"—no inheritance nor definite proof of heritage—the effect will be worthwhile if "cover-ups and falsifications of records" are exposed.

Another court hearing takes place on January 14, 1985, in response to a request by Frances Lucille Mealbach for Dodge lawyers to produce a medical history of Frances Dodge Van Lennep. Dodge attorneys retaliate by complaining that Cunningham has failed to supply them with requested information. Getting information from Cunningham "is like pulling teeth," one attorney tells the judge. "We are running up against a February 20 discovery date and a March trial."

When Cunningham responds that he had told opposition attorneys where the requested census and baptismal records could be found, Judge Gragg admonishes Cunningham. "We should adjourn for one hour and you can go and get them."

The arguments continue, each side accusing the other with failure to produce records until the judge orders Cunningham to be back at one p.m. the next day—with the records.

In defense of their own delay in supplying Cunningham with a medical history for Frances Dodge Van Lennep, a Dodge attorney claims that Cunningham "is putting the cart before the horse." He adds that "Mr. Cunningham should first produce evidence that Mrs. Mealbach was a Siamese twin." With a partial apology that he is only a "lay person" in medical matters, he insists there would have been a need, back in 1914, "for a C-section and for blood transfusions" at the birth of Siamese twins. He completes his argument with a charge of "preposterous," and with his personal opinion that "I don't think there were Siamese twin cases back then."

Although this opinion ignores the fact that Siamese twins, Daisy and Violet Hilton, were born in 1911 and lived unseparated, but productive, lives into adulthood—among other similar sets of twins, Jim Cunningham does not pick up on this point. Strangely, none of the Dodge attorneys quote any medical opinions that Siamese twins must come from one egg nor do they state that fraternal twins cannot become joined at an early stage of gestation.

Judge Gragg now rules that Cunningham must present his records—medical, baptismal, and census data—within five days, or else the records cannot be used at the trial. He rules, also, that Dodge lawyers need not produce Frances Van Lennep's medical history because such information is "irrelevant."

Stunned by the ruling, Cunningham leaves the courtroom, admitting to reporters that he is "very disappointed."

We are back in court in the first week of February as Cunningham presents two reasons for a requested 30-day adjournment of the March trial, and extension of the discovery deadline. The court, he charges, has not ruled on his December 14 petition for Mrs. Mealbach to review and inspect her adoption records which, he believes, will contain valuable evidence. Also, he must produce Mrs. Mealbach on February 12 for a physical examination and tests by doctors selected by the Dodges, even though the taking of depositions that he has requested from Frances Van Lennep's children has not yet been scheduled.

A Dodge attorney complains that Cunningham's motion is "premature." If the judge denies the request to see the adoption records, "then there is no need for additional discovery," he says, "because there won't be anything to discover."

Cunningham persists, stressing his need to get all his evidence before the court. Judge Gragg appears to be uncomfortable with the course this hearing is taking. He is well aware that if he rules the records should be opened, a legal precedent will be established. Never before, in a MIchigan court, have adoption records been ordered opened as part of a court case. Any such decision will result in a change in state law.

Judge Gragg shows irritation at Cunningham's next statement that "...the court may rule today, tomorrow, next month, I don't know." He complains that the ruling may come so late that the discovery date will occur immediately afterwards. "Then they will say to me," he argues on behalf of his request for an extension, "the court set a discovery date and I asked for a change, afterwards."

"Mr. Cunningham, how did this come to you, this information?" Judge Gragg demands.

"Your Honor," Cunningham responds, "we have been arguing for eight weeks..."

A Dodge attorney seizes his opportunity to interrupt with a complaint. "And the expense is being borne by our clients."

"I don't want to change this date," Judge Gragg says, looking sternly at Cunningham. "I'll have the ruling in writing."

The ruling has not yet been handed down when, a few days later, I drive along Dearborn's Calhoun Street, lined with modest homes on lots separated by narrow driveways. I enter the small vestibule of the Mealbachs' house, and am waved into the living room by Frances Lucille, who is taking a phone call from USA Today. She advises the caller to check with her lawyer, then hangs up the receiver.

She will be very much relieved, she tells me, just to have the entire court case over and done with—whatever the decision might be. To have the phone stop ringing with calls from all parts of the country, including Hollywood. To enjoy her family, her work, her home, and the remaining years of her life in peace. "I'm old enough to know that money can't buy happiness," she tells me, her clear blue eyes reflecting her desire for understanding. Her children, she adds with a shrug, are not willing to give up the quest. And who can blame them? After all, they are convinced they are grandchildren of John Dodge—entitled to their heritage.

"It would be nice to have a new car," she admits, adding that an automobile is the only thing she really needs. She has had problems with her current, used Nova. "And my car insurance has gone up," she says, explaining that as she was backing the car out of the backyard garage to take her husband to the doctor's office, "he opened the door on the passenger side before we were out of the garage, to the tune of $2000 worth of damage to the car door and the garage."

I hear her husband moving about in the kitchen, but he stays out of sight. "I do what I can for him," she says, "but he's not really <u>aware</u> any more. So everything is up to me."

Her gaze shifts to the front window, curtained with sheer, patterned panels and framed with green drapes and a valance. Looking outside to the quiet street dotted with cars parked near ice-rutted sidewalks, she reflects that "the sight of neighborhood children, playing outside, is rare now." Today's children, she offers, "seem to stay indoors and watch television." The Calhoun Street neighborhood is changing, like much of southeast Dearborn. When a house is listed for sale, it is likely to be bought by an Arab family. Southeastern Dearborn is populated, now, by the largest contingent of Arabs in the United States.

It is not the changing neighborhood, but coping with snow and ice and yardwork that has compelled Frances Lucille to list her name for an apartment in the city-owned, senior-citizen, housing complex. The high-rise apartment building is located only two blocks from the bridal salon where she works. When an apartment becomes available, she will sell her house and opt for convenience.

When she sees a van puling up in front of the house, our conversation is interrupted. Frances Lucille urges me to stay—to be a part of the interview with Rick Matyn of WDIV-TV. Thanking her politely, I choose to leave. But Frances Lucille is, again, partly excited and partly discomposed at the attention from the media.

Although Judge Gragg has ruled the medical records of Frances Dodge Van Lennep "irrelevant" to the case, Frances Lucille must go to Ann Arbor in the second week of February to be examined by doctors selected by the Dodge family. A Dodge attorney is present when she arrives in Ann Arbor, with daughter Sharon, to undergo blood tests. The elevators are not working, so they must walk up seven flights of stairs to a second office where a specialist examines the scars at the back of her skull and base of her neck. The scars are old, the doctor says warily, and it is difficult to be certain of their origin.

Sharon, who now is enrolled in nursing college, bristles at the vagueness of the remark. She points out what she insists are "suture marks" at either side of the scars—a transverse scar of three centimeters over the upper back and a 1.5 centimeter lateral scar over the occipit of the head. The pediatric surgeon is noncommittal.

The Dodges soon will have a medical report on Frances Lucille Mealbach to compare with whatever medical information they have on Frances Dodge Van Lennep. But since the judge has ruled the Van Lennep medical records "irrelevant" to the case, Frances Lucille can make no such comparisons.

At the middle of February, Judge Gragg effectively squashes the case by finally ruling to grant "accelerated judgment" as requested by Dodge attorneys. Gragg denies Frances Lucille's petition for access to her adoption records and her original birth certificate on the basis that, once "accelerated judgment" was rendered, her requests for the records became "moot."

Mealbach delayed too long in filing her claim, the judge tells reporters. Dodge heirs have been designated by an earlier court order, and that order was final.

Frances Lucille is at work in the bridal shop when she is notified of Gragg's decision. She expresses little surprise, telling reporters that she is "tired of fighting the establishment" and is not sure she wants to be "bothered" with an appeal of the verdict.

The five Mealbach children have no such doubts. Youngest daughter Sharon, most fiery of the three sisters, grabs a newspaper carrying a front-page story of a thoroughbred dog, King Boots, who bit an aged woman, causing her death. The dog escaped a death sentence after well publicized court hearings. "King Boots" now becomes the battle cry of Sharon and her siblings. Frances Lucille echoes the same challenge. "King Boots," she says, "had his day in court. That just shows how crazy they (the courts) are. Why can't they give me the same opportunity?"

Sharon agrees vehemently, shaking her blond head as she remarks that the dog has papers denoting his pedigree. "My mother is simply 'Jane Doe'," she complains.

The Mealbach sisters point out that million of people are now seeking the right to have access to adoption records...that many new organizations have been founded to assist adoptees in their search for information—Adoptees Search Connection, Adoptees' Liberty Movement Association, Operation Identity and others...that some legislators and attorneys are joining the clamor for open adoptions and open state records.

All the children insist that they "want to know who we are." Roots are important, they say. Not only for reasons of genetics, because of advances in medical science, but to satisfy emotional needs. Nothing, they think, can be worse than not knowing.

By June of 1985, Cunningham has filed his brief with the Michigan Court of Appeals in an attempt to get a reversal of Gragg's decision. In this same month, Frances Lucille lists her home for sale and moves into city-owned housing for seniors—Hubbard Manor East. Her tenth-floor apartment has a flower decked balcony from which she can see downtown Detroit silhouetted against the skyline. It is a comfortable, pleasant, and convenient apartment—one bedroom, large bath, living room, and kitchenette. In the downstairs lobby, other apartment residents sit in lounge chairs, watching television or having conversations about memories of earlier, more active times in their lives. Frances Lucille is friendly to everyone, but has no time to sit and talk.

Still, she is more relaxed now that the dispensation of the Dodge-Mealbach case rests with the slow moving court of appeals. Her current problem is her ailing husband who "cried for two days," she says, when she brought him up to the apartment.

William Mealbach is staying at the house on Calhoun, now, with the eldest son. But when the house is sold...She shrugs her shoulders. In the meantime, she walks up Calhoun every morning to fix her husband's breakfast, then returns after work to cook his dinner before going back to her apartment. Her husband is failing fast, she says. And she and her son do the best they can to care for him.

By October, the house on Calhoun is sold and the Mealbachs must move, permanently, into the senior citizens' apartment. When Frances Lucille brings her husband to the apartment for the second time, he is totally disoriented. Within days, he is so ill that he must be moved to a Dearborn nursing home where his condition rapidly deteriorates until he recognizes no one and must be fed with a syringe. His social security payments go directly to the nursing home for his care. Frances Lucille pays for his medication and such essentials as occasional haircuts from her earnings.

Christmas, 1985, is a difficult time for the Mealbachs. Bill Mealbach's condition is the same; he is tied into a wheelchair each day for a short time—head lolling, eyes staring vacantly, Frances Lucille has spent several weeks previous to the holiday season dealing with guilt—disposing of furniture and clothing, and sorting out a 46-year accumulation of family mementos and miscellanea...most of which is assigned to the junk pile. Her small apartment will not accommodate such collections—nor will it accommodate her children and grandchildren for the traditional Christmas turkey dinner. Instead, Sharon invites everyone to her home for dinner and a get-together, which her brothers and sisters enjoy. But things are no longer the same; everyone sadly recognizes that.

Time goes by rapidly for Frances Lucille whose work schedule keeps her occupied. In January, 1986, the Michigan Court of Appeals denies her plea to inspect her adoption records. But still pending, Cunningham says, is a second appeal—this one of Gragg's order that had denied Frances Lucille's request to be declared a Dodge heir.

"The court of appeals has said it will hear the appeal, and that I can incorporate into it her requests to open the adoption records," the attorney explains.

The wait for the appeal-hearing continues. Even when Frances Lucille falls and breaks her right arm in March of 1986, she misses only a day at the bridal shop before returning to the store with her arm in a cast.

"I must work," she says with no trace of self-pity, "to pay my rent and meet my expenses." She retains pride that she has supported herself for so many years, and now accepts only a minimum of help from other, younger saleswomen at the shop while her arm mends. Younger employees have tried to help, on occasion, before the broken-arm incident, only to be gently but firmly reproved by Frances Lucille when she found that someone else had rehung a wedding dress for her.

"I enjoy working," she says as she moves about the store on high-heeled pumps that she wears, daily, on the job. "When I can't carry my share of the workload—every bit of it, that's the day I'll hand in my resignation."

For only a couple of months, the broken arm prevents her from spending her free time at her sewing machine where she makes the skirts and blouses and capes that give her own wardrobe such a distinctive touch.

On March 13, 1986, Frances Lucille and her family are astounded to read media reports revealing that the Michigan Judicial Tenure Commission has filed a complaint with the Michigan Supreme Court, asking for suspension of Judge J. Robert Gragg from the bench. The commission charges that Judge Gragg is "mentally impaired," adding that he had been assisted and prompted in his rulings by his staff, after Gragg had "demonstrated confusion, disorientation, forgetfulness, and difficulty in comprehending" court proceedings.

Medical reports, cited in newspapers, refer to the judge being unable to name the vice-president of the United States. A respected neurologist, Dr. John Gilroy, writes his opinion that, since having blood clots surgically removed from the brain in 1981, Gragg has suffered severe brain damage and "is demented."

When Frances Lucille phones me, her voice rings with indignation. This man, she says, who cannot give the name of the governor who recently appointed him, was screened and approved by a State Bar of Michigan committee. Yet we—lay people—had questioned, among ourselves, the judge's apparent lack of comprehension on some of the basic issues brought before him at the Mealbach-Dodge hearings.

We wonder, now, about the self-protective links within the legal profession that form a secure and defensive barrier spiked with verbosity and legal terminology. True, the commission is now investigating Judge Gragg, but only after blatantly unprofessional behavior was evidenced.

Frances Lucille is outraged that her case has been tossed out of court by an incompetent judge. If the Michigan Court of Appeals also rules negatively on her appeal, when it is finally heard, she will, she says determinedly, "go to the media" with her complaints against the judicial system and it sufferance of what she terms as "collusion and hiding records." Her earlier, phlegmatic attitude toward pressing her case has largely disappeared. Lawyers' references to her "coming out of the woodwork" and to her "fantasy of sharing in a large estate" have stiffened her resolve to banish her image as "a crazy lady" she says, and to win her case.

Now, as the media seize upon the ridiculous combination of a "demented judge" and a discarded "Siamese twin" heiress, the peace-loving Frances Lucille is transformed into an aggressive tigress. She must wait, though—wait, again, until she learns whether the case will be returned to probate court because of Gragg's "incompetence," or whether the appeals court will deal with the matter.

Whatever is decided, we are sure that the entire matter must soon be concluded. Only Dodge attorneys are profiting, financially, from the prolonged battle.

Chapter 22

Up Against "The System"

Soon after the attention of the media focuses on Judge Gragg's "incompetence," Frances Lucille's attorney files a motion with the Michigan Court of Appeals for Peremptory Reversal of Gragg's decision to throw the Mealbach-Dodge case out of court. The basis for the motion is the report of Dr. John Gilroy, neurologist, that Gragg had suffered brain damage as a result of surgery for bilateral subdural hematomas in 1981. Subsequently, the doctor noted, Gragg experienced "difficulty with both intellectual and cognitive functioning."

Cunningham's motion quotes the neurologist's opinion that "the brain damage is of such a severity that Judge Gragg is demented..." The attorney also cites 30 examples of confusion demonstrated by the judge during the Mealbach-Dodge hearings.

By this time, Gragg has taken a voluntary medical leave from the bench as the Michigan Judicial Tenure Commission files an ouster complaint with the state supreme court. In May, the high court denies the ouster petition because Judge Gragg has agreed to "voluntarily remain off the bench while pursuing medical treatment and a resolution of the Commission's complaint..."

Since Frances Lucille has hope, now, that her case may be reactivated after the disclosures about Gragg, she goes with this writer to St. Joseph and Niles to search for more information. There, we learn more about the history of the Michigan Children's Home where Frances Lucille spent the first months of her life. At the branch of Child and Family Services at the outskirts of St. Joseph, we are given a photograph of that early orphans' home, but are denied any further information.

On September 4, the court of appeals denies Frances Lucille's motion for Peremptory Reversal because of her "failure to persuade the Court that reversible error is so manifest that an immediate reversal...should be granted without formal argument or submission." Frances Lucille has her own opinion about this—that a favorable decision might "open a whole can of worms" in regard to other cases on which Judge Gragg has ruled.

She is hopeful, though, that the same court will rule on her previously filed appeal before the end of the year.

A touch of glamor brightens the routine of pouring through library files and scanning convolutions of microfilm when, in the third week of September, 1986, DBA Associates of Hollywood sends two television-documentary producers to the metro-Detroit area to talk with Frances Lucille, her daughters, her attorneys, and this writer. Pro- ducers Terry Maurer and John Cosgrove are friendly, attractive people who meet with us at Sharon's home. Their enthusiasm for the project is contagious; they revitalize the flagging energies of those of us who are exhausted by the search for answers and the waiting for court rulings.

In later afternoon, we drive to Meadow Brook Hall so that the producers can have a quick survey of the magnificent Tudor-styled mansion—its lawns and gardens and its Sunday streams of touring visitors. The Hollywood people must rush off to catch a plane back to California in an hour, so they cannot join carefully regulated files of tourists entering the mansion under the supervision of docents, dedicated to fascinating memories of a stately Dodge-Wilson family. Instead, we wander the winding walks until the producers must dash away, promising to return within a month. On their return, they will film Frances Lucille's segment of an hour-long program, called "Unsolved Mysteries," for NBC-TV.

On October 16, the producers and a crew of four technicians fly to Detroit from Hollywood. They descend on this writer's house at five p.m. in two rented vans and accompanied by Frances Lucille and her daughter Brenda. The TV crew shuts off the refrigerator—noisy clicks are unwelcome. They move the furniture, hang lights from the ceilings, and set up a huge white dish (reflector) in the living room. No matter. Hollywood is calling. And when they complete their filming at 8:30, they must get ready for three more days of work in the area.

Early Friday morning, the crew arrives at the Grosse Ile home of the Ken Porters. Roberta Porter has been hard at work, setting up and decorating two huge Christmas trees, preparing hors d'euvres, and inviting some of the same guests who attended an earlier Christmas cocktail party—for a re-staging of that 1981 holiday affair when Brenda first saw the Dodge book photographs. The only fake detail at the 1986 party, apart from the date, is the contents of the cocktail glasses. Water.

Refused permission to film the interior of the Dodges' former Boston Boulevard home, still owned by the Catholic Archdiocese of Detroit, the television crew photographs the exterior of the house. The crew also films Frances Lucille and her daughters at the Meadow Brook estate, but they do not enter the Hall.

The camera crew then travels on to the old house on Hogarth Street in Detroit where Lucille was brought by her adoptive parents. To Woodlawn Cemetery and the ornate tomb of the Dodges. To the Mealbachs' former house on Calhoun. To the Bloomfield Hills offices of Frances Lucille's attorneys. To the Ann Arbor offices of the pediatric surgeon, selected earlier by Dodge heirs, who had examined Frances Lucille's scars. The physician is affable, now, under the glare of television lights and the stare of the camera as he responds to questions posed by the Hollywood producers. He repeats his opinion that, because the scars are old, their origin cannot be accurately determined. He thinks it unlikely, however, that they are scars from a Siamese-twin separation. But producer Cosgrove says that, off camera, the physician adds that separations of superficially attached Siamese twins were not unknown in the early part of the century.

Finally, the producers and crew squeeze into Frances Lucille's senior-citizen, 10th floor apartment where they pile her sofa and chairs on the small, wrought-iron balcony to make room for cameras and sound equipment. When they complete their work, they fly back to Hollywood to work with actor-narrator Raymond Burr in preparing their pilot program for NBC television.

In early November, the Michigan Court of Appeals schedules a hearing on Frances Lucille's appeal. Flanked by her younger son, Tom, her daughter Sharon, and son-in-law Larry, Frances Lucille attends the presentations by her attorney and by six Dodge attorneys before three judges—the Honorable Harold Hood, Honorable Thomas Burns, and Honorable John Theiler.

Everyone rises at the entrance of the robed judges to the triple summons of "Hear Ye." It is clear, immediately, that conduct within this courtroom will be decorus and orderly as Judge Hood states the ruling—saying that he recognizes the presence of six attorneys, representing the respondents (recognized Dodge heirs), who have asked for extra time for their oral presentation. The judges, he emphasizes, are granting 30 minutes "collectively" to Dodge attorneys. Each of the first two Dodge attorneys must limit their remarks to 12 minutes, retaining six minutes for any additional comments from the other four lawyers.

Judge Hood reminds the attorneys that the judges have read briefs and are informed about the case, then permits Cunningham to highlight the paramount factors of his client's appeal. "May it please the court..."Cunningham begins, calling Judge Gragg's earlier "accelerated judgment" a "harsh ruling." He reminds the court that "...we were asking only for a hearing to determine if she (Frances Lucille) is an heir." He cites a 1944 case (In Re Moores Estate) to back his claim that "as a matter of law, she is entitled to this determination."

Cunningham attacks his opponents' repeated references to his client's "so-called 'delay' from 1982 to 1984," claiming that the delay was caused by the court itself. He discounts the "too late" angle by asserting that "in 1980, Mrs. Mealbach didn't even know she was connected with this estate."

He reminds the court that when Frances Lucille first went to the Guardian Ad Litem for the Dodge estate, "he quite properly told the court that 'this woman has a case,' and asked 'what should I do?'" The court then discharged the Guardian Ad Litem's services, Cunningham adds, on the basis that Mrs. Mealbach was now a "known party."

"My client has never had a hearing," he insists, contending that when Frances Lucille did file her claim, she met "incredible opposition" from attorneys for the Dodge family. He points out that the recently discharged Guardian Ad Litem had revealed that Frances Lucille's adoption records "contain information helpful to this case," and that, legally, all an adoptee must do to get information from adoption records is to show "good cause." He adds that Frances Lucille has already presented five reasons why she has "good cause."

Judge Hood asks, now, for those reasons, and Cunningham lists them.

1. Frances Lucille's psychological need to know.
2. The inconsistent explanations of her adoption and other birth facts from the State.
3. The knowledge that whomever her biological parents are listed to be in the records, there is evidence that her father is John F. Dodge, and that the records will produce evidence and information leading to further evidence of this fact.
4 and 5. There are both inheritance and medical reasons which contribute toward "good cause."

Cunningham concludes by saying "something is fundamentally unfair" that his client did not receive a hearing; that he and his client were refused Frances Dodge Van Lennep's medical records, although Frances Lucille was required to offer her records to Dodge attorneys.

"Do you want Frances Dodge's medical records laid out on the table for the public to see?" a judge asks.

"No," Cunningham responds, adding that they can be privately viewed.

The judge then asks if Cunningham has had deep resistance from opposing attorneys on this point. Cunningham answers affirmatively.

"What if the court simply permitted reviewing of the adoption records...if that were all it did?" the judge questions.

Cunningham responds that a review of the adoption records would certainly "open the door" to other documents and information. Dodge attorney, Joseph A. Sullivan, then takes his turn at the microphone.

Sullivan relies on a quote to make his first point that "there may be a modicum of the layman's sense of equity here," but that the doctrine of res judicata is binding, thereby prohibiting a hearing for Frances Lucille Mealbach on her petition for determination of heir. "It is difficult," Sullivan says, "to keep up with the zigging and zagging of Mrs. Mealbach" who, he adds, has had many days in court on this same issue.

Sullivan gathers up more indignation as he wonders, aloud, "how sincere she (Mrs. Mealbach) is" since she did not appeal that first decision in the juvenile division of probate court, when she was denied access to her adoption records.

"She slept on her rights from 1982 to 1984," Sullivan persists, adding that "there is a proclivity here to try to tie in the adoption records to the determination of heir in the Dodge matter...they do not belong together." He expands on this point, stating that everything asserted by Mrs. Mealbach regarding her relationship to Dodge is based on speculation and that "there is no single fact indicating she is a Dodge heir." He is determined to stress, once more, that "merely telling a titillating story that captures the fancy of the press is insufficient to bend or bypass the principles of law."

When the attorney is reminded by a judge that he has used all of his time, Sullivan is reluctant to stop talking. "At the risk of taking my brother's time," he says, "I want to make a point..."

"That's up to your brother," the judge insists to the amusement of listeners. Sullivan takes his seat.

Dodge attorney Henry Grix now approaches the podium. He admits that "this is a controversial and complex case," but says that "the controversy is of the appellant's own making." He reinforces Sullivan's previous comment about the doctrine of res judicata and its binding powers.

A judge responds to this by admitting that "it's hard to quarrel with Attorney Sullivan's remarks on upholding the principles of law," but adds that "if the adoption file were made available, it would answer a lot of questions that would foreclose further action."

Grix will not accept this premise. "No further action is necessary," he claims.

"I thought you said you had no interest in whether the adoption records were opened," the judge reminds him.

Grix merely stresses, again, the irrevocability of previous "final and binding orders." He says the declared Dodge heirs have already paid taxes on the money they have received, and have spent much of the remainder. "The world must move on..." Grix concludes.

Attorney Charles Nida, representing Frances Van Lennep's daughter Judith McClung, claims the remaining few minutes to state that "Mrs. Mealbach has failed to prove that John Dodge's failure to include her in the will was by negligence."

Again, the judge has a comment. "If she is, in fact, a child of John Dodge, there is some question as to whether she is included," he says, referring to the wording of the will which states "...to the heirs of my said children."

Judge Hood points out that Cunningham has already given reasons why the doctrine of "laches" is not a proper ground for dismissing the case. He gives Dodge attorney Nida opportunity to respond, but the questions seem to confuse him.

Cunningham makes a short rebuttal in which he takes up the criterion of res judicata, pointing out other cases by name and number to reinforce his view that Frances Lucille "is entitled to have her petition heard and granted." By this time, he also is presenting a new interpretation of the birth certificate, filed in Lansing, for Frances Dodge (Van Lennep.) A new copy of the document, duplicated with the use of more advanced techniques, has disclosed a line through the word Triplet as well as the line through the word Twin. According to Cunningham's interpretation of the better copy, Frances M. Dodge was the "first born of an 'other'."

When Cunningham concludes by insisting that "the adoptive issue is alive and well," Judge Hood tells the participants that they will be informed of the court's decision. The Mealbachs talk among themselves as they leave, expecting that the decision may come within three months. Sooner, rather than later, they hope.

In newspaper stories about the appeal hearing, Frances Lucille is described as "intrepid," although her remarks to a Detroit News reporter are tinged with pessimism as she expresses doubt that she has "much of a chance" and says she is "really disenchanted with the whole system." She refers to missing papers and records and wonders, aloud, why the Dodge family is fighting so hard "if there is nothing to hide."

She is described in a news account as a "champagne-blond, well-dressed client"—an accurate portrayal that, nonetheless, suggests the kind of wealthy and sophisticated background that has not been a part of Frances Lucille's life.

Weeks pass by quickly for Frances Lucille who leaves for Florida to attend her granddaughter's wedding near Orlando, and returns in time to spend Thanksgiving with her family at Sharon's home. While she is out of town, a scandal breaks with the suicide of Michigan Court of Appeals Judge S. Jerome Bronson immediately following his arraignment in circuit court on charges of accepting a $20,000 bribe and of conspiring to accept another $20,000 bribe. Public confidence is shaken in the court system, and Frances Lucille, on her return from Orlando, feels reinforced in her opinion that "the system" is a self-protective one that sometimes covers up aberrations within its judicial fraternity.

Taking turns with her two sons, Frances Lucille visits the nursing home where her husband's condition is rapidly deteriorating. Attendants no longer tie him to a wheelchair...he remains in bed, drawn into a fetal position and fed through a tube.

A week before Bill Mealbach's death on December 10, Judge J. Robert Gragg resigns his Wayne County Probate Court post as hearings begin on whether to remove him because of mental impairment. Although Gragg refuses to admit incompetence, the attorney representing him concedes that "the judge is very ill." The Judicial Tenure Commission expresses its willingness to honor Gragg's retirement wishes, apparently relieved to avoid the notoriety of further testimony from Gragg's physician, his court staff, and from attorneys who have appeared before him in court.

By the time "Unsolved Mysteries" debuts on prime-time NBC television on the night of January 20, 1987, there has been no decision from the court of appeals. Because the Mealbach-Dodge appeal is still under consideration, the television segment dealing with Frances Lucille's story is handled carefully—but effectively, opening and closing with cemetery scenes near the Dodge mausoleum to set the mood. Feedback from many people among the national television audience indicates that viewers were impressed by likenesses, shown in television photos, between some of the Mealbachs and the Dodges... impressed by Attorney Cunningham's review of the facts, and by the presentation of research data. Telephone calls and letters, regarding the program, arrive from many parts of the country at Meadow Brook Hall. At Frances Lucille's apartment. At the law office. At this writer's home. All pose the same questions. Why is the opposition fighting so hard to prevent Frances Lucille from gaining access to adoption and medical records, if there is nothing to hide?

The court has not ruled yet on the appeal when Frances Lucille and her attorney are interviewed, February 23, on Detroit's popular television show, Kelly and Company, where the attorney acknowledges that "much of the evidence we used in court was provided by Jean Pitrone." Again, numbers of viewers respond with telephone calls and letters.

One of the calls impels Frances Lucille and this writer to drive north past Port Huron to the farming community of Yale and the home of Joseph and Wanda Batz. They relate the story of Joseph's father, Henry Batz (Andrea Bozzio), and his name change when he went to work at the Dodge shop in 1907. They tell of Henry's pride in working side-by-side with John Dodge in those early years...of his boasts that he had helped build the first Dodge automobile in 1914...of his loyalty, in 50 years of employment during which "he never took a sick day," to the Dodge and Dodge-Chrysler corporations...of his ownership of Dodge automobiles, although he never learned to operate a car and had to depend on his sons to take him for Sunday drives.

They tell of Henry Batz's pride in owning a drill press removed from that early Dodge shop when the Dodge brothers had moved into their newly equipped Hamtramck factory. Of his pride in a Detroit News article about his retirement from the Dodge Division of Chrysler Corporation in 1957. But of his disappointment in never receiving the $10,000 he expected at John Dodge's death. And, most important to Frances Lucille, of Batz's often expressed bewilderment at the John Dodges for having given away a child—one of twins.

From Yale, we drive to Roseville, just east of Detroit, to talk with Henry Batz's son Jerome and his wife. They tell us that they donated Henry's drill press, from the Dodge shop, to the city of Roseville in 1977, from which it was transferred to the Henry Ford Museum at Greenfield Village. They also tell us that until his death in 1969, Henry Batz was embittered because he never received his expected "inheritance" from John Dodge. They remember him muttering and complaining in his late years about waiting all his life to collect his $10,000.

Jerome's mother-in-law, "Nanny" Trombino, would remind "Pa" Batz, as he complained, that he had supported his family for 50 years on his earnings at Dodge Brothers. And "Pa" Batz would reluctantly agree, only to add that he hoped to receive a car from the company when he retired, but was given a wristwatch. And, always, he shook his head in disbelief when he muttered, in Italian, about the give-away of the twin baby.

"Nanny" Trombino did not attempt to pacify the old man with any explanation about possible reasons for giving away a baby. She could not imagine any such reasons. Nor could she explain to Henry Batz that he might have misunderstood John Dodge's intentions to leave money to his tool room employees. She did not know that John and Horace Dodge had set aside a private fund of $5 million to care for faithful and needy former Dodge employees. Batz had been a faithful employee. But did one have to be both faithful and needy to draw from the fund?

1987 drags along into late April, with no decision from the Michigan Court of Appeals, when this writer makes a surprising discovery during a visit to a private collection of Dodge papers. Among the unfiled stacks of papers and memorabilia is a record, in Amelia Rausch's handwriting, of the John Dodge family's links to Harper Hospital in the years beginning with 1914 and the birth of Frances Matilda Dodge at Harper, followed by the birth of Daniel in 1917 and Anna Margaret in 1919. All were "born in Harper Hospital" according to the carefully written words of the meticulous Amelia, in contradiction to the home-birth records for Frances Dodge on the official birth certificate.

I remember how eagerly and tenaciously Amelia pursued any information about the Dodges...how carefully she guarded her "papers" and pondered what should be done with them at her death...how clearly she recalled past events...how accurate were her facts and dates...how important it was to Amelia that the John Dodge history should be preserved. Could Amelia have been mistaken, then, about the place of birth for her niece...the first child of her only sister? Not likely—unless, for some reason, Matilda had lied to Amelia. And why would there be any reason for Matilda to lie, unless she were trying to shroud the circumstances of the child's birth in secrecy?

The protests of a Dodge attorney, in court, come to mind...that it was ridiculous to think that, in 1914, a woman could be successfully delivered of Siamese twins at home, and that the joined twins then could be separated at home.

But suppose, as Amelia had notated, Matilda's delivery did not take place at home? One certificate for Frances Dodge's birth had given the home address for the birth; the other had given no address at all.

Through research, I have learned that Dr. Max Ballin, Harper's most prestigious surgeon—trained in Berlin and Munich universities, had been on the hospital's staff since 1906 and was known as a "surgeon's surgeon" and "Prince of the operating room." Ballin, who specialized in thyroid surgery, instructed other physicians in surgical techniques and was always called upon "for the heroic measure" in Harper's operating rooms.

Dr. Ballin and Dr. William Chittick, close friend of the Dodges, served on many of the same hospital committees, and had offices on Woodward Avenue which were only a block apart. Dr. Ballin had operated on Anna Margaret Dodge in 1924 to try to save the child's life. He had been consulted when Frances was hospitalized after putting her fingers through the wringer, and had performed Frances' appendectomy in 1930. The same Dr. Ballin had operated on Margaret Rausch in 1927 for cancer. And it was Dr. Ballin who made a public announcement, in 1927, that Matilda was the first donor for operating rooms for a new Harper Hospital building on Brush Street, contributing $125,000.

Would Matilda, expecting her first baby at age 31, have chosen the pathologist, Dr. Chittick, to deliver her child when Harper Hospital had obstetricians such as Dr. Jenks on its staff? Or if there were complications, and surgery were necessary, would not the John Dodges have called for the "heroic measure" from the finest surgeon available—Dr. Ballin?

I recall the firm friendship between "Doc" Chittick, who also had a daughter named Frances, and John Dodge. Could it be possible that because of Chittick's friendship with the Dodges, he had filled out the birth certificates as ambiguously as possible? Was it even possible that another doctor—perhaps Dr. Ballin—might have done whatever surgery was necessary at the time of the birth? The money left to Chittick in John Dodge's will reinforces this speculation, but the questions remain unanswered and, certainly, the speculations remain exactly that—only speculations. For how long, no one knows.

Record-breaking heat in the summer of 1987 moves into July and almost into August before Frances Lucille is notified, on July 28, of the Michigan Court of Appeals decision. She may have her "day in court," the judges have decided, "to seek permission, on the basis of a 'psychological need to know,' to see her birth and adoption records."

Her attorney is encouraged, confiding that this important decision will "open a lot of doors" as the case returns to Wayne County Probate Court, with a different probate judge. Frances Lucille expects to receive a court date without undue delay.

The court date is still pending in September, 1987, when Pope John Paul II visits Detroit and stays overnight at the former John Dodge home on East Boston Boulevard—now the residence of Archbishop Edmund Szoka. The City of Detroit, plunging into a flurry of preparations for the Pontiff's visit, has hauled away the assortment of rusted, abandoned cars that formerly littered Woodward Avenue in the vicinity of Blessed Sacrament Cathedral. Bulldozers have razed a row of unsightly, vacant storefronts opposite the Cathedral. And the

Cathedral, itself, bathed in a battery of floodlights, is, for now, untainted by the usual presence of prostitutes who solicit customers on Woodward and who stop to rest on the steps of the great church.

For the one night of the Pontiff's visit, an eight-block area surrounding the church is sealed off until the next morning when John Paul II departs from the former Dodge mansion in his Popemobile, escorted by 40 police motorcycles. With the roaring departure of Popemobile and cycles along East Boston Boulevard, the spotlight of brief public attention is removed from the John Dodge manor as the great, aging house resettles into its quiet life among the boulevard's crumbling mansions...as the prostitutes return to their usual nearby beats...as Frances Lucille waits to learn the date of her next appearance in court.

Three months after Pope John Paul's visit to Detroit, Wayne County Probate Judge Martin T. Maher refuses to hold a hearing on Frances Lucille's request to see her records, despite the July, 1987, ruling by the Michigan Court of Appeals that she could have her "day in court"—probate court, that is. Frances Lucille immediately is advised by her attorney to file a motion for Maher to reconsider his refusal to conduct such a hearing.

Four months later, in April, 1988, the Michigan Supreme Court issues a one-sentence order. The order is a refusal to review another ruling, also made by the Michigan Court of Appeals in July, 1987, when the appeals court had refused to overturn an earlier probate court decision—that the Mealbach suit was filed too long after the assets of John Dodge's trust fund were distributed to heirs.

"We are not persuaded that the questions presented should be reviewed by this court," the Michigan Supreme Court order states without addressing the merits of Mealbach's claim. Frances Lucille makes no comment to the press on this development. But her attorney is surprisingly unreluctant to admit that, although his client is disappointed by the ruling, she is, at the same time, relieved that she can now "return to the normal existence she had before this whirlwind" and can "return to being a private person." He adds that the supreme court decision is "unfortunate" in that "Mrs. Mealbach will be fore- closed from displaying her evidence before a jury."

This disappointing news from the Michigan Supreme Court is followed by another blow one month later. In May, 1988, despite the Mealbach plea to Probate Court Judge Maher to reconsider his refusal to hold a hearing on her request to see her birth and adoption records, the judge again defies the Michigan State of Appeals Court order to preside over such a hearing. Maher claims that a similar hearing already had been conducted, much earlier, by former Judge Gragg in probate court . Gragg's "incompetence" is not mentioned.

A clerk at the Michigan Court of Appeals tells a newspaper reporter that the probate judge "can't overrule a decision of a higher court." A state court administrator, however, offers a different opinion of what he calls an "unusual decision." If Judge Maher felt, the administrator says, that "there was something the Court of Appeals overlooked, he is justified in entering an order that is contrary to the Court of Appeals order."

Once again, Frances Lucille's ambivalence is displayed when she has a different reaction, now, than the reaction reported by her attorney one month previously. "I'm tired of this powerful family fighting me, but I intend to appeal and re-appeal until my story can be heard," she tells a newspaper reporter. "I need to have the truth confirmed for my family's peace of mind. It's my right to know who my parents are."

One month later, the Mealbach attorney files another appeal with the Michigan Court of Appeals—this one asking the court to disallow Judge Maher's order and to clear the way for a hearing of Frances Lucille Mealbach's plea to have her birth and adoption records opened.

The year moves into 1989, through spring and summer. In November, Cunningham and one Dodge attorney finally appear before the Court of Appeals. In January, 1990, the Court's ruling is issued— because of recent changes in Michigan's adoption laws regarding adoptees' rights, Frances Mealbach may inspect her birth and adoption records.

"Unsolved Mysteries" reports on this breakthrough for Frances Mealbach on its "anniversary" show on February 7, 1990. There is great excitement among the Mealbachs, mixed with apprehension that the Dodge family might file an appeal that will delay or even prevent the opening of the records.

Dodge heirs do not file an appeal and, in late February, Frances Mealbach and daughters Brenda and Sharon go to Lansing to inspect Frances' birth certificate. They stare in disbelief at the certificate—the first of several pages of records they will see later that week, all of which pose more questions than answers. The father is "unknown." The 18-year-old mother's name is listed as Emma Jane, a "factory girl" born in Ontario. Could this be Emma Nelson, the maid at the Dodges' Boston Boulevard home, they wonder. And why is no last name listed? Why does it look as if there were erasures and write-overs, they ask the state employee who gives them the certificate.

The baby's name is listed as Remilda May, born at Woman's Hospital (Detroit) on November 20, 1914—but Brenda complains that

1914 is nearly scratched out. And why is the date—November 20—unlike the November 23 date listed on that registration of birth filed with the state by Judge Thomas L. Murphy in 1941?

When they learn the certificate is a copy, Sharon loudly demands to see the original. Inspection of original records is not permitted, is the implacable answer.

On the following day, they inspect the adoption papers. Here, the mother's full name is listed as Emma Jane Nelson. The Mealbachs learn that the papers were certified by Judge Thomas L. Murphy in 1941 and sent to the state—in the same year that the same Judge Murphy settled the $13 million Daniel Dodge estate and ordered five percent of it returned to the John Dodge trust fund principal for the benefit of "undetermined heirs"...the same year that Judge Murphy officially registered the November 23, 1914 birth of "Frances Lucille Manzer" with the state. The significance of this strangely coincidental, triangular cleanup of records is not lost on the Mealbachs who are convinced that Frances Lucille's birth and adoption records are closely linked with the John Dodge family.

Brenda Eilers ventures the opinion that perhaps her mother "is not legally adopted," since she was 27 years old when the papers were certified and "an adult can't be adopted without permission from the adoptee."

The Mealbachs decide to go public with two important bits of information they have acquired. A Texas horse-trainer, who formerly was employed by Frances Dodge Van Lennep, has signed an affidavit, the Mealbachs announce, stating that he overheard the daughter from Frances Dodge's first marriage quarreling with her stepfather after Frances Dodge Van Lennep's death.

"You'll rot in hell before you get my mother's money," former trainer Stanley Hammond declared he heard the daughter say. "I'll find her twin first."

And the Mealbachs state, on television, that they have learned that an Emma Nelson, of an age corresponding to that of the woman named in the adoption papers, later married an Ethan Kimball of Detroit. The Mealbachs appeal to Kimball descendants for information.

At the same time that their attorney, James Cunningham, is saying that Frances Mealbach is "satisfied" to have her records and wants to remove herself "from the public arena" to enjoy her privacy, Frances Lucille is telling Detroit News reporter Brenda Ingersoll that "there's a force pushing us on ."

The Mealbachs appear on still another television newscast, claiming they have found proof that the state birth certificate given to them only a few days previously is "phoney," as Frances Mealbach puts it. They have obtained an affidavit from the director of medical services at Hutzel Hospital (formerly Woman's Hospital) stating that no Emma Nelson gave birth at the hospital, according to its 1910-1917 records.

"We believe Emma Nelson is a pawn, to cover the fact that mom is a twin," the daughter Sharon tells the reporter.

Since 1982 when she first became convinced of her Dodge connections, Frances Mealbach never has changed, but only reinforced, her opinion that the wealthy Dodges had ways and means to cover up the facts of her birth. Attorney Frederick Buesser Jr. now points out to a reporter that "...1914 was a different world and things could be handled then in ways that would be unthinkable today."

"It's an illegal certificate," says the eldest Mealbach daughter. The family makes no effort to hide its disgust with the system that provided them with a "phoney" birth record. They will take their complaint "to Michigan's Attorney General Frank Kelley," they say.

The fight will go on. It is possible that Frances Lucille never will be able to uncover documented evidence of a Dodge relationship, but not from lack of trying. If a breakthrough suddenly occurs, however, and if Frances Lucille is recognized by the courts as a Dodge, another series of lawsuits could begin if she is forced to sue the present Dodge heirs to try to acquire some of the fortune she feels should be hers.

In the meantime, the assorted, unique facts and the long chain of strange coincidences remain unchanged.

Unexplained.   Unproved.   Unanswered.   Unsolved.

Bibliography

Books

Anderson, Rudolph E. *The Story of the American Automobile: Highlights and Sidelights.* Washington, D.C.: Public Affairs Press, 1950.

Barnard, Harry. *Independent Man: The Life of Senator James Couzens.* New York: Charles Scribner's Sons, 1958.

Beasley, Norman, and Stark, George. *Made in Detroit.* New York: Putman's Sons, 1957.

Brough, James. *The Ford Dynasty.* Garden City, New York: Doubleday, 1977.

Burlingame, Roger. *Henry Ford: A Great Life in Brief.* New York: Alfred A. Knopf, 1966.

Clancy, Louise B., and Davies, Florence. *The Believer: The Life Story of Mrs. Henry Ford.* New York: Coward-McCann, 1960.

Dahlinger, John Cote, and Leighton, Frances Spatz. *The Secret Life of Henry Ford.* Indianapolis: Bobbs-Merrill, 1978.

Detroit Public Library. *Detroit in Its World Setting: A 250-Year Chronology, 1701-1951.* Detroit: Detroit Public Library, 1953.

Donovan, Frank R. *Wheels for a Nation.* New York: Thomas Y. Crowell, 1965.

Gedda, Luigi. *Twins in History and Science.* Springfield, Illinois: C.C. Thomas, 1961.

Gentry, Curt. *The Vulnerable Americans.* New York: Doubleday, 1966.

Hill, Frank Ernest. *The Automobile: How It Came, Grew and Has Changed Our Lives.* New York: Dodd, Mead, 1967.

Bibliography

A History of Berrien and Van Buren Counties, Michigan. Philadelphia:
   D. W. Ensign & Co., 1880.

Holli, Melvin G. *Detroit.* New York, Franklin Watts, 1976.

Jenks, Wm. Lee. *St. Clair County, Michigan: Its History and Its People, Vol. II.* New York: Lewis Publishing Co., 1912.

Lacey, Robert. *Ford: The Men and the Machine.* Boston: Little, Brown, 1986.

Lasky, Victor. *Never Complain, Never Explain: The Story of Henry Ford II.* New York: Richard Marek, 1981.

Leland, Mrs. Wilfred C., with Millbrook, Minnie Dubbs. *Master of Precision.* Detroit: Wayne State University Press, 1966.

Lewis, David L. *The Public Image of Henry Ford: An American Folk Hero and his Company.* Detroit: Wayne State University Press,
   1976.

Lochbiler, Don. *Detroit's Coming of Age, 1873 to 1973.* Detroit: Wayne State University Press, 1973.

Lord, Walter. *The Good Years.* New York: Harper & Brothers, 1960.

MacManus, Theodore F. *Men, Money, Motors.* New York: Harpers,
   1929.

Michigan Through the Centuries, Vol. VI. New York: Lewis Historical Publishing Co., 1955.

Nevins, Allan, and Hill, Frank Ernest. *Ford: The Times, the Man, the Company, Vol. I.* New York: Charles Scribner's Sons, 1954.

Niemeyer, Glenn A. *The Automotive Career of Ransom E. Olds.* East
   Lansing: Michigan State University, 1963.

Rae, John B. *American Automobile Manufacturers: The First Forty Years.* Philadelphia: Chilton, 1959.

Bibliography

Rae, John B. *Henry Ford.* Englewood, Cliffs, New York: Prentice-Hall, 1969.

Richards, William C. *The Last Billionaire: Henry Ford.* New York: Charles Scribner's Sons, 1948.

Sorenson, Charles E., with Williamson, Samuel T. *My Forty Years with Ford.* New York: W. W. Norton, 1956.

Stark, George W., and Campbell, Anne. *Two Heads Are Better Then*
   One. Detroit: Alved of Detroit, Inc., 1947.

Sward, Keith. *The Legend of Henry Ford.* New York: Russel & Russel, 1948.

Thomas, Gordon, and Morgan-Witts, Max. *The Day the Bubble Burst.*
   Garden City, New York: Doubleday, 1979.

Woodford, Frank B., and Mason, Philip P. *Harper of Detroit.* Detroit:
   Wayne State University Press, 1964.

Woodford, Frank B., and Woodford, Arthur M. *All Our Yesterdays: A Brief History of Detroit.* Detroit: Wayne State University Press, 1969.

Booklets, Pamphlets, Brochures

Detroit Federation of Women's Clubs Directory, 1918-1919.

Detroit, the City of the Straits, Souvenir Edition.

Hartwick, Jeanne. *Sumpter Township, 1840-1910.*

A History of Dodge, 1914-1964. Chrysler Corporation.

Horst and Wilson. *Water Under the Bridge—A History of Van Buren*
   Township. 1946.

Guide to Meadow Brook Hall. Rochester, Michigan: Meadow Brook
   Hall Publication.

Bibliography

Marzolf, Marion, and Ritchie, Marianne. *Matilda R. Wilson: Mistress*
    of Meadow Brook Hall.

A Pictorial History of Chrysler Corporation Cars. Chrysler
    Corporation, 1968.

Robbe, Samuel H. *History of Van Buren Township.* 1930.

Savage, Mrs. James. *Memories.* 1930.

Vinton, John Adams. *Upton Memorial.* 1874.

General References

Burton. *History of Wayne County, Michigan.*Vol. 3.

Cowles, B. *Berrien County Directory and History,* 1871: Niles,
    Michigan.

Dearborn City Directories. 1950 and others.

Detroit City Directories. 1870 and others.

Luedder's City Directory. Niles, Michigan.

New York Times Index. 1914 and on.

Port Huron City Directories. 1883 through 1888.

St. Clair County Directory. 1888.

White, J. T. *The National Cyclopaedia of American Biography.*
    1937.

Who's Who in Commerce and Industry. 1939: Detroit, Michigan.

Bibliography

Archives and Private Collections

Amelia Rausch Cline Collection.

Child and Family Services, Southwestern branch, St. Joseph, Michigan. Historical collection.

Chrysler Corporation archives.

The Detroit News Library.

Ford Motor Company archives.

George McCall collection.

Meadow Brook Hall archives.

Mealbach, Frances L. Manzer papers.

St. Joseph Memorial Hospital, St. Joseph, Michigan. Historical collection.

Interviews

Batz, Jerome
Batz, Joseph
Batz, Mary
Batz, Wanda
Boutell, Mike
Boutell, Vivian
Brooks, Marylin
Burgett, Mabel
Clemens, Gary
Clemens, Maxine
Cline, Amelia Rausch
Cosgrove, John
Cunningham, James
DeBusschere, Margaret
Deering, Esther
Eilers, Brenda

Bibliography

Folsom, Dick
Jackson, Ronald A.
Hope, Gertrude Woodbridge
Love, Mary
Mabley, Theodore
McCall, Nancy
Mealbach, Frances L. Manzer
Milligan, Thelma Banta
Perry, Dick
Porter, Roberta
Savage, Joanne
Smith, Marion
Stadja, Sharon
Trombino, "Nanny"
Sullivan, Veronica
Upton, Viola
Velliky, John
Wilkie, Margaret
Wilson, Richard
Woodbridge, Miriam Leland

Newspapers

Detroit Evening News. October 4, 1901 and others.

Detroit Free Press. March 17, 1914 and others.

Detroit News. December 7, 1914 and others.

Detroit Times. April 26, 1922 and others.

New York Times. December 30, 1904 and others.

New York Tribune. January 7, 1917.

News Herald. Wyandotte, Michigan. October 29, 1986.

Niles Daily Star. Niles, Michigan. March 24, 1936 and others.

Rochester Clarion. July 1, 1953 and others.

Bibliography

Periodicals

Automobile Topics. January 17, 1920.

Automotive Industries. Vol. 54, Part I. January 21, 1926.

The Club Woman. March, 1925 and others.

Detroit Historical Society Bulletin. No. 24. July, 22, 1967.

Detroit Magazine. November 16, 1986.

The Detroit News Magazine. February 5, 1978.

Detroit Historical Society Bulletin. Fall, 1986 and others.

Detroit Saturday Night. November 6, 1915 and others.

Dodge News Magazine. Vol. 29, No. I. 1964. Golden Jubilee Souvenir Issue.

Ford Times, 75 Anniversary Issue. Vol. 71, No. 6. June, 1978.

Iron Trade Review. May 6, 1915.

Livingston County Press. Farm Supplement. March 31, 1971.

Michigan Magazine, The Detroit News. August 10, 1986.

Michigan Manufacturer and Financial Record. January 27, 1913.

Parade Magazine. October 27, 1985.

The Port Huron Companies' Weekly. Vol. 3, No. 11. October 13, 1903.

Power Boating. January, 1921.

The Swallow. Hot Springs, Virginia. May 20, 1925.

Telescope. September / October, 1976. Vol. XXV, No. 5.

Bibliography

Public Records and Collections

Automotive Collection, Detroit Public Library.

Bellm's Cars of Yesterday Museum, Sarasota, Florida.

Berrien Springs Historical Museum archives.

Burton Historical Collection, Detroit Public Library.

Census records. Detroit, 1910. St. Clair County, 1880.

Harper Hospital Archives.

Michigan Court of Appeals. Brief No. 83736.

Michigan Public Libraries. Belleville. Dearborn. Detroit. Niles. Port Huron. St. Joseph.

Niles Historical Museum.

Oakland County Probate Court, Will and Estate Papers.

Oakland University Kresge Libreary archives.

Public Health records. Berrien County, Detroit, Lansing, and Van Buren County of Michigan. Ontario, Canada.

Silver Brook Cemetery records. Niles, Michigan.

University of Michigan, Dearborn. Historical Collection.

Wayne County Probate Court. Will and Estate papers. Court Hearings.

INDEX

Addams, Jane, 67
Allen, Reverend C. S., 37
American Red Cross, 38, 86
Anchor Realty Company, 133
Anti-Saloon League, 6, 77
Ashbaugh, Delphine (see Dodge, Della)
Ashbaugh, Rie (see Eschbach, Uriah)
Automobiles (See Ford Motor Company, Dodge Motor Car)

Cadillac, 10, 95
Dodgeson, 123, 126
Graham-Paige, 160
Haynes, 95
Jewell, 42
Lincoln, 125-126
Oldsmobile, 10-11, 95
Packard, 44, 53-54, 95
Peerless, 42
Pungs-Finch, 42
Premier, 95

Avenue Theater, 15
Baker, U.S. Secretary of War Newton D., 82
Ballagh, Heath, 158, 170
Ballin, Dr. Max, 117, 122, 130, 284-285
Barsamian, Judge Y. Gladys, 258
Battle Creek, Michigan, 21
Batz, Henry (Andrea Bozzio) 36, 66, 97, 141, 283-284
Batz, Jerome, 283
Batz, Mrs. Jerome, 283
Batz, Joseph, 283
Batz, Wanda (Mrs. Joseph) 283
Berg, Zona, 77
Berlin, Irving, 59
Book-Cadillac Hotel, 54, 146

Bovee, Helen, 65, 80, 88-89, 98, 100, 102, 156
Bryan, William Jennings, 67
Bryant, Lloyd, 173-176
Bryant, Mrs. Lloyd, 174-176, 184
Buesser, Frederick III, 257
Buesser, Frederick Jr., 258-259, 279
Burgett, Andrew, 151, 267
Burgett, Ida, 66, 151-152, 267-268
Burgett, Mabel, 151-152, 266-268
Burgett, Silas, 50, 65-66, 151-152, 267
Burnham, Sara, 104, 123, 146
Burr, Raymond, 278
Castle, Vernon and Irene, 59
Castleton Farms, 199-201, 211, 237
Churchill, Charlie, 51
his saloon, 51, 69
Cherry Sisters, 15
Child and Family Services of Michigan, 64, 250, 252, 256, 276
Children of John Dodge, 9, 24, 30, 35, 37, 42, 47, 71
Chittick, Adele Kent, 69
Chittick, Dr. William R., 12, 41, 63-65, 69, 96-97, 101, 252, 285
Chrysler automobile, 143
Chrysler Corporation, 131
Chrysler Corporation, Dodge Division, 91, 97, 150, 197, 242, 283
Dodge Main, 150-152, 243
Chrysler, Walter, 131, 137
Clay, Eleanor (Mrs. Edsel Ford) 56, 74-75, 109, 154, 190

INDEX

Clay, Eliza, 74

Clay, Josephine (Mrs. Ernest Kanzler) 55, 154

Cline, Amelia (see Rausch, Amelia)

Cline, John, 72-73, 125, 130-132, 142-144, 177, 182, 208, 222

Codd, Mayor George P., 45, 69

Continental Motor Company, 91

Cosgrove, John, 277, 278

Couzens, James, 17-19, 32, 89

Cromwell, James H. R., 103-104, 106, 128

Cromwell, Oliver, 103

Cunningham, James P., 2-4, 259-262, 264-270, 272-274, 276-277, 279-283, 285-287

Curtiss, Lena, 107, 119, 135

Dahlinger, John, 239

DBA Associates, 277

Dearborn, Michigan, 5, 68

Delphine I (yacht) 79

Delphine II (yacht) 110, 123

Detroit Athletic Club, 91-92

Detroit Automobile Company, 9

Detroit, city of, 1, 6, 9, 12, 16, 22, 44, 50-51, 59, 85-87, 128-129, 143, 150, 163, 197, 285

Detroit Federation of Women's Clubs, 38, 53, 86, 213

Detroit Historical Museum, 209

Detroit Historical Society, 185, 230

Detroit Hunt and Fish Club, 52

Detroit Institute of Arts, 87, 154, 237
    Founders' Society, 185
    Wilson Memorial Gallery, 237

Detroit Lumber Company, 29, 34

Detroit-Michigan Stove Company, 165, 215-216

Detroit Symphony Orchestra, 45-46, 53, 87, 91, 104, 106, 230

Detroit Street Railway Commission, 49

Detroit Water Board, 45

Dickinson, Governor Luren, 192-193

Dillman, Hugh (Hugh McGaughey) 127, 154-155, 168, 200

Dillon, Read and Company, 121, 131

Dimmer Machine Works, 9

Dodge, Anna Margaret, 89, 99, 101-102, 110, 112, 114-119, 122-123, 125-126, 131, 139, 181, 197, 229, 231, 238, 260, 284-285

Dodge, Anna Thomson (Mrs. Horace E. Dodge) 9, 12, 23, 28-31, 35-37, 43, 45-46, 49, 55, 69, 78, 88-89, 91, 94, 96-97, 100, 103-106, 109-110, 115, 117, 121, 123, 125, 127-128, 154-156, 168, 194, 223-224, 227, 229-230, 236-237

Dodge, Annie Laurine MacDonald (Mrs. Daniel Dodge) 159-162, 167, 169-170, 173-177, 179-180, 182-184, 193, 195, 243

Dodge attorneys, 2-3, 5, 75, 85, 109-111, 142, 170, 182, 186, 243, 261-262, 264-268, 270-272, 275, 278-281, 284

Dodge automobile, 54, 56, 58, 61- 63, 66, 70, 73-74, 77-78, 82, 88-89, 91-92, 95, 111, 116, 125, 283

INDEX

Dodge brothers (John and
Horace) 11-12, 16-23,
25-29, 32, 35, 42, 44-45,
52-54, 56- 57, 59, 61, 64, 68,
73-77, 81- 83, 91-92, 95-96,
98, 106, 249, 267
Dodge Brothers (see also
Dodge Brothers, Inc. and
Dodge Motor Car Company)
6-8, 10, 13-14, 16-18, 27-28,
30-31, 34, 36, 39, 44, 50, 56,
63, 66, 78, 82-84, 95, 98, 108,
114, 116, 121, 131, 142, 283
Dodge Brothers, Inc. (also
Dodge Motor Car Company)
57, 61, 65, 71, 73-74, 77-78,
80, 82, 87-90, 97, 100, 105-
106, 109, 111-112
Dodge Brothers Industrial
Band, 66
Dodge Brothers munitions plant
(ordnance factory) 83-84
Dodge, Caleb, 20
Dodge, Charles, 21, 101
Dodge, Daniel George, 80, 84,
87, 102-103, 109, 110, 112,
114-118, 122, 124, 129, 132,
138, 143, 145, 157-162, 168-
171, 173-185, 191, 197, 201,
229, 231, 237, 284
estate of, 184, 186, 192-
193, 195-196, 235, 262
Dodge, Daniel Rugg, 20-22, 52,
253
Dodge dealers, 95, 131
Dodge, Della (Mrs. Uriah
Eschbach) 20-21, 23, 33-34,
37-41, 53, 65, 79-80, 88-89,
98, 100-102, 106, 109, 115,
156, 224, 229
Dodge, Delphine Ione, 12, 43,

103-106, 110, 128, 155-156,
197
Dodge, Edwin, 20
Dodge Estates Corporation, 156
Dodge, Frances Matilda (Mrs.
Frederick Van Lennep) 3, 63,
65,68, 71, 76, 84, 86, 89,
98, 102, 110, 112, 114-115,
117-118, 122, 124, 129, 132,
134, 138-140, 143-148, 153,
156-157, 160-162, 167-171,
179-180, 182, 184-186, 191-
195, 197-201, 208-212, 223-
224, 227-228, 232, 236-237,
243, 251-254, 260-261, 263,
265, 268-269, 271, 279-281,
284
Dodge, Gregg Sherwood,
227-228
Dodge heirs (designated) 2-3,
256, 262, 266, 271-272, 278,
287
Dodge, Horace Elgin (see
Dodge automobile; Dodge
brothers; Dodge Brothers,
Inc.)
biography of, 244
childhood in Niles, 20
his clothing, 19
closeness with brother
John, 11, 35, 51,
68-69, 98, 134
reaction to John's
death, 97, 100
companions of, 45, 50,
52, 57, 65, 76, 87, 91,
267
daughter's wedding,
103-104
death and funeral of,
105-106, 236
and Detroit Symphony
Orchestra, 53, 87, 91

his dislike for name, 13
and Dodge Brothers
machine shop, 6, 9-12
and Dodge Hamtramck
    factory, 44, 66, 73, 110
    employees' pension
    fund, 284
and Dodge munitions factory,
    84
drinking habits of, 12, 40, 46
estate of, 121
and his family (wife and
    children) 9, 43, 78, 128
his fascination with boats,
27,   45, 52, 71, 79-80, 103
finances of in early days,
    15-16, 23
and Henry Ford, 13-15
and Ford Motor Company,
    16, 41, 44, 51, 88
    sale of company shares,
    88, 91
and Grosse Pointe Country
    Club, 155
homes of, 28
    Rose Terrace, 43
illness of, 95-96, 98, 103-105
influence on brother John,
    30-31
and Jefferson Avenue
    Presbyterian Church, 92
and Henry M. Leland, 10
loyalty to John, 36-37, 94
abilities of as machinist,
9-10,   14, 57, 73, 82-83
    with ball-bearing
        mechanism, 23
    problems with Ford
        Model A., 18
at Meadow Brook Farm, 52
personal habits, 24
move to Port Huron, 21, 33
and sister Della, 38

temperament, 11
travels, 49, 89, 100
visits to Niles, 52
Dodge, Horace Elgin, Jr., 12,
    43, 77-78, 106, 109-110,114,
    117, 121, 128, 155-156, 174,
    227-228
Dodge, Isabel Cleves (Mrs.
    George Sloane) 38-39, 48,
    54-56, 68, 89, 96-97, 102-
    103, 105, 109, 111-113, 123,
    133, 153-154, 182, 184, 193,
    224
Dodge, Isabel Smith, 9, 29-33,
    35-37, 55
Dodge, Ivy Hawkins, 9, 13, 23-
    24, 38, 60, 224, 236
Dodge, John Duval, 38-39, 43,
    48-49, 54, 58, 68, 77-79, 84-
    85, 89, 98, 100-101, 105,
    109, 111-113, 121-124, 126,
    133, 153-154, 183, 186, 192-
    193, 195-196, 243, 261
Dodge, John Francis,
    antagonism toward unionism,
        50, 71
    biography of, 244
    companions of, 45, 54-55,
        71, 75-76, 94
    and court suit against Henry
        Ford, 74-75, 88
    and children of first marriage,
        9, 23, 37-38, 42, 47-48,
        54-55, 58, 65, 68-69, 77-
        78, 85, 87, 96-98, 102,
        123, 184, 224, 236
    and children of third marriage,
        58, 61, 68-69, 76, 80, 87,
        89, 102, 115, 117, 123,
        161, 184, 224, 251
    civic responsibilities of, 45,
        49, 64
    death of his father, 20

INDEX

death of his mother, 34
death and funeral of, 4, 97-98
death of wife, Ivy, 9, 13, 60
divorce from wife, Isabelle, 35-36
and Dodge Brothers, Inc., 57
plans for expansion of, 90-91
and Dodge Brothers machine shop, 9-19, 23, 25-26, 36
and Dodge Motor Car, 54, 56, 62-63, 66, 73-74
and early life in home-town of Niles, 19-21
attachment to Niles, 52, 226
and early years in Detroit, 22
escapades of, 12, 24, 46-47, 54-55, 91-92
estate of, 142, 195, 258
fears of, 27, 71
and Ford Manufacturing Company, 31-32
and Ford Motor Company, 16-19, 25-27, 31, 35, 41-42, 44, 51, 54, 56, 74, 88
sale of his stock, 88
and Henry Ford relationship, 13-17, 31-32, 42-44, 53, 57-59, 65, 67, 74-75, 78, 83, 91, 113
his friendship with employ-ees, 36, 39-40, 50, 65, 267
generosity of,
to charities, 63, 86, 92, 101, 213
to employees, 50, 77, 98
to mother, 33
to sister Della, 33-34, 38-41, 53, 86

Hamilton, Alexander—
collection of, 45-46
and Hamtramck factory, 11, 44, 50, 57, 61, 73-74, 238
homes of:
East Boston Boulevard house, 33, 39, 41, 48, 65, 89, 94, 133-134, 245
Grosse Pointe mansion, 87-88, 90, 92, 102, 110, 116, 125, 130, 198
Meadow Brook Farm, 40, 42-43, 47-48, 52, 57, 71-73, 91, 102, 132, 232
Trumbull Street house, 32-33
Horace, relationship with, 11-13, 19, 27, 36, 51-52, 71, 76, 79, 94-96
illnesses of, 12, 23-24, 96-97
marriages of:
to Ivy Hawkins, 23
to Isabelle Smith, 29-30, 181
to Matilda Rausch, 36-37, 229, 232, 239
as possible father of daughter given up for adoption, 2-4, 151-152, 247, 249-250, 257, 261, 266-268, 281, 283-285
in Port Huron, 21-22
Rausch,
Amelia—relationship with, 49-51, 60, 70-71, 92, 102, 125-126, 141-142, 250-251
and recoil mechanism for Howitzer gun, 82-84
and secretary, Matilda

Rausch, 6-7, 11-12, 15,
19, 22, 24-25, 27-32
travels of, 42, 49-50, 89,
94-95, 139
will of, 101-103, 243, 252,
281, 183-184
working in Canada, 22-23
Dodge, Lois Knowlson (Mrs.
Horace E. Jr.) 110, 128
Dodge, Laura (see Stineback,
Laura)
"Dodge Law," 111
Dodge, Maria Casto, 9, 20, 30,
33-34, 253
Dodge, Marie O'Connor (Mrs.
John Duval Dodge) 84-85,
113, 153
Dodge Memorial Hall of
Industry, 209-210
Dodge Power Building, 80
Dodge Stables, 157, 199
Dodge, Silas, 21
Dodge trucks, 82, 95, 111
Dodge, Winifred (see Seyburn,
Winifred)
The Dodges: The Auto Family
Fortune and Misfortune, 246,
278
Dominion Typography
Company, 22-23
Dorsey, Tommy, 162-163, 186
Dressler, Marie, 15
Drolet, Dick, 158-159, 173,
177-178, 183
Dry Dock Hotel, 20-21, 72
Duke, Doris, 155
Duveen, Lord Joseph, 154-155
East Boston Boulevard home,
32-34, 37-41, 43, 47-48, 50-
51, 53, 61-63, 68, 71, 76,
83, 85, 89, 94, 97-98, 100,
102, 105, 110, 116, 133-134,
244, 246, 261, 278, 285-286

Eccles, Barbara Jean (see
Wilson, Barbara Jean)
Eccles, Thomas, 210, 224-226
children of, 224, 231
Edison, Thomas A., 67, 74-75,
137
E.J. Kruce Cracker Company, 7
Elwart, Joan P., 244
Enricht, Louis, 75-76
Epworth League, 135, 148
Eschbach, Della (see Dodge,
Della)
Eschbach, Uriah, 22, 33-34,
40-41, 65
Eschtruth, June, 120, 172, 214,
219-221, 259-260
Evans, Dr. Mark, 252
Fair Lane, 67, 154, 212
Fidelity Bank & Trust
Company, 118-119, 140, 142,
155
First Presbyterian Church, 86,
92, 119, 123, 133, 225, 230-
231
Fish, Marvin, 107, 120, 149,
171-172
Fitzgerald, Ed, 94
Floranada, 128
Foch, Marshal Ferdinand, 111
Ford & Malcomson Ltd., 16
Ford, Anne McDonnell, 190
Ford, Benson, 195
Ford, Clara (Mrs. Henry) 44,
53, 55, 68, 74-75, 113, 154,
190, 228
Ford, Edsel, 44, 56, 68, 74-75,
77-79, 88, 98, 113, 154, 190-
191, 194-195, 197
Mrs. Edsel Ford (see
Eleanor Clay)
Ford, Henry I, 9-10, 13-19, 27,
31-32, 35, 41-45, 52-59, 65,
67-68, 71, 74-79, 81-83, 85-
91, 96, 98, 113, 137, 154,

156, 168, 190-191, 195, 197, 209, 239, 244
Henry Ford II, 190-191, 195, 197, 209
Ford Manufacturing Company, 31-32, 35
Ford Motor Company, 16-19, 25-27, 31-32, 35, 41-42, 44, 50-51, 54, 56, 67, 74-75, 78-79, 81, 86, 88, 113, 190, 203
   Car Models:
      Model A (first product of Ford Motor Company) 13-14, 16-19, 25
      Model A (of late 1920s) 128
      Model B, 26-27
      Model C, 26-27
      Model F, 16-27
      Model K, 31-32, 35
      Model N, 32, 35
      Model T, 41-44, 51-53, 56, 59, 63, 67, 75, 88, 128
   Tractor Division of, 204
Ford, Williams, 44
Frances (yacht) 92, 110, 116
French 155-millimeter Howitzer gun, 82, 84, 111
Gabrilowitsch, Ossip G., 87, 91
General Motors, 121
Gilroy, Dr. John, 274, 276
Glinz, Harry, 29, 37, 130, 239
Gore Bay, 159-160, 169, 176
Gorsline Business College, 7
Gragg, Judge J. Robert, 1, 3-4, 260-262, 264-266, 268-277, 279, 282, 287
Graham brothers, 111, 131
Graham Brothers Truck Company, 131
Graham Paige Motor

Corporation, 131
Grandt, Rudolph, 50-51
Gray, John S., 16-17, 35
Gray, William J., Jr. ("Jack"), 65, 68, 103, 111-112
Graystone Ballroom, 163, 165-166
Greenfield Village, 137, 283
Grosse Pointe Country Club, 144, 155
Grosse Pointe mansion of John Dodges, 87-91, 103, 109-110, 116, 122, 125, 130, 133-134, 198
Hamilton, Alexander, 45-46
Hamtramck, Michigan, 44, 50, 54, 61, 66, 73, 83, 150-151
Hannah, Dr., 213
Harmonie Club, 52
Harper Hospital, 63-64, 69, 80, 116, 130, 284-285
Harroun, Motor Car Company, 80
Harroun, Ray, 80
Haynes, Frederick, 100, 109, 111, 114, 116
Henderson, Dr., 204-206
Henneman, Mary, 259-260
Henry Ford Hospital, 86, 197
Highland Park, Michigan, 44, 56, 59, 74, 79
Hilltop Lodge, 129, 132, 147
Hilton, Daisy and Violet, 269
Holmes, Mr. and Mrs. Frederick, 170
Hoover, President Herbert, 137
Hornet I, 27
Hornet II, 45
Hubbard, Mayor Orville, 215
Hudson, J.L., 12, 55-56, 75
   J.L. Hudson Department Store, 149-150, 164

INDEX

Hudson Motor Car Company, 90-91

Industrial Home for Girls, 89, 100-102

IWW (Industrial Workers of the World) 50

Jefferson Avenue Presbyterian Church, 92, 104

Johnson, James, 161-162, 167-169, 179, 182, 184-185, 197-200, 210, 263, 266

Johnson, Judith, (McClung) 193, 197-200, 223, 228-230, 236, 281

Joncas, Edmund, 46-47

Kagawong Lodge, 159, 173-174, 177

Kelly and Company, 283

Knole House, 130, 138, 147

Lamborn, Fred, 267

League of Women Voters, 118

Leland, Faulconer & Norton, 10

Leland & Faulconer Manu-facturing Company, 9, 10

Leland, Henry, M., 10-11, 24

Leland, Wilfred, 10

Leland, Mrs. Wilfred, 10

Liggett School, 39, 47-48, 54, 68

Lincoln Road home, Grosse Pointe, 110, 116-117, 123, 128

Lotus, 27

MacDonald, Annie Laurine (see Dodge, Annie Laurine)

MacDonald, John, 159-160, 170, 183,
Mrs. John MacDonald, 159, 170, 176, 183

Maher, Judge Martin T., 286-287

Mahon, Thomas J., 46-47, 55

Malcomson, Alexander, 13, 15-18, 26-27, 31-33, 35, 74

Mamie-O, 71

Manitoulin Island, 161-162, 170, 177

Manzer family, 76, 92, 106-108, 119-120, 134, 148, 165, 171, 186-187, 217, 247, 249-250, 255, 278
foster child of, 107-108, 119, 255

Manzer, Florence, 219-221, 232

Manzer, Frances Lucille (see Mealbach, Francis Lucille)

Manzer, Minnie, 64, 76, 80, 92-93, 99-100, 106-107, 119- 120, 134-136, 149-150, 163- 164, 166, 171-172, 186-189, 195-196, 201-203, 214, 219, 241, 252, 255, 260

Manzer, Robert, 64, 76, 80, 92-93, 100, 106-108, 119-120, 134, 148-150, 163-164, 166, 172, 187, 201-203, 214, 219-221, 233, 259

Manzer, Robert Jr., 120, 135, 149, 172-173, 201-203
his wife, Lillian, 203

Maple Leaf Bicycle (Evans and Dodge Machine) 23

Marx, Oscar (Mayor) 45, 54-55, 75-76, 94, 96

Matthews, Mary, 58, 114, 138

Matilda R. Wilson Hall, 228

Mazey, Gail, 258

Maurer, Terry, 277

Meadow Brook Farm, 40, 42-43, 45, 47-49, 52, 57, 60-61, 65, 70-73, 84, 91, 98, 102, 122, 124-125, 128, 132, 137, 141, 143, 146-147, 158, 168, 185, 199, 209, 212-213, 222, 251

INDEX

Meadow Brook Hall, 129-131, 133-134, 137-141, 143-148, 155-157, 160-163, 167-170, 173, 177-180, 185-186, 194, 198-199, 201, 207, 210, 213, 222-223, 225, 227-228, 230-232, 237-238, 255-256, 277, 282

Meadow Brook Music Festival, 230

Mealbach family, 201, 214, 217, 220, 233-234, 240-241, 253-258, 266, 272-273, 277-278, 282, 287

Mealbach, Frances Lucille, 1-6, 64-65, 76, 80, 92-93, 99-100, 106-108, 119, 134-136, 148-150, 163-166, 171-173, 186-189, 195-196, 201-206, 214-221, 232-235, 239-242, 245-266, 268-283, 285-287

    daughter, Brenda, 189, 214-215, 217, 220-221, 232-234, 244-252, 255-257, 268, 277

    daughter, Linda, 203-204, 232, 240, 260

    daughter, Sharon, 1-4, 206, 214, 234-235, 239, 244-245, 249-250, 255, 257, 260, 265, 271-278

    son, Thomas, 215, 217-218, 234, 240, 278

    son, William Jr., 189, 232, 240

Mealbach, William Sr., 165-166, 171, 186, 189, 201, 203-205, 214-218, 233-234, 239-242, 254, 270-271, 273, 282

Methodist Children's Home, 64, 107, 241, 247, 250, 255, 276

Michigan Children's Home Society, 64

Michigan Circuit Court, 81-82

Michigan Court of Appeals, 272-278, 283-287

Michigan Judicial Tenure Commission, 274, 276, 282

Michigan State Board of Agriculture, 143, 212

Michigan State Superior Court, 82, 88

Michigan State University, 194, 208, 212-213, 232

Michigan Supreme Court, 2, 274, 286

Miles Business College, 28

Miller, Marilyn, 132

Model Development Company, 158

Murphy, Judge Thomas C., 184-186, 193, 196, 235, 241, 246, 262

Murphy, Tom (boiler shop) 22

Muscagong Lake lodge, 52, 76

Nardin Park Methodist Church, 108

Nation, Carry, 6, 21

National Automobile Show, 94-95, 126

National Register of Historic Places, 238

NBC television, 278, 282

Nelson, Emma, 233, 246-247, 250-251

Nevins, Allan, 16

Newspapers and magazines:
    Cats Meow, 162
    Detroit Free Press, 117, 151, 208, 220
    Detroit Journal, 51
    Detroit Monthly, 91
    Detroit News, 2, 117, 161, 283

INDEX

Detroit Saturday Night, 68

Detroit Times, 123, 148

Globe, 267

Horseman, 237

Michigan Manufacturer and Financial Record, 56

National Examiner, 2

New York Times, 23, 122, 127

Star, 2, 263

USA Today, 270

Niles, Michigan, 19-22, 27, 40, 47, 52, 57, 64-65, 226, 253-254, 276

Nokomis I, 52

Nokomis II, 79-80, 103

Oakland University, 223, 227-228, 231-232

branch of Michigan State University, referred to as Oakland County College, 213

Oakman brothers (Robert and Milton) 46-47, 94, 96

O'Brien, Judge, 233, 246

Oldfield, Barney, 13

Olds, Ransom, 10-11, 14, 27

Olds Motor Works, 9-10

Pancho Villa, 73

Patton, George S., 73

Peace Ship, 67-68, 75

Pershing, General John J., 73

Pitrone, Jean M., 244, 246-254, 259-260, 262, 265-266, 268-271, 274-277, 282-285

Pontchartrain Hotel, 55

Pope John Paul II, 285-286

Port Huron, 21-22, 33, 45, 65

Porter, Ken and Roberta, 234, 244, 277

Princess Saloon, 60, 115

Prohibition, 85-86, 143, 192

Prohibition Party, 77

Rausch, Amelia (Mrs. John Cline) 7-8, 12, 15, 18, 21, 17-32, 34-37, 40, 44, 46-47, 49-51, 53-54, 56-58, 60-61, 63, 70-72, 80-89, 91-92, 98-99, 102, 104-106, 110, 114-116, 118, 122-127, 130-132, 138-139, 141-144, 167, 177-178, 180-182, 207-208, 222-223, 225-226, 228-231, 238-239, 248, 250-251, 284

Rausch family, 6-8, 20-21, 29-30, 34, 37, 40, 46, 48, 60, 229

Rausch, George, 6-7, 20-21, 29, 34, 40, 47-48, 60, 141, 213

Rausch, Margaret, 6-8, 20-21, 29, 32, 40, 43, 46-48, 60-61, 72, 80, 89, 98, 102, 114-118, 122-126, 130, 141, 144, 252, 285

Rausch saloon, 6-8, 12, 15, 34, 112, 141

Republican Party, 38

Ritz-Carlton Hotel, 94-96

Rose Terrace, 43, 88, 104, 106, 123, 155-156, 194, 223, 237-238

Rothschild, S.K., 88

Russell House, 15, 22

St. Joseph, Michigan, 57, 64, 250, 253, 276

Salvation Army, 92, 143, 185, 194, 200, 230

and Women's Auxiliary to, 38, 86, 118, 140, 143, 200, 213

Schwimmer, Madame Rosika, 67

Seyburn, Wesson, 112-113, 123-124, 133, 154

Seyburn, Winifred Dodge, 38-39, 48, 54-55, 65, 75, 87,

INDEX

89, 96-97, 102-103, 109, 111-114, 123-124, 126, 133, 153-154, 182, 184, 193, 224, 236, 242

Sheen, Monsignor Fulton J., 191

Siamese twins, 66, 151, 252-254, 259, 261, 263, 267-269, 275, 278, 284

Sloane, Isabel (see Dodge, Isabel)

Stein brothers, Christopher and Edward, 45, 87

Standard Electric Company, 29, 31

Stevenson, Elliot, 81, 82

Stineback, Laura Dodge, 21, 47

Stotesbury, Lucretia, 103-104, 106

Stoyanovich, Dr. Angelo, 252

Strelow, Albert, 17, 32, 35, 44

Sullivan, Joseph A., 264

Sullivan, Veronica, 198-199

Sun City, 226, 231

Sunset Terrace, 210-213, 224-225

Szoka, Archbishop Edmund, 285

Thomson family, 109, 125

Timken-Detroit Axle Company, 91

Trombino, Nanny, 283-284

Trust fund of John Dodge, 2-3, 102, 112, 121, 131, 144, 179, 183-185, 192-193, 195, 228, 236, 243-244, 256-257, 260, 266, 286

UAW-CIO, 156, 215-216

U.S. War Industries Board, 83

University of Michigan, 212

"Unsolved Mysteries," 277, 282

Upton, Edward Frank, 21

Upton family, 57

Upton, Frank, 57, 64, 80, 108, 120, 156, 186, 196, 219, 247, 249

Upton, Floyd, 57

Upton, Frederick, 211

Upton, James S., 21

Upton Machine Company, 57

Upton Manufacturing Company, 21

Upton, Sally, 21

Upton, Viola, 80, 108, 120, 247, 249

"Upton Works," 21

Uptonville, 21

Valiquette, Frank, 173-176, 184

Vance, Reverend Dr. Joseph, 68-69, 98, 119, 123, 168, 170, 182

Vandenberg, Arthur H., 45

Van Lennep, Frances (see Dodge, Frances)

Van Lennep, Frederick, 200-201, 211-212, 223-224, 227, 236- 237, 243

Van Lennep, Fredericka, 4, 211, 227, 236, 244

Van Lennep, John Francis, 211, 227, 236

Watson, Ruby, 194

Wayne County Probate Court, 1- 2, 258-259, 285-286 Juvenile Division of, 257

Westminster Presbyterian Church, 87

Wills, C. Harold, 13-14, 17, 42, 44

Wilson, Alfred G., 119, 122-133, 138-140, 143, 145, 146-147, 153, 155, 167, 170, 177, 179, 180-182, 185, 194, 201, 208-213, 222, 224-225, 227, 229, 231, 238

Wilson, Barbara Jean, 140, 143, 145-146, 158, 168, 193-194,

INDEX

207-211, 222-228, 231-232, 243

Wilson, Elinor, (Mrs. Richard Wilson) 209, 211, 226

Wilson family (senior) 123, 132

Wilson, Donald, 132, 173, 182

Wilson, Matilda Rausch Dodge, and Alfred Wilson, 119, 122-125, 132, 177, 181, 194, 211, 224-225, 229

  appointment of as Michigan's lieutenant governor, 192-193

  as business woman, 100, 109, 118-119, 131-133, 140-142

  accumulation of wealth by, 101-103

  appearance of, 7-8, 129, 146

  aversions of, 7, 12, 24, 39-40, 46, 111, 141, 200

  and her children, 112, 115

    Anna Margaret, 89, 99, 101, 114, 119, 122-123, 126, 131, 229

    Daniel, 80, 84, 116, 118, 124, 129, 145, 158, 160-162, 169-170, 177-180, 182, 185, 191, 229

    Frances, 63, 68-69, 76, 84, 86, 114, 122, 124, 129, 132, 139, 145-146, 148, 161-163, 167-168, 180, 184-185, 191-192, 198, 200, 211- 212, 227

    and her children by adoption, 139-140, 145-146, 150, 193-194, 201, 207, 212, 222, 227

  desire for wealth, 8, 33, 56

  at Dodge Brothers machine shop, 6-7, 9, 11, 13, 17-18

  quits job at Dodge Brothers, 29

  and Dodge Memorial Hall of Industry, 209-210

  death of, 230-231

  early life, 20-21, 40, 46

  education, 18

  guilt feelings of, 34

  estate of, 231, 232, 237

  and Grosse Pointe mansion, 88-91, 103, 109-110, 116, 125-134

  at Lincoln Road home, Grosse Pointe, 116, 128

  and her horses, 129, 143, 199, 222

  and Henry Ford, 113, 190-191

  honors accrued by, 212-213

  illnesses of, 97-99, 129

  her Howell horse farm, 222, 230

  and Horace Dodge, 103-106

  John F. Dodge, her relationship with, 43, 45-48, 51, 58, 75, 77, 83-84, 89, 94, 229

  courtship of, by John Dodge, 16, 19, 22-24, 27

marriage to John, 37
    summoned to hus-
    band's bedside, 96
John's death and
    funeral, 97-98
reaction to John
    Dodge's secret
    marriage, 30-31, 36
reconciliation with
    John, 32-33
love of Meadow Brook
    Farm, 71-72, 84,
    128-129, 143
Meadow Brook Hall,
pride   in, 125, 129-130,
    133-134, 137-139,
    143, 145-146, 154-
    156, 162, 167, 180,
    198-199, 207, 225
and Michigan State
    University, 212-213
and National Council of
    Women, 133
Oakland University, her
    gifts to, 223, 228
penchant for neatness,
8-9,   39, 144
philanthropic works of,
    118, 140, 185, 200,
    213, 230
her pragmatism, 25
pregnancy of, 61, 76, 129
relationships with other
    family members:
        with Anna Dodge,
        28-29, 36, 104,
        110, 117, 123,
        127, 167, 223-
        224, 227
        with Daniel's wi-
        dow, 179-180,
        182-183, 195

        with John's sister,
        Della, 38, 65, 80,
        115, 224
        with granddaughter,
        Judy, 193, 199,
        223, 228-230
        with Horace Dodge
        family, 128, 156,
        200, 228
        with her mother,
        Margaret, 37,
        115, 117, 130
        with her sister,
        Amelia, 12, 27-
        30, 35, 37, 40,
        49-50, 60, 70-
        72, 115, 118,
        125-127, 130,
        141, 167, 180,
        207, 222, 225-
        229
        with her stepchild-
        ren, 38-39, 55-
        56, 65, 68, 78,
        84-85, 105, 109-
        113, 123, 133,
        153, 183, 196-
        197, 224
sale of Dodge business, 121
self-improvement measures
    taken   by, 34, 39, 45,
    91, 199
sensitivities of, 8, 20-21, 28,
    54-55, 72, 112, 117-118,
    130, 141, 210
and Sunset Terrace, 211, 225
temper of, 8, 11, 39, 46, 132,
    200
travels of, 49, 114, 122, 124,
    127, 130, 147, 153, 228,
    230
and threats of danger to fam-
    ily, 89

INDEX

women's independence,
admiration of, 86
Matilda R. Wilson Fund, 2,
232, 237, 243, 256
Wilson, Richard, 139-140, 143,
145-146, 158, 168, 193-194,
201, 208-212, 223-226, 228,
231-232, 243, 263
Richard Wilson children,
212, 231
Wilson, Reverend Samuel N.,
122, 132
Wilson Theater, 131-132, 140,
198
Wilson, President Woodrow,
67, 77
Williams, Schaefer, Ruby &
Williams, 258, 278
Women's National Farm and
Garden Association, 228
Wood, Gar, 177
World War I, 62, 66, 77-80, 82,
86-87
World War II, 193-194,
198-199, 201, 203